CITY OF GOLD

DUBAI AND THE

CITY *of* GOLD

DREAM OF CAPITALISM

JIM KRANE

ST. MARTIN'S PRESS

NEW YORK

For Clonut and Jay Bone

www.stmartins.com

Book design by Phil Mazzone

Maps by Paul J. Pugliese

Library of Congress Cataloging-in-Publication Data

Krane, Jim.
     City of gold : Dubai and the dream of capitalism / Jim Krane.
               p.   cm.
     Includes bibliographical references and index.
     ISBN 978-0-312-53574-2
     1. Dubayy (United Arab Emirates : Emirate)—History.   2. Dubayy (United Arab Emirates : Emirate)—Economic conditions—21st century.   3. Captialism—United Arab Emirates—Dubayy.   I. Title.
     DS247.D7K73   2009
     953.57—dc22

                                                              2009013188

First Edition: September 2009

10   9   8   7   6   5   4   3   2   1

CONTENTS

FOREWORD

THIS IS THE story of a small Arab village that grew into a big city.

It was a mud village on the seaside, as poor as any in Africa, and it sat in a region where pirates, holy warriors, and dictators held sway over the years. There was even a communist uprising for a time, right next door. But the village was peaceful, ruled by the same family generation after generation.

No one thought the village would become a city. It sat on the edge of a vast desert, surrounded by a sea of sand. There was no running water, no ice, no radio, no road. The village drifted in an eddy of time. While other nations launched rockets into space, the villagers fished and napped. They and their slaves dove for pearls in the sea.

The villagers trusted the family that ruled them. The family produced generous men who ruled by three principles: what is good for the merchant is good for the village; embrace visitors, no matter what their religion; and, you cannot win if you do not take risks.

The ruling family and their villagers were sorely tested during the hard times of the 1930s and 1940s. People starved. Slaves fled, because masters had no food. Rivals rose against them. Schools crumbled into the earth. The only blessings came as clouds of locusts, which the villagers toasted and ate.

But the villagers were a gregarious and hardworking bunch. They pulled themselves together. They enlarged their sailing fleet and began trading and smuggling. They borrowed money and dredged a little port. They invited foreigners to settle, promising freedom from taxes and turmoil. Foreigners who ventured in liked the village and its ambitious leader, a man named Rashid. The village grew into a town. The foreigners told Rashid of the wonders of the modern world, the skyscrapers of New York and the London Underground. He listened intently.

Rashid and his townspeople were dismayed to learn that no one in the outside world had ever heard of them. Rashid decided this would change.

Rashid wanted the name of his town, Dubai, on the lips of every person on earth. When a family sat down to dinner in America, Rashid wanted them to discuss the happenings of Dubai. And when two Englishmen paused for a glass of beer, it was Dubai that he wished them to talk about. Farmers in China, bankers in Switzerland, and generals in Russia: All of them must know of Dubai. For this to happen, the town couldn't stay small and poor. Rashid made a wish. Dubai must become the most luxurious city the world has ever known: the City of Gold.

In 1960 Dubai set off on a journey that was more exciting than anything the Arabs had done in seven hundred years. The town grew bigger and more dazzling with each passing day. Rashid's son Mohammed took over and pressed forward with even more passion. The villagers whose parents ate locusts donned gowns embroidered in crystal. Illiterate elders went shopping by private jet.

Arabs everywhere admired Dubai. A people down on its luck found pride flooding back. They asked their own leaders why they couldn't be more like Dubai.

But like all great wishes that are granted, the success of Rashid's quest brought unforeseen trouble. Lives were trampled by the city's growth. Greed eclipsed common sense. The old ways were lost, and simplicity disappeared, never to return. The dream of capitalism brought them a new city, unlike any other. It also wed Dubai to the fickle ways of the global marketplace, which, as the desert-dwellers learned, can inundate you with wealth and then, even more quickly, take it away.

The story of Dubai's wild ride contains powerful lessons for all of us. It starts long ago, when a great migration took place in Arabia's most isolated corner.

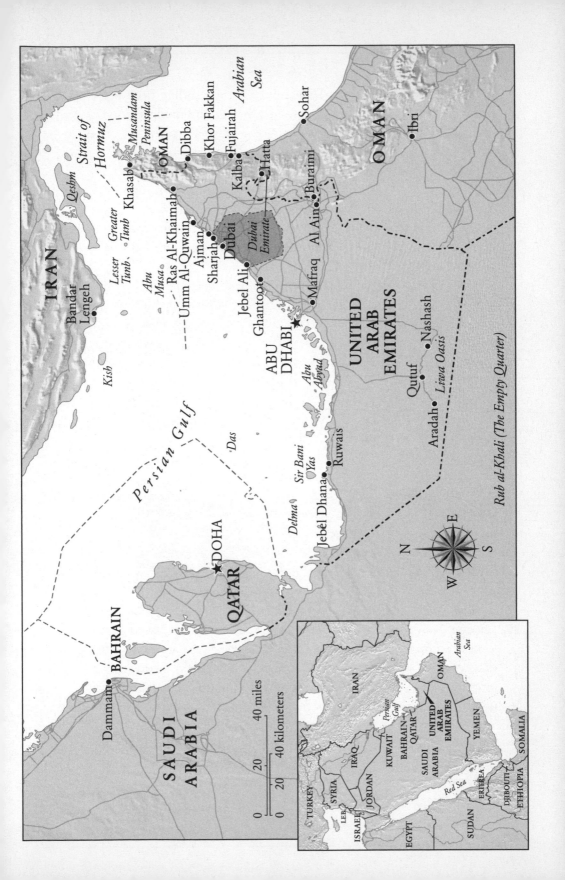

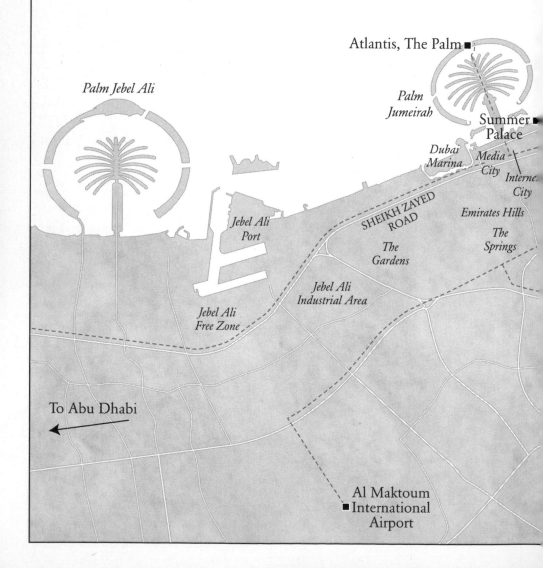

Persian Gulf

Atlantis, The Palm ■

Palm Jebel Ali

Palm Jumeirah

Summer ■
Palace

Dubai Marina *Media City* *Internet City*

SHEIKH ZAYED ROAD *Emirates Hills*

Jebel Ali Port *The Gardens* *The Springs*

Jebel Ali Industrial Area

Jebel Ali Free Zone

To Abu Dhabi

Al Maktoum
■ International
Airport

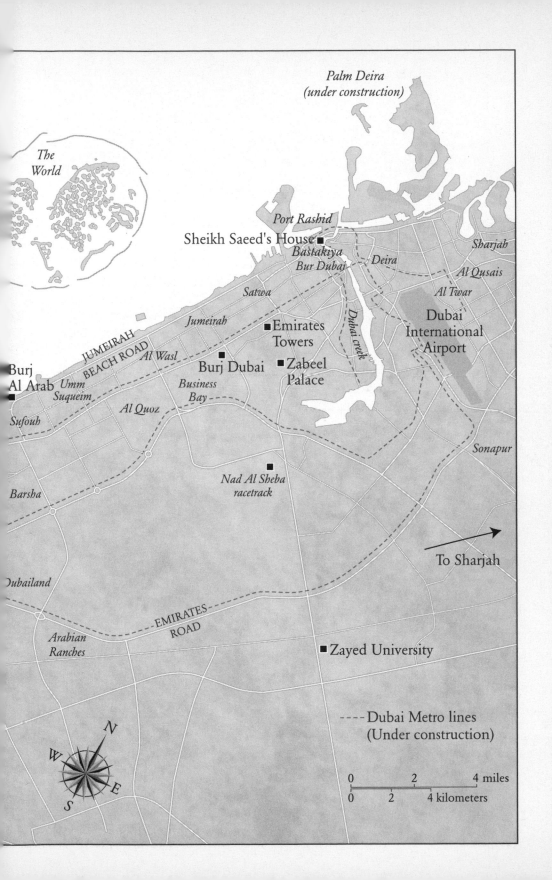

Palm Deira
(under construction)

The World

Port Rashid

Sheikh Saeed's House ■

Bastakiya
Bur Dubai

Deira

Sharjah

Al Quasis

Al Twar

Satwa

Dubai
International
Airport

Jumeirah

■ Emirates
Towers

JUMEIRAH
BEACH ROAD

Al Wasl

Burj Dubai ■

■ Zabeel
Palace

Burj
Al Arab ■

*Umm
Suqueim*

*Business
Bay*

Al Quoz

Sufouh

Sonapur

Barsha

■ Nad Al Sheba
racetrack

To Sharjah

Dubailand

EMIRATES
ROAD

*Arabian
Ranches*

■ Zayed University

- - - - Dubai Metro lines
(Under construction)

N
W   E
S

0   2   4 miles
0   2   4 kilometers

I

DUBAI STIRS

1

THE SANDS OF TIME

Isolation: The Safety of the Undesired

THE ARABIAN PENINSULA is a sun-hammered land of drifting sands and
rubble wastes. Ranges of unnamed peaks slash across the landscape,
their sun-shattered rock sharp enough to cut skin. Salt flats shimmer in
the moonlight night after night, untouched by humans for eternity. It's a
forsaken landscape, this *Arabia Deserta,* with more in common with the
planet Venus than with Earth.

Arabia is as big as Alaska, California, and Texas combined, and it has
not a single river. There are places where the earth cracks open to reveal
savage gorges as spectacular as the Grand Canyon. In others, the landscape is covered in peach-colored dunes that look like blobs of Dairy
Queen frozen custard, except that they rise nearly as high as the Appala-
chians. And then there is the weather. Dry storms rage for days, sending
gusts of sand scouring the earth for a thousand miles. Arabian summers
are hot enough to kill healthy men.

Dubai and the United Arab Emirates sit on the southeastern corner
of Arabia, the most desolate corner of a desolate land. Elsewhere on the
peninsula, civilizations managed to defeat the tough conditions and
build cities. But the odds of survival were so low in the Maine-sized territory that formed the UAE that the population hovered around 80,000

for more than a millennium, from the arrival of Islam in AD 630 until the 1930s.[1]

Even the sea conspired to keep man in isolation. Along much of the coast, it's difficult to distinguish land from water. Tidal flats extend for miles, covered in a white salt crust called *sabkha*. The monotonous *sabkha* belts are useless for agriculture and treacherous for travel. Step in the wrong spot and the crust disintegrates like thin ice, pitching man, camel, or Land Rover into a pit of salty mud. Many a camel was butchered on the spot after such a fall.

Offshore, the lower Gulf coast is interwoven with coral reefs and meandering sandbanks that rise to become low-lying islands. Much of this coast is not conducive to seafaring. The main exception is the far northern end, near the Strait of Hormuz, where the Hajjar Mountains plunge to the sea created harbors for a seafaring Arab clan, the Qawasim. Those living along the rest of the coast had to make do with shallow tidal inlets known as *khors*, or creeks. Dubai's creek is the best of these, making a fine shelter for small boats and dhows. But the creek was so shallow for most of history that ships needed to anchor offshore, with visitors sculling to shore in rowboats.

There isn't much known about southeastern Arabia further back than a few hundred years. Before the discovery of oil—and the arrival of air-conditioning—these lands were simply too harsh for all but a few especially tough people. Those who eked out a living were, until about fifty years ago, among the planet's most undeveloped societies. No one envied their existence of perpetual hunger and thirst, nor their diet of dates and camel's milk. The ragged folk spent nights around the campfire, reciting poetry and recounting intricate tribal genealogies that stretch back thousands of years. Few came to visit and fewer stayed long.

Elsewhere, empires rose and fell, and civilizations were transformed by conquest and colonization. Just across the Gulf, the mighty Persian Empire emerged in the sixth century BC to become the most powerful force on earth. The Persians made halfhearted incursions, controlling bits of the coast and most of neighboring Oman for a time. But they largely ignored the desert tribes across the Gulf, and focused on richer lands.

Even the advances of the golden age of the Arabs, between the eighth and thirteenth centuries, passed the lower Gulf by. The Arabs took their turn as the earth's most powerful race, ruling an empire that stretched from China to Spain. They leveraged their *lateen*-sailed ships and astrolabe navigation tools to master the sea. But the chief Arab seaports were far away. The small ports of southeast Arabia lay close to trade routes, and a few outside influences filtered in. Archaeological evidence unearthed by UAE experts like Peter Hellyer shows trade with Mesopotamia starting around the sixth century BC. Local mariners traveled as far as China by the birth of Christ, judging by unearthed shards of porcelain. But these ancestors left little behind. No major ruins or monuments mark their bygone presence.

Few of the shockwaves of science and learning that molded human civilization penetrated the Gulf. History simply happened elsewhere.

"They have enjoyed the safety of the undesired, and have lived lives to which a hundred generations have specialized them, in conditions barely tolerable to others," wrote British military administrator Stephen Longrigg in 1949, in the *Journal of the Royal Central Asian Society*.[2]

The other side of the Arabian Peninsula, the west, was where the action was. The vibrant caravan cities near the Red Sea supported people and commerce. In one of them, Mecca, an orphan born around AD 570 grew into a merchant who enjoyed bouts of solitude in the mountains. On one of his meditation sojourns, an angel brought him God's revelations. The merchant returned to Mecca a changed man. He began to preach and became known as the Prophet Mohammed. The people of Mecca were skeptical of his message. So in 622 Mohammed took his few followers to the nearby city of Medina. This event, the Hijra, marks the start of the Islamic calendar. From Medina, of course, Mohammed and his followers returned to conquer Mecca, and, by the time of his death in 632, the religion of Islam had swept across most of the Arabian Peninsula, claiming even the few souls in the remote patch of desert that became Dubai.[3]

The Final Frontier

As late as the 1940s, the West still had little clue what lay in the lands that now form Oman, Saudi Arabia, and the United Arab Emirates. Africa and Antarctica had been crossed, the source of the Nile pinpointed, and the North Pole conquered. The interior of the Arabian Peninsula was the last major blank spot on the map, the earth's final frontier.

In the 1940s, people speculated that the center of the terrible Arabian Desert, the Texas-sized Empty Quarter, or Rub al-Khali, was the source of the plagues of locusts that ravaged East Africa. The final great British explorer, Wilfred Thesiger, used the locusts as an excuse to explore the unseen region. Thesiger was a British officer born in Africa and stationed in Sudan's Darfur region, where he developed a love for desert life.

Rather than return to England after World War II, Thesiger lit out for Arabia. In Oman, he coaxed a band of desert Bedouin to lead him by camel across the Rub al-Khali in 1948. Thesiger, wearing the robes and beard of a Bedouin, found no evidence of locusts and not much else. He and his companions trudged barefoot up and down dunes for months, finding almost nothing—no shade, almost no water, and few signs of humanity.

Thesiger's two crossings of the Rub al-Khali were little different from those done a thousand years ago, or at any time since the domestication of the camel in the late second millennium BC. Camels gave eastern Arabians a far broader range, encouraging migration, trade, and the mingling of isolated cultures. The swath of desert that became the UAE even attracted some migrants in the second and sixth centuries when waves of Arab pioneers wandered in from what is now Yemen and Saudi Arabia. Those settlers gathered themselves into tribal clans that still govern society in the UAE today.

The Arabian wastes of the UAE may have been a bit more attractive in those days. The land wasn't always as powder-dry as it is now. Traveling by caravan was probably easier.[4] The evidence for this is bolstered when the drifting sands part to reveal dried riverbeds and long-abandoned frankincense caravan routes deep in the desert. In 1992, an expedition in remote Oman discovered the lost ruins of the fabled city of Ubar, which, according to the Quran, was so full of sinners that God destroyed it. Part of Ubar did collapse when an underground cavern gave way, but its residents were more likely driven off when its water source dried up.[5]

As late as the 1930s, the British explorer Bertram Thomas, who roamed southeast Arabia for six years, met tribesmen who told him the rains had stopped in their lifetimes, with the date crop dropping by half and farmers abandoning the land.[6]

There isn't much left in the UAE from the ancestors of the Arabs beyond a few beehive-shaped burial tombs made of piles of rocks, some primitive settlement foundations, archaeological finds—including Central Asian ivory and Greek pots—and the ingenious irrigation channels still in use called *falaj*.

Moon Worshippers, Christians, and Muslims

There are few experiences more enchanting than spending a night in the desert. As the sky darkens, a giant moon rises above the dunes like a dinner plate just out of reach. The moon's craters are so clear, it seems as if someone just scrubbed the sky. Scattered behind the moon, billions of stars glisten like polished crystal. Heaven never seemed so near. It's practically a religious experience.

In fact, it is a religious experience—or it was before Islam arrived. Many Arabs of the lower Gulf worshipped the moon and the stars. Some prayed to the fearsome sun, which makes a powerful entrance in the clear sky each morning. A temple to the sun god once stood in the town of Al-Dur, now Umm Al-Quwain, probably the largest settlement on the lower Gulf coast at the birth of Christ.[7]

Gulf Arabs also worshipped Jesus. There are churches scattered around the area that is now the UAE, including an important monastery of the Nestorian Church, built in honey-colored stone carved with crosses, grapes, and palm trees. The remains, unearthed just a few years ago on Sir Bani Yas Island in Abu Dhabi—not far from Dubai—may date to the fourth century. A village of Nestorian Christian monks lived on the island in what must have been stark isolation, with little fresh water. Besides praying, they sold pearls to their brethren in India. The monastery reached its peak in the eighth century, well after the arrival of Islam. Christianity in southeastern Arabia fizzled out by the ninth century.[8]

Islam arrived in the lower Gulf in the form of a handwritten letter from the Prophet Mohammed. In 630, Mohammed sent an emissary to the mountain town of Nizwa, in Oman, to deliver a forceful invitation to convert. The Omanis knew the ascendant Muslims of western Arabia were too strong to ignore. The Omani princes felt it was time to befriend them. They sent a delegation to the Prophet in Medina, where they embraced Islam on behalf of all Omanis, which included Arabs living in what is now the UAE. Mohammed accepted these distant tribes into the fold. He sent the converts home with a tutor who showed them the proper way to pray and wash.[9]

But the Omanis' blanket acceptance of Islam had been hasty. There were skeptics who weren't ready to stop worshipping an idol called Bajir.[10] When the Prophet Mohammed died in 632, anti-Muslim rebellions flared around the Arabian Peninsula, including one in what is now the UAE. In the east coast port of Dibba, now a two-hour drive from Dubai, a sheikh named Laqit bin Malik took advantage of the chaos to announce he'd abandoned Islam. Laqit led his followers back to worshipping Bajir.[11]

Laqit's rejection of Islam set off one of the bloodiest battles that ever took place on the land that became the United Arab Emirates. In 633, the Prophet Mohammed's successor, caliph Abu Bakr, sent an army of holy warriors on a grueling 1,200-mile march to reconvert the apostates. The Muslim army converged with allied forces from Oman and Bahrain and swept into the coastal plain of Dibba, a swath of palm groves and villages that sit between the mountains and the sparkling blue Arabian Sea.

The site makes the city a poor choice for a military defense. On the north end of town, the mountains plunge directly into the sea, with faces so sheer that no roads penetrate them. The rebels were thus boxed in between sea and crags. The battle was a short one, lasting little more than a day. Abu Bakr's troops mowed down the unbelievers. As many as ten thousand were killed. The dead wound up in a hardpan cemetery where scattered rocks still mark their graves. The Muslim warriors tore apart Dibba's souk and tramped home with booty and prisoners. Dibba never regained its prominence, a fate many blame on the disgrace of apostasy. Afterward, southeastern Arabia became nearly 100 percent Muslim. Religion dominated life as never before. The guttural Arabic language and the austere land of Arabia that gave life to Islam are considered hallowed, to this day.

As Muslims, divided Arab tribes found unity. The faith's equanimity brought leaders closer to their people. The religion swept out of Arabia. The Muslim faithful overran Persia and the richest provinces of the Roman Empire, building a vast empire. Knowledge of this conquest instilled in the desert Arabs a towering sense of pride that endures today. Centuries later, after isolated Arabs understood how underdeveloped they were compared with outsiders, Gulf Arabs still held themselves with striking self-confidence. In the late 1940s, Thesiger remarked upon this sense of superiority, especially among Bedouin, who took pride in hardship and valued freedom above all else. Thesiger introduced these men in ragged cloaks and long braided hair to cars and airplanes and other trappings of modernity. The Bedouin wanted none of it. The only modern convenience that interested them was the rifle.[12]

Frontier Democracy

For centuries that extend into the fog of unrecorded history, tribes in the lands that formed the UAE spent alternating periods as villagers and nomadic Bedouin. A tribe might spend a hundred years growing dates and raising animals, and then be uprooted and take to the desert as nomads, raiding towns and stealing animals. After a few generations, roles switched. Bedouin would overrun an irrigated area and start farming. The villagers they'd chased out would become wandering outlaws.

Either way, it was a lean and unstable existence. There wasn't enough arable land or water to sustain everyone who wanted to farm, and people were too poor to support commerce. Few had the luxury of a single career. A tribesman might winter with livestock in the desert, and in summer he might fish or dive for pearls, harvest dates, or tend a patch of millet in the mountains.

Life, such as it was in southeast Arabia, was made possible by the camel. The bellowing, foul-tempered beasts provided the only means to cross long, waterless stretches of territory, right into the 1950s. Bedouin might travel a thousand miles carrying only a rifle, pots for cooking and coffee, goatskins loaded with water, and reed bags jammed with dates. The Bedouin knew they would die if their camels died, so the animals drank first. Arabs also roasted camels, sometimes whole, and ate their meat. Camel's milk sustained them far from water sources. Right into the 1990s in urbane Dubai, people kept camels in their yards and milked them. Every grocery store in the city still sells fresh camel's milk because many Arabs find cow's milk lacks a certain tang.

In the days before the British took an interest in the coast in the nineteenth century, the lands that became Dubai and the UAE were tribal territory, not part of any state. Tribal sheikhs had none of the hereditary claims on power enjoyed by the UAE's leaders today. Their authority came from a frontier form of grassroots democracy. A sheikh had to prove that he was braver, wiser, or more generous than any rival.

Tribal chiefs ran their fiefs like Chicago ward bosses. They handed out jobs and gifts and demanded loyalty in return. When a dispute flared, the sheikh and his men rode their camels to the troubled village and erected a tent to be used as a *majlis*, or council chambers. They invited locals to present complaints and handed down decisions on the spot.

Sheikhs sometimes fell out of favor. When that happened, subjects would either back a rival or move to a place governed by someone they liked better. This happened as recently as 1968, when eight thousand members of the Zaab tribe decided they'd had enough of the ruler of Ras Al-Khaimah and moved en masse to Abu Dhabi.[13]

Nowadays, frontier democracy is a relic. Dubai and the other sheikhdoms are still led by tribal rulers, but in a less democratic fashion. Dubai ruler Sheikh Mohammed bin Rashid al-Maktoum still holds *majlis* sessions where he hears complaints and business offers, but the city has swollen far beyond his ability to give personal attention to individual problems, which are now handled—or not—by bureaucrats.

The UAE's rulers now maintain power and legitimacy by giving generous subsidies to their citizens, known as Emiratis, essentially buying their support. The majority is happy with this unspoken bargain, which holds sway in most of the Gulf. The sheikhs get public backing in return for improvements in living standards, including jobs, homes, health care, and education. Tribal autocracy is one of the oldest ways of organizing society and the only form of governance the UAE has ever known.

The Portuguese Arrive

Portuguese sea captain Alfonso de Albuquerque was a short man with a long beard. For convenience' sake he kept his beard tied in a knot. In good company, Albuquerque was known for his wit. But the Arabs of the Persian Gulf saw little of the captain's humor. In 1506 the Portuguese crown handed Albuquerque a job he didn't want: forging a trade route around Africa and Arabia, to India. His mandate called for setting up way stations in the Arabian Sea and the Gulf that Portuguese ships could call upon on trade voyages between Indonesia and Europe.

At the time, Arabs of the lower Gulf knew little or nothing of Europe. When the billowing sails of Albuquerque's five-ship flotilla appeared on the horizon, it was the first major European arrival in the lands that formed the UAE. The pioneering Portuguese had the unique privilege of introducing the Gulf Arabs to European civilization. No matter what he did, Albuquerque's actions would be remembered for centuries as the behavior of Europeans and Christians.

Albuquerque made the impression a lasting one. Rounding Africa and reaching Arabia, the mariner destroyed every Arab vessel he saw. When Omanis refused him permission to land, he sacked their towns. When Albuquerque's fleet arrived in Khor Fakkan—his first stop in what is now the UAE—crowds gathered on the beach, beating drums and shouting. Horsemen galloped up and down the shore, and spectators climbed atop the town's wall and the hill behind, to catch their first glimpses of the European visitors.

Albuquerque and his men peered at the spectacle from their decks. They decided Khor Fakkan's raucous reception wasn't submissive enough. The Portuguese waded ashore, unsheathed their swords, and began hacking off noses and ears, bayoneting men, capturing or killing women and children, and putting the torch to every one of Khor Fakkan's handsome houses, with their lemon and orange trees and horse stables.[14]

The Portuguese made sure the next century in the Gulf wasn't a pleasant one for Arabs who had the misfortune of meeting them. Albuquerque's compatriot, the great mariner Vasco da Gama, burned a ship crammed with hundreds of Muslim pilgrims bound for Mecca.[15]

While the Arabs of the remote Gulf knew nothing of these warlike Iberians, the Portuguese, like their Spaniard cousins, had plenty of experience with Arabs. Just over a decade before their arrival in Khor Fakkan, the Portuguese and Spanish had put an end to seven hundred years of Muslim rule of their homelands. When Granada fell in 1492, the last Arab-governed city in Europe had been captured and the Reconquest was complete. Now the Iberians were in a mood to conquer and colonize. They viewed Arabs and Muslim civilization as heathen enemies. They killed thousands. If a town didn't hand over its harbor, ships, and forts, the entire population risked death or mutilation.

Historians like Abu Dhabi-based Frauke Heard-Bey believe the unnecessarily cruel Portuguese occupation soured Arabs on Westerners in general and Christianity in particular. "The memory of the indiscriminate killing of women, children and the old, and the mutilations inflicted on their prisoners by the Portuguese became engraved in the minds of Arabs living anywhere between the Red Sea and the Persian coast, and were remembered as the deeds of Christians," she writes.[16]

The Portuguese showed little staying power. In 1631, after defeats by the surging navies of the Dutch and British, the Portuguese began to fade away. They anchored off Ras Al-Khaimah and fought running battles with the Arabs, and built a short-lived fort. Soon they were gone.

Beyond memories of their cruelty, the Portuguese legacy is minimal. A few crumbling forts and rusty cannon remain, as well as a handful of Portuguese words that still cling to the patois of the remote villages in Oman's Musandam Peninsula, at the Strait of Hormuz.

When the British arrived in earnest two hundred years later, they were unwelcome. In the Arab view, there was no reason that one Christian power would act less barbarically than another.

Arabia's Venice

Dubai today is a classic city-state, built on trade and liberal laws that have left competitors scrambling to keep up. Dubai's admirers regularly compare the city's dynamism to that of Singapore and Hong Kong, or even the Hanseatic city-states like Hamburg.

But Dubai bears even more similarities to the great entrepôt city-state of Venice, especially during the twelfth and thirteenth centuries, when Venice was the most prosperous city in Europe. Venice, like Dubai, lacked natural resources, but grew ostentatiously wealthy and studded with palaces and cutting-edge architectural icons. Both cities leveraged duty-free trade and lured investment and the smartest minds from the surrounding region.

Dubai, like old Venice, survives as an island of enlightenment in a sea of religious fundamentalism. Both cities provoked a backlash for their tolerance. Venice was pilloried by the papacy for trading with Muslims. Dubai gets excoriated by Muslim hardliners for catering to Christians—and a hedonistic lifestyle replete with pork, alcohol, and prostitution.

But there is also an historical connection between the two cities. The first written reference to Dubai appears in the sixteenth-century journal of Gasparo Balbi, who happened to be the court jeweler of the Most

Serene Republic of Venice. Balbi set out to discover the source of pearls and sailed up the Gulf to find the world's richest oyster pearl beds. Balbi's 1590 *Viaggio dell'Indie Orientale* mentions a fishing settlement in the lower Gulf called "Dibei."[17] Back then, Dubai was probably just a few palm-thatched *barasti* huts. It's unclear whether Balbi landed.

Until the late eighteenth century, Dubai was overshadowed by mercantile ports like Sohar, in Oman; Hormuz and Bandar Lengeh, in Iran; and Dibba and Khor Fakkan, on the Arabian Sea; and Ras Al-Khaimah, just up the coast.[18] For the next two hundred years Dubai rated only fleeting references in the archives of the British and Portuguese.

Dubai's recorded history begins around 1800. Then, the tiny town with its coral fort was an outpost on the remote Persian Gulf, associated with Oman, but not part of any recognized state. The British branded the entire area "the Pirate Coast," the source of attacks on their shipping. After the first set of peace treaties with Britain in 1820, the sheikhdoms that eventually became the UAE began to be called Trucial Oman, the Trucial Coast, or the Trucial States.

Trucial States is somewhat of a misnomer. The seven and sometimes eight sheikhdoms in the group were tribal lands of shifting sizes and shapes. They weren't organized as nation-states. They lacked standing armies, central bureaucracies, and diplomatic relations with other states. There was no central authority, as exists now in the UAE federal government in Abu Dhabi. And there were no borders demarcating the limits of the sheikhdoms. Instead, territory was based on tribal leaders and the realms they could control. When the British started drawing borders of these sheikhdoms, the surveyors followed fault lines between tribes. For instance, when demarcating the border between the UAE and Oman, surveyors asked tribes to declare whom they preferred as overlord, the sheikh in Abu Dhabi or the sultan in Muscat.

In 1800, Dubai was the northeastern anchor of the vast realm of the Bani Yas tribe. Bani Yas territory with its headquarters in Abu Dhabi, extended deep into the desert and hundreds of miles along the coast, to the base of Qatar. Thus Dubai was under the control of Abu Dhabi but sat on the border of the lands of the Qawasim clan, the finest Arab sailors of the Gulf. A few times the Qawasim in the neighboring sheikhdom, Sharjah, occupied the town. But the Bani Yas always recovered Dubai.[19]

The British Conquest

By the early 1800s, the Persian Gulf's strategic value was beginning to tantalize the Europeans and Ottomans. Britain, especially, agonized over the Gulf. It saw that it could not secure its lucrative trade lines to India without controlling the nearly landlocked sea. India lay just a few hundred miles across the Arabian Sea from the Gulf coast—easy striking distance. In those days, the rough-and-tumble Gulf harbored pirates and roving Wahhabi warriors, members of an ultraconservative Muslim sect now synonymous with Saudi Arabia. The Wahhabis stoked hostility to the British and any Muslims who befriended them. Rival powers were already extending their tentacles into the Gulf. The Ottomans held Iraq, including the Gulf port of Basra, and they carried influence in parts of what is now Saudi Arabia. The rest was uncolonized and fair game.

Britain's East India Co., which governed India, made the first major move. It launched new trade routes to Gulf ports, which, besides establishing British power, had the added benefit of profitability. This gambit for trade and influence put the British squarely into conflict with Arab traders, especially the Qawasim, those with the family name al-Qassimi.[20]

The Qawasim were the most powerful group of families in the lands that formed the UAE, and their cities were the largest, overshadowing the Bani Yas settlements of Dubai and Abu Dhabi, which were just dots on the map. The Qawasim owned nearly a thousand ships and boats, with twenty thousand men based in Ras Al-Khaimah, Sharjah, and other ports north of Dubai, and Bandar Lengeh, now in Iran. Their ships ferried goods to East Africa, India, and ports throughout the Gulf.[21]

The cheap and maneuverable Qawasim dhows proved nimble competition for British shipping. Pirates, some allied with the Qawasim, preyed on British merchant ships. In 1805, pirates boarded two brigs belonging to the British political resident in Basra. They slaughtered most of the crew and chopped off the arm of one of the ship captains. The brigands then reflagged the hijacked ships as pirate vessels. The gruesomely wounded commander saved his life by shoving the stump of his arm into a pot of scalding ghee and cauterizing the wound.[22]

The Qawasim got the blame for this attack and many others, although they were probably responsible for few of them. Much of the Gulf piracy stemmed from the anarchic disintegration of the Persian Empire. But the British ignored this source of attacks to take on the trading clan.

In 1809, the British attacked Ras Al-Khaimah, the seat of Qawasim power. The town's inhabitants simply melted into the mountains and returned when the British left. In 1816, a fleet of British warships again parked itself off Ras Al-Khaimah and bombarded the city. The shelling was so ineffectual that, as the British weighed anchor to depart, townsmen mocked them with victory dances on shore.

In 1819, the British returned in earnest—in a fleet of twelve warships led by the frigate HMS *Liverpool*. The ships brimmed with three thousand marines, largely Indians under British command. Their attack on Ras Al-Khaimah was one of history's first major amphibious assaults. This time the Qawasim stayed to fight. Their slaughter at the hands of red-coated Indian fighters is enshrined in watercolors at the Sharjah Art Museum. The British raiders went on to smash Qawasim strongholds in Bandar Lengeh and Sharjah. When it was over, the proud Qawasim trading empire was a smoking ruin.

Historians differ on their views of the British assaults. Traditionally, the narrative follows the British line that the attacks were a justified response to Arab piracy. Recent research disagrees. Using documents from the East India Company's archives, historians—including Sharjah ruler Sheikh Sultan al-Qassimi—say the British decision to destroy Qawasim shipping was made to snuff the competition. The incessant alarms over Arab piracy were more smoke than fact, used to justify sending the Royal Navy on its punitive mission.[23]

Whatever the truth, the British swooped in to dominate Gulf trade. Exports from British India to the Gulf doubled within two years.[24] The Qawasim never recovered. Their powerful sheikhdom of Ras Al-Khaimah shattered into several pieces, with the towns of Ajman, Umm Al-Quwain, and Fujairah declaring independence, and Sharjah becoming a separate sheikhdom. Today, Ras Al-Khaimah is one of the poorest of the seven emirates of the UAE. For this, they hold the British responsible.

The British ended their 1819 campaign by demanding that the ruling sheikhs of coastal tribes sign truces renouncing any sort of naval hostility. The ruler of Sharjah signed first, in 1820. He agreed to surrender pirate ships and arms, destroy the town's fortifications, and release British prisoners. In exchange, the British returned all the pearling and fishing boats they had seized. The other six ruling sheikhs soon followed Shar-jah's lead, although two of them needed a bit of British shelling to make up their minds.[25] British supremacy over the coast was sealed. The seven sheikhdoms that later formed the UAE—Dubai, Abu Dhabi, Sharjah, Ajman, Umm Al-Quwain, Ras Al-Khaimah, and Fujairah—fell under British dominance that lasted until 1971.

The 1819 assaults are significant for other reasons: They mark the start of a major Western military presence in this strategic sea. After the assaults, the British kept six warships on patrol in the Gulf. That presence grew over the years until, after World War II, America largely replaced the British. In 2008, the U.S. military kept around 40,000 American soldiers, sailors, and airmen in the Persian Gulf, not including the U.S. forces in Iraq.[26]

The downfall of Ras Al-Khaimah also left a commercial vacuum in the lower Gulf. The Qawasim port of Sharjah would take over some of the slack for a while, but the opening left room for Dubai to emerge and later, to dominate. Dubai's leaders learned a lesson from the 1819 raids: The English were a force better befriended than fought.

The Qawasim of Ras Al-Khaimah held a grudge against the British for nearly two hundred years. But in the late 1990s, the two sides made amends. The HMS *Liverpool*, albeit in a new incarnation, made a spe-cial voyage back to Ras Al-Khaimah harbor. And the British ambassa-dor to the UAE, Anthony Harris, escorted the emirate's leader Sheikh Saqr bin Mohammed al-Qassimi aboard the frigate for lunch in the cap-tain's cabin. After receiving a twenty-one-gun salute, Saqr gave Harris a tour of his palace, showing him an oil painting of the earlier HMS *Liver-pool*, hung as a reminder of the British assault that devastated his sheikh-dom.[27]

While the Qawasim were left to stew over their fate, the British would find no better friend in the lower Gulf than the ruling sheikhs of Dubai. The rewards for their friendship would soon be apparent.

The Mud-Walled Village

In December 1819, a British ship anchored off the Dubai creek and a scouting party rowed ashore. The sailors wandered around a dusty vil-lage with fishing and pearling boats resting on the beach or nodding in the tidal creek. Lording over the settlement was the Al-Fahidi Fort, a castle of coral and mud. The fort's two watchtowers—one square, one round—rose above its thirty-foot walls, giving riflemen a clear shot at anyone walking up from the creek. The British sailors faced no such threats, exchanging warm handshakes and brief words with the man in charge. He was a Bani Yas noble named Mohammed bin Hazza bin Zeyl al-Nahyan, a cousin of the Abu Dhabi ruling family, the al-Nahyans. When it came his time to sign the British truce a few months later, Mohammed bin Hazza was ill. He sent his uncle, Zayed bin Saif bin Mohammed, to sign.

In 1822, a British naval surveyor, Lt. Cogan, returned to the village at the mouth of the languid creek. Cogan took the time to jot down a description of Dubai. He found a thousand people living in an oval-shaped town ringed by a mud wall, with goats and camels throughout. The site was barren, barely clinging to a low peninsula just a few feet above the waterline. The map he sketched shows three watchtowers poking up above a wall with several breaches.[28] Two small groves of date palms grew outside the wall, harboring the town's only fresh water wells. Dubaians lived in huts of thatch or mud. They dressed in crude cloaks and turbans. Their exposed skin was so deeply tanned that it cracked like old cowhide. Men and women daubed black *kohl*, mascaralike, on their eyelashes, to protect their eyes from the relentless sun. It helped, but not enough to prevent most from getting cataracts. The men spent their days fishing, pearling, and collecting shark fins.

The dozen streets Cogan found in Dubai were sandy footpaths that cut across the village. On one side the paths led down to the anchorage on the reedy creek. On the other, they converged outside the walls, where they trailed off into the desert as caravan routes. There was nothing about Dubai that suggested a spark of greatness; nothing that hinted at future skyscrapers and palaces, thrumming ports and glittering resorts that would cover the blinding sands that stretched beyond the horizon. Dubai was as primeval and timeless as any seaside village in Africa.

The lethargy wasn't to last. Two hundred miles away, deep in a lost desert oasis, a tribal clash was brewing. The outcome brought big changes to Dubai, providing the spark that sent the village on a course of incredible growth.

The Maktoums Take Over

The dispute happened in a place called Liwa, the ancestral homeland of the Bani Yas tribe.[29] The Liwa Oasis is a long arc of four dozen villages that lies so deep in the desert—more than seventy-five miles from the coast—that outsiders didn't know of its existence until 1906.[30]

Liwa now sits on the Saudi border, the last outpost before the endless sands of the Rub al-Khali, the Empty Quarter. Then as now, palm grove villages nestled in the hollows between towering orange dunes that rise to seven hundred feet, giving Liwa the look of West Virginia done in sand. Groundwater made the settlement possible, supporting villages and palm plantations.

The Bani Yas—whose name, in translation, means the Sons of Yas—is the biggest of the tribes claiming Liwa as its homeland. Two Bani Yas branches are worth mentioning: the Al Bu Falah branch, which houses the al-Nahyan ruling family of Abu Dhabi; and their cousins, the Al Bu Falasah, which includes the al-Maktoum family, the rulers of Dubai. Collectively, the Bani Yas dominates the UAE.

In 1833, the tribe's leader, Sheikh Tahnun, was murdered by his brother Khalifa, who then slew several others who rose up against him. The Al Bu Falasah were said to be so disgusted by Khalifa's repression that eight hundred of them fled north, heading for a frontier province on the coast.[31] There, they must have known, al-Nahyan rule was so weak that they could take control and govern themselves.

Their weeks-long journey to the Dubai creek took the settlers out of territory that was later found to hold some of the world's richest oil fields. When they descended on Dubai, this mass of rough tribesmen and their camels and livestock overwhelmed it, nearly doubling the village's population in the space of a few months. The newcomers took control of the settlement and its fort. The two Al Bu Falasah sheikhs, Obaid bin Said and Maktoum bin Buti, declared Dubai a new sheikhdom, independent of Abu Dhabi and its al-Nahyan rulers. The British soon recognized the new regime, cementing the Maktoum family in power. Sheikh Obaid died just three years after his arrival, leaving Sheikh Maktoum bin Buti to rule Dubai until his death in 1852.

Why the Al Bu Falasah risked their future on a little-known fishing village on the coast is a forgotten detail of history. Whatever the reason, the clan's decision to gamble on Dubai was the first recorded evidence of the Maktoum family's knack for bold decisions. The family's skill in backing these decisions with quick action would pay off incredibly well, making the Al Bu Falasah and its ruling Maktoum house wealthy beyond belief, anchoring them in control of a Rhode Island-sized patch of desert that grew into one of the world's great sea-trading city-states.

The year 1833 was a watershed year in the history of Dubai. It signaled the start of the Maktoum family's long and profitable friendship with Britain. That relationship served both parties, but the British nurtured Maktoum leaders and kept them in power through virulent challenges. It was also the year in which Dubai would receive the first of dozens of waves of immigrants who would strengthen and remake the settlement time and again, leaving it, by 2008, one of the world's most cosmopolitan cities, with some two hundred ethnic groups living in a rare atmosphere of tolerance.

Most importantly, the 1833 takeover heralds the start of the Maktoum dynasty, which has ruled Dubai with remarkable stability for 175 years. A quick succession of Maktoum sheikhs ruled Dubai after Maktoum bin Buti's death in 1852. Life expectancy wasn't long in Dubai those days; up until the 1960s, few people lived beyond the age of forty-five.

Maktoum bin Buti's brother Said bin Buti ran the village until he died in 1859. His nephew Sheikh Hasher bin Maktoum ruled until his death in 1886, and his brother Rashid bin Maktoum held control until 1894. His death gave way to Sheikh Maktoum bin Hasher, who died in 1906 and was succeeded by his cousin Sheikh Buti bin Suhail, who held power until his death in 1912.[32]

The three Maktoum men who ran the city from 1912 until 2006—sheikhs Saeed bin Maktoum, Rashid bin Saeed, and Maktoum bin Rashid—all died natural deaths while on the job. In 2006, the city anointed its eleventh Maktoum ruler, Sheikh Mohammed bin Rashid. Not one of the sheikhs who governed Dubai since 1833 was overthrown or murdered. By the chaotic standards of the region, 175 years of uninterrupted succession is probably unprecedented. Dubai's immediate neighbors are more typical. In Abu Dhabi, it was rare for a ruling sheikh to die in office. Fratricidists and coup plotters took out most of them. And Sharjah has been fraught with palace murders and coup attempts right into the 1980s. Much of the Gulf is the same.

In fact, Dubai's record of peaceful transition even puts America's to shame. Assassins gunned down four U.S. presidents in that period: Abraham Lincoln in 1865, James Garfield in 1881, William McKinley in 1901, and John F. Kennedy in 1963.

Stable rule and predictable succession is one of the fundamentals of Dubai's commercial success. Stability is the bedrock of commerce, of course, but so are laws and incentives. And Dubai's sheikhs, who had been living in rags in the deepest desert, were somehow shrewd enough to build an environment conducive to business. A few decades after the Maktoum takeover, the lonely outpost got its first chance to show what it could do.

2

A FREE PORT GROWS
IN THE DESERT

Siphoning the Wealth of Iran

DUBAI'S LEADERS HAVE a knack for hitting risky bets. The city's airline, ports, sail-shaped hotel, and man-made islands confounded common sense and prevailing advice. Even in a place where politics is nonexistent, they kicked up gales of protest. The leaders wisely ignored the dissenters and went ahead with their gambles. All of them have created value that has soared beyond best-case predictions. But not all of Dubai's winnings come from mortgaging the city's future. On a few occasions there was low-hanging fruit to be picked, and all Dubai had to do was spot it, reach, and pluck.

Around 1900, an opening presented itself like a purse drifting in on a cloud. Dubai was able to turn an evolutionary corner, moving from an insular fishing and trading village to an international port, albeit a small one. The town won healthy boosts in population, wealth, and industrial capacity. All it took was a few policy moves from a ruler named Sheikh Maktoum bin Hasher.

And, like so many of Dubai's gains, it came at the expense of the stumbling giant across the Gulf, Iran.

A few decades earlier, a cash-strapped Iranian administration began collecting taxes in the Arab-run ports along its coast. One of those cities, the thriving port of Bandar Lengeh, then known as Lingah, was a haven for Qawasim merchants. This especially rankled the Persians because the Qawasim paid no allegiance to the Persian regime in Tehran. Their metropoles were Ras Al-Khaimah and Sharjah, on the Arab side of the Gulf.

The situation in Bandar Lengeh looked like Havana in 1959. Dubai, like Miami, sat just ninety miles across the water. Lengeh was a vibrant port with smart people who knew how to make money. But the freewheeling environment that attracted them was slipping away as the government tightened the screws. Around 1887, the Persians began to forcibly kick out the Qawasim merchants and brought Bandar Lengeh under direct rule.[1]

Disgruntled Qawasim began moving across the Gulf. But unlike the case with those fleeing Havana, Dubai wasn't as obvious a destination as Miami. Many of the merchants returned to their tribal homelands, Ras Al-Khaimah and Sharjah. The Dubai leader at the time, Sheikh Rashid bin Maktoum, understood the value of the capitalist brain trust that was looking for a new home. He did his best to divert the refugee merchants to Dubai, and lured a few dozen.[2]

In 1894, Sheikh Maktoum bin Hasher took over in Dubai. He wanted to do more to coax merchants from Iran. In 1900, the Persians made his job easier. They raised taxes in Lengeh and another Iranian port, Bushehr. The exodus intensified and included Arabs as well as Iranians.

Sheikh Maktoum saw the low-hanging fruit. He launched a plan to make Dubai the most business-friendly port in the lower Gulf. He abolished the 5 percent customs duty and slashed fees, turning Dubai into a free port. At the same time, Sheikh Maktoum sent his agents across the water to sweet-talk the biggest merchants, whether Arab or Persian, into moving to Dubai. The agents offered free land, guarantees of a friendly ear in the leader's *majlis*, and a hands-off government policy.

The incentives worked. The heads of a few of the biggest Iranian businesses agreed to relocate, and as the Dubai sheikh planned, their business partners and customers followed. By 1901, a census found five hundred Persians in Dubai.[3] Within a few years it was clear that most of the Iranian traders who'd packed up and left Lengeh were unpacking in Dubai.

The Dubai ruler gave each a plot of land on the south bank of the creek, and the Iranians built the Bastakiya neighborhood, named for the ancestral town of Bastak in south-central Iran. Besides their businesses, the Persian migrants brought their language, their pomegranate-laced food, their melancholic music, and social customs like enormous weddings that raged for days. The Iranian influx was the second mass-migration to transform Dubai after the 1833 arrival of the Al Bu Falasah. There would be many more.

Free trade was mother's milk for Dubai. Wharves now lined the creek, and the newly built Iranian souk was crammed with goods from British-run India. Cargo was reexported to ports nearby or strapped onto camels bound for inland bazaars like the Buraimi Oasis. Within a few years, Dubai was closing in on larger ports like Sharjah, Ras Al-Khaimah, and Bandar Lengeh to become the chief trade center between the Strait of Hormuz and Qatar.[4]

Links with the outside world began to mount. Prior to 1901, British cargo and passenger vessels visited Dubai no more than five times a year. Two years later, Dubai was a scheduled destination. Steamships stopped twice a month. By 1908, Dubai was home to 10,000 Arabs, Persians, Indians, and Baluchis—as well as 1,650 camels, 400 shops in two bazaars, and more than 400 ships and boats. The town had long since burst out of its mud walls, which lay in ruins. Sheikh Maktoum ruled from his palace in the beachfront Shindagha neighborhood, backed by a hundred tribesmen who roamed the town with Martini rifles.[5]

Like the Cubans who fled to Miami, the Iranians who settled in Dubai dreamed of returning home. They hoped the Persian government's clampdown on commerce was a temporary move. Many of the merchants had left their families in Iran and commuted across the Gulf for holidays. But the reforms never came and the Persian ports slipped into an idle torpor.

By the 1920s, most Iranians accepted Dubai's invitation to settle permanently. They brought their families across and adopted the customs and dress of the local Arabs. Dubai was happy to have them. The Iranians brought their entrepreneurial savvy and trading links with Africa and Asia, and removed those assets from Iran, a competitor.

Iranians brought prosperity and worldliness to a town that had known little of either. Most Dubaians still lived in thatch huts and gathered their water at a communal well. But the town had a modern quarter now, Bastakiya, which showed off the latest imported cooling technology: the wind tower. Most of the big new homes had at least one of the square towers that rose a story or two above the roof, with openings on all sides to catch the breeze—whether blowing off the sea or from the desert. The wind towers funneled the breezes indoors and, sometimes, directly onto the hammock of a merchant taking his midafternoon nap. The fresh air might be hot, but the Bastakis called the indoor relief "God's breeze."[6]

Bastakiya is now an historic district, and some of the old Iranian merchant homes still stand, rescued from wholesale bulldozing in the 1980s. Unfortunately, the government's heavy-handed restoration of the once elegant neighborhood has destroyed most of its charms.

The best place to see wind towers is across the Gulf in Bandar Lengeh, where the old port has been frozen in time. Lengeh's coral homes are still in use, and the town retains a bygone air of another century, thanks to the exodus of its merchant class and the drying up of the economy. The Lonely Planet travel guide to Iran describes Bandar Lengeh as "an infectiously lethargic place" that shuts down for a five-hour siesta every afternoon. Dubai, in effect, siphoned away Lengeh's lifeblood.

Dubai's leaders took a lesson from Sheikh Maktoum bin Hasher's free trade and business incentives. They know that, but for a few changes in circumstance and wisdom, the fortunes of Bandar Lengeh and Dubai could have been reversed.

Since the 1920s, Iran's cascading missteps have showered Dubai with wave upon wave of Iranian entrepreneurs and their savings. In the 1970s Iran raised import tariffs to nearly 40 percent on some goods, triggering another exodus. In the 1980s and since, the Islamic revolution pushed liberal-minded Iranians and much of its academia across the Gulf. Dubai's free ports have even cut into Iran's retail sector. Iranian importers learned it was easier to serve their customers from tax-free Dubai, so Dubai now takes a profit on reexported goods sold in the Islamic Republic.

Much of Dubai's Iran-bound cargo gets ferried across the Gulf in colorful wooden sailing dhows, now chugging under greasy diesel smoke. Hundreds of these old ships with their jutting prows and grizzled sailors glide into the Dubai creek every day, loaded with pistachios, watermelons, raisins, and zucchini from Iran. They return home with televisions, Colgate toothpaste, Clairol shampoo, and Teflon-coated frying pans.[7]

Nearly half a million Iranians have fled to the good life in the UAE. In Dubai, Iranians outnumber local Emiratis by around three to one.[8]

Iranian parliamentarian Hadi Haqshenas blames the exodus on Tehran's failed social and economic controls. "Since these wrongheaded policies won't be reversed any time soon, we can expect the UAE to attract many of our specialists, medical doctors, engineers and other experts," Haqshenas said in 2006.[9]

Iranians are a key cog in the machinery that has created this marvel in the desert. Dubai now hosts nearly ten thousand Iranian-run businesses[10] that have diversified beyond the Iranian market and now ship anywhere in the world. Iranians are among the city's largest developers and merchants, its top buyers of homes, and one of its biggest sources of investment.

All of this comes at huge cost to the Iranian economy, which has seen its citizens investing tens of billions of dollars in the UAE rather than at home. Some $15 billion flowed out of Iran and into Dubai in 2007 alone, estimates Jean-François Seznec, of Georgetown University, who has researched the links.[11] Dubai is also Iran's largest trading partner. Iranians spent some $14 billion importing goods that sailed across the Gulf from Dubai that same year, Seznec believes, rather than the $10 billion tallied in official figures.[12]

"Prosperity in Dubai is based squarely on trade with Iran," says Anthony Harris, a former British ambassador to the UAE, now a Dubai-based insurance broker. "Dubai merchants speak Farsi to this day. They feel totally at home doing business with Iranians."[13]

The Wisdom of Pearls

The mighty Persian Gulf curves like a fat banana for six hundred miles, from the Iraqi port of Umm Qasr in the west to the Gibraltar-like narrows in the Strait of Hormuz. There, the Gulf empties into the Arabian Sea and the broader Indian Ocean.

The Gulf is a gentle and shallow sea, never more than three hundred feet deep. Hot sunshine makes it one of the world's warmest, with surface temperatures between 75 and 90 degrees Fahrenheit.[14] High rates of evaporation make it one of the saltiest. It is so salty, in fact, that before air-conditioning, Dubaians used to take advantage of the extra buoyancy by taking cool naps while floating in the sea.[15]

Seagrasses wave in the currents on its well-lit sandy bottom, making a perfect oyster habitat and ideal grounds for finding pearls—the priceless anomalies known as *lulu* in Arabic.

Even before oil, the countries surrounding the Gulf[16] squabbled over jurisdiction over the sea off their coasts, vying for access to undersea beds where pearls could be collected by divers with no more equipment than a nose clip, a leather sack, and a rock tied to one leg. Milky Gulf pearls with their faint blush of pink were must-have accoutrements for the world's wealthy—from India's maharajahs to the fashion elite of Paris and New York.

By the 1800s, pearls were far and away the main business pursuit of the lower Gulf. Buyers from Bombay sailed into Dubai, Sharjah, and Bahrain to greet arriving pearling ships and buy up the best specimens. When the business peaked in 1897, British surveyor John Gordon Lorimer reported that Gulf pearl exports ran to three-quarters of a million British pounds, ten times their value just two decades earlier.[17] By the early 1900s, pearls commanded 95 percent of the Gulf economy[18] and supported 1,200 pearling boats, each with a crew of fifteen to eighty sailors. A quarter of those boats sailed from Dubai.

The pearling business grew complex, creating a native capitalist class that outfitted boats and lent money for the expedition in return for a large cut of the haul. These financiers sent representatives to sea known as *nokhadas* to claim the pearls as crews pried open oysters on the boat deck.

"While the shells were being opened I would have four people, two on either side, to make sure no one took any pearls," says Saif al-Ghurair, one of Dubai's wealthiest businessmen and a former pearl boat *nokhada*. "If we were lucky we would catch them."[19] At the end of the day, al-Ghurair locked the pearls in a wooden box, placed the box in a compartment under his mattress, and slept on top.

Pearl merchants grew wealthier than some ruling sheikhs, building mansions with multiple wind towers and carved wooden verandahs. The wealth imbalance caused instability. In Sharjah in 1884, pearl merchants overturned the ruling sheikh and replaced him with a favorite. Cautious voices warned that the pearl economy was unstable in other ways. Dubai and the Gulf were growing dangerously dependent on a single export, an expendable luxury item.

But the Arab natives of Dubai were proud of their ways. They felt it was beneath them to diversify into real estate or shopkeeping. They left a fat wedge of the economy open for migrant Indians, who soon controlled Dubai's retail sector.[20]

The British policy of isolating the Trucial States narrowed Dubai's already razor-thin economic base. As a reward to ruling sheikhs who relinquished control of foreign affairs, the British announced in 1905 that the rich seabed would be reserved as a Gulf Arab monopoly. The catch: Pearls had to be marketed through British India. The British also banned modern technology—such as trawling or diving gear—to protect the traditional industry.[21]

Over the long term, it was a disastrous move. The British protected the Arab pearl beds from outside intruders but forced Dubai and other sheikhdoms to maintain their primitive ways, sending divers to sea for months, risking—and sometimes losing—their lives when safer methods were the industry norm.

Dubai's pearl divers are still celebrated for their toughness in plunging to the seabed up to thirty times a day, holding their breath for two minutes while stuffing oysters in leather bags tied around their necks. One diver says he distracted himself by imagining his fiancée was a mermaid swimming in front of him.[22] On the way up, with lungs bursting, divers swam through schools of stinging jellyfish and risked the deadly decompression sickness known as "the bends." But the divers were unwitting participants in a monopoly that left their economy balancing on a house of cards. In 1929 the house collapsed. That was the fateful year when the New York stock exchange crashed and America, then Europe, spiraled into the Great Depression.

When life got hard in the West, it turned brutal in Dubai. The economy depended on a capricious ornament that was of no practical value. When times get tough, luxuries like pearls are the first things people stop buying.

The pearl industry wasn't just ravaged by the drying up of demand. At the same time, Japanese researchers figured out how to "culture" pearls that looked nearly the same as natural ones. Culturing pearls had been tried for years by inserting a speck of grit into the oyster and allowing the animal to cover it with secretions of nacre, the mixture of calcium carbonate and protein that hardens into pearls. But those early cultured pearls usually turned out to be "blister pearls" mounted to the shell. They could be chipped off and used, but only on rings or mountings where a half a pearl would do.

In the early twentieth century, Japanese researchers who inserted grit into oysters' genitals found that the creatures would excrete nacre and build round pearls inside themselves.

Cultured pearls flooded the market and killed pearling in the Gulf and everywhere else—permanently. If Dubai had built a backup industry, it might have preserved a reasonable standard of living. It did not. Dubai sprawled like a turtle on its back. The pearling fleet still sailed out in the spring and returned in late summer, and the town turned out to watch the *nokhadas* row ashore carrying strongboxes jammed with shimmering pearls. But the buyers no longer greeted them when they stepped ashore. So the pearlers turned their boats toward Bombay. There they sold their collections, but at a sliver of the price. Pearling in Dubai was dead.

A Diet of Bugs

In a town that had grown dependent on a one-trick industry and imported food, the return to hand-to-mouth subsistence was devastating. The seventeen years between the 1929 crash and the end of World War II in 1945 were the toughest in Dubai's history.

The pearl crash triggered a famine, with malnourishment widespread in Dubai in the 1930s and 1940s. With war on the horizon in Europe, the British, who could normally be counted on to help, had bigger things to do. Goatherds had gone to work in pearling. Now they were looking for food, not selling it. Bankruptcies tore into the souk, wiping out business. The Indian merchants gathered their families and wares and boarded the steamer for Bombay. Slaves deserted masters who could no longer feed them. Dubai's first schools that had opened during in the 1920s collapsed. Foreign teachers fled.[23]

As World War II ground on, the famine grew desperate. When there was no rice, fish, or dates, people ate leaves or the ubiquitous dhub, a spiny lizard that may have given Dubai its name. Plagues of locusts became a blessing. People would net the bugs and fry them, crunching on them by the handful. "They were very delicious," says Fatma al-Sayegh, a history professor from Dubai who ate locusts as a girl. "They taste like French fries." A town can't survive on bugs, leaves, and lizards. Inevitably, some Dubaians starved to death.[24] In the northern sheikhdoms like Ras Al-Khaimah and among nomads in the interior, deaths from starvation were even more common.[25]

The Mellow Sheikh

Governance during an economic crisis requires a strong-minded leader with bold ideas. Unfortunately, Dubai was stuck with easygoing Sheikh Saeed bin Maktoum al-Maktoum, who presided from 1912 until his death in 1958. He was the grandfather of Dubai's current ruler, Sheikh Mohammed bin Rashid, who grew up in Sheikh Saeed's rambling house on the creek.

Sheikh Saeed's nonconfrontational style bears little resemblance to the determination of Dubai's strongest rulers, his son Rashid and his grandson Mohammed. A comparison with British rule at the time is apt: Saeed played Neville Chamberlain to his son Rashid's Churchill.

Sheikh Saeed looked like a melancholy warlock in his long white beard, his body hidden in the folds of curtainlike robes. A silver-handled *khanjar*, a ceremonial dagger, hung from his waist. Saeed's tired eyes rested in a wrinkled face that gathered around a bulbous nose. In one happy picture, Dubai's ruler sits on the ground among friends and slices up a bird carcass for his falcons.

Dubaians prized Saeed's kindness. Once he caught a servant stealing a carpet and warned the thief to return it because "the guards will surely catch you."[26] But Saeed's submissiveness provoked plots and coup attempts. His cousins, a rough bunch who scorned his authority, schemed openly, ridiculing the ruler as a man dominated by his wife and son. Rivals fed on discontent with the hard times, which bared the ruling family's privileges.

The first attempt to depose Saeed came with the pearl crash in 1929, when a band led by his cousin Mani bin Rashid forced him to resign. Mani declared himself Dubai's ruler and informed the British, but they refused to accept him. Saeed maintained power.[27] In 1934, rebel cousins tried another tack: murdering him. The failed attempt left Saeed shocked and desperate. He begged help from the British, who sent a squadron of warplanes to buzz Dubai. More convincing was the show of support from eight hundred menacing Bedouin, who set up camp on Dubai's outskirts.[28] The rebels stood down—for a while.

The respite didn't last long. Saeed's cousins tried to extort a share of his income by organizing gangs who beat his night watchmen. In 1938, he faced street demonstrations.

Saeed's eldest son, Sheikh Rashid, was better matched to take on his unruly cousins. Pictures of young Rashid show an intense man with a full black beard, eyes brimming with vitality. As a young man, Rashid held a monopoly on Dubai's taxi service. One of his cousins mounted a challenge by opening a taxi service of his own. In 1938, Sheikh Rashid led an armed posse that ambushed the competing business, wounding a driver and locking others in stocks.[29] The attack incensed the Maktoums' rivals, pushing them to develop an alliance with Dubai's influential merchants.

The Dubai Reform Movement

The merchants understood that Sheikh Saeed's tribal rule was inadequate, and that the city needed deep reforms to climb out of the depression. Together, the merchants and the rebellious cousins channeled their opposition into a remarkable democratic reform movement. The short-lived movement, which had popular support—but crucially not that of the British—hacked away at Saeed's powers, backing him into a corner that nearly ended his rule.

Saeed allowed the merchants to set up a fifteen-member *majlis*, led by his cousin Hasher bin Rashid. The council approved progressive reforms including health care, garbage pickup, and the reopening of schools. It voted to abolish the taxi monopoly and other privileges, and required Saeed to contribute seven-eighths of his income to the town treasury.

When Sheikh Saeed ignored the demands, the rebels occupied rooftops around Dubai. The city divided into armed camps trading sniper fire. The ruling family kept control of the southern Bur Dubai side and the rebels held Deira, the commercial center on the northern creek bank.

It was then that Sheikh Saeed decided to destroy the *majlis*. It's unclear whether he was pushed to do so by his eldest son, but Rashid would soon scatter the council, end its reforms, and restore his family's full power. Maktoum rule would never face a serious challenge again.

The Wedding Massacre

March 29, 1939, was Sheikh Rashid's wedding day. He dressed that morning in his white *kandoura* robe and covered that in a gold-trimmed black cloak. His bride-to-be was Sheikha Latifa, a refugee of the al-Nahyans, the Abu Dhabi royal family. Latifa's father was Hamdan, Abu Dhabi's ruler from 1912 until 1922. When Sheikh Hamdan was assassinated by two of his brothers, Latifa and her mother fled to Dubai. In 1939, her home sat deep in rebel-held Deira.

The rebels agreed to a temporary truce, a conciliatory act that allowed Rashid's wedding to go ahead as planned at his fiancée's home. Foolishly, the reformers also welcomed Rashid's entourage, including a band of armed Bedouin who, it was explained, would fire their rifles in celebration at the ceremony's climax.

The climax came ahead of the wedding. The Bedouin, calloused men with long tangles of hair and wild beards, were crack shots with their ancient single-shot rifles. Once they were in place, Dubai's only democratic reform movement would be cut down in a burst of bullets and blood. The Bedouin first gunned down Saeed's cousin, the *majlis* leader Hasher bin Rashid, along with his son and eight others.[30] Then they set upon the coup plotter Sheikh Mani, besieging his home. Mani escaped, bolting for the safety of Sharjah. When the gunsmoke drifted off, Deira was no longer rebel territory. The reformers who'd challenged the Maktoums' rule sprawled dead in the sand or had fled to Sharjah.[31] The audacious attack was a total success. The bloodshed didn't postpone the wedding of Sheikh Rashid and Sheikha Latifa. The couple went on to lead a full life and Latifa bore Rashid five daughters and four sons, two of whom followed their father to rule Dubai.[32]

By the early 1940s Saeed slipped into retirement and Rashid began assuming his father's duties.[33] The wedding strengthened Maktoum rule in another way. It tightened their bonds with the al-Nahyan rulers in Abu Dhabi. The children of Latifa and Rashid became cousins of the Abu Dhabi royal family.

A few months after the wedding, Dubai got another display of the

Maktoums' brutality. Saeed heard rumors of another coup plot. This time he didn't hesitate. He arrested five suspects and put out their eyes.[34] The gruesome punishment triggered an outpouring of disgust with Maktoum rule. But instead of rising up, dissenters packed up and moved away in the time-honored fashion. Saeed and Rashid were in total control.

Sheikh Rashid's use of violence to maintain power is nowadays seen in Dubai as an embarrassing bit of family history. Discriminating folks don't mention it in public. Local books gloss over the event. But in the context of 1930s Arabia—or, for that matter, Europe—the killing of political opponents was hardly unusual.

More remarkable was the success of the operation. Sheikh Rashid's wedding fusillade rescued his dynasty. It was as if the Maktoum penchant for risk taking had ebbed under Sheikh Saeed and needed a flash of violence to get it back.

The rebel *majlis* might have been destroyed, but Rashid realized the ideas it spawned had merit. He enacted every single one of them—except the royal pay cut—once he took power. But Rashid didn't just co-opt the merchants' ideas. He eventually co-opted the merchants themselves. As Dubai grew, Rashid secured their loyalty in exchange for business contracts and exclusive trade licenses. Onetime opponents built monopolies in branded goods like Mercedes cars or Frigidaire freezers. Some descendents of rebel merchants are now billionaires.

The British, too, were winners in the massacre. After the showdown, the British political resident issued a deceptive statement saying the democratic movement had grown "unpopular" and collapsed.[35] The British preferred the friendly Maktoums to the merchant radicals, who exhibited a distinct anti-imperialist air. The massacre was a nasty business, but it took away the need for the British to tackle the rebellion themselves.[36]

Truces and Consequences

The Maktoums' dogged staying power owes itself less to gun battles than to British buttressing through the treaties, or truces, they signed with them and the other ruling families of the Trucial States. Rulers like

Sheikh Saeed earned legitimacy through ties to the British. And the British, in turn, depended on their allied sheikhs to fend off advances by foreign powers like France and Germany.

The truces of 1820 and the following decades quashed piracy and hostilities at sea. In later treaties, the ruling sheikhs traded Britain much of their sovereignty in exchange for protection. In 1892, the rulers gave Britain command of their foreign affairs. In 1922, the sheikhs relinquished the right to sign oil exploration contracts with the United States and other countries, and agreed to deal only with Britain.[37]

The treaties turned out to be incredible stabilizers. They replaced strife-prone "tribal democracy" with monarchies that evolved into some of the most stable regimes in the developing world. The hereditary authoritarian rule that Britain backed in the Trucial States continues today. Rulers of Dubai and the other UAE sheikhdoms still choose their successors from sons and brothers, preserving a system that is one of the least democratic in the world.

The British didn't bother colonizing the impoverished sheikhdoms, which, until the late 1950s, showed no signs of mineral wealth. The British Empire, overstretched around the globe, did the minimum to keep the Gulf Arabs under its thumb. That amounted to six warships patrolling the Gulf part-time. Until the early 1900s, just one white Briton watched over the lower Gulf—from Iran—buttressed by three residency agents who were local Arabs or Indians. That makes just four full-time representatives.

The British kept order by maintaining the illusion of power, by making threats, and by occasional shelling of rulers' forts. They kept up their bombardment diplomacy far beyond the period that it was politically acceptable.

One such barrage came in 1925. The ruler of Fujairah, Sheikh Hamad, obsessed over a Baluchi slave girl he met in Muscat, in Oman. Hamad convinced the girl's mother, also a slave, to sell him the girl. The sheikh smuggled his mistress home in violation of the British ban on importing slaves. When the English found out, they demanded that Hamad release the girl. Hamad refused, but offered to pay a fine that would allow him to keep her. The British decided to punish the insubordinate sheikh. The gunboat *Lawrence* blasted his fort and knocked down two of its towers, but Hamad kept his slave girl.[38]

The British also bullied rulers by holding their boats for ransom. In 1930, the British seized the entire pearling fleet in Ras Al-Khaimah, relinquishing it only when the sheikh agreed to allow the Royal Air Force to open a refueling base.[39]

Overweening British agents treated Arab leaders like children. Lt. Col. T. C. Fowle, who oversaw the Trucial States from his base in Iran for most of the 1930s, liked to say he was civilizing a people stuck in the seventh century.[40] In reality, the opposite was true. Fowle and his contemporaries did nothing to advance Gulf Arab society, giving no encouragement to reforms of health, education, or politics. By the time the British left in 1971, illiteracy was above 70 percent, life expectancy wasn't much more than fifty years, and there wasn't a single university.[41] Life improved dramatically after their departure.

The stability that Britain brought to the Trucial Coast was, for the first hundred years, stagnation. The sheikhdoms remained Third World outposts because the British enforced their isolation and blocked foreign ideas. Dubai's links to the world came despite—not because of—the British presence.

But Britain's truce-enabled stability was crucial. It allowed the ruling sheikhs to develop seven robust monarchies that eventually banded together as the UAE. The British also prevented the expansionist Saudi Wahhabis from swallowing up the tiny sheikhdoms. By the time oil arrived, the monarchies were strong enough to drive their country through one of the fastest and most thorough modernizations in history. Political stability has held up through thirty-eight years of independence with no serious hitches. It is a key reason Dubai and the UAE have generally outperformed the rest of the Middle East.

Money for Nothing: Oil and the Rentier State

On a scorching day in July 1937, a deep-throated rumble intruded on Dubai's afternoon siesta. Stumbling out of their thatched *barasti* shacks and looking up, Dubaians saw a lumbering aircraft, its silver aluminum skin shimmering in the sun. Dubai had seen aircraft passing overhead before, but nothing like this. The plane was as fat as a blimp, with an arched bottom that made one think of a pelican. Alarmingly, the plane wasn't passing by. It swung behind the town and began a low approach as if to land. But Dubai had no airport. Worse, the four-engine behemoth wasn't even heading for land. It looked like it was going to crash into the creek.

Aboard the Imperial Airways flying boat, the distress was equally grave. The craft was the pinnacle of luxury travel, with two decks, like those of a Boeing 747, only civilized. It was an airborne gentlemen's club with a smoking room, promenade saloon, and, for those who'd had a tipple too many, berths where one could sleep it off. Few of the two hundred or so passengers knew anything about Dubai. From the air, it looked like the end of the world. Certainly not a place that warranted a break in a game of gin rummy, let alone a stop on their journey to India. But not only were they making a fuel stop, they would spend the night.

The passengers, who'd left Southampton four days earlier, gazed down at the empty desert and sparkling sea and wondered what sort of depredations awaited. The creek's S-bend marked the site of the town, but where were the buildings? The land was white in the afternoon sun. Slowly, walled compounds that looked like animal pens revealed themselves. The buildings were barely discernible from the surrounding sands. There was no greenery, not a single concrete building, nor a bridge or a paved road. The town had no electricity, no telephone service, not a pane of glass or a cube of ice. Drifting lower, the passengers saw humans in long, loose cloaks moving among camels. Goats scampered like tossed dice.

After a dramatic splashdown in the creek, with gaping onlookers lining the banks and bobbing in sailing dhows, the passengers were whisked to Imperial Airways's guest house in neighboring Sharjah, where the airline had landing rights at a British airbase built in 1932.[42]

Dubai's aviation history started with these flying boats that made the four thousand-mile trip from England to India in short hops, across Europe, Turkey, Iraq, and the Gulf.[43]

But the 1930s flying boats also represent a less salubrious side of Dubai's economy: the start of what economists call "the rentier state." In Dubai and elsewhere in the Gulf, the British made payments for landing rights directly to the ruling sheikhs, handing them wealth that they could use to make allies among their subjects. Imperial Airways paid Sheikh Saeed 440 Indian rupees a month (about $150, or £30), plus a landing fee of 5 or 10 rupees—a small sum in British terms but a lifesaver in depression-racked Dubai.[44]

The rentier state was a product of "economic rent," a financial reward for a gift of nature such as mineral deposits or, in Dubai's case, location. The first rents came as payments for landing rights, which didn't require any labor or expertise on Dubai's part.[45] In one way of looking at it, economic rent is money for nothing.

Sheikh Saeed and the other rulers on the Trucial Coast considered the payments personal income that could also be used for public benefit. Initially, the money staved off some of the ravages of the depression, while angering merchants who argued the money belonged to the state. In coming decades, Sheikh Saeed's successors would distribute those economic rents with skill, using them to neutralize political opponents. The ruling sheikhs fortified themselves by trading money—subsidies—for the support of their opponents, and later for the backing of the population at large.[46]

A second concession Sheikh Saeed signed in 1937 was far more lucrative. This was an oil exploration contract that ignited hopes that Dubai would be rescued from the poverty of its pearl bust by another gift from God—sludgy crude oil. The contract granted seventy-five years' exploration rights to London-based Petroleum Development (Trucial Coast) Ltd. in return for an annual royalty of just over 30,000 Indian rupees (about $10,000, or £2,000).[47]

Dubai might've done better if Sheikh Saeed had dealt with one of the American oil companies working across the border in Saudi Arabia. But treaties bound him to Britain. The oil contract cemented the pattern of granting concession income to the ruling sheikhs. The sheikhs' grasp on power strengthened.

In those days, gusher oil strikes came year after year. Each one brought undreamed-of prosperity to some of the world's most hard-bitten lands. The first Arab jackpot erupted in northern Iraq in 1927 and the big strikes crept ever closer to Dubai. Bahrain, a Gulf island just west of Dubai, struck oil in 1932. Wildcatters tapped huge flows in Kuwait and Saudi Arabia in 1938. Each find raised hopes in Dubai that the economic depredations were over. If a drilling rig struck oil, the British concession promised to pay Sheikh Saeed 200,000 rupees (about $75,000, or £15,000) on the spot, and a further payment for each barrel exported. Dubai was waiting to bathe in a shower of oil wealth.

But exploration got off to a fitful start in the lands that now form the

UAE. Geologists pored over the desert in Dubai, Abu Dhabi, and Ras Al-Khaimah. They noted interesting geological formations, but drillers never arrived to punch holes. When World War II broke out in 1939, the teams left.[48] The company eventually relinquished its Dubai concession. It would be twenty-seven years before anyone struck oil in Dubai.

3

OIL, SLAVES, AND REBELLION

The Big Sleep

IN THE DEVELOPED world, the 1950s brought prosperity and progress. America's postwar baby boom roared into full swing. City dwellers fled to the suburban good life. They tuned in to *Leave It to Beaver*, slicked their hair with Brylcreem, and careened down the highways in tail-finned Chevys. Air conditioners triggered a population shift from slushy Detroit to sunny Florida.

Technology was on the march. In the 1950s, IBM launched its Fortran computer programming language. But the Russians made the biggest splash, firing their Sputnik satellite into orbit. That kicked off a space race and, a decade later, Americans were bounding on the surface of the moon.

Imagine, then, the surprises that greeted George Chapman when he arrived in Dubai in 1951. Chapman, an Englishman, soldiered in India during World War II and returned to Britain after the war. There, he found life gray and boring. England's colonial empire was in collapse and the battered country focused on rebuilding itself. Chapman dreamed of returning to the East, where the days were bright and freighted with adventure. He couldn't go back to India. The country was off-limits to Brits since having gained independence in 1947. But the company Chapman interviewed with, a shipping firm called Gray Mackenzie, had an opening in Dubai. Chapman was in his twenties. He decided Dubai—a place he'd never heard of—sounded better than the dreary confines of London.

He sailed from England to Bahrain, where he transferred to an India-based steamship that hopped between the major towns in the Gulf. The ship was too big to land in Dubai, so it parked off neighboring Sharjah and hoisted its cargo of rice to a wooden sailing dhow. Chapman rode to the beach on the dhow, lying on a sack of rice until the dhow ground itself onto the sand and Chapman, a wiry red-haired man full of energy, leaped ashore. It was dark. He could see nothing beyond the beach and the sea and the few men around him.

An Englishman named John Hoffman collected Chapman in his Land Rover, the first such four-wheel drive in the Trucial Coast, where most travel was still done by camel or sailboat. Hoffman took Chapman bouncing over the empty dunes between Sharjah and Dubai. At some point that wasn't marked by anything to see, Hoffman welcomed Chapman to Dubai.

Lurching into Dubai village, Chapman could see the orange light of kerosene lamps. The flickering glow revealed the ragged outlines of palm-thatch *barasti* shacks and adobe houses sprouting vents like oversized chimneys. Men in beards and rough turbans led camels through the sandy lanes. The air smelled of smoke and dung. Nearing the center of town, squares of bright light in two houses revealed the presence of electric bulbs. One was the oil company headquarters. The other was Chapman's new home, the creekside office of Gray Mackenzie, known as the Beit Wakeel—the agent's house.

Dubai in the 1950s was little different from how it was in 1850s. Nearby, Egypt was in the midst of its cinematic golden age. Beirut was a swank destination for the jet set. Iran was delving into nuclear power[1] while its upper classes washed down caviar with iced vodka.

Dubai, by contrast, sat in darkness. Literally. At night the town gave off so little light that it couldn't be seen by those aboard a plane flying overhead or a ship passing offshore. This primitive darkness became a problem for Gray Mackenzie. Every two weeks, a steamship called at Dubai. If it arrived at night, the ship's pilot couldn't find the town. So Chapman, one of six resident Europeans, had an idea. He climbed the flagpole mounted to the roof of his house and at the top he clamped a light socket loaded with a 200-watt bulb, the brightest he could find. He fired up his gasoline-powered generator and turned on the beacon whenever a ship was due after dark.

"There were no other lights, no electricity in the place at all," Chapman says in his Bur Dubai office, as sharp and energetic as ever, but now in his gray-haired eighties.

Chapman's makeshift lighthouse allowed ships to anchor offshore and shift cargo to a shallow-draft barge. But to reach the town's wharf, the barge had to find the creek entrance, a tidal wash whose mouth shifted after storms. At night, Chapman would send an *abra* rowboat to the creek mouth and pay the boatman to stand there like a lawn jockey, holding a kerosene lantern to mark the channel.

The town woke up by daylight. Dubai's creek was as wide as London's Thames, but far busier. Its turquoise water churned under a cavalcade of zigzagging boats and ships. Wooden dhows, with their upwardly raked prows, still powered themselves with dramatic triangular *lateen* sails, in use in Arabia since the sixth century. Sailors rounding the creek's S-bends hurriedly pulled down the sail and worked it under the spar. Pilots navigated a thicket of *abras,* the two-oared ferries that carried passengers from one bank to another, with gulls wheeling and shore hands shouting in Farsi, Hindi, and Arabic.

Much of Dubai's center was a clamorous Arabian souk. Alleys shaded by straw roofs let tiny beams of sunlight poke through the murk. The lanes were too narrow for cars, but donkey carts, camels, and even stray herds of goats could get inside, and it was by all accounts cacophonous. Shop owners sat crosslegged on the ground, offering customers a stool and tea. Men with daggers and rifles wandered, Iranians in their suit jackets and Omanis in their colored scarves. Roguish Bedouin from the desert, overconfident in their ragged cloaks, strutted like they owned the place. The Bedouin were the poorest of them all, but held themselves above town folk.

Butchers hacked at stringy goat carcasses and kicked up cascades of flies. Vendors piled dented cans of sardines and beans into pyramids. Meat scraps sizzled on the grill. Carpenters cobbled furniture from Indian lumber. Halfway down the souk, a bright passageway offered stairs to the creek, where the *abras* sat—just like today—with pilots yelling for passengers to choose a boat. Nearby, men built wooden dhows on the creek bank, sealing their hulls with fish oil.

Even then, Dubai's merchants were scheming. Edward Henderson, a British oil executive, wrote of meeting a man who unlocked a ramshackle warehouse and showed him hundreds of new bicycles. Henderson scoffed at the possibility that robe-wearing Dubaians would ride bikes in a city without a paved road. The merchant explained Dubai's budding reexport trade.[2]

"My friend, of course I shall not sell them here," he said. "One or two perhaps. I shall ship them into Pakistan. I got a similar number of Singer sewing machines off my hands in the same way."

Dubai held only fifteen thousand people in those days, and Chapman reckons 60 percent of them were Iranians. Farsi was the language spoken most. Chapman liked the rough-and-tumble ways of the little port. Rifle shots rang out a few times a day, mostly just Bedouin potshots at sea birds. A stray bullet once flew through Chapman's window and slammed into his dining room wall.

Staying Cool

Life was good at the Beit Wakeel. The house's generator allowed Chapman to run lights and a fan for a few hours each evening. It would be nearly a decade before Chapman or anyone else in Dubai would know the cooling breeze of an air conditioner—even though more than a million of them had been sold by 1953 in the United States.[3]

The house's toilet was another Western luxury: an oil drum cut in half with a crude wooden seat. Most Dubaians simply squatted over the creek—or above a pit in their yards. Not even the home of Dubai ruler Sheikh Saeed, his son Sheikh Rashid, and baby grandson Sheikh Mohammed had flush toilets. Going to the bathroom in Dubai could be dangerous. Privies were deep, open pits with bricks marking a foothold on either side. But Dubai's sandy soil does not hold its shape well. Soaked cesspits sometimes caved in. Elderly Dubaians still tell of townspeople buried alive.

Then there was the heat. Despite the arid landscape, Dubai bastes in the sickening heat of the tropics, with smothering air and searing sunshine. It's uncomfortable five months of the year. In July and August Dubai is a steam bath. It's 95 degrees at midnight.

Nowadays the city air-conditions everything, even curbside bus shelters. But before electricity arrived in the early 1960s, there was no escape. Most people took siestas between noon and 4:00 p.m., when businesses closed. Chapman took showers to cool off. He changed his shirt three times a day. But at sundown in Dubai, just as the air begins to cool, a bank of sea mist rolls in and drenches everything. It's the curse of the Gulf.

"In one minute you'd go from being reasonably comfortable then you were soaking wet. There was no getting out of it," Chapman says. "In the evening, you'd have a bath or shower and you could never dry yourself."

Chapman tried sleeping on the roof, like the rest of Dubai. Most houses had sleeping platforms on the roof or in the yard, raised woven mats that could accommodate a family. But Chapman never got used to waking up soaked with dew. Bibiya Sharif, who lived a few houses down from Chapman in Bastakiya, says her family would sleep lined up on their broad verandah overlooking the creek. The older children took turns fanning the little ones to sleep.

In a hot place like Dubai, you learn the value of a cold drink. But almost no one in Dubai had ever seen ice or known the refreshment of an iced drink until an ice plant was built sometime around 1960. Chapman was lucky enough to have a kerosene-powered fridge that he shipped from Australia. It kept things cold, but only produced tiny amounts of ice. Chapman's was one of perhaps two or three fridges in town.

Sharif ordered a kerosene fridge in the mid-1950s and waited six months for a ship to bring it. She froze bowls of water and distributed ice to neighbors who had never seen it. She showed them how to chip it into shards and jam them down the necks of their clay water jugs. "The neighbors used to kill each other to get at it," says Sharif, now a vigorous seventy-two and a resident of Dubai's fashionable Umm Suqeim section.

Until electricity arrived in the 1960s, most people in Dubai cooled water through the time-tested method of evaporation: Water in an earthenware jug or a goatskin would evaporate through the container's pores, naturally cooling the liquid. Maryam Behnam, an Iranian diplomat who fled to Dubai after the revolution in Iran, collects the old jugs. She wandered her garden one steamy afternoon in May 2008, pointing to orange pots resembling the amphorae of ancient Greece. The jugs bear names according to size and shape, like *jalla* and *quzza*, names that now mean nothing. Some are decorated with swirled patterns of dots. Behnam spent months in Dubai in the 1950s and 1960s with her family in Basta-kiya and remembers the best cooling method was to wrap a clay jug in wet rope, then lower the filled jug into a well, where it would dangle in cool dampness. "After a few hours the water was icy cold," she says.

To Behnam, who lives in a home jammed with carpets and furniture of her Iranian hometown of Bandar Lengeh, the pots are a reminder of a simpler time, when ladies gathered to sing the Quran, or her personal slave, Jameela, spent hours braiding her hair. "I cling to these old pots when I see them," she says, caressing a bulbous terra-cotta jug shaped like a Gallo wine bottle.

Dung, Soap, and Whiskey

Some Arab women in Dubai did a curious thing with their hair, caking it in a mixture of mud, henna, and incense and perhaps a bit of dung—at least, that was what Chapman thought. The mixture hardened like a hel-met and stayed on for weeks. It was supposed to be good for the hair.

"The ladies used dung for their hair. They would rub big lumps of it in," Chapman says, roaring with laughter at the memory. "If you passed a *barasti* and looked in you might see someone with their head all cov-ered in dung. Apparently it had good qualities."

Most people didn't have soap, so they cleaned themselves with mud. Dubaians considered a special red oxide mud healthy for the scalp and good for hair growth. Problem was, the red mud was tough to rinse out, which wasted water. "It used to be torture, literal torture, to wash the hair," Behnam says. Most people washed their hair once or twice a month. She bathed in a room with a floor drain, using a basin of water drawn from a ceramic urn. Slaves kept bathrooms stocked with water.

Drinking water was a big problem. It was easy enough to dig a well and find water, but most of it was salty. In the 1950s, the town had only a few wells with passable water. One was in Bur Dubai under a tree where the Astoria Hotel now stands. Another few sat near today's Ra-mada Continental Hotel in Deira. Vendors loaded well water into drums, which they carried around town on donkey carts, selling it by the large tin measure. Chapman found it undrinkable, even for tea. He imported barrels of Tigris River water from Iraq. He would unload a few drums for the sheikh and one for himself.

When a ship came in, thirsty men sometimes stormed the vessel, climbing the mooring ropes to get aboard and steal a precious drink of clean water. Chapman saw several fights, with crew members bludgeoning water-mad Dubaians with wrenches.

In the 1950s, if you wanted a bottle of whiskey or gin, you went to see Chapman, the only liquor vendor in town. He kept his hoard in a primitive storeroom under padlock and chain. Dubaians needed a license to buy drink, as is the case today. In those days the British political agent approved liquor permits, denying those with Muslim names. In the early 1950s, only twelve people in Dubai were licensed drinkers.

"People would come to me at midnight on Thursday. I'd go down and laboriously undo the chain. I'd sell them a bottle of whiskey for two-and-a-half rupees," Chapman says with a laugh. "There wasn't much money in it." But liquor helped build Dubai. Sheikh Rashid was cobbling together a municipal government in the 1950s and needed revenue to pay salaries. His representative asked Chapman to agree to a 10 percent tax. "That's a bad idea," the Englishman replied. But he soon changed his mind and started sending the authorities 80 rupees a month. It was a pittance, but enough to fund one low-level salary. "We paid the wages for the first clerk in the municipality," Chapman says. Liquor still funds Dubai's government, but the tax has risen to 30 percent.

In 1950, 130 years after the British arrived, Western medicine finally reached Dubai in the form of the Al Maktoum Hospital. The tiny clinic sat in a fenced compound surrounded by dunes and gnarled scrub. Local Arab women refused to give birth there. Rumors said the doctor would cut open stomachs to take out the baby. Arabs bore children at home with help from an elderly midwife who was nearly blind. Infant mortality rates—and hygiene—were appalling.

"They used to suffer in such a way, I can't tell you," says Sharif, who moved to Dubai in 1952. "But they wouldn't go to the hospital."

When Sharif grew pregnant, she told her neighbors that she would deliver at the hospital. She returned home with a healthy baby girl and showed her neighbors that her stomach was intact. "Now you all must go to the hospital. It's more hygienic," Sharif admonished them. After that, Arab mothers began visiting the hospital.

The Education Gap

Dubai may have been the most advanced town east of Bahrain, but it offered no opportunities to get an education. Schools that opened during the pearl boom closed in the 1930s. In the 1950s Dubai had a couple of simple schools that taught the Quran, rudimentary math, and history. Most people couldn't write. Some learned to read the Quran. Anyone wanting more had to study in Iran, India, or Pakistan.[4]

People were suspicious of education. In his autobiography, Dubai native Easa Saleh Al-Gurg wrote that his father denied him permission to study English, considering it un-Islamic. Al-Gurg's mother intervened and the tutorials, by an Indian doctor, went ahead. English gave Al-Gurg a huge advantage. He traveled with Sheikh Rashid to handle his dealings in English and eventually became the UAE's ambassador to Britain.

Dubaians' disdain for school caused the city to develop one of the world's widest education gaps, which, together with its complementary wealth gap, makes for some extreme juxtapositions. To this day, many older Emiratis cannot read or write. They still sign papers with a thumbprint and close business deals on their word of honor. Their immediate children, who grew up with schools, may have gone on to get PhDs.

Emirati political scientist Abdulkhaleq Abdulla, who earned a PhD at Georgetown University in the 1980s and now teaches at UAE University in Al Ain, is one of them. Abdulla was raised in a mud-and-thatch home by parents who made fun of his penchant for reading. "Where do you think that reading is going to take you?" Abdulla's mother would tease him. To her, there was no reason to read anything but the Quran.

"They were always making fun of us," says Abdulla, a relaxed talker with a salt-and-pepper beard and wire-frame glasses. "It would've been better to do something worthwhile than sit for hours, reading books that made no sense to them."

Parents who grew up in stark poverty also raised children who've become billionaires. Mohammed Ali Alabbar, the chairman of real estate giant Emaar, is a billionaire tycoon and one of Dubai's most powerful men. He, too, is the son of poor illiterates who raised him in a *barasti*. He went to college in Seattle and, when he returned, became one of Sheikh Mohammed's favorite entrepreneurs. Alabbar's father, a dhow captain, never learned to read and write. He didn't need to. He navigated by the stars.[5]

Forsaken No More

Elsewhere in the Gulf, the modern world was barging in. The West wanted oil, and the realization set in that the Persian Gulf countries, with some of the most backward societies on earth, had most of it. The chasms between civilizations weren't quite as deep as those between the Europeans arriving in, say, aboriginal Australia or lost civilizations of the Pacific, but they were close.

Saudi Arabia, a nation so poor that its king, Ibn Saud, could carry his entire national treasury in the saddlebags of his camel, was also so traditional that the trappings of modernity that found their way into the kingdom—the telephone, the radio, the automobile—were shunned as tools of the devil.[6] Ibn Saud tried to temper the foreign influences of the modern world on his deeply religious subjects, but it proved impossible. Saudi Arabia got roads and buildings and hotels, along with electricity and telephones. The Westerners who flooded in brought air conditioners.

Dubaians moved to Saudi Arabia, Kuwait, and Bahrain to work. Oil exploration resumed in the Trucial States in the 1950s, but drillers found nothing. Abdulkhaleq Abdulla's family joined the migration north, taking up residence in the eastern Saudi oil town of Dammam in 1959. Abdulla, just six years old, traded his thatched *barasti* with kerosene lamps for a concrete house with electric lights. For a time, the modern world still lay outside the Trucial States.

In August 1958, the first offshore drilling barge in the Trucial States, the *Enterprise*, parked in the shallow waters off Abu Dhabi's Das Island. The sea floor held a promising formation. The crew lowered the barge's legs, and a drill as big around as a tree trunk began grinding its way through the seabed. In a while, the crew noticed blobs of black scum bobbing to the surface.

"A nice, sweet crude," is how the *Enterprise*'s engineer described the lucky first-hole strike, the equivalent of a hole-in-one in golf.[7] The Umm Shaif strike was the first oil discovery in Abu Dhabi or any of the lands that, in thirteen years, would become the United Arab Emirates.

Two months later, Abu Dhabi's cantankerous ruler, Sheikh Shakhbut bin Sultan al-Nahyan, sat in the backseat of a Cadillac fishtailing over the sand at Murban, in the windswept flats of western Abu Dhabi. A parade of Land Rovers followed Sheikh Shakhbut's car, carrying a band of royals and retainers to oversee the spudding of a new well.

The bearded sheikh, wearing a dagger and robes that billowed in the wind, took his seat in an armchair on the drilling rig, surrounded by Bedouin wearing bandoliers of rifle cartridges and falcons on their wrists. The oilmen and the sheikhs ate lunch together, then someone flipped a switch. The men watched the drill start to chew into the sand. It wasn't much to see. Shakhbut soon gave the order and his entourage piled back into their cars and drove off in a cloud of dust.

The first Murban well turned out to be a bust, yielding only gas. A year later, though, probing hit pay dirt. There was yet more light, sweet crude: low-sulfur oil that is easy to refine and therefore valuable. Drillers hole-punched the landscape around the underground limestone feature known as the Bab Dome until they tapped what turned out to be an enormous reservoir of oil.[8]

The barren wastes of Abu Dhabi, it turned out, were not worthless after all. The drifts of dust and the poisonous plains of salt had preserved a sea of oil for a tiny segment of humanity, the few thousand souls who defied nature and made their homes in that forsaken landscape. For their hardships, and those of their ancestors, they would be rewarded with custody of 8 percent of the world's proven oil reserves. When the extent of the deposits became known, it was clear that Abu Dhabians were immediately among the richest and most privileged people in history. At $50 a barrel, Abu Dhabi's 92 billion barrels of proven reserves[9] are worth $46 trillion. Divided among Abu Dhabi's roughly 200,000 citizens, each person's share is nearly $23 million.

By 1963, Abu Dhabi's oil was flowing from twenty-five wells offshore and another dozen on land. In 1965, drillers forty miles from the Umm Shaif oil field connected again. This time they found the Zakhum field, the biggest of all, and the third largest in the Middle East. It held 66 billion proven barrels.[10] Abu Dhabi exported 2.5 million tons of crude that year, an amount that rose nearly ten-fold by 1968, when the sheikhdom shipped out 24 million tons of petroleum, earning tens of millions of dollars—incredible wealth for a sun-wizened people who knew nothing beyond gnawing poverty.[11]

Oil in Dubai

Abu Dhabi's good fortune led those in Dubai and the other five Trucial States to believe that they, too, bobbed on an ocean of oil.

Dubai's well-spudding days started in 1950, when British geologists and drillers set up in Jebel Ali, a sandy rise on Dubai's southern outskirts. They found nothing.[12] The team shuttled between Dubai, Abu Dhabi, and Sharjah, moving tons of gear and men and perforating the desert at huge cost and effort. The British exploration company Petroleum Development, finally got tired of pouring its money down dry holes and gave up, abandoning its Dubai concession in 1963.

For thirteen years after Abu Dhabi began pumping oil, Dubai drilled hole after dry hole. One can only imagine how the Maktoum family must have cursed the ancestors who fled Abu Dhabi in 1833. But Sheikh Rashid was a relentless optimist. Dubai built a consortium of local and international firms and redoubled its drilling on land and at sea. Everyone felt it would only be a matter of time before Dubai spiked a gusher and people would toss money like confetti. In 1964, with no oil in sight, Dubai issued postage stamps emblazoned with derricks and bearing the message "Oil Exploration."

Finally, in 1966, a crew drilling fifteen miles offshore proved everyone right. Planes buzzed Dubai, scattering leaflets with the news.[13] One crewman turned up in Sheikh Rashid's *majlis* with a gift: a jar of coffee-colored crude. Rashid named the offshore field Fateh, translating roughly to "conquest." The first export of Dubai crude came in September 1969, forty-two long years after Sheikh Saeed signed the first exploration agreement in the Trucial States.

In 1970 and again in 1972 and 1973, drillers in Dubai's territorial waters hit new oil fields. Dubai was in business. But when the finds were assessed, they looked more like a letdown. Dubai had just 4 percent of the UAE's oil, or 4 billion barrels of reserves. Nearly all the rest was in Abu Dhabi. Sharjah and Ras Al-Khaimah found paltry deposits and the other sheikhdoms found nothing.

Oil is a curious substance. It's one of the key drivers of economic life, but few people ever see it. The crude oil underground is pumped into pipelines and holding tanks and then hauled across the globe in ships, offloaded into refineries, converted to products like gasoline and diesel fuel, and then trucked to filling stations or heating oil distributors, from where it is dispensed into gas tanks or boilers and burned. The entire lifecycle of a barrel of crude is hidden from view.

Sheikh Rashid wanted to make sure Dubaians got to see their oil. Not for novelty's sake. Dubai, like most of the Middle East, is a rumor mill where conspiracy theories run wild. The leader might claim he'd struck oil, but until people saw it, there would be doubters sowing rumors. So Rashid ordered a barge to haul some of his crude down the creek. He called a gathering of news reporters, advisers, his sons, and sundry photographers to the creek bank. And there, the bearded sheikh directed the barge crew to start pumping. The hose's six-inch nozzle coughed and spat and then burped forth a gush of black sludge onto the ground.

A photo taken by Dubai chronicler Noor Ali Rashid records the event. There is Sheikh Rashid squatting on his haunches next to the nozzle, closely examining the black flow. Behind him stands his dapper son Maktoum, fingering prayer beads, his *agal*—the black bands around his headscarf—jauntily askew. Two dozen others watch, including Europeans in bow ties and crewcuts, and a woman in a skirt.[14]

Word of the oil strike reached the Abdulla family in Dammam. The family, like many others, pulled up stakes and returned to Dubai, flying into the new airport. Abdulkhaleq, then twelve, drove with his family on a paved road to a new home, built of concrete. The old *barasti* homestead with its kerosene lamps was gone. So was the wandering water vendor and his donkey. The family still slept on the roof in summer, but most other trappings of modernity were in place.

By 1975, oil earnings dominated Dubai's economy, bringing in nearly two-thirds of gross domestic product. That year stood as the peak of oil's importance. By 1985 oil's contribution slipped to 50 percent of GDP.[15] A decade later it was down to 18 percent. By 2000, it slid to 10 percent. In 2006, oil sales brought a minuscule 3 percent of Dubai's overall economy.

Dubai wasn't exactly running out of oil. It hit peak production in 1991 at 410,000 barrels per day. But it had other prospects. Trade, construction, and services rose in relation to oil as a portion of the economy. By the time oil production dropped as reserves began running dry, oil was already losing its importance. In 2008, Dubai's daily draw was 60,000 barrels. Abu Dhabi's was 2.5 million.[16]

Dubai isn't an oil town. Oil fever never caught like it did in Kuwait City, Houston, or Baku. Perhaps it was memories of the collapse of the pearl economy that made people shy away from banking on a primary export. Oil was nice while it lasted. Because it came so late, Dubai had other sources of income. When it started to run out, few noticed. Dubai moved from oil dependence to independence, becoming the first post-oil economy in the Middle East.

Oil did give Dubai a shot in the arm. Sheikh Rashid invested the proceeds in overbuilding roads, factories, and ports that he imagined would serve the city for the next fifty years. Oil income allowed Dubai to create the state-run business base that grew into the foundation of its economy. Oil has always been a mixed blessing for producer countries. Prices spike and plummet in cycles, pushing oil economies into inflationary booms and dragging them into recession at the whim of the marketplace. Dubai succumbs to those cycles, as in 2009, but not usually as acutely as its neighbors. As its economy diversified, Dubai kept busy amid most of the downturns.

Dubai's commemoration of its oil discovery sums up its attitude. By way of gratitude, the city installed an eternal flame in a roundabout at the intersection of two roads in Deira. But that roundabout was torn up when the roads were widened. The eternal flame was moved to a small park near the airport. Few people know about it.

Slaves

One morning in October 2008, I phoned Fatma Essa, a tour guide at Dubai Heritage Village. The village is a collection of *barasti* and coral huts in the old style, where retirees weave palm mats and bake flatbread for tourists. It sits in the Shindagha section, next to Sheikh Saeed's house.

"I hear you have an old man working there who used to be a slave," I tell Essa. "I'd like to interview him."

She doesn't understand the word "slave." I use the Arabic *abd*, or *abeed* in the plural.

"We have no *abd*, only handicrafts," she says drily.

Slavery in the UAE is a touchy subject. As an institution, it was only banned in 1963. Hundreds or thousands of former slaves are still alive. Many black Dubaians are descendants of African slaves. They took UAE citizenship after independence in 1971 and now reap the same privileges as any other Emirati citizen. It's considered rude—to the point of starting a fight—to ask black Emiratis whether they are African or descended from slaves.

Essa grudgingly invites me to Heritage Village. It's her job, as a guide, to explain Dubai's history, even the dark chapters. "The *abeed* came from Africa," she says as we stroll through the village. "We needed strong people, strong men to help with the work. There weren't enough people here. They worked on the pearl dhows, the trading dhows."

Essa is a twenty-something woman in a black *abaya* and *shayla* scarf over her hair. She wears oversized sunglasses. Her skin is coffee brown. She quickly assures me she's descended from Bedouin. You can spot non-original Emiratis, she says, by the color of their skin. If they're too white, they're probably from Iran. Too brown, and they're African.

"When you see people with African faces and dark skin, these are from *abeed*. They're locals like us now," she says with no hint that it should be any other way.

Fatma Essa leads me into a copse of trees where a brown bullock and a wiry old man stand together in the shade. The man rakes eucalyptus leaves. His bandy arms are tightly muscled and his neck is ribbed with carrotlike cords. He's wearing a checkered *lunghi* and a dirty T-shirt that is disintegrating at the seams. An embroidered skullcap is crushed on his head, accenting a kinky salt-and-pepper goatee. He is a black man and his name is Juma Khalaf Bilal az-Zari.

Az-Zari says he's unsure of his age, but he figures he's somewhere around seventy. His eyes are milky yellow, from cataracts and malarial jaundice. He was born in the east coast sheikhdom of Fujairah. He's the only Emirati I've ever seen doing manual labor. I ask az-Zari if he's got African ancestry.

"No, I'm pure-blooded Emirati," he says bluntly. I don't follow up by asking if he was once a slave.

But az-Zari knows all about the lives of slaves. He went to sea as a boy, sailing to the South Indian port of Calicut before he could grow a mustache. He launches into slave chants he sang, miming the rowing and sail-rigging and sundry hard labor he performed. Slaves in the Trucial States sailed to African ports like Mombasa and Zanzibar, where they could speak the language. They handled the bartering of Arabian dates for African lumber and spices. He tells of building a road through the Hajjar Mountains and farming in Kuwait.

"There were no machines back then. Black people did all the work by hand," he says. "We ate dates and fish. It's the perfect food. Makes you strong."

Az-Zari is a proud man. Not once does he say he'd been a slave. He thrusts out his chest and speaks with his chin pointed to the sky. I ask him about the buying and selling of slaves, the markets, and the transport. Was there a slave market in Dubai? "Like today, if you want a house or a car, there were people you could visit. You just said, 'I need *abd*.'

"The big market for *abeed* was in Buraimi. From there they went to Saudi," he says. "I saw them with chains on their wrists. Like this," az-Zari crosses his forearms behind his back. "They put the cuffs on them, so they couldn't go anywhere. If any *abd* refused to work, they chained his legs to keep him from running away. Stolen children also, they sold them through Buraimi. They stole them from Dubai and they sent them to Saudi Arabia, Yemen, or Kuwait."

Wealthy Dubai families owned slaves. Men handled outdoor chores and the women slaves cooked and cared for children. Slaves married each other and bore children who were enslaved by the same families. In the famine of the 1940s and 1950s, owners sold off their slaves. Few people could afford to feed themselves, let alone slaves.

"There was no rain, no fish, no food. People sold their *abeed* to get money for food," az-Zari says.

Az-Zari remembers the 1963 emancipation like it was yesterday. By this point he's given a demonstration to a group of schoolchildren of the ancient *falaj* irrigation system, whipping his bullock to draw well water into the stone channel, which directs it to the shade trees. Afterward he douses himself and mops his face with a towel.

"Sheikh Rashid and Sheikh Zayed said, 'Every *abd* is free to go.' They gave them land and houses. They said, '*Khalas*—enough—it's not allowed to be *abd* anymore. If you want to stay and work, okay. But you must be paid.'"

Essa explains that former slaves are no longer called *abd*. After 1963, they became *kadhim*, which means helper or servant. Freed slaves often took their owners' family names, as in America. Black Emiratis now bear some of the most prestigious names in the country. But, unlike in America, integration was quick and nearly total. Black Emiratis face little discrimination.

Slavery is deeply ingrained in Arabia, pre-dating Islam.[17] It was big business during the pearl boom. Arab captains delivered East African slaves to the ports of Sharjah, Ajman, Umm Al-Quwain, and Dubai. Merchants sold slaves locally and assigned them to caravans bound for what is now Saudi Arabia, where they were especially prized. The Bani Yas tribe in Abu Dhabi controlled many of the slave routes into the interior. The ruler of Sharjah levied a $4 tax on each slave brought through his domain.[18]

The British tried to thwart the practice and banned slave imports by sea in 1847.[19] But slavery in the Trucial States carried on in legality until 1963, when laws readied for independence outlawed ownership of humans. That date—a century after the U.S. Emancipation Proclamation—sounds barbaric, but slavery wasn't usually the brutal institution it was in the United States.

Slaves sometimes became the masters. In the 1860s, when American slavery was about to be contested by the Civil War, Sharjah was ruled by a pair of half-brothers, including the son of a slave woman.[20] In the east coast city of Dibba, an African slave named Bakhit bin Said governed between 1924 and 1926.[21]

An African slave named Barut ran the east coast enclave of Kalba for decades. Barut was Kalba's summer governor starting in 1903, when his owner, the *wali* Said bin Hamad, stayed in Ajman. When Said bin Hamad died in the 1930s, the crown prince, a boy named Hamad, was too young to rule. Barut took over as full-time ruler. In 1937, the British resident pressed Kalba to choose a real leader. Reluctantly, the tribesmen chose twelve-year-old Hamad. When the British rejected the boy as too young, they picked Barut the slave. Ironically, the British—who had campaigned against slavery for the previous seventy-five years—rejected Barut, presumably because he was a slave. Still, Barut managed to run Kalba until around 1950.[22]

Slaves worked aboard pearling dhows and lived in the walled compounds of prominent families. Most were more like second-class family members or trusted domestic servants. In the early days of oil exploration, slaves even toiled with the crews of international oil companies,[23] and Thesiger ran across them several times in his travels. One elderly

Dubaian told me of seeing a group of slaves manacled to a wall in Al Ain in 1951.

A tour of Sheikh Saeed's house, where Dubai ruler Sheikh Mohammed spent his first ten years, turned up a history of slaves. Abdulla al-Mutairy, the fifty-year old director of the museum that operates in the old coral-walled house, mentioned that the room where he and his staff chatted over coffee was the slaves' quarters.

"The slaves lived here—where you're sitting—this was the slave room," al-Mutairy says. "The black people living here did the housework and the cooking."

Emirati historian Fatma al-Sayegh describes her family's ownership of slaves as "domestic slavery." The slaves took the family's last name and were considered members of the tribe. "We used to have a whole family working for us. They called themselves al-Sayegh, but they were from Africa," she says. "Even middle-class families kept slaves." Gulf Arabs' current over-reliance on foreign labor and disdain for physical work and service jobs stems partly from their thousand-year history of slave ownership, al-Sayegh believes. The 1963 ban wasn't much of a hardship for slave owners. They switched from slaves to low-paid Asians who find themselves mistreated in much the same way.

British policy in the Trucial States was to grant freedom papers to any slaves who presented themselves at their mission. The ceremony was simple. A slave would grasp the flagpole inside the compound and ask to be freed. In 1958, Dubai's political resident Donald Hawley reported that two women slaves turned up to ask for freedom papers. One slave bared her back to reveal welts from a whipping she'd received from her mistress. "Not too serious but many and unpleasant," Hawley wrote in his 2007 book *The Emirates: Witness to a Metamorphosis*.[24] Hawley freed the women and gave them asylum inside the mission. The next day, the owner asked for the slaves back. Hawley refused. They stayed in the British mission until Sheikh Rashid intervened and guaranteed their freedom.[25]

Maryam Behnam, an Iranian-born Emirati, says her family kept "hundreds" of slaves around their home and farm in Bandar Lengeh, in southern Iran. When the family came to Dubai, they brought slaves with them. Everywhere they traveled, slaves accompanied them as integral members of the family. Behnam had a personal slave, a girl her age named Jameela. The girl turned up on the family doorstep in Bandar Lengeh one day. Behnam's grandfather was never able to find her parents, so they kept her.

"She would clean my shoes and put them on me. She helped me with my dress. She brushed my hair for me. I didn't do anything in the house. These things were done by servant people," Behnam says. "Lamps had to be cleaned and filled with oil. Water had to be brought in. Everywhere you looked, you saw three or four slaves."

Behnam's Dubai relatives freed their slaves in the 1960s. "They're still in Dubai. They used to visit me," she says. "Some of them are better off than we are. They've got children studying in America."

Kings for Life

In the 1960s, political scientists in the West declared the end was nigh for the world's traditional monarchs. The theorists, including Daniel Lerner, Karl Deutsch, and Samuel Huntington, wrote that the kings and sheikhs clinging to power were hopelessly out of step with modernization.[26] Either they would surrender power peacefully, perhaps retaining scraps of their privilege, as in Europe, or face overthrow.

The march of evidence backed this theory. Egypt's king lost power to an army colonel named Gamal Abdel Nasser in 1952. Iraq's army executed King Faisal II after overrunning his palace in 1958. Yemen's King Muhammad al-Badr was overthrown by revolutionaries in 1962. In Libya, a coup in 1969 tossed aside King Idris in favor of Col. Muammar Ghaddafi. Just across the Gulf from Dubai, Islamic revolutionaries drove out Iran's shah in 1979.

The Gulf monarchies, with their anachronistic sheikhs, looked like teetering dominoes. As societies grew wealthy and educated, there was no way a tribal chief could keep them happy. Given the modernization under way, the sheikhs would cave in to political reforms that gave citizens a greater say in governance.

The 1950s and 1960s were trying times for the Gulf-ruling families, with Arab nationalists like Nasser in Egypt calling for Arab unity and self-rule. Nasser's message resonated deeply in Dubai and the Gulf, stoking opposition to the British first, and the ruling sheikhs second. The Soviet Union egged on the radicals. Colonial empires withered. A slew of independent states emerged, especially in Africa.

For a while, it looked like the political scientists would be right. The Trucial States sat as fat targets for revolution. Gulf Arabs traveled to Egypt to meet with the Arab League and foment colonial overthrow. The league opened an office in Sharjah that imported nationalist teachers from Iraq and Syria. The radicals made plain their goal of expelling the British and upending absolute tribal rule. Pan-Arab and anti-British graffiti sprouted everywhere.

Much of the opposition focused on Hawley, the British political resident in Dubai. Hawley would attend a seemingly innocuous event, like a school sports day, and, instead of greeting him with the Union Jack, jeering students would wave flags of the United Arab Republic, Nasser's short-lived union of Egypt and Syria. One morning Hawley woke to find the Union Jack missing from his residential compound. He found it floating in the creek. The British knew the end of their 152-year "colony-on-the-cheap" was near. The air smelled of rebellion, and many among Dubai's prominent families became Nasser's acolytes.[27]

"It's impossible to overstate Nasser's effect," says Anthony Harris, a British diplomat in Egypt and Sudan during Nasser's time. Later, he became UAE ambassador. "It was the first time an Arab leader stood up to the West. He had this honeyed voice. People fell into trances when he spoke. The British were scared that Nasserism would sweep them out of the Arab world."

Nasser's revolutionaries might have ousted the British and carried off the Gulf sheikhs. But their timing was bad. Competing with independence fever were new opportunities to get rich. Abu Dhabi had oil, and the ruler suddenly had income to distribute. In Dubai, which had not yet struck oil, Sheikh Rashid understood that a boom was on the way, requiring construction and huge imports of goods. Without oil income, he bought off his opponents with business concessions. The families fomenting revolt were the first recipients. Christopher Davidson, an English scholar who has written extensively on the end of British rule, says that the largest Dubai merchant families whose names now adorn shopping malls and car dealerships were the most vehement Arab nationalists of the 1950s.

"The British advice was not to give blatant handouts, but to give prominent families exclusive trade licenses. If you make one family, say, the sole importer of Mercedes cars, you make them billionaires very quickly," he says. The revolutionaries gave up their fight to get rich.

Perhaps nowhere begged for revolutionary change more than did Abu Dhabi before 1966. This sheikhdom had one of the world's largest underground reservoirs of oil, and it was governed by Sheikh Shakhbut, a ruler who lived in a mud fort and, by several accounts, kept his money in his mattress because he didn't trust banks.

Shakhbut's moment in the sun came when drillers hit oil in 1958. All eyes were upon him. Was he going to use the money to raise his people up with dignity? Or was he going to squander it on trifles? As it turned out, Sheikh Shakhbut wasn't going to do either. He feared the modern world and knew the ageless traditions of his land would be dashed by riches. He was considered stingy, rare for a Bedouin leader. Shakhbut wanted Abu Dhabi to keep its frontier edge and reject the soft clutches of the West.

In his defense, Sheikh Shakhbut understood the delicacy of the situation. His subjects had lived in primitive isolation for millennia. They weren't ready for the Rolling Stones and miniskirts. Shakhbut wanted to ease his people into wealth and preserve their culture.

Shakhbut even rejected practical improvements, like roads and schools. For instance, by the end of his reign in 1966, he had only just started building a bridge to the mainland from Abu Dhabi island. Until the Maqta Bridge was finished, visitors had to wait until low tide to drive or wade across the channel. There was still no paved road between Abu Dhabi and Dubai. People drove more than sixty miles along the beach and the salt flats, which was only possible when the sea was calm.[28]

Shakhbut could be unreasonable. He sparked a diplomatic row by refusing to repay a loan from the British Bank of the Middle East. He considered the money a gift and used it to buy rifles and a generator. When the bank asked him to repay, he accused it of stealing his money. Shakhbut settled only after the British sent a diplomat from London.[29]

Shakhbut was eventually overthrown. But it was no revolutionary uprising that toppled him. He'd become an embarrassment to his own family, the ruling al-Nahyans. On August 6, 1966, with the urging of the British, Shakhbut's youngest brother, Zayed, took control of Abu Dhabi in a bloodless coup. Sheikh Shakhbut went quietly, apparently relieved to relinquish the headaches of rule. But Sheikh Zayed's coup didn't end tribal rule in Abu Dhabi. It strengthened it. Zayed went on to become the UAE president, ruling until he died in office in 2004. He is revered as the father of his country. His son Sheikh Khalifa is now UAE president and Abu Dhabi leader.

It turned out that the political scientists who'd predicted an end to Gulf monarchies had got it wrong. In the UAE, as well as in Saudi Arabia, Kuwait, Bahrain, Qatar, and Oman, the same tribal families in power in the 1950s were still locked into power in 2009. Of the six, the UAE has enjoyed perhaps the greatest stability despite offering the fewest political freedoms. The other five Gulf countries allow some form of elections, although in Saudi Arabia only men vote. The sole vestige of democracy in the UAE is an advisory body in which half the members are elected by a hand-picked caucus. Political parties and civil society organizations are banned. Yet the tribal leaders in the UAE, especially Dubai's Sheikh Mohammed, are broadly popular, seen as competent and benevolent. There is precious little political grumbling. How could the theorists get it so wrong?

In the short term, agitators were put down. Witness Sheikh Rashid's 1939 smashing of the rebel *majlis*. After independence, Sheikh Zayed made clear that he brooked no talk of democracy. Abdulkhaleq Abdulla, the professor who is one of the UAE's few democracy activists, got a personal demonstration. Abdulla had written about UAE tribal rule at Georgetown. The articles weren't flattering, but they weren't distributed widely. One of them came to Zayed's attention in 1991. Zayed got angry. The UAE president stripped the professor of his passport. It was a mild punishment, but Abdulla, who suddenly couldn't leave the country, got the message.

"We tried to be daring but it wasn't a good time. We knew we were testing the limit," Abdulla says while crunching on a Caesar's salad at the Novotel Hotel in 2008. "It could've been much worse. I said 'Okay, take my passport. I don't want to go anywhere anyway.' "

Dubai leader Sheikh Maktoum quietly intervened, speaking to Sheikh Zayed and getting Abdulla's passport returned. The professor got a personal warning from a security man. "You can talk about anything else but don't mention democracy. Sheikh Zayed doesn't like it," the official said. "Anybody can bring it to his attention and you're in trouble, guy."

A tiny political opposition has developed in Dubai, but its activists still run into trouble with Sheikh Zayed in his grave. Mohammed al-Roken, a lawyer and rights activist, has been arrested twice and forced out of his job as a professor at UAE University. His newspaper columns and speeches have been banned by the government, his passport seized. Al-Roken's main offense has been speaking out about what he describes as a government that caters to the foreign majority. He says Emiratis shouldn't feel like strangers in their own country, shouldn't have to stomach immodest dress and rampant boozing. Al-Roken's conservative critiques are considered political activism, which is not tolerated.

In the longer term, rulers in Dubai and the UAE have stanched dissent the nice way, by paying off their opponents. In practice, a wealthy populace is a happy populace and not one to clamor for political rights. In the UAE, the calculus is easy because the number of citizens is tiny, around one million, and the budget surplus is huge. The UAE earned $71 billion in oil revenue in 2007, enough to dole out $55,000 a year in subsidies to the average male Emirati.[30]

Subsidizing away the political opposition isn't so easy in other Gulf states. Bahrain discovered oil in 1932, when prices were low. It has since pumped out most of its reserves and has little left to pamper its people.[31] The tiny country is now embroiled in a slow-burn rebellion led by its underprivileged Shiite majority.

Neighboring Saudi Arabia may sit atop the world's largest oil reserves, but it must share the proceeds among 25 million citizens. Saudi per capita income is $23,000 per year, a third less than the UAE average of $37,000, and far lower than Abu Dhabi's towering $74,000.[32] Not surprisingly, there is far more political opposition in Saudi Arabia.

Emirati sheikhs also survived because there was no one to unseat them: no army, trade union, or party that could start a conspiracy or grassroots movement. Dubai didn't even have a police force until 1956.[33] The only people in arms were desert Bedouin, who, by their nature, wanted to remain free and nomadic; and the tiny British-led Trucial Oman Scouts, created to prop up British-backed rulers. The sheikhs were safe because no one, save the British or their own families, could topple them. When Sheikh Zayed formed a national army in the 1970s, he staffed the officer corps with tribal leaders loyal to his family.[34]

There is another reason the sheikhs confounded those predicting their downfall. People are happy with them. There may not be much political freedom, but that doesn't mean the country is oppressive. The UAE enjoys broad social freedoms which substitute for its lack of political ones. People raised under democracy feel at home in Dubai. Women are encouraged to work and there is little of the separation of the sexes seen in Saudi Arabia, even in Bahrain. Alcohol is freely available. Speech is relatively free, in comparison with censored media in Saudi Arabia and Egypt (but less free than in Kuwait). UAE leaders are seen as progressive. Sheikh Mohammed encourages—even subsidizes—entrepreneurship and scholarship. These social liberties compensate those who might grumble about a lack of a political voice.

"People don't want to replace tribal rule. It is my absolute conviction that they are happy with it," says Anthony Harris. "The sheikh makes sure he's a river to his people, through property, jobs, and sponsorships. Certainly there's no threat to that system, no threat at all."

II

DUBAI EMERGES

4

IT'S SHEIKH RASHID'S WORLD—WE JUST LIVE IN IT

Death at Dawn

IT WAS A silver dawn that broke on September 10, 1958. A suffocating mist enveloped the town and the sun appeared to be working in concert with it, cranking up the heat and basting everyone in sweat.

British political agent Donald Hawley, an Oxford-educated Arabist in his mid-thirties, was eating breakfast when a knock came at the door. The caller was Dr. Desmond McCaully, the local physician. McCaully looked a state. His pressed tropical outfit of white linen trousers and jacket were rumpled, and his face glistened with the oily sheen of a sleepless night. McCaully said that he'd spent the night tending to the ill Sheikh Saeed and that, despite his best efforts, the eighty-year-old ruler of Dubai had died. The old sheikh's attendants were, at that moment, preparing his body for burial.[1] Muslims, especially in the Gulf, waste little time burying their dead. In the days before refrigeration, the reasons were practical as well as religious.

Hawley donned a somber suit and tie and walked with McCaully to Sheikh Saeed's sprawling home on the creek. Arriving, he found a silent crowd of white-clothed mourners sitting on the ground, clustered in patches of shade. The dhows in the creek swayed silently in the tide as if respecting the end of a benevolent man and his era. The anguished wail of a mourning woman rose from inside the house. The death had defied at last the inscription over the door: "O house, let no grief enter you and let not time betray your owner."

The carved wooden doors on the coral house swung open for Sheikh Saeed one last time. The ruler emerged flat on his back on a wooden bier, his body covered in a red-checked cloth. Pallbearers carried the corpse along the creek to the cemetery. The crowd fell in behind, including Sheikh Saeed's sons, Rashid and Khalifa, wearing simple white *kandouras*. Men led the group in Quranic chants as muezzins at Dubai's mosques announced the death in melancholy cadences. Women in black robes and masks wailed on the streetcorners and joined the procession as it passed. Hawley heard a Saudi telling the women to get lost, that it was *haram,* forbidden in Islam, for females to join a funeral march. No one paid him any mind.

Townspeople surrounded the grave to watch the lowering of the old man's body. Sheikh Saeed had been born in 1878, one of a thousand or so inhabitants in an unknown town on the far edge of the world. He survived as an infant against the odds. He took over as ruler in 1912 upon the death of his uncle, Butti bin Suhail al-Maktoum. The town's business leaders, Europeans, Indians, and Iranians, were paying respects to his son Rashid, now officially in charge. Hawley found Dubai's forty-six-year-old leader squatting in the shade of a tree and murmured to him in Arabic, "May God give you consolation."

A Pakistani photographer named Noor Ali Rashid was one of those in the crowd, but he'd purposefully left his camera at home. Noor Ali Rashid had only arrived in Dubai a few days earlier, and he'd had a bad experience taking pictures of the dead. In Karachi, he'd snapped a photo of a little girl killed in a traffic accident and a mob had chased him through the streets. He'd barely escaped with his life. He swore off corpse photography after that.

The simple burial was over by 10:00 a.m. Locals gathered around Sheikh Rashid, kissing him, according to custom, on the nose. The new ruler looked exhausted and disoriented. By the end of the morning, he collapsed. Dr. McCaully had to visit the royal residence a second time.

Rashid in Command

The death of Sheikh Saeed and the end of his forty-six-year rule marked the final stage of Dubai's long slumber in old Arabia. Very little changed on his watch. His death came like a catalyst, a dam burst that allowed fifty years of pent-up modernity to flood Dubai.

Sheikh Rashid, who had been running things unofficially for nearly two decades, would use his mandate to put this unknown city on the map. Within a year, Dubai would have a modern port. Within four years, electricity, running water, and telephones. A bridge would span the creek in five years, and street lights would illuminate the town a year later. Queen Elizabeth II would pay Sheikh Rashid not one but two visits, touring Dubai's new airport terminal in 1972 and then returning to inaugurate the Middle East's tallest building in 1979.

The British threw a recognition ceremony for the new leader, complete with a naval artillery salute. Rashid stood on the creek bank amid a smattering of British officials and sheikhs, looking nervous as Hawley read a letter from Queen Elizabeth recognizing him as the legitimate ruler of Dubai.

This time Noor Ali Rashid brought his camera. The wiry man strode up to Sheikh Rashid and snapped his picture, then asked him to pose with Hawley and snapped a few more. Soon he was stage-managing the event, herding merchants to pose with Dubai's ruler. A few days later he dropped off a few prints. He'd developed them in his makeshift darkroom with chemicals he'd brought from Pakistan. He filtered the water himself because it was so full of grit that it scratched the film. The Dubai ruler was impressed with the pictures. From then on, any time there was an official function—luncheons, visiting warships, falcon demonstrations, ribbon cuttings—Sheikh Rashid would send for the Pakistani photographer.[2]

Sheikh Rashid had a crooked hawk's nose and beady eyes that danced when he smiled. His shaggy beard and the creases around his eyes lent his smile a grandfatherly allure, even when he was a young man. He was self-educated and had had little schooling. He spoke only Arabic. Rashid was skeptical of certain bits of modernity, but he was openly disdainful of the stagnant past.

The new ruler kept himself in good shape, maintaining the bandy physique of a horseman his entire life. He'd already proven his toughness in the 1939 attack that rescued his father's administration. But the ruthlessness of his younger years had mellowed. Rashid now exuded the simple confidence of the Bedouin, or *Bedu*.

Rashid disdained certain comforts. He rode his horse even after he owned a car. He preferred to sit cross-legged on the floor in the Bedouin style. When offered a seat on a couch, he'd draw his legs up underneath him. He smoked a tiny pipe, a *midwakh*, common in the Gulf, and held it absentmindedly as he spoke, filling it with green tobacco from a small aspirin jar.[3] Rashid's charm was infectious and disarming. His *majlis* was as much a forum for teasing and gags as for serious business. His jokes were often self-deprecating. He'd ask people to explain things in detail, saying with a smile, "I am a *Bedu* and do not understand complicated modern ways."[4]

Behind the modesty was a skilled politician who managed to stay on good terms with just about everybody, including the Saudis and Iranians, despite territorial disputes. He'd allied himself with the ruling al-Nahyan family of Abu Dhabi when he married Sheikha Latifa, a cousin of ruling sheikhs Shakhbut and Zayed. Rashid earned enormous respect in Britain and, in his later years, in Washington. He even managed to out-maneuver Saddam Hussein in the 1980s while remaining on cordial terms. During the Iran-Iraq war, Saddam demanded that Dubai halt trade with Iran, which, he complained, was giving his enemies an economic lifeline. Sheikh Rashid's sympathetic noises managed to mollify Saddam while keeping up the profitable trade with Iran.[5] The Bush administration put the same diplomatic pressure on Dubai after 2006, haranguing Sheikh Mohammed to heed the U.S. trade embargo on Iran. Like Saddam, Bush got friendly responses and little action.

Sheikh Rashid maintained a punishing work ethic in a region known for languor. He rose while it was dark and toured the city before dawn prayers. Afterward he held daily *majlis* meetings with movers and shakers. He brought Dubaians under his spell, demonstrating a knack for sizing people up, and then investing trust in men who found themselves working to impress him, if only to extend the magical sensation of Sheikh Rashid's attention.

"Those of us foreigners that came here, we all got the same infection from Sheikh Rashid. Dubai had to become a place on the map," George

Chapman says, reeling off a list of names of Englishmen who pitched in. Bill Duff handled finances. Eric Tulloch became the state engineer and developed Dubai's municipal drinking water. The surveyors of Sir William Halcrow designed major projects and mapped out the city's growth. And Chapman handled shipping.

Dredging for Dollars

In the 1950s, Dubai was in trouble. The creek, its lifeline to the world, was being choked with silt. Ships had to anchor in deep water a mile offshore and transfer goods to barges, which ferried them into the creek. This could only be done when weather and tides cooperated. The creek mouth was only two and a half feet deep at low tide, far too shallow for most boats. Barges could only get in at high tide. Even then they ran aground. Breakers rolled in and swamped the barges, ruining sacks of rice and flour.[6]

Ship captains on tight schedules skipped Dubai, which could only handle tiny cargoes. The creek debacle was a constant theme in Sheikh Rashid's *majlis*. He agreed with the merchants: If the waterway was deeper and had moorings, ships could enter and they'd only be unloaded once.

In 1954, when Sheikh Rashid was still crown prince, he commissioned a feasibility study that called for dredging the creek and building up its banks with bulkheads and sheet piling. But the estimated cost, £600,000 (about $3 million), was far beyond Dubai's means, representing years of the town's total economic output. Sheikh Rashid decided to raise the cash. He gathered £200,000 by levying special taxes, selling bonds, and strong-arming donations from merchant families who relied on the creek.[7] And the rest, £400,000, he borrowed from newly wealthy Kuwait, which played the role of Gulf big brother in those days.

Aerial photos from the era show how the dredging barges, with their backhoes scraping the creek bed, swept away the shoals from the creek's mouth. Crews shored up the banks with steel and concrete, allowing boats to moor. From a shallow tidal wash whose mouth shifted with each storm, the creek became a defined channel. It could handle ships with eight-foot drafts, carrying seven thousand tons of cargo. One ship could deliver triple the cargo Dubai imported in all of 1951.[8]

Sheikh Rashid used the dredging spoils to reclaim new land along the banks, which he sold to merchants for warehousing. When Dubai's largest public project finished in 1961, Dubai was the most accessible and important port on the Trucial Coast.

The dredging cleared away the obstructions to Dubai's modernization as if they were bowling pins, catapulting the growing port into the commercial leadership of the lower Gulf. Weather was no longer a big problem, since there was no need to transfer cargoes offshore. Shippers knew their vessels could visit and stay on schedule. Dubai became a profitable destination. Merchants could order hundreds of tons of concrete, for example, or block, steel, glass, and plaster. No one built from palm fronds or coral anymore.

Dubai's entrepôt business, its reexports, caught like a gasoline fire. The town became the chief port for southern Iran and the supplier for the rest of the Trucial Coast, warehousing goods that were transshipped down the coast in dhows or humped into the interior by camel. From then on, Dubai would ride an incredible growth spurt that has yet to stop. The dredging of the creek was the spark that started the whole thing.

Sheikh Rashid was able to repay the merchants and the Kuwaitis ahead of time. Locals who shared the risk became some of the richest in the city and in some cases, the world. The al-Ghurair family, the al-Rostamanis, the al-Futtaims, and others were repaid with exclusive import licenses and business contracts. To this day, Sheikh Mohammed pays tribute to the families who risked their personal wealth to build Dubai.[9] A few of their descendants, men like Abdul Aziz al-Ghurair, are now on the *Forbes* magazine "world's richest" list.[10]

Brightening Up

Rashid's next task was to brighten up the place. In his initial year as ruler, he set up a municipal electric company. It built a rudimentary 1,440-kilowatt generating plant and strung the town with wires.[11] The bright lights of Dubai flickered to life in 1961. It was about time. Not far away, Israel had already launched a rocket into space. The Soviets sent a satellite zooming past Venus. Dubai's municipal power came eighty years after the lights went on in Niagara Falls, New York, and long after Cairo, Beirut, and even Saudi Arabia. Electricity brought all sorts of unknown comforts. The souks were suddenly awash in fans, refrigerators, radios—even air conditioners. That same year, technicians cobbled together the town's first telephone exchange and spliced it into the international network. Dubai was now a phone call away from anywhere in the world.[12]

Dubai's good fortune often looks like a gift. In some cases, this is literally true. Its first paved road, first bridge, and municipal water system came as dowry presents from Sheikh Ahmad bin Ali al-Thani, the emir of the nearby sheikhdom of Qatar. Sheikh Ahmad helped his upstart neighbor in gratitude for being given the hand of Sheikh Rashid's eldest child, Mariam, in 1958.

In 1961, Sheikh Ahmad paved a sand track that ran between the creek and Sheikh Rashid's new Zabeel Palace, a few miles inland. Zabeel Road was Dubai's first tarmac street.[13] Engineers soon began laying out roads and roundabouts in the English fashion. At first, Dubaians drove like Brits, on the left. When it became apparent that neighbors had adopted right-side driving, Sheikh Rashid ordered everyone to switch.

In 1962, the Qatari emir plunked down £162 million to pay for Dubai's first creek crossing, the Maktoum Bridge.[14] For the first time, people could walk from Bur Dubai to Deira, and driving didn't mean an hour-long sand rally around the far end of the creek.

A few years later, drillers found an aquifer of fresh water at Al Aweer, fifteen miles south of the city. The clean water was delicious compared with the brackish swill in town. Sheikh Ahmad bankrolled the system that brought the water into Dubai, with underground pipes fanning out to nearly every building by 1968. Finally, Dubaians had running water. Nobody mourned the demise of the donkey cart vendors.

New amenities swept Dubai one after another: an ice plant, radio and television broadcasts, streetlights, municipal government, a police force, even the use of concrete. Dubai was among the last places in the region to get these things. Sheikh Rashid knew it was part of his ruling bargain to bring water and power and pave the streets. That would have been enough to gain public support as the tribal patriarch. But, of course, Sheikh Rashid wasn't content to bring Dubai to par with the region. Dubaians got a lot more than the ruling bargain called for.

Outpacing the Neighbors

In the 1950s, Dubai was overshadowed by next-door Sharjah, a larger city with a bigger port and a long maritime history under the Qawasim. But Sharjah drifted in indecisiveness. Its ruler refused Kuwaiti assistance to stop the silting up of its own tidal creek, its chief port.

One night in 1960, a hot *shamal*, a summer wind, blew down from Iran, kicking up booming surf that filled the mouth of the Sharjah creek with sand. Sharjah's port was sealed shut. Overnight the tidal creek became a saltwater lake. Chapman had a barge in Sharjah and it was now stranded, like every other vessel in port. He only reclaimed it during a high spring tide with twenty men digging and pushing on their hands and knees. The closure of Sharjah port lasted a decade, devastating the commercial viability of Dubai's closest rival. Sharjah merchant families, including the powerful al-Yousuf clan, shifted their businesses to Dubai. Sheikh Rashid welcomed them with land grants. Even the British decamped, moving their political agent's office from Sharjah to Dubai. A few years later, the British decided Dubai was best suited to host its development offices for the Trucial States.[15] To this day, Sharjah is a poor city, playing Tijuana to Dubai's San Diego.

Dubai's economic tussle with Sharjah didn't end there. It was in Sharjah that the British built their airbase in 1932, paving a runway that grew more valuable as aviation progressed. Dubai had backed the wrong technology in 1937 by giving the British permission to land flying boats on the creek. Sea-based aircraft were being phased out. Sheikh Rashid, who began flying from Sharjah on his own travels, knew Dubai needed an airport. He knew it would be a moneymaker, too, even if it was only a refueling stop.

"If a person lands in Dubai, he will take a taxi, buy a pack of cigarettes, have a meal, and we will all benefit," he said.[16]

But when he sought permission from the British political agent, Rashid got nowhere. The agent said Dubai didn't need an airport with Sharjah's just a few miles away. At the time, Dubai had developed into a major smuggling port. Merchants imported gold from England and the United States at market prices around $35 an ounce, and then smuggled it into India where its import was banned, so it sold for more than $70 an ounce.

There was one hitch. The gold flights landed in Sharjah, where the ruler imposed duty on air cargo, effectively taking a chunk of Dubai's business. Sheikh Rashid knew he could pay for an airport of his own with the money he would save in taxes to Sharjah. In 1959, he hired a British aviation consultancy, International Aeradio Ltd., to design an airport. In the meantime, a British pilot named Freddie Bosworth began flying gold-laden planes onto a makeshift airstrip on a Dubai salt flat.

Dubai's wily sheikh brought Bosworth in on his plan to circumvent the agent's restrictions. One day he handed Bosworth a Rolex watch. Then he asked the daring flier for a favor: fly to Bahrain and charm the British political resident, who was the Dubai agent's superior, into supporting an airport. To the consternation of the Dubai agent, the plan worked.[17] Sheikh Rashid's airport opened in 1960, and Dubai has expanded it relentlessly ever since. By 1968, it could handle Boeing 747s.[18] By contrast, Sharjah's airport slipped into anonymity as a hub for cargo flights, arms merchants, and budget airlines.

Smugglers' Notch

Dubai has always been a freewheeling place where bureaucrats and inspectors get little traction because they slow commerce. Smugglers ran guns, gold, slaves, diamonds, and drugs through Dubai in the past and still do today.[19]

"Dubai, city of merchants. Anything goes. They smuggled gold into India and silver out. That's how it survived," says Charley Kestenbaum, a retired U.S. diplomat who was based in Dubai and Abu Dhabi. "Its whole economic function was aimed at evading the rules and regulations of other countries in the region."

Venerable merchants swap stories about their smuggling escapades. Saif al-Ghurair, head of one of Dubai's banking and shipping families, piloted a smuggling dhow in the 1940s and 1950s. He tells of buying forty cases of stolen British ammunition in Mombasa, Kenya, "for almost nothing" and smuggling it into Dubai, where he sold each bullet for 5 rupees.[20]

After Indian independence, al-Ghurair and other dhow owners smuggled Dubai gold into India, where it is prized as a holiday gift and store of value. Al-Ghurair said he and others would sew gold pieces into vests they wore under their jackets. When they rendezvoused with Indian mobsters in boats off Bombay, the Indians would make their payments and don the vests.[21]

Dubai's exploits grew infamous in 1976, when the American novel *Dubai* appeared, written by *French Connection* author Robin Moore. The novel's fictitious smugglers ferried tons of gold into India while fighting off the Indian navy with stolen U.S. military gear.[22]

Sheikh Rashid himself, meeting with British Foreign Office officials in London in 1958, acknowledged that the city supported itself on "uncertain smuggling."[23] Dubai and Sharjah were then major import-export destinations for hashish and opium from Afghanistan and Iran, and still are today, with seizures of Afghan heroin still common.[24]

London, Meet the Maktoums

Sheikh Rashid's first trip outside the Gulf was a grand tour. He brought two sons, Maktoum, seventeen, and Hamdan, fourteen, along with customs chief Mahdi Tajer and banker Easa Al-Gurg. The arrangements called for the British government and the Iraq Petroleum Co. to split the costs of putting up the entourage at the Savoy Hotel for two weeks.

The royal party made the trip in hops, stopping at Bahrain, Amman, Jerusalem, Damascus, and Beirut, then flying across to Rome. There, the entourage rented cars and drove across the heart of Europe, finally reaching London on June 8, 1959. It had been a grueling trip, but Rashid wasn't one to relax. The very next day, he met Queen Elizabeth II for the first time. He greeted her in her box at the Royal Tournament, a military pageant steeped in empire nostalgia. In keeping with the occasion, Rashid handed the queen, her prime minister, and several other top officials a collection of Arab swords and curved *khanjar* daggers. In return, he was given a few photographs in silver frames and an umbrella, a novelty for a desert sheikh.

London made a big impression on Sheikh Rashid. He enjoyed the Royal Tournament's pomp, but was more taken by the London Underground, which he boarded for a ride at St. James's Park. He admired the sense of order, the magnitude of the buildings and elevated sense of politeness that seemed to stem from the British pride of accomplishment.

The only dim spot was his son, Sheikh Hamdan, who, according to Foreign Office intelligence reports, assumed a teenager's typical surliness for most of the visit.

But Sheikh Rashid wasn't just sightseeing. He also wanted to light a fire under oil exploration in Dubai. In one closed session with Minister of State for Foreign Affairs John Profumo, Rashid expressed "extreme frustration" that the British oil company refused to act on its exploration rights or reveal the extent of the sheikhdom's oil prospects. The Dubai leader complained that he was locked into the 1937 deal signed by his late father. The contract prevented him from bringing in American oil firms working across the Saudi border which were eager to extend their string of big strikes.

In the meantime, Rashid worried that Abu Dhabi, which had struck oil the previous year, would soon challenge Dubai's newfound maritime supremacy, taking away his chief source of income. Dubai, he told Profumo, would again be impoverished.

"Sheikh Rashid pleaded again and again that we should not treat his country as a little state in the back of beyond, but that we should regard him as part of our own country. (I think he really meant that he wanted a larger slice of cake!) He used the word 'guardian' to describe our relationship and said he had no other friends to which he could turn. He said anything we wanted from him would be granted," states a Foreign Office memo.[25]

Sheikh Rashid got no satisfaction from the British. So he took action on his own. Perhaps he was pushed by Abu Dhabi's challenge, or maybe it was the success of his dredging bid. But as soon as his plane touched down at home, Sheikh Rashid embarked on a remarkable string of gambles. Dubai's desert was an empty palette. He was going to start painting.

The Gambler

Sheikh Rashid's motto is famous in Dubai: "What's good for the merchants is good for Dubai." But he had another unstated philosophy: Move first and outrun the competition. He did this even after Dubai struck oil in 1966. The current ruler, Sheikh Mohammed, has taken these mantras to new heights. But Rashid knew Dubai's prosperity meant keeping ahead of Abu Dhabi, a neighbor with more resources than Dubai could hope for. To do this, Dubai jumped at every opportunity, cornering industries and economic sectors.

The curving creek remained Dubai's chief port for only a decade. Even dredged, it was too small for the ships that dominated international trade in the 1960s. Dubai's growth was hurtling and vessels again sat at anchor a mile off Dubai and transshipped cargo in barges.

In 1967, Sheikh Rashid vowed to fix this problem. He hired Halcrow, the British planners that handled the dredging, and asked them to design a deepwater port named after himself: Port Rashid. It was the biggest earthmoving project in Dubai's history, but, with the oil discovery, Dubai had the cash to make it happen. The sheikh wanted to press his advantage in infrastructure. The first port designs, built by digging away the beach of his ancestral neighborhood in Shindagha, called for four berths. Sheikh Rashid tore up those plans, quadrupling it to sixteen berths. By the time those drawings were done, Rashid ordered the port doubled again, to thirty-five berths.

In 1971, when Port Rashid's first berth opened, it brought immediate relief. The first of 120 ships anchored off Dubai began to discharge cargo.[26] The state-run operator that ran the port would eventually grow into the world's fourth largest.

Queen Elizabeth II arrived to inaugurate the port in 1972. Her arrival was a bit of serendipity. She happened to be flying across the region and planned to refuel in Bahrain, but she had heard about Sheikh Rashid's new airport terminal in Dubai. Recalling her meeting with the Dubai leader in London three years earlier, she ordered her pilot to stop at Dubai instead.[27]

Dubai in the 1970s was a city erupting onto the earth. Foreigners poured in: businessmen, laborers, investors, and fast-buck chasers. The city spread over the desert like an oil stain. In 1960, Dubai's 60,000 residents lived in an area of just two square miles, the size of a few city blocks. By 1970, the city held 100,000 people in a seven-square-mile area—roughly the size and density of present-day Cambridge, Massachusetts. Five years later, Dubai more than doubled in size again, reaching eighteen square miles, with 183,000 people—about like Providence, Rhode Island. By

1980, it doubled again, to thirty-two square miles and 276,000 people, nearly the size of Buffalo, New York. In those two decades, Dubai's area grew sixteen-fold and its population nearly quintupled.[28]

Dubai's first big hotel, the Intercontinental, coped with occupancy rates approaching 200 percent. Staff housed strangers together as a matter of policy. Businesses imported laborers from India and Pakistan to cope with the work. Hendrik Bosch, a thirty-three-year-old Dutchman overseeing construction of the five hundred-room Dubai International Hotel, tried a different tack. He toured Southeast Asia looking for six hundred workers. He liked those in Thailand, except few Thais spoke English. His next stop was Manila. In the Philippines, Bosch found a veritable mine of service-oriented people willing to live in Dubai. And, as citizens of a former American colony, they spoke English. Bosch worked out a deal with the Philippine government and in 1978 imported six hundred workers in three planeloads.

Bosch was the first major recruiter of Filipinos, a group that soon came to dominate jobs in hospitality, retail, and nursing. Filipina women also took jobs once held by slaves: as housemaids and nannies.

Sheikh Rashid wanted Dubai to be more than a port. He wanted it to be a center for the shipping industry. In 1971 he commissioned a feasibility study on building a dry dock, a yard where the largest vessels could be hauled out of the sea and repaired. But nearby Bahrain also had dry dock ambitions, and it got backing of the chief Arab oil exporters' group.

Rashid bulldogged ahead. Dubai's British advisers said the project was ridiculous. Global shipbuilding was in recession. Dubai was too small to absorb such a huge industrial investment. And there was simply no call for two dry docks within a few hundred miles of one another.[29] "Everyone told him this was too big. Why were we spending all this money? Why didn't we make a joint venture with the dry docks in Bahrain?" says Qassim Sultan, the longtime head of Dubai Municipality.

Sheikh Rashid wasn't going to invest $500 million of Dubai's oil revenues in Bahrain, Dubai's main competitor. He was intent on diversifying his own economy. His answer: "Why don't we compete with them instead?"[30]

The Dubai Dry Docks exhibited ambition that bordered on folly. But

Sheikh Rashid's next three announcements made people think he was a bit crazy. In 1979 he commissioned the mammoth Dubai Aluminum smelter—which recycled the plant's heat to distill fresh water from the sea. He launched the Dubai World Trade Centre, a skyscraper in the empty desert. The building was so tall that some Dubaians felt a frisson of fright when their gaze fell upon it. They thought the bone-white building would bring the evil eye upon Dubai, in the form of envious attention from those who thought Dubai was overinflating its profile.

"Everybody told Sheikh Rashid that the Trade Centre was a waste of time. Nobody would ever use it," says George Chapman. "I never said that. But I did query him. I would say, 'Have you costed it out? Have you thought it all out?' But you see he was very wise. He built things when they were cheap. That's the way Sheikh Mohammed thinks. 'Let's get it while the money's around.'"

The Middle East's tallest building had little trouble finding tenants. Its thirty-nine stories housed offices for some of the biggest corporations of the day, including IBM, Union Carbide, United Technologies, and British Petroleum. The honeycomb skyscraper, engraved onto the 100-dirham note, also hosts the U.S. consulate and several others, as well as Dubai's local stock market. On September 11, 2001, two of Rashid's countrymen would ensure Dubai's World Trade Centre would outlast New York's.

The third project was the biggest. Sheikh Rashid told the world he would build another port in Dubai's farthest scrap of empty beach, Jebel Ali, about twenty miles from the creek. There was no natural harbor at Jebel Ali, just a beach of broken coral where locals camped. Every square inch of the new port would have to be dug from the sandy shoreline, and a channel dredged through the coral beds offshore. The excavations were visible with the naked eye from outer space. Satellite pictures reveal a notch chiseled from the Gulf shore. Tiny Dubai would soon have more berthing capacity than San Francisco Bay.[31]

In 1980, the *Wall Street Journal* chided Sheikh Rashid in a front-page article titled "Is Dry Dock in Dubai to Be High and Dry and Pie in the Sky?"

> So, you thought risk-taking was out of style? Meet the entrepreneurs of Dubai, the fellows who put their petrodollars behind such sure-fire winners as:

- A dry dock so big that no ship afloat can fill it.
- A $1.4 billion aluminum smelter whose power plant has five of the largest gas-fired turbines in the world.
- A 66-berth seaport where freighters will steam into a 1-1/4-mile-long rectangular basin carved out of the desert at a cost of $1.6 billion.

Blue-chip investments, right? Now consider that not one of these investments is in an industrialized country . . . Checkbooks still ready?

The article, written by *Journal* reporter Ray Vicker, went on to state that the only way to explain Dubai's building boom was that Sheikh Rashid suffered "an edifice complex." Nearly thirty years later, the same accusation gets leveled at Rashid's son.

Vicker wasn't the only skeptic. Dubaians themselves had reservations, especially about Jebel Ali port, so far from the city center.[32] This time, Sheikh Rashid's own sons broke ranks with him. As Sheikh Mohammed relates in his autobiography, Dubai merchants pleaded with him to talk sense to his father. Young Mohammed agreed, bluntly asking his father to stop the job before the city went bankrupt. The old sheikh puffed on his pipe and told his son: "I'm building this port now because there will come a time when you won't be able to afford it."[33]

The Jebel Ali port is the world's largest man-made harbor, Dubai's greatest financial asset, and the U.S. Navy's number one overseas seaport. From the air, its mile-long container stacks resemble furrows of a vast cornfield. The fifty-two-square-mile tract of warehouses, factories, and container storage is some of the earth's busiest real estate. To call it bustling is an understatement. The level of activity is relentless and disorienting. Cranes swing shipping containers overhead, trucks rumble past, forklifts dash around like houseflies, and tugboat teams nudge juggernaut ships to their berths.

Many believe that Sheikh Rashid's steel-gut gambles on infrastructure were *the* pivotal decisions that make Dubai what it is today. Dubai's massive investments set the tiny emirate apart from its oil-rich neighbors. Abu Dhabi, Saudi Arabia, and Kuwait used mineral wealth to subsidize cushy lifestyles and overpaid bureaucracies, or they parked it in overseas stocks and bonds. Their investments earned maybe 10 cents on the dollar, while Dubai made $5 for each dollar invested in infrastructure, says Essa Kazim, who heads Dubai's stock exchanges.

In hindsight, Sheikh Rashid's ideas were the best use of Dubai's small oil reserves. Dubai had one chance to get it right, and, instead of following its neighbors, it chose a new route. It invested to diversify its economy. The more Sheikh Rashid poured into ports, industry, and airports, the faster the economy grew. State spending triggered a larger torrent of private investment.

"Everything he did was visionary and everything he did was criticized at the time," says Charley Kestenbaum, the retired U.S. diplomat. "The thirty-nine-story tower: 'What do you need a thirty-nine-story tower for in the desert?' The dry dock: 'Oh my God, what a white elephant!'"

Why did Dubai's mega-investments succeed when so many others in the Third World failed? Maybe the price of failure was too high: The cash was Dubai's own, and not on loan from the World Bank. Maybe Sheikh Rashid's sons made sure their father's priorities were given maintenance and attention, not left to rot.

"Time and again the British advisers said, 'This is risky. Don't do it.' Or 'Don't do it on such a large scale.' Time and again the rulers in Dubai got it right," says Davidson, the British academic.

Dubai today is the Middle East's capital of commerce, one of its biggest recipients of foreign direct investment, its top financial center, biggest port and airport, and home of the largest number of foreign businesses. Sheikh Rashid's investment gambles in the 1950s, 1960s, and 1970s are largely responsible.

5

THE ROAD TO DOMINANCE

Independence

IT'S 1971. BLACK Sabbath is pounding out "Iron Man." NASA's fourth moon launch is under way. The Israelis are busy assimilating territory captured from Egypt, Jordan, and Syria. And the British Empire is disintegrating.

Three years earlier, Britain announced the jettisoning of its territories east of the Suez. The Trucial States would have to fend for themselves in a tough new world. No one thinks they can do it, not even their own leaders. The seven weak sheikhdoms have no experience with central rule. There is no government infrastructure, no tradition of private property, no currency, no roads stitching them together. There are few laws and fewer books. Most people are illiterate. Women cover their faces in metallic masks that resemble helmet visors of medieval knights. The territory's only protection is a tiny band of paramilitaries called the Trucial Oman Scouts. Outside the main cities of Dubai, Abu Dhabi, and Sharjah, the country is as primitive as sub-Saharan Africa: Tribesmen raise families by lantern light in thatched huts or goat hair tents. Bedouin roam the desert in search of water and grazing.

Dubai and the sheikhdoms that would form the UAE had languished in isolation for centuries. The idea that they could catch up with the developed world appeared preposterous. Independence was a problem, not an opportunity. Sheikh Zayed of Abu Dhabi and Sheikh Rashid of Dubai pleaded with London to extend British protection. They'd pay all expenses.

The Gulf beyond Britain's embrace was a cutthroat neighborhood in 1971. Saudi Arabia's royals were looking to expand their undefined borders. And Iran, across the narrow sea, had its long-running claims to bits of the Arab side, including Shiite-majority Bahrain.[1] When the Trucial sheikhdoms came together as the United Arab Emirates, they stood little chance of fending off these powers. American and British diplomats expected the untested UAE, including Dubai, to be subsumed into a new regional empire. Joseph Sisco, the U.S. undersecretary for political affairs, told Congress he had grave doubts the UAE would remain in one piece.[2]

The British decision to pull out was final. Recovery from World War II had overstretched the British economy, and the public wanted the government to pare down its expensive colonial empire. So the preparations moved toward UAE independence day, December 2, 1971.

And then, electrifying everyone's fears, Iran swooped in. The day before independence, Iran captured three islands governed by the Trucial States. Two of the islands, the Tunbs, were held by Ras Al-Khaimah. The third, Abu Musa, was governed by Sharjah. It wasn't a good omen.

The Iranians planned a clever takeover. The shah sent a flotilla on maneuvers in the lower Gulf under the cover of Navy Day celebrations. Hours before the British mandate expired, on November 30, 1971, an Iranian destroyer group broke from the maneuvers and sailed to the Tunbs. Iranian marines landed in hovercraft and jogged toward the police barracks. Instead of surrendering, the Arab police opened fire with machine guns, mowing down the invaders. The burst killed three Iranians and wounded a fourth. The Iranians responded by assaulting the post, killing five and wounding a sixth. The invaders soon captured the remaining Arab defenders, who were allowed to join civilians fleeing to Ras Al-Khaimah.

A pair of British warships idling nearby did nothing to intervene. A British government spokesman said the Royal Navy couldn't be expected to exercise her treaty responsibilities toward the Arab sheikhdoms on the final day the treaties remained in force.[3] The UAE's diminished standing in the regional power structure was all too clear.

The Iranians also sent a destroyer group to seize Abu Musa. There, however, the wheels had been greased. The Sharjah ruler, Sheikh Khalid bin Mohammed al-Qassimi, perhaps understanding that Iran would invade anyway, leased the island to the Iranian navy for $3 million a year.[4] The Iranian force staged a similar amphibious landing on Abu Musa, but instead of being greeted by bullets, the Sharjah ruler's brother met the Iranian officers with handshakes. Tehran quickly exceeded its mandate, building a port, setting up a customs post, and incorporating Abu Musa into Iran. Abu Musa and the Tunbs have been held by Iran ever since.

Sheikh Khalid's family never forgave him for the traitorous selling off of Qawasim land. In January 1972, Khalid's brother Saqr launched a coup and murdered the Sharjah leader. But a new way of governing was already afoot. The UAE's month-old federal government intervened and sent Saqr into exile. Khalid's brother Sultan took over as Sharjah's ruler.

The Iranian aggression wasn't the only event spawning doubt about the UAE's longevity. Saudi Arabia still claimed broad swaths of Abu Dhabi and decided to withhold diplomatic recognition. Across the border in Oman, a full-blown communist insurgency was under way, with leftist rebels fighting to overturn the royal family and British warplanes bombing insurgent bases. It was a mess.

A decade earlier, Omani rebels mounted several attacks inside the Trucial States, bombing British troop carriers. In 1961, the rebels planted bombs on a passenger ship, the *Dara*, carrying 800 people between Basra and Bombay. As the ship approached Dubai, two blasts tore through it, killing 236 passengers and crew. The *Dara* sank two days later.[5] That bombing stands as the worst terrorist attack in Dubai history. The Omani insurgency grew stronger in the following years and many worried the war would destabilize the neighboring UAE. The rebels weren't defeated until 1976.

Competing internal interests also endangered the union. Sheikh Rashid himself was lukewarm on joining a federation that would be dominated by Abu Dhabi, with 88 percent of the land and 90 percent of the oil. Dubai was clearly the most advanced of the seven shcikhdoms, but the energetic Sheikh Zayed was proposing to fund the partnership. Dubai's chief aim was to preserve its autonomy. A compromise constitution bowed to these interests, allowing each sheikhdom—known henceforth as emirates—to control its own oil resources and politics.

On December 2, 1971, the leaders of six of the seven sheikhdoms— Dubai, Abu Dhabi, Sharjah, Ajman, Umm Al-Quwain, and Fujairah— met in Dubai's Union House, overlooking Jumeirah Beach, and signed the proclamation declaring themselves part of a new country called the United Arab Emirates. Ras Al-Khaimah joined the following year. A towering flagpole mounted with a colossal flag marks the spot. Sheikh Zayed became president and Abu Dhabi city was named temporary capital. Sheikh Rashid assumed the roles of vice president and prime minister. The United Arab Emirates became a tribal confederation, its ruling sheikhs the owners of all land and mineral wealth. For the few outsiders who took notice, independence was a nonevent. People described it as the federation that was born to die.

A Whiff of Nationalism

The gloomy outlook did not infect the new country's few hundred thousand citizens. Everyone but the rulers, it seemed, was happy to be rid of the British.

Iran's takeover of Abu Musa and the Tunbs put a charge into people. The land grab spoiled independence celebrations but gave citizens, now known as Emiratis, a chance to show national unity. Across the emirates, anger at Iran turned into nationalist fervor, a new phenomenon for a new state.

Dubaians took to the streets to protest the Iranian takeover. Students marched across Deira, shouting, waving, and blocking traffic. When they reached their rally point, speeches were cut short by the arrival of twenty-two-year-old Sheikh Mohammed. The young graduate of Britain's Sandhurst military academy had just trained as a fighter pilot. He returned home to take the post of UAE defense minister, the world's youngest ever. The sheikh wore a full beard and carried himself with charisma and authority well beyond his years.

The marchers gathered around Sheikh Mohammed and grew quiet. They hoped that he would say something sympathetic. He thanked the students for their nationalist pride. And that was it. Street demonstrations would be as unwelcome in the UAE as they were before independence. "Everything is being taken care of," Sheikh Mohammed assured the students. "Thank you very much. Now it's about time for you guys to go home."[6] So the students thanked the young sheikh and went home.

Qualms about the UAE's viability didn't last long. As the oil discoveries mounted, the country's wealth—and its strategic value—was increasingly hard to deny. The economy was sizzling, and the world soon discovered that Sheikhs Zayed and Rashid were impressive leaders.

Much of the credit for the country's postindependence stability is due the British. Whatever the faults of their enforced isolation, their buttressing of the same ruling families for 152 years wound up creating strong leadership institutions, however archaic and undemocratic. Tribal-based family rule survived the British departure without serious challenge.[7] The same can be said for the other Gulf Arab sheikhdoms, where British policy cultivated strong monarchies that have gone on to govern stable independent countries. Elsewhere in the Middle East, colonial powers left behind shaky ruling institutions that disintegrated in strife after independence.

Sheikh Zayed, Father of the Nation

In this world, a man with unlimited charisma and unlimited cash can go a long way. That's essentially how the UAE became a nation, cobbled together by an uneducated guy who had both.

Sheikh Zayed bin Sultan al-Nahyan was a rare human specimen. He was a true Bedouin chief, riding out of the Abu Dhabi desert on a white stallion. Zayed wore bandoliers of rifle cartridges across his broad chest and gripped his rifle in his fist. The sheikh spent his early decades in a mud fort in the inland oasis of Al Ain, his seat as governor. He spent his days meeting with tribal allies and hunting with falcons. He and his men ate while sitting on the ground around a crude platter of meat and rice, everyone tearing at the carcass with his right hand.

In the early 1950s, Zayed's reputation as a wise frontiersman reached British explorer Wilfred Thesiger and the Bedouin guides leading him across the Empty Quarter. When Thesiger reached Al Ain, he was keen to meet the governor. He describes the encounter in his brilliant book *Arabian Sands*. Thesiger asked a bystander to take him to Zayed. The man pointed to a throng seated under a thorn tree and said the man at the center was Zayed.

He was a powerfully built man of about thirty with a brown beard. He had a strong, intelligent face, with steady, observant eyes, and his manner was quiet but masterful. He was dressed very simply in a beige-colored shirt of Omani cloth and a waist-coat which he wore unbuttoned. He was distinguished from his companions by his black head-rope, and the way in which he wore his head cloth, falling about his shoulders instead of twisted round his head in the local manner. He wore a dagger and a cartridge belt; his rifle lay on the sand beside him.

I had been looking forward to meeting him, for he had a great reputation among the Bedu. They liked him for his easy informal ways and his friendliness, and they respected his force of character, his shrewdness, and his physical strength. They said admiringly: "Zayed is Bedu. He knows about camels, can ride like one of us, can shoot, and knows how to fight."[8]

In those days, Zayed roved the Abu Dhabi outback, rallying the tribes to stay allied with al-Nahyan rule. It was a challenging task. The Saudis offered buyouts to tribes who changed allegiance, thereby bringing their territory—and any oil underneath—under Saudi control. Zayed had little means to counter the Saudis in those days but appealed to tribesmen through their sense of history and honor. In 1952, the Saudis set to work on Zayed himself, offering him a staggering bribe of $42 million to back their claim to Al Ain and the rest of the Buraimi Oasis, which Zayed governed on behalf of his family. Zayed, with an income of just a few thousand dollars a year, spurned the bribe and redoubled his efforts to keep the oasis inside the al-Nahyan family's lands.[9]

"Zayed was very proud he'd rejected it," says Peter Hellyer, the Abu Dhabi leader's onetime press handler. "He didn't want much publicity of it—there were enough problems with the Saudis already—but he was very proud that when he had nothing, he told them to get stuffed."

The bribe was chump change compared to the fortune Zayed would compile after Abu Dhabi struck oil in 1958. When he died in 2004, Sheikh Zayed was one of the world's richest men, leaving behind a fortune that *Forbes* magazine estimated at $24 billion. And this was despite his best efforts to give money to anyone who would ask.

Zayed wasn't a tall man, but he was calm and decisive, with a dominant personality. He could read and write, unusual for a chief of his generation. But he didn't enjoy writing and ordered an attendant to jot notes on his behalf. He loved to hunt, but gave up shooting game as the antelope began disappearing.[10] He was a curious man, fascinated by the work of European archaeologists and naturalists who began arriving during the 1950s. One of these scientists wound up naming a subspecies of bat after him.

British naturalist David Harrison was chatting with the Al Ain governor one evening in 1954. When dusk fell, tiny bats with gossamer wings began to flit above the men. Harrison told Zayed he'd like to examine one of the bats, since little was known about Arabian species. Zayed called for a rifle. He aimed at the sky and blasted away until he'd downed one of the zipping creatures. Harrison declared it a new subspecies and named it *Taphozous nudiventris zayidi*, or Zayed's sheath-tailed bat.[11]

In the mid-1960s, after Zayed had traded his camel for a Land Rover, he'd make the six-hour dune drive from Al Ain to Abu Dhabi. On arrival, he liked to look over the exotic goods at a new department store. The store was opened in 1964 by an Indian merchant named Mohan Jashanmal.[12]

"Jashanmal," Zayed would say. "Show me the films."

"Which ones?" Jashanmal would ask, adding in jest, "Films of girls?"

"Show me the films with the tall buildings!" Zayed would thunder, and Jashanmal would hand over the red plastic View-Master, a child's 3-D viewer with binocular eyepieces and a lever that turned a slide wheel. Sheikh Zayed, sitting in a sandy town with its camels and mud fort, would hold the View-Master up to the light, thumbing his way through slides of the Empire State Building, the Statue of Liberty, and the UN Headquarters. On other occasions Zayed wanted to see English gardens or the California redwoods, and Jashanmal would oblige.

"Jashanmal! One day, you will see. The gardens will be here. The tall buildings will be here," Zayed would say.

"If you are saying so, okay," Jashanmal would reply. "But it's very difficult to believe."

Zayed deeply wanted for Abu Dhabi to develop, but with his grouchy brother Shakhbut in charge, that wasn't going to happen. He grew frustrated watching Dubai build itself up while the oil capital of southeastern Arabia remained a village of thatched huts. Finally, in 1966, Zayed gave his big brother the hook. The unseated sheikh fled to Bahrain and wandered rootlessly around the Middle East, moving to Iran and Lebanon before resettling into anonymous retirement in Al Ain.

Once in power, Zayed was an energized man. One of his first acts in office was to throw open the palace strongbox, giving away all the money that his brother had stockpiled. Zayed made an incredible announcement: Anyone in the seven Trucial States who needed cash for any reason should come see him. People streamed in from every corner of every sheikhdom, traveling to Abu Dhabi by camel, by car, by dhow, and on foot. They lined up outside the leader's palace, waiting for their turn to ask, and receive. Zayed kept up the handouts until he emptied the coffers.[13]

The big giveaway sounds like a crazy idea, especially coming as it did before the UAE emerged as an independent nation, so that most of the recipients were, essentially, foreigners. But Zayed's gifts weren't mislaid. Local Arabs considered such over-the-top generosity as the behavior of their kind of leader. The upstarts in Dubai couldn't match the gesture, nor could the has-beens in Sharjah. Zayed's giveaway went a long way toward welding disparate sheikhdoms into a nation—and toward positioning Zayed as the paternal über-sheikh who should rule.

Sheikh Zayed didn't disappoint. Each year for the rest of his reign, he made a splashy tour around the emirates, visiting even the dust bowl towns of Ajman and Umm Al-Quwain. People yelled, "The president is coming! The president is coming!" and lined up to greet the great sheikh. He would ask what they needed. "Anything you want, tell me," Zayed would say. His subjects asked for houses, overseas medical treatment, or the release of a jailed brother. Some handed requests scribbled onto sheets of paper, lest the great sheikh forget.

Zayed's handlers from the *diwan*, his royal court, compiled names, phone numbers, and requests. Over the next few weeks, the *diwan* would send officials knocking at each door with cash, whether 10,000 dirhams or 100,000 dirhams.[14] It was a fantastic nation-building tool. Not just the handouts of cash, but the in-person availability of the national ruler, who would respond like a kind father to personal needs. How could anyone speak against the union if it put cash in your hand?

"We used to think he was too generous, that he was wasting money. But he knew the money wasn't lost because it bought loyalty for the union," says Emirati historian Fatima al-Sayegh. "In the West, people couldn't reach the government. Here you could. Today, loyalty is stronger in the small emirates because of Sheikh Zayed."

In 1966, it fell to Zayed to bring Abu Dhabi and then the UAE out of the dark ages. He built the underpinnings of a modern state from scratch. He pieced together a government by drawing up a list of departments and staffing them, one after another, and ordering offices to be built to house them. He hired planners who laid out Abu Dhabi's avenues on a sensible grid, running sewer and water lines, power and phone wires beneath them. Zayed directed a British firm to erect a pair of diesel generators to bring power, and ordered construction of a desalination plant to distill drinking water from the sea.

Abu Dhabi looked like a film set under construction. Development milestones came even later than Dubai's. Electricity arrived in 1967; so did telephones—just three hundred lines for a town of fifteen thousand. The phones connected directly to the international network, putting London and New York in reach, but it took two more years before anyone in Abu Dhabi could dial the emirate's second city, Al Ain. All the concrete, steel, pipe, and everything else imported into Abu Dhabi had to be landed on the beach. Shakhbut's intransigence left the town without a port or an airport until Zayed had them completed in 1969. Until then, barges and dhows ground their hulls into the beach and laborers carried everything ashore by hand.[15]

Sheikh Zayed didn't just hand out cash, he institutionalized it. His government subsidized almost every aspect of life. He gave every Abu Dhabian three or four pieces of land. One was for a home, one for a commercial building, one for a workshop or industrial project, and the fourth was for a farm. To the would-be farmers, Zayed gave tractors and irrigation gear. He sent engineers to design productive farms, and laborers to work them. He gave homes to those who needed them.[16] He built schools and a university and set aside overseas scholarships for the smartest.

"There was a feeling that after a long period of deprivation and poverty it was about time that we enjoyed ourselves," says Abdulkhaleq Abdulla, the Emirati political scientist. "The government's duty was to establish the best subsidized welfare system on earth."

As UAE president in 1971, Zayed cleaned up his frontier image, losing the cartridge belts and rifle. He trimmed his full beard to a point on his chin, giving him a slightly villainous look. Any hint of a sinister nature was offset by his crooked million-dollar grin of white teeth. The sheikh of Abu Dhabi also favored mirrored aviator sunglasses that reflected bursts of blinding sunlight. Together with his beard and flowing robes, the shades and grin made him look like a rock star. Sheikh Zayed not only exuded charisma, he was cool—Mick Jagger take note—right into his seventies. He never got fat, preserving his broad wrestler's chest and washboard waist. Five years after his death in 2004, Sheikh Zayed's grinning face is a Warhol-style pop icon; plastered on key fobs, coffee mugs, and sunshades that cover the rear windows of 4x4s.

Zayed was a sheikh's sheikh, with a passel of wives who delivered him an enormous brood. His offspring and their children and handlers could fill a stadium. British diplomats did their best to keep track of Zayed's wives and counted nine by his death, but that figure could be inaccurate. The Abu Dhabi ruler never kept more than three wives for long, one less than the legal limit, so he had a slot open when he found an eligible mate. He fathered nineteen boys and perhaps twelve girls, but the number of Zayed's daughters, like his wives, is unclear.[17]

Zayed's spending dazzled people everywhere he traveled, including my hometown, Cleveland, Ohio. Zayed visited Cleveland regularly for heart treatment and, at one point, decided he wanted a house. He and his entourage drove through streets lined with fine mansions in the suburbs near the hospital. When Zayed saw the one he wanted, he ordered his men to make an offer. They immediately knocked on the door and asked the family whether they could buy the house. When the occupants refused, Zayed doubled his offer—more than $1 million is the rumored price—and the family agreed to move out within two weeks.[18]

The UAE's founder died in 2004 at the age of eighty-six, triggering a nationwide paroxysm of grief. In Abu Dhabi, mourners lined the streets weeping openly, some women throwing themselves to the ground as his cortege passed. Zayed's sons buried him beneath the site of what has become a vast white marble mosque with fanciful arches and flower-bulb domes tipped in gold. The Zayed Grand Mosque is the third largest in the world, but also one of its most beautiful, reminiscent of the Taj Mahal. The desert Bedouin with his rifle and side-cocked grin had come a long way.

Sheikh Zayed may have passed on, but there's a strong family resemblance among the men now running the federal government. Zayed's eldest son, Khalifa, is the UAE president, the head of state. His son

Mohammed, who spent two days with President Bush at Camp David in June 2008, is the Abu Dhabi crown prince and the country's top defense official. Zayed's sons Sultan and Hamdan are the deputy prime ministers. Abdullah is foreign minister. Saif is interior minister. Mansour is minister of presidential affairs.

To this day it is common for Emiratis to profess love for Sheikh Zayed. A young Emirati woman I worked with in 2007 told me she and some friends from university visited Sheikh Zayed in 2004. The sheikh was on his deathbed. He asked the young ladies whether they needed anything before he died. They all responded that they only wished him a long life. He asked them the same question twice more. Each time, the girls refused any gifts. "I love him. I really adore him. W'allah," the woman told me, using an Arabic word that means "I swear to God."

Zayed had his pitfalls, of course. He lost territory to Saudi Arabia that he should have fought harder to keep. One is a wedge of the Empty Quarter that sits atop the huge Shaybah oil field. And his family name was tainted by scandal when a bank it owned, the Bank of Credit and Commerce International, or BCCI, collapsed in 1991. U.S. Senate investigators found BCCI officers—including some of Zayed's financial advisers—involved in a sleazy matrix of kickbacks, money laundering, prostitution, and even terrorist financing.

The life's visions of Sheikh Zayed and Rashid were distinct. Rashid dedicated his life to Dubai, but didn't concern himself much with the wider federation, even after he became prime minister. Zayed's quest was for a unified state, and he accomplished this in the time-honored manner of his al-Nahyan clan, by cultivating the tribes. After independence, Zayed treated the entire UAE to his formula of tribal generosity. It worked. The uncertainty that shrouded the UAE at its birth faded away.

But that didn't erase the fact that the new country sat in a war-prone region. And it was about to heat up.

The Salvage Business

On September 22, 1980, the Iraqi dictator Saddam Hussein launched an invasion of Iran, sending troops pouring across the border and warplanes blasting Iranian airfields. Saddam took advantage of the chaos in the opening days of the Islamic revolution led by Ayatollah Khomeini, who had ousted the U.S.-backed shah. The Iraqi leader hoped to grab some oil-rich territory, but the Iranians rushed to defend their land. The invasion wound up unifying Iran behind Khomeini. The war descended into a stalemate that harkened to the senseless gore of World War I, complete with human wave attacks and poison gassings.

In 1984, the Iraqis tried a new strategy: They attacked Tehran's economic jugular, the tanker ships taking on crude oil at Iran's Kharg Island terminal. Iran then did the same, sending aircraft and small boats to rocket tankers carrying Iraqi oil exports. The Iranians widened their targets to tankers visiting terminals in the Gulf Arab states. The tanker war was on. Over the next four years, more than five hundred commercial vessels, mostly Kuwait-owned ships, took damage from rockets, shells, and mines, mainly those of Iran. More than four hundred civilian sailors died in the attacks. The war on oil exports ground on in the Gulf until the U.S. and Soviet governments agreed to post their own flags on the tankers, which, under international law, allowed their militaries to retaliate.

For Dubai, the war was an economic lemon. So Sheikh Rashid made lemonade. In a feat of serendipity, the giant Dubai Dry Docks—opened fully in 1983, a year ahead of one of history's most devastating campaigns against civilian shipping.

The tanker war was a different class of conflict than the German U-boat onslaught on Allied shipping in World Wars I and II. Most of those vessels, once torpedoed from below, sank in the ocean's depths far from shore. In the busy shipping lanes of the Gulf, help wasn't far away. Few wounded vessels actually sank. Iran's French-made Exocet missiles punctured the ships well above the water line, setting tankers and cargo alight. Raging oil fires made the strikes look bad but damage was often slight.[19]

Each detonating Exocet sent cash to Dubai's coffers. Sheikh Rashid's spanking new dry dock sat on the edge of the fray, easy limping distance for a stricken tanker. In a new twist on ambulance chasing, salvage tugs patrolled the Gulf and towed the victims to Dubai. Once again, opportunistic Dubai reaped an Iranian windfall. The dry docks grew so busy that damaged ships waited months for repairs, or got patched up just enough to steam to a yard outside the Gulf.[20]

This kind of foresight earned Sheikh Rashid an aura of clairvoyance. I asked Emiratis how Sheikh Rashid could have known the completion of his dry dock would be greeted with a sudden supply of damaged ships. "Sheikh Rashid prayed every day. Maybe he saw a sign from God," one said.

Trading Land for Ambition

The word people use most often to describe Sheikh Rashid is "farsighted." The Dubai leader's reputation was partly a product of his cagey leadership style. He offered people business tips or free land—on condition they develop it. He assured them that the locations would be profitable one day. But he often withheld full details, so the recipients of his largesse had to proceed on blind trust. When the investments paid off, recipients praised Sheikh Rashid's farsightedness. But the flipside meant that people sometimes rejected the Dubai leader's gifts.

Sheikhs are supposed to distribute land and wealth. That's exactly what happened in most of the sheikhdoms that formed the UAE, with few strings attached. In Abu Dhabi, Sheikh Zayed's gifts of homes and farms didn't even require their owners to occupy them. But the recipients of Rashid's largesse were required to contribute to the city's expansion. An American might say Rashid offered Dubaians a hand up, not a hammock.

One Emirati merchant family migrated from Sharjah to Dubai in the 1960s to take advantage of Dubai's business climate. In the late 1970s, Sheikh Rashid gave the family's head fifty plots of land in what became the upscale neighborhood of Mirdiff, on condition he build on the plots. The merchant thanked Rashid but declined the offer, believing the plots were too far from central Dubai to warrant investment. That decision wound up shortchanging the family hundreds of millions of dollars.[21]

Sheikh Rashid's murky ways also made fools of foreign investors. In the 1970s, a self-important Kuwaiti businessman declared that he wished to invest in booming Dubai. Sheikh Rashid welcomed the Kuwaiti, handing him a business card, and telling him he did indeed have a plot available. He drove the Kuwaiti deep into the desert and showed him the excavation in the sand that would become the World Trade Centre. He drove a quarter mile further, to the edge of a caravan track, and offered the Kuwaiti a patch of the undulating scrub surrounding him. It was a place where Bedouin grazed camels.

The Kuwaiti was incensed. His answer was immediate: "No." He stomped into the office of Dubai mayor Qassim Sultan to declare that Sheikh Rashid's vaunted generosity was a myth. Here was a city full of bustle, and he was being offered barren land in the middle of nowhere. "That Bedouin was trying to cheat me!" the Kuwaiti yelled.

Sheikh Rashid gave the land to another developer who built four high-rise apartment blocks there. The buildings became known as the Hilton Apartments, one of Dubai's fanciest addresses for years, home to diplomats and businessmen working in the just-finished World Trade Centre. The Kuwaiti returned a year or two later and saw the apartments under construction. The desert track had been paved as the Dubai-Abu Dhabi highway, later renamed Sheikh Zayed Road and expanded to twelve lanes.

The proud Kuwaiti realized his folly. He returned a chastened man to Sheikh Rashid's *majlis*. "Hello, Kuwaiti!" Sheikh Rashid greeted him. "Too bad you didn't take that land!" The Kuwaiti assured the Dubai leader that he was now ready to accept the site he'd spurned. Sheikh Rashid apologized, saying the land was taken. But he offered the Kuwaiti another plot. Again it required a leap of faith. The new plot was another quarter mile into the desert, and had no road frontage. Today the site houses the twin Emirates Towers skyscrapers, which surpassed the Dubai World Trade Centre in 1999 as the tallest buildings in the Middle East. But in the mid-1970s, the land was desolate. Again, the Kuwaiti demurred. "Why does he want to take me to the desert again?" He gave up and went home.

The Kuwaiti didn't return for fifteen years. By then Qassim Sultan was nearing retirement and Dubai was the most dynamic of Gulf cities. The Kuwaiti turned up in the mayor's office. This time his hubris was only a memory. He'd gone to see the Emirates Towers and admire the silver triangular spires that resemble razor cartridges. The businessman realized he'd doubled down on his shortsightedness. "This land could've been mine and I didn't take it," he told Sultan. "I'm such a fool."

There are dozens of Sheikh Rashid stories that circulate in Dubai. Some are so improbable that any wisp of truth has long since slipped out. But they're useful in gauging the enormity of Sheikh Rashid's influence on the mentality of Dubaians.

Dubai's physical shape is one of Sheikh Rashid's legacies. He bequeathed us a linear city with multiple centers, rather than a traditional metropolis that radiates outward from a central core. The World Trade

Centre anchored a new business district in the southwest desert, away from the creek. The Dubai-Abu Dhabi highway became a grand entrance. And the building of Jebel Ali port on a faraway beach created a new development anchor. Jebel Ali ensured Dubai would stretch along a narrow coastal strip. Sheikh Rashid's sons set about filling the space in between with housing, golf courses, resorts, parks, warehouses, racetracks, industrial zones, factories, and malls.

Sheikh Rashid's investments transformed Dubai into a low-cost hub of global trade. But the days when Dubai would have to finance its own expansion were ending. Dubai's second phase of growth, which took place under Rashid's sons Maktoum and Mohammed, would lean on the wealth of foreign investors who saw the emerging city as a strong bet.

Losing History

Sheikh Rashid showed no compunction about erasing the past. He fought against huge odds to modernize Dubai, to improve his subjects' lives—but also to win respect, even if it meant only that outsiders would know his city's name.

Modernization comes at the expense of heritage, of course, and Dubai's heritage was bulldozed without hesitation. Sheikh Rashid began by demolishing the old cloth bazaar, a souk on the south bank of the creek that sat just behind the Beit Wakeel, the Gray Mackenzie office where George Chapman lived. The Indian vendors in the covered alley brought a welcome clamor, as well as a stream of people pissing on the beach next to the house. Chapman says he could tell who was squatting below his window by the pattern of his *lunghi*.

The bazaar was a touch of old Araby, reminding visitors of Damascus or Tehran. At night, the vendors locked the great wooden doors at either end of the souk and climbed to their sleeping quarters above their shops, safe from Bedouin who might be tempted to a bit of looting. Steamship passengers liked to wander the souk while their ship refueled. Chapman asked Sheikh Rashid to halt the demolition. "I bring people off ships and they like to see old Dubai. Now you're knocking it down."

Rashid was unrepentant. "What do you want that old place for? Let's have a proper road in the town so people can get through."[22]

The ambitious sheikh did the same thing with the neighborhood of palm-thatch *barasti* houses that crowded behind Bastakiya's big coral homes. Many of Dubai's greatest citizens grew up in a *barasti*, which were perfect for pre-electric Dubai, their loose thatching allowing cool breezes to penetrate. Most were built as compounds, with a palm fence surrounding the home, giving privacy to women who cooked outdoors on kerosene stoves. But ramshackle *barastis* were more like tents than houses, too primitive and fire-prone to electrify.

Sheikh Rashid saw them as a ghetto that stood in his way. He planned a new commercial center, the Bur Dubai of today, with paved streets and concrete buildings. One day, trucks descended on the neighborhood and crews picked up the huts and dumped them in the desert. The residents rebuilt in the desert, and the new district became known as Satwa.

Now, thirty-five years later, Satwa is a quaintly anachronistic neighborhood hemmed in by skyscrapers, where goats still romp in fenced lots. Satwa teems with Filipinos, Iranians, and South Asians, and is home to Dubai's best curry houses, tailors, and used book shop. It's one of the few neighborhoods conducive to strolling. Sidewalk cafés sell cups of tea for 30 U.S. cents, fresh Indian *naan* bread can be bought hot from the clay oven, and a bowl of Iranian *ash*—a lamb and dill stew—costs $1.25.

But Rashid's sons who ruled after him, Maktoum and Mohammed, have pressed Dubai's redevelopment just as their father did. In 2008, Sheikh Mohammed decided Satwa would go the way of the *barastis*. Landlords gave tenants a year to move, telling them most of Satwa was to be bulldozed to make way for Jumeirah Gardens, a futuristic district of sparkling towers on canals. Government men with clipboards banged on doors, giving residents their demolition dates. The men used green spray paint to number each house for the wrecking crews.[23] The news caused a clamor of lament in the press and local blogs. To be fair, Satwa's low-rise concrete block houses are a poor use of valuable land in the city center, and hold little of architectural interest.

Another neighborhood, the Shindagha section that housed the original Maktoum migrants from Liwa—perhaps the most heritage-rich district in the city—was razed in the 1980s during Sheikh Maktoum's de facto rule. Wrecking crews with bulldozers and backhoes also ripped down a large section of historic Bastakiya. The destruction, captured in the photos of Iranian architect Dariush Zandi, is heartrending. The filigreed *mushrabiya* screens, carved wooden doors, and the coffinlike wind towers that told of the sophisticated Iranian lifestyle, all destroyed.

The bulldozing of these architectural treasures was akin to New York's 1964 demolition of historic Penn Station. The city woke up and realized its loss, and the lamenting started right away. A few of the wind tower houses were saved and renovated, including the ruin of Sheikh Saeed's house, where the old sheikh died and his children and grandchildren grew up. A handful of Bastakiya's old buildings remain, but the city forced residents out and turned the homes into offices. Excessive renovations destroyed the detail and turned the neighborhood into a soulless husk.

The Fires of Damnation

Sheikh Rashid's thirst for modernity often brushed against his Bedouin roots. In 1969, the Dubai ruler and Easa Al-Gurg, the Emirati banker, happened to be staying at the Dorchester Hotel in London when the first moon landing took place. Sheikh Rashid dismissed the event as a stunt, saying it was impossible to put men on the moon. Al-Gurg turned on the television and showed him the pictures being broadcast. Still, Rashid was convinced the event was a hoax. The landscape looked curiously like the empty terrain in Ras Al-Khaimah. Maybe it was filmed there, he said.

Later, flying home to Dubai, Al-Gurg tried to convince Sheikh Rashid that men had indeed walked the moon. "We were sitting together eating a delicious Lebanese meal served some 40,000 feet above the ground. Had he enjoyed his meal, I enquired? He had. Could our fathers ever have imagined eating such a delicious meal in such circumstances? He agreed that of course they could not have done so. I grasped his arm and asked how he could explain the accomplishment of this miracle, when he so firmly believed that the miracle of landing on the moon was an illusion?" Sheikh Rashid didn't answer.[24]

Dubai's ruler put a huge value on the skills and contributions of expatriates. He understood that Western engineers and advisers wouldn't invest their time in Dubai if they had to live an ascetic life, or if they couldn't follow their own religions. So Rashid granted land for churches and schools, and he allowed non-Muslims to drink and open taverns. He appeared to tolerate prostitution.

Though Dubai's ruling sheikh welcomed those of other faiths, he believed they, as unbelievers, were doomed to burn in hell for eternity.

One day Al-Gurg and Sheikh Rashid were lunching at the Hotel du Rhône in Geneva, sitting with a group of Arabs in their native *kandoura* robes in the picture window. A group of pretty Swiss girls caught sight of the men and stood there, intrigued by the sight of the Arabs in their traditional dress. The men and girls stared at each other in mutual fascination. One of the Arab diners praised the exquisite charm of the Swiss girls. Al-Gurg decided to tease the sheikh. Were such pretty girls as these destined to roast in hell?

"Of course," Rashid said.

"In that case, why did God make all the people of the world who are not Muslims if it was only to condemn them all to hell? How many millions are there in China, India, America, Russia?"

"Now I know you're a communist," Rashid replied, half in jest.

These sentiments aren't spoken in public in a city that has been built and operated by non-Muslims, and in which non-Muslims (Hindus, Christians, Buddhists, Bahai, Jews, and others) form around half the population. But in 2008, the textbooks of every Muslim child in Dubai said much the same thing, irresolutely condemning non-Muslims to the eternal fires of damnation. It's an anomaly in an otherwise tolerant city. A friend of mine, a liberal Muslim, showed me the passages in his daughter's textbook one afternoon as we drank beer in his backyard.

"This is really bad," he says. He'd complained to the teacher that the curriculum violated Dubai's spirit of tolerance. He asked the teacher to soft-pedal the brimstone because it scared his daughter. The teacher told him the descriptions of hell and damnation were required state curriculum.

The Sheikh's Secret

The Warba Centre is a forlorn mall in blue-collar Deira. Inside, it smells pleasantly of *oudh* incense and apple-flavored *sheesha* smoke. The mall's main draw, besides the smoky café, is the commercial office for Iraqi Kurdistan. It was in the Warba Centre that I met Ali al-Sayed, a beefy Emirati man who speaks in a rambling, mystical style while chain-smoking

Captain Black cigarillos. I'd heard about al-Sayed through several Emiratis who told me he had the best insights on Sheikh Rashid's legacy.

"I can tell you the secret of Sheikh Rashid, how he built Dubai. I have it," he says, relighting a cigarillo stub while taking care not to ignite his paintbrush mustache.

"What's the secret?" I ask, sipping mint tea and soaking up the surroundings. It's a typical *sheesha* house, full of idle men in their fifties, the Gulf version of guys who hang around the off-track betting parlor. Except that *sheesha* smoking is now hip with Arab women in their teens and twenties, so there were also Lebanese and Syrian girls wandering past in eye-popping outfits.

Rashid's secret, Ali al-Sayed says, was his bureaucracy-killing management style. "Sheikh Rashid did something the Arabs couldn't do for hundreds of years: He kept lawyers away from the decisions. The biggest sickness in the Arab world is legal advisers saying, 'This is forbidden, this is forbidden, this is forbidden.' If a certain contract violated the law, he didn't care," al-Sayed says.

"Instead of waiting to choose among bidders for a project, he just chose a qualified company. He didn't care if he paid a higher price," he says. "Time was more important."

Sheikh Rashid visited Europe and said, "'Why aren't we like this?'" He asked how long Europeans spent crafting their cities. "The answer was, 'Hundreds of years.' That was too long for him. How could he make it shorter? The answer was to create a new management paradigm."

"People say management is the art of the possible. Not in Dubai," al-Sayed says with a penetrating stare. "In Dubai, management is the art of the impossible."

End of Days

On May 9, 1981, Sheikh Rashid finished one of his punishing eighteen-hour days with a banquet for visiting Indian Prime Minister Indira Gandhi. The next morning, the sixty-nine-year-old didn't rise for *fajr* prayers at dawn. He left his breakfast untouched. Sheikh Rashid struggled through the next few days feeling sick, then decided to take a break in Hatta, Dubai's picturesque enclave in the Hajjar Mountains. A few days in the mountain air had no effect, so he decided to return to Zabeel Palace and try to work. On the two-hour ride back to Dubai, the ruler's illness spiked. He vomited several times. The next day doctors declared he had suffered a severe stroke.

Word swept Dubai. Rashid's four sons, Maktoum, Hamdan, Mohammed, and Ahmed, kept a bedside vigil.[25] Sheikh Zayed phoned his concern, and his son, current UAE president Sheikh Khalifa, drove up from Abu Dhabi. Phone calls expressing support came in from around the world, from Egyptian president Anwar Sadat, Jordan's King Hussein, the Reagan White House, and Margaret Thatcher's office in London.[26]

Dubai's longtime leader eventually made a partial recovery. In 1982, the aging sheikh made his first public appearance since the stroke, touring a new highway underpass. Dubaians lined his route to catch a glimpse. Sheikh Rashid waved as he drove past. He had become gray and frail. The crowds waved and cheered, but some Emiratis cried.

A year later, Rashid's wife of forty-four years, Sheikha Latifa, died while undergoing routine medical treatment in London. Sheikh Mohammed broke the news to his father. It came as a total shock. The loss of his only wife and the mother of his nine children devastated the old sheikh. It was the only time anyone had seen him weep. Sheikh Rashid never regained his old spark, his dancing eyes, his joking confidence. He doled out his tasks to his sons, who took control of Dubai in all but title.

Sheikh Maktoum, the eldest, took his father's role as Dubai's ruler, as well as his functions as federal vice president and prime minister. Sheikh Hamdan took the helm of Dubai's industrial plants and the Dubai city government. Sheikh Mohammed was entrusted with the city's vital organs: Dubai's police and military, its oil production, the airport and its ports. His *majlis* grew into a key power center.

Sheikh Rashid spent the last days of his thirty-two-year rule sitting outside his Zabeel Palace, a low-key whitewashed building that still sits on a small rise in central Dubai. A much larger mosque faces the palace from across the street. The seventy-eight-year-old's grizzled beard had gone white, hiding the sunken mouth below his falcon's nose. The father of modern Dubai kept an eye on the progress he'd started, watching new skyscrapers rise alongside his World Trade Centre as his life ebbed. On October 7, 1990, he died in his sleep.

News of his death brought more than ten thousand mourners to Zabeel Palace, where his sons spent days receiving condolences. Ali al-

Sayed was one of the mourners. He rushed to the palace to join the crowd of pallbearers who held Sheikh Rashid's coffin aloft, sometimes just reaching a hand or a few fingers to touch the casket. Dubaians lined the streets leading to Umm Hurair cemetery, where Sheikh Rashid, wrapped in a white shroud, was laid into the sandy earth. Halfway around the world, at UN headquarters in New York, the General Assembly and Security Council observed a minute of silence. The U.S. representative was among those who rose to pay tribute to Dubai's leader.

"We cried for Sheikh Rashid even after he was dead a long time," al-Sayed says. "At first we didn't understand what he was doing. But after we saw everything growing more and more beautiful around us, we realized he was giving his life for Dubai."

6

SPRINTING THE MARATHON

Turning Hell into Paradise

BY 1985, DUBAI had come a long way. Just about everyone lived in an air-conditioned home. The creek bank held a phalanx of trophy office towers. Dubai's offshore oil platforms were pumping. And the dry docks were fixing tankers almost as quickly as Iraq and Iran could rocket them.

Dubai didn't have many hotels. There was one main tourist resort, the Chicago Beach Hotel. The strange name came from the Chicago Bridge & Iron Co., which welded giant floating oil storage tanks on the beach. It became known for a while as Chicago Beach.

Expats found Dubai little different than Kuwait City, Bahrain, or Doha: dull. It was best visited only long enough to replenish a bank account. Of course, old-timers now talk of the 1980s as the good old days, when expatriates and locals knew each other and the city was manageable.

The Iran-Iraq war, which left a million dead, was killing Dubai's economy, despite the bounty of damaged vessels. Business was slow at the airport. The Jebel Ali port sat in silence. Sheikh Mohammed's friend Sultan bin Sulayem ran the port, sitting at his desk with a flyswatter, pining for a real job. The oil price that spiked in 1979 dove into the doldrums and stayed there. The 1980s were Dubai's slowest decade since the 1950s.

Sheikh Mohammed, in his mid-thirties, sought an answer. He'd taken over a large portion of the city's daily affairs after his father's stroke. The city's airport and tourist sector was under his charge. And when Sheikh Rashid died, Mohammed took over most of the city's governance, which his easygoing elder brother Maktoum, the official ruler, was happy to entrust to him. It was Sheikh Mohammed, Dubai's crown prince until becoming the emirate's ruler in 2006, who would steer the next phase of Dubai's development.

The young sheikh tinkered with the idea of pitching Dubai as a vacation spot, as he describes in his book *My Vision*. In the mid-1980s, he attended a meeting of Gulf Arab government officials. Sheikh Mohammed, who regularly professes distaste for politics, sat quietly as ministers bloviated on crises in Palestine and Iran.

"I was keen to change the subject. I said to the ministers, 'Why don't we try to develop this region, and particularly Dubai, as a tourist destination to attract people from all over the world?'" The officials ignored the young upstart. When Sheikh Mohammed repeated the question, one of them scoffed, "What is there in Dubai to make it a tourist attraction? You have nothing but humidity, red-hot sun, burning sand and barren desert!"[1]

There is no motivator like ridicule. When the young sheikh strode out of the gathering, he was formulating the opening moves of one of the most sudden and lucrative tourism plays in history. Turning Dubai into a vacation destination was the first step in the second phase of Dubai's development, a phase that Sheikh Mohammed led. Sheikh Rashid had started the process. His ambitious third son would bring Dubai to heights that no one could imagine. And, when it came to governing Dubai, the triumph of Sheikh Mohammed's tourism project gave him a leg up on his two elder brothers.

Sheikh Mohammed, like his father, was blessed with an uncanny knack for timing. In the 1980s, sun-starved Europeans were flying farther afield to escape the continent's winter gloom. Their needs were simple: hot sun, a lounge chair, and cold beer. Tour operators flew them to Spain, Greece, or North Africa.

Dubai is sunnier and hotter than those places. The city gets around 350 sunny days a year. Six months may pass between rain showers. In January, the coldest month, the average high is 75 degrees. Dubai's guaranteed sunshine wasn't a turnoff, it was an asset. Dubai also had forty miles of fantastic beach washed by a warm turquoise sea. And Dubai stocked plenty of beer. Sheikh Rashid's pragmatism wasn't matched in Saudi Arabia or Kuwait—or even neighboring Sharjah, where alcohol was banned.

Dubai also had a midsized international airport. Sheikh Rashid's "open skies" policy allowed any airline to fly in without restriction, giving the airport the feeling of a duty-free port. Sheikh Mohammed upgraded the airport in the early 1980s, and it became a refueling stop between Europe and Asia. The city already had most of the tourist infrastructure it needed.

On one count, the Arab minister who had chided Sheikh Mohammed was right. Dubai is one of the few places in the Middle East without historic sites. It can't touch the ruins and ancient quarters in Syria, Iraq, Egypt, or Israel. As it turned out, Dubai didn't need them. It had practical advantages, like public safety and visa-free entry. It lacked hassles with touts, thieves, and corrupt bureaucrats. And Dubaians genuinely welcomed foreigners. Problem was, they lacked an efficient means of hauling them in.

Learning to Fly

In the early 1980s, Dubai had no airline of its own. Foreign carriers were supposed to meet demand for flights because Dubai's ruler had given them unfettered access to his airport. This wasn't good enough for his son's tourism push. Sheikh Mohammed needed more flights, especially from Europe.

In those days, Gulf Air was the chief carrier. It was owned by the governments of Bahrain, Oman, Abu Dhabi, and Qatar. At the time, Gulf Air was embroiled in a dispute with Pakistan, which refused to grant it landing rights in the northern cities that supplied many of the Gulf's workers. Pakistan preserved those rights for its state carrier, Pakistan International Airways, or PIA. Gulf Air fought back, leaning on Dubai to unwind PIA's landing privileges. Sheikh Mohammed and his father refused, citing their open skies policy.

In 1984, Gulf Air retaliated by cutting its weekly Dubai schedule from eighty-four flights to thirty-nine. The cutbacks triggered a standoff.

Sheikh Mohammed had been lobbying for an increase in traffic. He demanded the airline restore the canceled flights. When Gulf Air refused, he closed the airline's local office.

Dubai didn't have many options. But it did have Maurice Flanagan, a British Airways executive who ran the Dubai National Air Travel Agency, which handled ticketing and supplied ground staff.

Flanagan is a burly eighty-year-old with a ruddy face and a hearing aid tucked behind his ear. His white hair is long enough to curl at the ends, giving him a cherubic look. He's the airline's executive vice-chairman. In 2008, with a mug of coffee in his fist, he sat on the edge of his buttery leather cube chair, and told me how he helped Dubai build an airline.

In 1951, Flanagan joined the British Royal Air Force as a navigator, flying in DC-3s and Bristol Brigands, a problematic dive-bomber that entered service in Malaysia. The Brigand's twin engines had a dangerous knack for losing propeller blades. This would unbalance the propeller, which would wrench the engine off the wing and send the plane plummeting into the jungle. Fortunately, this didn't happen when Flanagan was aboard.

After the air force, he signed on with BOAC, the airline that became British Airways. Flanagan ran BOAC's operations in Bombay in the 1960s, increasing the number of Bombay-Dubai flights after Sheikh Rashid guaranteed a minimum number of passengers. By 1978, he found himself on loan to Dubai.

When the Gulf Air standoff began, Flanagan wrote a memo outlining three options. Each was disagreeable. First, do nothing and wait for the market to respond. Second, give in to Gulf Air's pressure. Third, start a Dubai-based airline. A fledgling carrier would need government protection, which, he wrote, spelled the end of open skies.

Flanagan and his wife were celebrating their thirtieth wedding anniversary in England when Sheikh Mohammed summoned him back to Dubai. He'd read the memo. It was time to start planning. "I'm not saying to start an airline, but prepare to start an airline, just supposing I decide that we need one," the sheikh said. Flanagan allowed that the best launch time was in October, when carriers publish their winter schedules.

In a few months, Flanagan returned to Zabeel Palace to describe his progress. This time, another young royal was present. He was twenty-six, nine years younger than Mohammed, but, strangely, he was Mohammed's uncle. It was Sheikh Ahmed bin Saeed al-Maktoum, Sheikh Rashid's young half-brother.[2] Ahmed, who had just graduated from the University of Denver, looked up to his nephew. Flanagan wasn't told why Sheikh Ahmed was there. But the newcomer paid rapt attention.

Sheikh Mohammed had hired Deloitte & Touche, the international consultancy, to look into the feasibility of a state-owned airline. He was waiting on their findings before making a final decision. But in the interest of time, he asked Flanagan to hire staff and start building a carrier. The Englishman said he'd need $10 million. The airline also needed a name. The men tossed out suggestions like Air Dubai and Dubai International, but Sheikh Mohammed declared it would be called Emirates, with the UAE flag on the tail.

Many people say that was a mistake. Dubai missed a giant opportunity to introduce its name to the world. But at the time, there were hopes that Emirates might become the UAE's flagship airline. That hope was laid to rest in 2003 when Abu Dhabi launched a rival, Etihad, and declared it the UAE's national carrier.

Sheikh Mohammed swore the men to secrecy. Flanagan hired designers to create paint schemes for Emirates jets, staff uniforms, ticket covers, everything that got the logo. By July, word had leaked out that Dubai was working on an aviation project. Gulf Air executives asked for a meeting to patch things up. At the meeting, Sheikh Mohammed cleared up the ambiguity. "Gentlemen," he told them, "I'm going to start my own airline."[3]

The plan was on. In the spring of 1985, Flanagan got his $10 million in seed capital. Emirates was to be headed by Sheikh Ahmed, who'd never held a job. It fell to Flanagan to train the sheikh as his boss. "Tell Ahmed everything," Sheikh Mohammed commanded. He warned Flanagan that $10 million was all the help he'd get. The airline would have to fly on its own. "Don't come back for any more," the sheikh said.

"What about protection against competition?" Flanagan asked, referring to the recommendation in his memo.

"Forget it," the sheikh said. "That's not the way Dubai works."

In fact, Emirates did get more subsidies. Flanagan estimates the carrier got $90 million in gifts from the royal family. That includes two barely used Boeing 727s that the royal air wing handed over in 1985; payment help with another aircraft purchase; and a building to house its training quarters.

When word of Emirates' launch leaked out, the skeptics brayed. Airlines were a tough business, and few expected the carrier to survive without subsidies. But Emirates appears to have proven them wrong. Flanagan leased two jets from Pakistan International Airlines—delighted to help after the Gulf Air hostilities. With the four-plane fleet, Emirates shoehorned its way into the air routes in the Middle East and South Asia, a region that would soon bear some of the world's fastest-growing economies. The carrier made its maiden flight to Karachi on October 25, 1985. Again, Dubai's timing was sharp. Emirates would develop at a torrid pace, just like the city and region it served.

By 1990, Emirates was flying to twenty-one cities, including London, Frankfurt, and Singapore. A year later, the carrier started buying—big time. The manufacturers got their first look at the chain-smoking sheikh with the gruff voice who would soon become one of their biggest customers. In 1991, Sheikh Ahmed slapped down $64.5 million for seven Boeing 777 long-range jets. It was a big bite for a six-year-old carrier, especially given that the triple-7s wouldn't begin to arrive until 1996. But the growth in passengers warranted the investment. Emirates would carry 1.5 million by 1992.[4]

In 2001, when terrorists crashed four airplanes in the United States, the industry fell into a panic. Emirates had been negotiating a $15 billion purchase of fifty-eight aircraft, one of the biggest civilian deals ever. The sale was to be a milestone for France-based Airbus, a vote of confidence in its new A380 Superjumbo, designed to carry six hundred passengers. Emirates wanted twenty-two of the double-decker jets, the first firm order for what was then a concept.

But the airline sector was hurting. Ticket sales plummeted amid endless TV footage showing planes slamming into skyscrapers. Carriers cut routes and canceled orders. The U.S. government bailed out its money-losing airlines. All told, some 200,000 aerospace jobs were cut and the industry took a $12 billion loss.[5]

Emirates, with fifty-eight aircraft on the block, found itself in the catbird seat. Airbus and Boeing went from suppliers to supplicants. Airbus bosses phoned Emirates in a near-panic. Jobs hinged on Sheikh Ahmed's order. Was Dubai going to pull the plug?

Perhaps Emirates managers were less afraid of turmoil than the rest of the industry. Emirates was one of the last airlines out of Kuwait when the Iraqis invaded in 1990 and the first back in 1991 when the U.S-led coalition chased the Iraqis out. It made money flying to places others avoided, like Iran, Ethiopia, and Libya.

In November 2001, Sheikh Ahmed stepped into the breach. He proclaimed that Emirates would go ahead with its purchase, not mentioning that the price dropped in the interim. "We will maintain our plans to take delivery of 11 aircraft in 2002 and expect to weather the present crisis in the same successful way as we have other situations of the past 16 years," Sheikh Ahmed told the press.[6] The announcement went a long way toward restoring confidence in the airline industry. That year brought Emirates a record profit of $128 million.

Emirates has been wowing the industry ever since. In 2003, it bought seventy-one planes worth $19 billion. In 2007, Emirates ordered ten more A380 Superjumbos, for a total of fifty-eight. In 2008, as its first superjumbo entered service on the long Dubai-New York route, Emirates' order book stood at 177 aircraft worth $58 billion.[7]

At the time of writing, Emirates operated 119 aircraft to 101 cities in 61 countries. It earned a profit of $1.45 billion in 2007, carrying 21 million passengers. Over two decades, the start-up grew into the world's fifth biggest international airline. It handled more international traffic than American and United airlines, but less when the U.S. carriers' domestic flights were included.[8] Dubai's airline looked set to move up the rankings, perhaps overtaking Singapore Airlines and British Airways.

The carrier has been indispensible to Dubai, a city that depends completely on air travel. Dubai could never become the world's fastest growing city without one of the world's fastest growing airlines. In 2007, Emirates says it made nearly $13 billion in indirect contributions to the Dubai economy. "It's a massive virtuous circle," says Flanagan. "Neither can succeed without the other."

Emirates swears it gets no special treatment from its owner, the Dubai government. Executives at competitors like Air France and Qantas beg to differ. They say Emirates benefits from hidden subsidies that keep expenses far below the industry norm. A 2003 study by Switzerland's UBS found costs 40 percent below those of Dutch carrier KLM.[9]

For examples, it's hard to look past the fact that Sheikh Ahmed is the government's top aviation official as well as the airline's chairman. The government built Dubai airport's new Terminal 3 and, in October 2008, handed it to Emirates for its exclusive use. Emirates' home in tax-free Dubai means the airline and its staff pay no corporate or income tax. Government ties mean it borrows at low rates for which it wouldn't otherwise qualify. It cuts costs by recruiting low-paid Africans and South Asians for cabin crews and ground staff. It houses catering staff in a gritty labor camp in Sonapur, Dubai's poorest neighborhood.

Flanagan calls such claims "utter rubbish," and reels off a list of costs that Emirates carries that most airlines do not. For the past five years, Emirates has paid a $100 million dividend into the city budget. And Emirates lures pilots and executives from U.S. and European airlines with unmatched perks like free housing and children's tuition.

Flanagan puts the airline's success down to decision speed and freedom of action. "We're a Maktoum family business, run by a brilliant Maktoum, Sheikh Ahmed. We don't have a board to slow us down." Sheikh Mohammed only gets involved for purchases in the multiple billions of dollars, Flanagan says.

The carrier's ambition matches that of Dubai. Simply stated, Emirates wants to take over the world. "Any city with a conurbation of five million plus, we could probably serve. The further distant from Dubai, the better," Flanagan says. "We can link any two points in the world now with one stop in Dubai."

Long routes are its most profitable, and Emirates has lots, including the fifteen-hour route to São Paulo, the seventeen-hour trips to Los Angeles and San Francisco, and the fourteen-hour flights to Sydney. It flies direct to most of the major cities in Europe that supply Dubai with tourists. It flies to almost every major city in Africa, the Middle East, and South Asia.

But as 2009 dawned, air travel began to plummet. Emirates, like many Dubai-owned companies began to look overstretched, its order book extravagant and its debt levels dangerous. It began to appear, again, like a carrier in need of government support.

In 1969, Dubai's airport was a flyblown patch with an open concrete shed where sweaty officials hand-stamped passports. Nine airlines served twenty destinations. In 1980, just after Flanagan arrived but before the city's tourism push, the airport had more than tripled its destinations to 64 and airlines to 31. By 2007, Dubai International was heaving with passengers. It was the world's eighth largest international airport, with 118 carriers serving 202 destinations. In 2008, Dubai International received nearly 40 million passengers, nearly double the airport's design capacity.[10]

Flanagan stands on his office balcony and points out the shiny new Terminal 3, bigger than Heathrow's new Terminal 5. Adjacent is a hole in the ground that will become Terminal 4. Dubai airport will be wracked by permanent expansion until its operations shift across town. There, next to Jebel Ali port, the first of six runways at Maktoum International Airport are being paved. Dubai expects its new airport to be the world's busiest, with rail connections to Dubai International, and cargo synergies with the port.

With Dubai's airport madness seemingly mushrooming without end, I ask Flanagan when he'll call it quits. He's fifteen years beyond retirement age. "I should. There are other things I want to get on to." Flanagan could use a break. He's got a bum leg. Each time he stands up he presses his knee into place. His right middle finger is locked into a leather splint. He speaks in a whisper.

More disturbingly, every time he runs into Sheikh Mohammed, the Dubai leader shouts the same greeting—"Hello, old man!"—and grins and slaps him on the back.

"I don't know what kind of message he's sending. He's probably discovered how old I am." Flanagan laughs, stands up, and pops his knee into place.

Building a Landmark

In the early 1990s, the Chicago Beach Hotel sat alone, eight miles out of Dubai. The yellow concrete hotel was a cash cow. Year after year, it managed 80 percent occupancy. Its Bierkeller tavern and Beachcombers bar were two of the best expat watering holes in Dubai. "It's making a lot of money," Sheikh Mohammed said one day. "Why don't we put something else out there?"[11]

In 1992, a British engineering firm called W. S. Atkins submitted a proposal for a new beachfront resort, to be called the Jumeirah Beach Hotel. It was a two-dimensional wave design. It looked like the initial hill on a roller coaster, except glassed-in. Every room faced the sea. Atkins's architects showed Sheikh Mohammed the concept. The company wasn't really in the design business. It was more of an engineering firm that kept a few architects on staff.

"I like that," Sheikh Mohammed said, giving Atkins the go-ahead. "But we want a tower as well."

In 1993, Atkins assigned a thirty-six-year-old London-born architect named Tom Wright to work on Sheikh Mohammed's tower. Wright was a wild card. Atkins had hired him just over a year before. He'd never worked on a hotel. Neither had any of the others on his team. Wright knew only that the young sheikh wanted something tall and iconic. Without experience, Wright, a thoughtful and plain-spoken man who is an avid sailor, sought inspiration in structures that had won fame: the leaning tower of Pisa, the Sydney Opera House, the Eiffel Tower. He wanted his hotel to be instantly recognizable—by everyone on the planet.

"We decided that the test to determine if a building is symbolic is if you can draw it in five seconds and everyone recognizes it," he said. He was given two weeks to come up with sketches and a model.

One day Wright and his team were discussing La Défense, the modern square arch in Paris. Wright thought a giant arch in the Islamic style might make an iconic hotel. He folded a sheet of paper in half and cut out the center. He unfolded the sheet and showed the arch to his team. It wasn't right. But the paper cutout was interesting. It looked like the blade of a kitchen knife, a flat edge and a curved edge meeting at a sharp point.

"Hey, that's quite good," Wright said, holding up the scrap. It reminded him of a sloop sail. Since he wanted the structure to rise from the sea—perhaps on an island—the nautical theme made sense. "Let's push this modern sail idea," he told his team.

They started sketching it out. Early drawings showed a huge sail-shaped building 1,300 feet tall, jutting from the sea floor, waves lapping at its base. The building leaned over the sea—a sop to Pisa—and a cable car ran from shore to its peak. The other access came via an undersea tunnel. It was iconic all right, but structurally impossible. Wright straightened it up, moved it from the sea floor to a small man-made islet, and traded the cable car for a helipad. A causeway bridge replaced the tunnel. They scaled back the height to 1,000 feet.

"It didn't need to be the tallest building in the world, just the most interesting," Wright said.

Wright and his ten-man team drew their sail-shaped building and three others as alternates. The men didn't put much effort into the alternates. One, Wright said, was a pile of terraces, like a ziggurat protruding from the sea. It would have made a nice hotel with all those balconies, but the shape wasn't iconic.

In October 1993, Wright flew to Dubai and gave Sheikh Mohammed his first look at the drawings. He chose the sail-shaped one, just as Wright had hoped. His order was simple: "Build it."

Unlike today, when Dubai projects are launched with fanfare on overload, very little was said as work began in 1994. Those who noticed dubbed the project the new Chicago Beach Hotel. To Sheikh Mohammed, it was much more. The iconic tower symbolized his pride as an Arab. It would cement his legacy as one of the great Muslim builders. The sheikh's project would become the most significant Arab monument since the Alhambra, built in Spain during Muslim rule in the fourteenth century. He would call it the Tower of the Arabs—Burj Al Arab.

Wright rented a house in Satwa and bought a Jeep to drive the sandy track to the construction site. There was still no paved road along the beach. The neighborhood now known as Umm Suqeim was a fishing village.

Sheikh Mohammed had other projects under way, including the Emirates Towers skyscrapers, which would be taller than anything in the Middle East or Europe. But he obsessed over the Burj Al Arab. "It was his baby," Wright says. "We gave him presentations on details right down to the door handles. This was his chance to do something really special and he needed to get it right."

The Dubai crown prince was a dream client. He was enthusiastic. He understood engineering challenges. And he was decisive. "He had the ability to make big decisions without many facts, and to get them right," Wright says. "He had a sophisticated vision. He knew what was significant and what didn't make a difference. He could see the end result."

The budget was unlimited. The Burj's purpose was to put Dubai on the map. The tower had to be stunning enough to compete with the classic buildings that inspired it. Inside, it had to be luxurious beyond compare—a twenty-first-century version of the *Arabian Nights*. Sheikh Mohammed knew the hotel would never pay for itself. He didn't want pursuit of profits to cramp Wright's style. The hotel would be the world's tallest, but it would hold just 202 giant suites, two stories each. The smallest would be 7,200 square feet, larger than most private homes.

The Burj would shatter the hotel industry's five-star standard. It would be beyond classification.

One day, discussion centered on Wright's desire to locate the hotel atop a man-made island. The sheikh moved the model back and forth from island to mainland. Building it at sea would add cost and time, and the hotel's underground parking garage would be tricky, essentially lying under water. But a land location was less unique, and the tall structure would cast a shadow on its own beach. Mohammed decided to keep it on the island.

Another day he took issue with the helipad, which was to sit atop the tubular Sky Bar, facing the sea. The sheikh, who flew his own helicopter, knew the strong Gulf breezes would create a dangerous tailwind.

"A helicopter needs to land into the prevailing wind," he told the men, jabbing at their drawing. "You have to move the helipad to this side."

Some of the work was unique. The three hundred-foot-long steel trusses that buttress the Burj's exterior were assembled in the desert and trucked to the site on a giant flatbed with forty axles. Road crews took down streetlights, so the truck could turn corners without wiping them out. Since much of Dubai has no bedrock, the pilings that anchor the tower to the earth would not sit on rock but in hard sand, held there by friction.

Dubai lacked the capacity to build big in those days. Atkins and its contractors had to import cranes, trucks, engineers, and crews. They used Dubai companies whenever possible, passing along their knowledge. "One of our missions was to upgrade Dubai's entire construction industry and the technology they were using," Wright says.

By 1999, the Burj was creating a stir around the world. The blue-and-white tower is an arresting sight, especially in the soft afterglow at dusk. The building's land face is sheathed in white, Teflon-coated fabric that resembles a billowing sail. Flashing strobes race up the tubular frame that bows out in the middle stories and converges at its pointy summit. From the beach, the island-bound Burj casts its reflection on the water like a river of moonlight. Guests flick on their room chandeliers and wedges of glass light up like blocks of iridescent ice. Tucked under the spire, the Sky Bar looks like a roll of parchment laid horizontally, its soft cocktail lighting beckoning. A yawning eighty-foot cantilever attaches the tavern to the Burj's frame. The only thing between drinkers and the sea far below is a bit of steel plate. "That caused a few structural nightmares," Wright chuckles.

Burj Al Arab did exactly what Sheikh Mohammed wanted. It became an instantly recognizable icon. Dubai's skyline was famous. No one could confuse it with Bahrain or Kuwait anymore. The Burj lured in droves of big-spending tourists. The publicity has been genius. When Andre Agassi and Roger Federer happened by, they were photographed whacking volleys on the helipad. A year later, Tiger Woods drove balls from the same spot.[12]

But the Burj isn't perfect. Step inside and the clean modernity of its exterior disintegrates. Suddenly, you're in Vegas. The walls are fishtanks trimmed in gold piping. The lobby centerpiece is a fountain that explodes like a rocket-propelled grenade, firing off a fourteen-story geyser. The lobby's Al Iwan restaurant is a confused muddle. Its arches look Arab. Its red and gold tapestries look Chinese. "It's Chinese-Persian fusion," a tour guide explains.

Looking up, the atrium is dizzying, almost seizure-inducing, with scalloped balconies rising floor after floor—so high that the Eiffel Tower could fit inside the open space. Looking down, the floor is dizzying. It's covered in giant mustard tiles woven with arabesques of gold mosaic, blue wedges, and red swooshes.

There is a dichotomy in philosophies between Wright the architect, who likes things clean and white, and British-Chinese interior designer Khuan Chew, who doesn't. Sheikh Mohammed sides with Chew.

Wright says the interior isn't his taste. His team's designs roughly matched the exterior. It was white, with muted shades of blue. One day, Wright, Mohammed, and Chew walked into the hotel lobby and looked up at the scalloped balconies, stretching far up into the heights. Wright loved it. The boss did not.

"His highness came in and it was all white," my guide explains as we tour a residential floor with lozenges of sea color here and there. "He said, 'It's too white! Add more color!' So we painted it turquoise and aquamarine."

By that point, Sheikh Mohammed had turned into a difficult client. He'd arrive unannounced and order crewmen to change things. Wright couldn't keep track. "Sheikh Mohammed had strong feelings about color. He wanted a modern interior, not Arab looking, but colorful. His houses are like that, bright colors and polished wood."

The crown prince had long been an admirer of Chew, who had done the bold primary colors of the Jumeirah Beach Hotel lobby. Her style suited him, but Wright believes it clashes with the overall design. "It's so different than everything else. I'd never have done it. But Sheikh Mohammed insisted," Wright says. "It's as unusual in its own way as the exterior. And the shock when you enter is one of the things people comment on. It's a modern-day pirate galleon full of treasure. But it's also quintessential Arabic Dubai—Sheikh Mohammed's taste."

Dubai has no underwater hotel or restaurant. Several articles and at least one book state that it does. There were plans at one point to build one. It never happened.

The Burj Al Arab has a restaurant that feels like it's underwater. The eatery is stashed below the raised lobby, just behind the escalators. But to get there, you step into a slow-descending elevator shaped like a bathyscaphe. When the doors open, you're in a Jules Verne set: a circular room set in a massive fish tank with menacing sharks and rays gliding past. The waiters wear captain's garb. Diners, sitting unawares along the glass walls of the aquarium, are interrupted by a scuba diver blowing bubbles. Otherwise intelligent folks are fooled into thinking they are dining 20,000 leagues under the sea. "The hotel even has an underwater restaurant that's only a short internal submarine ride away," write Saeb Eigner and Jeffrey Sampler in their 2003 book, *Sand to Silicon*.

There is an oft-heard rumor about the Burj. It cost so much to build—estimates range from $650 million to $2 billion—that even at 100 percent occupancy for a hundred years, Sheikh Mohammed, who owns it, will never recoup his investment. That's impressive, giving that the hotel's three-bedroom suites go for $7,000 per night, double or triple that in high season. The royal suite is double that again. The cheapest room rents for $2,000 in low season.

The Burj is popular with Chinese, Japanese, and Korean tourists, but Russians positively obsess over it. It's *the* place for Moscow's *nouveaux riches*. The management has hired Russian speakers and caters to a preference for raw oysters and caviar.

The Burj, surprisingly, doesn't have much of a beach. But why go there? The management offers yachts from its marina—$14,000 for three hours. Or you can rent a Lamborghini or a Ferrari. But why do that? The hotel has a fleet of sixteen Rolls-Royces with chauffeurs to handle the driving. But why drive? The hotel will book you a helicopter from the saucer cantilevered to the roof. It's $2,500 to the airport. Check that no one is up there whacking golf balls first.

Dubai has achieved an unlikely feat. The city has become a Mecca for Western tourists, bringing them to booze and carouse in the Muslim heart of Arabia, not far from the real Mecca, the holiest place in Islam. It's the earth's most barren landscape, a land with nothing in the way of historic sights, and big-spending visitors fly halfway around the world to see it.

The Burj Al Arab is the centerpiece and exemplar of that tourism sector. It's part hotel, part attraction. The whole of Dubai's industry is built around the same concept: the hotel as destination.

Dubai had 42 hotels with 4,600 rooms when Sheikh Mohammed got started in 1985. By 2008, the city owned one of the world's highest concentrations of luxury hotels, 350 of them, with 40,000 rooms—nearly 10 times as many.

Vacationers have poured in to fill them. The number of overnight visitors to Dubai rose eighteen-fold, from 400,000 in 1985 to 7.3 million in 2008. The largest number were Brits, with more than 750,000 in 2007. But Americans also flocked to Dubai. In 1990, just 15,000 Americans made an overnight visit. In 2007, that number jumped to nearly 400,000.[13] Rooms aren't cheap. In 2007, with occupancy rates at 85 percent, rooms rented for an average of $270 per night. Those prices and occupancy rates dropped in 2009 as the global downturn swept into town.

Dubai couldn't have trusted the free market for such a grand entrance into the tourism business. Sheikh Mohammed kick-started the sector, building hotels himself and eventually launching his own hospitality brand, Jumeirah International, which owns and operates Dubai's best resorts.

In 2007, the World Economic Forum ranked the UAE as the world's eighteenth most competitive tourist destination, just behind Spain and ahead of Portugal and Japan. The closest Middle East rival was Israel, in thirty-second place.[14]

Tiny Dubai now brings in more vacationers than Australia, Brazil, or

India.[15] Tourism made up nearly a quarter of the city's economy in 2006, earning $8 billion.[16] The emirate's goal is to host 15 million tourists a year by 2015, bequeathing the economy an annual $23 billion.[17] The recession that was beginning to spread across the globe at the time of this writing looked likely to defeat that goal, even with hotel managers cutting rates. Still, Dubai's success is undeniable. One might ask: Who needs ruins?

Setting the Groundwork

In 1999, as crews were fitting out guest rooms in the all-but-finished Burj, the stock market, at stratospheric heights in the United States, was nearing its peak. The dot-com balloon was showing signs of trouble.

The Burj Al Arab was greeting its early guests when the tech-heavy Nasdaq Composite Index peaked in March 2000 and began its steep and jagged slide that shed savings and jobs as it tumbled. Money-burning Internet companies ran out of cash and shut down. Gulf Arab investors were among those holding crumbling U.S. assets.

It was the start of a rough patch for America. The Clinton era fizzed out with a disputed election, and cocky George W. Bush found himself in the White House. Shortly after, nineteen Arabs—including two from the United Arab Emirates—crashed passenger jets into the World Trade Center, the Pentagon, and a field in Pennsylvania. The battered U.S. stock markets keeled over again. All told, the dot-com crash wiped out $5 trillion in market value of technology companies. In the United States, the September 11 attacks were the catalyst for a period of fear, war, and economic worry that has yet to abate.

Not so in Dubai. In the Gulf, the September 11 attacks marked the start of a six-year economic boom that raged in gluttonous excess until finally losing steam at the end of 2008. In fact, the attacks played a role in triggering that boom.

The post-9/11 United States was not the place to invest, especially if you were an Arab. Gulf Arabs pulled tens of billions of dollars out of U.S. assets and sent the money home. American hostility toward Arabs rose after the attacks, and the U.S.-led wars that followed were broadly opposed in the Muslim world. "The Americans shot themselves in the foot by being so harsh," says Beshr Bakheet, owner of Bakheet Financial Advisers in Riyadh. "Do you want to put your money in a country that is involved in wars all over the globe?"

There were practical reasons to repatriate cash. Many Arabs thought the U.S. Patriot Act being drawn up at the time would freeze their assets on suspicion of terror links. That didn't often happen. But investors moved their money first and asked questions later. More elementary, U.S. markets were tanking. Those in the Gulf were on the upswing, kicked by oil prices that rose for the next seven years.

Before 9/11, World Bank figures show, Middle Eastern oil-exporting countries plowed as much as $25 billion a year into U.S. investments. Between 2001 and 2003, the figure only reached $1.2 billion. The missing money, a lot of it, was rerouted from America to Dubai. "I lost about $200,000 in the U.S. market," Mohammed al-Ghussein, a Dubai-based private investor, told me in 2005. "So I took it back to the Gulf and I made the money back."[18]

The Muslim-bashing in the States put Arabs on the defensive. Investing at home became a matter of pride. "If someone calls your cat ugly, you suddenly love your cat more," says Georges Makhoul, managing director at Morgan Stanley in Dubai. "It brought a sense of, 'I'm going to show you.'"

The results have been spectacular. Since late 2001, economies in the six Gulf Cooperation Council countries—Bahrain, United Arab Emirates, Kuwait, Oman, Qatar, and Saudi Arabia—billowed. The UAE's gross domestic product swelled more than 60 percent between 2001 and 2008.[19] The U.S. economy grew 18 percent during the same period.

Cash poured into Dubai, which became the poster child for the Gulf boom. Dubai's growth averaged a scorching 13 percent a year between 2000 and 2005, faster than China. The emirate's population doubled between 2001 and 2008, reaching 2 million.

In 2001, Dubai's urban area was a narrow ribbon along the shore, around the size of Milwaukee. By 2008, Dubai was nearly the size of Houston.[20] The area under development had quadrupled to 565 square miles, with man-made islands rising from the sea and construction sprawling deep into the desert. The emirate's population looked set to reach 2.5 million by 2010, until recession turned it around.

The scale of the post-9/11 investment in the Gulf was staggering. As of 2008, more than $2 trillion in construction and infrastructure projects were planned or under way, with nearly 40 percent of those in the UAE, largely Dubai.[21]

The repatriation of Arab holdings in America was the start of a bigger trend. Since 2001, a huge portion of global wealth has flowed to the Gulf. Most is due to the quintupling of oil prices since 2001 to levels of more than $140 a barrel in 2008. Even with the plunge in prices late in the year, Gulf oil revenues were expected to come in around $600 billion in 2008, up nearly tenfold over a decade. In 1998, oil brought them just $61 billion.

By 2008, the six Gulf states were on the receiving end of what American oilman T. Boone Pickens calls the biggest transfer of wealth in human history. The cash Americans and Europeans handed over when they fueled their cars correlates directly with the sprouting of the Dubai skyline, and those in Abu Dhabi, Doha, and Riyadh. By year end, Gulf states held $2.6 trillion in government reserves, banks, sovereign wealth funds, and assorted other holdings.[22] That money was equal to America's 2007 federal budget, before the value of some Gulf holdings was clipped in the downturn. This is the nest egg that will carry the Gulf countries through the global recession.

When the oil price started to climb in 2002, Dubai didn't have much crude left. But the city didn't need it. Its neighbors sit atop 60 percent of the world's known oil reserves. Sheikh Mohammed lowered barriers to investment. Oil revenue looking for a home found one.

Prior to 2000, most Gulf countries had no investment vehicles to soak up the cash that was coming in. Oil earnings were spent on social schemes, infrastructure, and simple consumption. Any surplus got invested in American stocks and bonds. But through the 1990s, Dubai and other cities began building the banking and financial infrastructure needed to transform their societies. When the September 11 attacks made America less attractive, the Gulf had opportunities at the ready.

By 2001, Dubai had a stock market. Now it has two, with a third in Abu Dhabi. The city has grown into a regional services and banking center, and, with the Burj Al Arab, a playground for the jet set. Investors had their choice. They could buy stocks or real estate, or start a business.

"Before, it had been barren land. You couldn't have planted seeds," says Morgan Stanley's Makhoul, forty-two. "Now, the land was well tilled. It was fertile. The money came pouring in. The main axis that was ready to receive it all? It was right here."

It wasn't just money that came back. Arab professionals who'd fled saw an opportunity to return to their neighborhood without suffering a pay cut. Dubai calls it the "reverse brain-drain."

"These were people who thought the West was alienating them because of their cultural background. Suddenly they could function just as well in their home region," Makhoul says. "You didn't have to worry about the stigma anymore. You were in a comfortable environment."

Makhoul is one of these people. He'd fled his hometown, Beirut, when he was twenty, figuring he was abandoning the Arab world. But in 2005, after two decades in New York, Tokyo, and London, Morgan Stanley asked him to move to Dubai. Most Arab bankers and lawyers came in similar circumstances. "I like living here," he says. "It's Arab enough for me and it's Western enough for me."

The Real Estate Boom

In 2002, Sheikh Mohammed made perhaps his single most momentous decision. It would catapult Dubai onto the globe and, within a few years, into the household vocabulary of nearly everyone on earth.

He decreed that foreigners could buy homes.

The city was already the Gulf's most desirable expatriate base. Suddenly it became the only place in the Gulf where foreigners could buy real estate. Sheikh Mohammed's message to foreigners was: I don't just want you to bring your money to Dubai. I want you to bring your skills and your family and contribute to our economy and society. And I want you to be comfortable.

The decree unleashed a typhoon of pent-up demand that was far stronger than anyone knew. A gold rush ensued. Expatriates jumped at the chance to buy. Investors followed, funneling cash into Dubai from ever farther away. Within a few years, developers turned the city into a giant construction site.

That year, London property consultants Jones Lang LaSalle released a report titled "World Winning Cities." Researchers studied a hundred cities around the globe, looking for the best performers to recommend to investor clients. They compared metrics like growth in economy, population and employment, and demand for real estate.

Three cities emerged from the pack: Dubai, Las Vegas, and Dublin. The paper turned out to be prescient for all three, which were just starting to erupt with growth. Each had attractive business environments, light regulation, favorable tax regimes, and plenty of inward investment.

Las Vegas was well known. Dublin less so. Dubai was the wild card—an unknown city that, it turned out, had grandiose visions of becoming a world player. Jones Lang LaSalle told clients that Dubai had led the world in population growth (nearly 6 percent a year) and employment growth (more than 8 percent a year) for the previous decade. In both categories, Dubai beat out fast-growing cities in China, the United States, and India.

"In 2002, Dubai wasn't really on the radar screen of real estate players around the world," says Jeremy Kelly, the consultant who directed the study. "But we saw an opportunity in Dubai at the time. We identified it as a key rising star."

Dubai's glamor was born in an explosion of dust, noise, and sweat. Dozers flattened the desert, and pile drivers sank columns deep into the sand. Cranes crammed the skyline and lined the highways, hauling up gray slabs of prefabricated wall, tureens of wet concrete, and spaghetti bundles of steel reinforcing rod. When the sun set, the night shift kicked into action and the bluish hue of sodium vapor lights lit the city. Observers have dubbed Dubai the world's fastest-growing city, as well as its largest repository of building cranes, between 10 and 20 percent of the world's total.[23]

Mohammed Ali Alabbar's Emaar typifies the housing boom. On vast tracts of rolling dunes once grazed by antelope and camel, Emaar built Levittowns of cookie-cutter townhouses and Moorish-themed McMansions. The neighborhoods were riven by meandering roads fringed with flowerbeds, with sidewalks for rollerbladers and baby strollers. Bulldozers sculpted golf courses, swimming pools, and tennis courts. The gated communities got names with a California ring: The Springs, The Lakes,

Emirates Hills, Arabian Ranches, The Meadows, The Greens. Western expatriates hungry for homes lined up at dawn, checkbooks at the ready. So did professionals from Iran, India, and Pakistan.

"The world decided that Dubai would become one of its center points," says Ryan Mahoney, the Canadian managing director of Better Homes, the biggest local realtor. "We didn't have any inkling it would ever be this big."

In 2000, Alabbar visited Vancouver, British Columbia, to glean ideas from a city perennially ranked among the world's most livable. Touring a development, he met Robert Lee, a developer's agent. Lee impressed Alabbar so much that the Dubaian hired him. The Canadian had handled big projects in Vancouver. But he'd never seen anything like Dubai. "When I came here and saw what was happening, my jaw literally dropped. Wow! It was an absolute stampede," Lee says. "It was like a fish market. 'Just give me a property, any property!'"

Not all the developers were as thorough or well capitalized as Emaar. The lack of regulation ignited a boom like the crazed 1920s speculation in Florida. Small operators were exhilarated to find that they could come to the city with a drawing of an apartment tower, buy a cheap plot, get government permission to build, and then sell all the apartments before they'd broken ground, sometimes even before owning the land they would build upon.

"People would buy the apartments and the investor would build the building with that money," says Mahoney. "This was risky. But it was a great way to excite the worldwide investor community." It also encouraged cost-cutting and shoddy work, with developers boosting short-term profit by skimping on materials, labor skills, and amenities.

The government did the same thing. It drew up plans for a palm-shaped island and sold off the plots in three days—while the plots were still open sea. With the money they'd collected, the Palm Jumeirah got built.

As the years passed, nothing could slake the thirst for Dubai property. Sheikh Mohammed designated tract after tract as development zones for foreign buyers. He sold the plots to foreign developers and let them build what they wanted. Speculators flooded in and the city grew like a patch of kudzu.

Contractors kept up with demand by switching from low-density townhouses to skyscrapers. Emaar got control of two square miles of desert, and Robert Lee used his Vancouver experience to put together Dubai's first neighborhood of apartment towers, the Dubai Marina. Lee drew up building lots, devised prices, and brought the scheme to Sheikh Mohammed for approval. The Dubai crown prince liked the project but not the prices.

"Cut them in half," he told Lee. "If you sell it low, there'll be a herd of people and excitement. Everybody will go around saying, 'Me, too!'"

Sheikh Mohammed had done the same thing with building plots alongside Sheikh Zayed Road. He would do it again on the Palm Jumeirah, setting launch prices artificially low. "He was actually playing the speculation market," says Lee.

The man from Vancouver dug a short canal, bringing a loop of the sea inland. Then, developers clustered the banks of this canal with a mini-Hong Kong. It rose so quickly, it was as if they'd adapted instant ramen noodles technology to building a city. The Marina district is now a dense forest of apartment towers, each with blinking lights to warn approaching aircraft. Some rise above 50 stories. One cluster, the Jumeirah Beach Residence, is a massive conglomeration of yellow concrete that looks vaguely Miami Beach. It's said to be the world's largest single-phase housing development, with 36 connected towers and 25,000 residents. All told, the Marina will house 400,000 people in 200 skyscrapers, each vying for a tiny patch of sky.

Buyers didn't care to see their apartments or townhomes before making downpayments. Developers sold tens of thousands by brandishing drawings of dream neighborhoods with homes, trees, elevated trains, and European families strolling with ice cream cones. It took a leap of faith to trust that empty desert would be converted into the renderings on display. But the theoretical homes sold out in hours, years before structures would be built. Values shot into orbit. In the speculative secondary market, prices on luxury homes quintupled in five years, with properties sold repeatedly before completion. Blocky three-bedroom homes overlooking an artificial lake in The Meadows launched for around $350,000 in 2003. Five years later, they cost $1.8 million.[24]

"This is pyramid selling by any other name," says former British ambassador Anthony Harris. New laws in Dubai have since limited the most free-wheeling of these practices.

Problem was, Dubai was creating jobs faster than it was building apartments. Despite six years of round-the-clock building, Dubai's housing supply could not keep pace with a population rising by 170,000 a year. The city faced yearly demand for 80,000 homes, but construction crews going flat-out could build just half that many.[25] The result was a wildly distorted housing market with prices that spiked up and up.

The housing boom bled into consumer goods and Dubai responded with malls, building them fatter and taller until the city had more mall space per capita than anywhere on the planet.[26] IKEA came. Harvey Nichols came. Ace Hardware came. Marks & Spencer and Saks Fifth Avenue came. France's Wal-Mart-style megastore, Carrefour, came. One mall resembled Venice. Another, the Giza pyramids. Another erected halls based on China, Egypt, Moorish Spain, and India. Another added an indoor ski slope.

Until September 2008, Dubai realtors could declare that no one had lost money in the Dubai property market. A month later, that was no longer true.

Designer Industries

If Dubai's housing boom caught people by surprise, its payoff for its free zone gambles would beggar belief.

The city's dalliances with free zones harkens to an attempt to kick-start the languishing Jebel Ali port. In 1981, no one wanted to work in Jebel Ali. Berths sat empty. The port was miles from anywhere on the far edge of Dubai. The cargo action was still at Port Rashid in the city center.

At some point, Sheikh Mohammed and the advisers that coalesced around him, Sultan bin Sulayem included, decided to convert Jebel Ali into a free port and manufacturing district. It was to become a special economic zone, where companies could import raw materials, assemble finished goods, and reexport those products. The area would be exempt from the federal government's 5 percent import duty, as well as the Companies Law, which prohibited majority foreign ownership of any business. That law was Dubai's biggest impediment to foreign investment. The UAE government in Abu Dhabi requires foreign companies to find a local partner to take a minimum 51 percent stake. Dubai got around the law by declaring the port a free trade zone.

The plan worked—slowly. A few dozen companies moved into the port in the early 1980s. That jumped to two hundred by 1990, and then seemed to achieve critical mass. By 2006, more than six thousand companies operated in the fifty-two-square-mile free zone, now packed with warehouses and trucks hauling goods for reexport to Iran, Africa, and the rest of the Gulf.

One thing irked the crown prince. The companies flocking to Jebel Ali weren't exactly high-tech. They were textile sweat shops, tire and auto parts importers, and the like. By the late 1990s, it was clear that Dubai was missing the Internet revolution. Gulf Arabs just didn't connect with computers and the Internet in the same way that Americans did. Sheikh Mohammed couldn't let this pass. He and his advisers racked their brains for a way to tap into technology and reap its productivity gains. The answer came in a study that he commissioned. It said the city would do well to set up cluster zones for two industries: information technology and media. It wasn't advice that the sheikh would ignore.

In the late 1990s, the northwestern edge of Dubai petered out along Jumeirah Beach. There were a few hotels and a smattering of Maktoum family palaces, including Sheikh Mohammed's summer villa, a sleek assembly of round buildings with a private island. Most of the area was empty desert and pristine shore. Just inland from the beach lay a salt-crusted lowland, flooded with ponds of brine. It was some of the least attractive real estate in the city.

In 1999, Sheikh Mohammed announced that this lowland would house Dubai's next free trade zone. Foreign firms would get the same relaxations of federal tax and ownership laws at Jebel Ali, except the enticements would be restricted to information technology companies. There would be unlimited visas for imported workers, no income or corporate tax, and no restrictions on repatriating capital. The swamp got a name: Dubai Internet City.

The job of building Internet City fell to a man named Mohammed al-Gergawi, a midlevel bureaucrat from a poor family who worked in the Dubai Department of Economic Development. Gergawi had the fortune to be discovered years earlier by one of Sheikh Mohammed's internal spies, known as "mystery shoppers." In his book, Sheikh Mohammed says he gave Gergawi a promotion when he learned that the young functionary planned to resign for a private sector job. When Gergawi turned up at Sheikh Mohammed's *majlis* to offer his gratitude, he learned the sheikh's agents had been monitoring his performance for four years.[27]

Sheikh Mohammed took Gergawi under his wing, testing him with ever-larger responsibilities. The young executive carried off several of Dubai's most successful tourist promotions, including the Dubai Shopping Festival and Dubai Summer Surprises event. Both send shopaholic tourists streaming to Dubai's malls, hotels, and airlines. The Summer Surprises festival manages to lure tourists to Dubai in the seething depths of summer. It's an impressive feat.

Gergawi, a bear of a man with an electric smile, is a rare personality. He exudes the energy of a man delighted with his lot in life. Women in Dubai—locals and expatriates—fawn over his George Clooney looks. Like Sheikh Mohammed, he has a reputation for giving wads of cash to strangers. I worked briefly as a consultant at the Executive Office, downstairs from Gergawi. One day he strode into my office with his arm extended and boomed "I am Mohammed al-Gergawi," and gave me a hearty handshake. We had an easygoing chat. When my son Jay was born in 2007, Gergawi sent a towering bouquet of flowers to the hospital room of my wife, Chloe, that took two men to erect. When I returned to work, his secretary handed me bags of baby clothes.

In 1999, with Internet City, Gergawi got the chance to show what he could do.

Even then, Dubai was an immature city with more ambition than accomplishment. The four-building office park wasn't huge—the buildings were to be four stories high—but it was supposed to bring dot-com millionaires to Dubai. Architects' renderings showed manicured grounds with café tables overlooking artificial lakes. Sheikh Mohammed, perhaps sensing that the tech bubble was about to burst, declared in October 1999 that Internet City would be built in a year. It was a ridiculous deadline.

Gergawi and his team rented an office in the Crowne Plaza Hotel and interviewed would-be contractors. The group had only a foggy understanding of the amenities needed. A survey of technology companies provided some answers: uncensored high-speed Internet and Starbucks coffee.

John Larson, an IT consultant from Winthrop, Massachusetts, was one of the contractors who met Gergawi and his team. Larson, an athletic man with jet-black hair and a sarcastic sense of humor, described the communications infrastructure the buildings would need, as well as the housing and lifestyle requirements of young Western and Asian techies. Larson, forty-six, got the feeling the Dubaians were in over their heads. But when a subcontracting offer came through, he took it.

Internet City was a government project, but Sheikh Mohammed refused to commit state resources. It got even less help than Emirates airline. The crown prince handed over the land and—other than his sales pitch—that was it. Gergawi bankrolled the project with a loan from HSBC.

To the developers in Dubai, the concept seemed like a good deal: modern offices, no tax. But no one signed up. Gergawi's bulldozers had cleared the land, dug the lake, and filled in the low spots, but construction was on hold. "They needed to build to suit. So they didn't move forward," Larson says. "They were waiting for people to sign up."

The site sat in eyeshot of Sheikh Mohammed's beach palace. He could see that crews were just pushing dirt around. One day, the crown prince drove onto the site and told construction managers to get moving. "He lit a fire under their butts," Larson says.

Tenants finally signed up when Dubai cajoled Microsoft to become Internet City's anchor tenant by offering fifty years' free rent in exchange for "the biggest Microsoft sign in the world," says government adviser Yasar Jarrar.

When construction kicked into action, it was like sprinting a marathon. Sheikh Mohammed refused to budge on his one-year deadline. It was Dubai's version of the Alaska Highway in 1942: Speed was the concern, the deadline paramount. "It was chaos. Plans were changing on the fly. Specs were changing from one day to the next," Larson says. "If there was a cost overrun, something got chopped out. Things got cut to get buildings done on time."

Funny thing: It worked. With Sheikh Mohammed riding herd, four blue glass buildings rose from the sand. Internet City held its grand opening in October 2000, just 364 days after launch, a day ahead of schedule. It was an early demonstration of the can-do Dubai work ethic that would emerge over and over. "You wonder how anything gets built. But you know what? It gets done," Larson says. "That's Dubai for you."

Larson got a card inviting him to the opening ceremony at Internet City, to be followed by dinner at Sheikh Mohammed's beach palace across the road. It was to be a gala bash with a thousand guests—contractors, the press, diplomats, and local bigshots. Larson knew Internet City wasn't ready for tenants, but that didn't stop the party. Laborers erected bleachers and draped a giant video screen from one of the buildings.

Larson arrived in a suit and tie, watching workers painting walls and heaving rolls of sod from trucks. Foremen barked at them: Get the grass down so guests wouldn't dirty their shoes. "They were literally unrolling sod in front of us as we walked. It was a red-carpet welcome," Larson says. Women in high heels and cocktail dresses tripped on the uneven turf. So laborers laid a walkway of plywood. "I said, 'Hey, they're trying like hell. Let's give them credit,'" Larson says.

Sheikh Mohammed toured one of the lobbies, with a TV cameraman following. Live video played on the giant screen, allowing guests to watch his inspection. It was a minefield. If the sheikh barged into an unfinished room, the crowd would witness it. At one point, the crown prince reached for a door handle. A spectator in the bleachers yelled, "No, don't go in there! The stairs aren't built yet!" The sheikh's guide must have whispered something similar, and led him away.

Afterward, buses whisked the guests to a night of Arab hospitality in the safer confines of Sheikh Mohammed's summer home. It was a magical experience just entering the walled grounds. Linen-covered tables spilled across the vast lawn and around the swimming pool. A breeze rustled the palms and carried the smoke of grilling kebabs. White-garbed attendants stood behind an enormous buffet table, carving roasts and serving Lebanese delicacies. Arab musicians with a stringed *oud* and hand drums played under the stars. A beaming Sheikh Mohammed mingled with guests, asking whether they enjoyed the food. Diners stayed as long as they could, hobnobbing in groups over espresso and glasses of juice.

The party marked a Dubai milestone. Sheikh Mohammed had opened another new development avenue, and it pointed to the direction the city would take under his leadership. Dubai would become the base for any company prospecting markets in the Middle East and South Asia. Sheikh Maktoum was still Dubai's titular leader, but Sheikh Mohammed was the ambitious one who, it was evident to all, pulled the strings. It was plain that the Dubai crown prince had inherited his father's drive and obsession with speed—and then some. Internet City forged a new development path, more durable than tourism and luxury real estate.

If Sheikh Mohammed had been the driver, Gergawi was the manager who pulled it off. He built an office park in a year. He brought Microsoft,

Oracle, and Hewlett-Packard to Dubai. From nothing, the city soon had three thousand knowledge workers and nearly two hundred new foreign companies. Dubai gained decades' worth of foreign investment in a year, simply by bundling offices with clever incentives. And it wasn't just any sort of foreign investor. These were clean companies that would inject productivity and skills into the economy. It was a coup.

Gergawi's profile and responsibilities skyrocketed. The rest of the Middle East would scramble to copy Dubai's free zone model. Even Iran aped the idea, opening three similar zones on its coast.

As in the housing boom, demand for Dubai offices was hotter than anyone predicted. The two expansions fed on each other, sucking in immigrants from around the world. International companies, it seemed, were desperate for a tax-free base, if only to book their global profits. Internet City's four modest buildings filled immediately. More companies wanted the same deal, but there was no room. The zone expanded. Sheikh Mohammed wanted technology to be given space in Dubai at all costs, to keep valuable firms from finding homes in a competing city. Builders struggled to keep abreast of demand for the next eight years. By 2007, Internet City had expanded to twenty-five buildings with twelve thousand workers and nearly nine hundred companies.

The hurtling success hides a crucial weakness. Internet City was supposed to bring research and development to Dubai. It did not. Companies like Microsoft and IBM do their regional software development in India and Israel, where schools produce smart engineers. Microsoft CEO Steve Ballmer hammered that point in May 2008 at the opening of Microsoft's expanded Israel Research Center. There, six hundred coders write the company's software. "If you do the math, Microsoft is almost as much an Israeli company as it is an American company," Ballmer crowed in front of the Israeli press. In Dubai, a few hundred Microsoft employees operate a government consultancy and service center, and they market software written elsewhere.

A month after the gala, Sheikh Mohammed announced that another free zone was in the works next door. This was Dubai Media City. Companies would get the same deal as those in Internet City: unlimited visas, no restrictions on capital, no tax. With Gergawi in charge again, building went smoother, but there was an oversight. Dubai invited television and film producers, but built only offices. There were no soundstages or production facilities. The omission would be rectified later by another free zone, the International Media Production Zone.

Media companies ran to Dubai. My company, the Associated Press, rented an office, as did Reuters, Agence France-Presse, BBC, Dow Jones, and lots of others. Saudi-owned news channel Al Arabiya put its headquarters in Dubai. Media City lured Arabic newspapers that faced censorship in their home countries. Besides the news outlets, comers included public relations firms, modeling agencies, book and magazine publishers, ad agencies, and Web developers.

It was a smart move. Journalists need to travel to war zones, and Dubai sits in the middle of most of them, with great flight connections. Afghanistan is a three-hour flight. Baghdad is two hours. Pakistan is three hours. Lebanon is three hours. There are direct flights to Sudan, Congo, even lawless Somalia, on a carrier called Jubba Airways, launched in Dubai by Somali exiles.

Media City also made marketing sense. With so many reporters in town, Dubai reaped international coverage of its big projects. Announcements like the Palm Islands, the Burj Dubai, and the international stock market got heavy play in the West. The world also learned about the city's ugly side, its exploitation of laborers and boys brought in to race camels. But the exposure did more to clean up the cruelty than anything else.

Sheikh Mohammed launched the zone with a speech telling reporters they were free to write and say what they wanted, but it had better be accurate. "I guarantee freedom of expression to all of you in the media. I give you the right to speak your minds, to be completely objective in your views and reporting," he said. "But I will hold the media accountable for its use of this freedom. You must thoroughly research and gather facts and make no accusations without evidence and cast no slurs without proof."

Sheikh Mohammed's pledge hasn't been ironclad. In 2007, the UAE government halted broadcasts by two Pakistani TV stations after Pakistan declared emergency rule and asked the UAE to muzzle the Media City-based broadcasters. One station vowed to move its operations to a freer market.[28]

Like Internet City, Dubai Media City started with humble office buildings beside an artificial lake. By 2008, the zone held a thousand companies in two dozen buildings, including two fifty-three-story copies of New York's Chrysler Building. The two free zones have become such hives of activity that they have helped reverse Dubai's rush hour traffic flow. Sheikh Mohammed would reuse the free zone model more often than Bo Diddley recycled his beat. A dozen times and more, Dubai demarcated vacant land for tax-free business zones—anything that might be a remote fit.

It now hosts Studio City, Silicon Oasis, Investment Park, and Sports City. There is DuBiotech, for the biotechnology sector. And there is Motor City, Golf City, Maritime City, Logistics City, Academic City, Humanitarian City, and many more. But none has repeated the rollicking success of Internet and Media cities.

Historically, rich Arabs who got sick fled to the West for treatment. The hospital in which I was born, the Cleveland Clinic, was a favorite. Perennial visitors included Jordan's King Hussein and Sheikh Zayed, who, upon his death, left behind a whole floor in one hospital building stuffed with his belongings.

Dubai saw the exodus as a business opportunity. If it could build a decent health care system, it could siphon off some of the trade. The city's outdated health infrastructure was overdue for an overhaul anyway.

In 2004, Harvard Medical School received an invitation to explore options in Dubai. Specifically, Dubai wanted it to anchor a cluster zone to be called Dubai Healthcare City.

Harvard was intrigued. The medical school hadn't had an overseas venture since the late 1930s, when its fledgling campus in Shanghai closed ahead of the Japanese invasion. The school was ready to try again, but it didn't like Dubai's concept. It looked like the city was building a health care mall and wanted Harvard Medical School as the anchor tenant. "That was a pretty lousy model for quality health care," says Dr. Robert Thurer, a surgeon who came to Dubai to head the Harvard Medical School Dubai Center. "Dubai wants to be a world-class city. Well, it can't do that without world-class health care." And that takes decades of institution building.

Thurer, sixty-three, a Long Islander, held meetings with Sheikh Mohammed, who eventually bought into Harvard's vision. The university would be allowed to restructure Healthcare City. Harvard agreed to operate a research hospital to teach doctors the latest advancements. At the same time, the school would help regulate the cluster zone. Instead of turning Dubai into a destination for sick tourists, Harvard aims to improve health care in the Middle East. Dubai is investing over $1 billion to build Harvard's hospital, which is supposed to admit its first patients by 2012.

"This is by far the biggest thing we've ever done," Thurer says. "No place in the world is doing anything like it."

7

ALMOST FAMOUS

Dubai Inc.

THE SYSTEM OF government in Dubai and the rest of the UAE is perhaps best described as tribal autocracy. It's autocratic because a single ruler, Sheikh Mohammed in Dubai's case, holds unlimited power. It's tribal because rule is based on tribe and family, with power handed down the generations.

Martin Hvidt, a Danish scholar who has studied Dubai's governance, describes it as a neo-patrimony, organized around the ruler as an individual. Those under him depend on his good graces for their jobs.[1]

Sheikh Mohammed probably wouldn't describe himself as a tribal autocrat. His advisers would never use those terms, which disguise the benevolence and pragmatism that also characterize his rule. He'd probably say it like this: Dubai is a big corporation and I am CEO, otherwise known as "the boss."

Dubai's government is a steep pyramid. Below Sheikh Mohammed sit his second and third sons, Hamdan, the crown prince, and Maktoum, the deputy ruler. Both are untested men in their twenties. That's where the royalty ends.

The bureaucracy begins with The Executive Office, Sheikh Mohammed's cadre of advisers. It sits on the forty-third floor of the Emirates

Office Tower. The Executive Office is comprised of a few dozen planners and managers who oversee every entity that reports to the ruler. These are the technocrats who plot the city's growth strategy and incubate its initiatives and state-owned companies. It's the home of Sheikh Mohammed's tough Delivery Unit, which follows up after a manager promises to, say, increase passenger throughput at the airport. The unit ensures the manager "delivers" on that promise.

Six floors down is the Dubai Executive Council, the ruler's Cabinet. The nineteen members—appointed by Sheikh Mohammed—exert direct control over the municipal government. They draft legislation and budgets, draw up development plans, and see that Sheikh Mohammed's policies are coordinated across all twenty-four government departments. Most department heads have a seat. That is the structure. In reality, council members are many of the same overstretched personalities who show up elsewhere. For instance, Sheikh Mohammed's uncle Ahmed— the chairman of Emirates Airline—is a member, in his capacity as chief of Dubai Civil Aviation. Police Chief Dhahi Khalfan has a seat. So does Sultan bin Sulayem, as chairman of the Ports, Customs & Free Zones. Mohammed Alabbar is a member, in his capacity as the head of the department of economic development. Dubai's crown prince, Sheikh Hamdan, chairs it.

Vying with these two offices for influence is the Ruler's Court, or *diwan*, on the creek. The new director, Mohammed al-Shaibani, was a rising force in 2008. Under him the *diwan* had taken control of the city's Department of Finance, which oversees the city budget, and several functions previously held by The Executive Office.

Least influential is Dubai's city hall, known as the Municipality, which sits across the creek from the *diwan*. The building is as thronged as any American city hall, with waiting rooms and take-a-number counters. The municipal director, Hussain Lootah—Dubai's mayor—is just one member of the Executive Council. The city's day-to-day affairs, its sewers and roads, take a backseat to the plotting of Dubai's growth and investment.

The contrast between the Municipality and The Executive Office is like the difference between GE's lightbulb and jet engine divisions. The municipal building is grimy and mundane, with vending machines and shoeshines. The Executive Office is swish and corporate, with espresso and teppanyaki.

Nabil al-Yousuf runs The Executive Office.[2] He's a big, fit man of forty, with a precisely sculpted goatee. He'd look like a biker if it weren't for the crisp white *kandoura* and *gutra* headscarf. Al-Yousuf is relaxed and eloquent, and his polite listening style belies his position as one of the city's busiest men. He sits back on his office couch, bare foot on his knee, clicking a string of milky yellow prayer beads. Behind, the plate glass that is his office window is a trophy case of skyscraper crowns.

Al-Yousuf is an industrial engineer with an MBA who studied at American and British universities. If Sheikh Mohammed is CEO of Dubai Inc., and his four lieutenants—Gergawi, Alabbar, bin Sulayem, and al-Shaibani—are the board of directors, al-Yousuf is the chief financial officer. He doesn't mind the comparison.

Al-Yousuf has spearheaded the introduction of corporate management tools into government. One is the Dubai Government Excellence Program, an intense and humiliating contest among city departments. Each year the boss rewards the top municipal departments and singles out the worst. Winning is great, but losing is so devastating—sometimes career-ending—that bureaucrats go to outrageous lengths to increase their scores. The award system has seen departments hiring consultants, spying on each other, and revamping their floor plans. They've raced to offer services online. They even compete over the freshness of the coffee and homemade buttermilk they offer visitors.

The government has also adopted—and tweaked for its own use—the "key performance indicators" introduced by Harvard Business School professor Robert Kaplan. The indicators measure a company's financial performance, customer satisfaction, and internal functions. Dubai relentlessly benchmarks itself against governments it sees as competitors. Hong Kong, Singapore, Ireland, New Zealand, and Australia are favorites. "This reflects the leadership style of Sheikh Mohammed," al-Yousuf says. "He really runs this country as a corporation."

Government jobs in the UAE used to be like those in the rest of the Arab world, a gravy train for life. The longer you stayed, the bigger your salary. Dubai's new human resources law—modeled after GE's—reserves promotions for those who outperform their colleagues. If a worker devises a technique that saves the government money, a portion of the savings winds up in his paycheck. "The reward is based on what you do rather than how long you've been in the job. It's a major shift in paradigm for our government," al-Yousuf says.

Sheikh Mohammed oversees a cadre of undercover mystery shoppers, like the one who discovered Gergawi. They pose as prickly members of the public seeking the government's help. Their reports are instrumental in firings and promotions. No bureaucrat can be sure the demanding customer across the counter isn't secretly reporting to the boss. Once in a while, Sheikh Mohammed turns up at 7:30 a.m. on surprise inspections. He's been known to fire late-arriving managers on the spot.

Dubai isn't run like a business for reasons of style. That's partly how it raises its budget. Dubai levies no income, property, or corporate taxes. Its tax base is small: hotel occupancy taxes, levies on restaurant meals and liquor sales, as well as a 5 percent duty on imports that aren't destined for free zones. There are fees for permits, road tolls, and a regressive renter's tax on apartments and offices. But part of the budget comes from the profits of government businesses like Emirates airline, Dubai Taxi agency, and the city's aluminum and glass plants.

The World Economic Forum ranks the United Arab Emirates as the most competitive economy in the Arab world. But Dubai, viewed on its own, rates much higher. Dubai's economy is more competitive than those of Japan, Britain, and Germany, and its government is more efficient, says a report by the prestigious Swiss IMD business school. Dubai beats the United States in government efficiency as well.[3]

"Dubai is successful because it is a government that is an entrepreneur at the same time," al-Yousuf says. "It can spot opportunities and immediately take advantage, unlike the rigid five-year planning and specific road maps that many developing economies follow."

The institutions that make Dubai hum function in obscurity. Their power isn't codified in law. They are driven by individual personalities whose influence rises and falls on the sheikh's favor. Most Dubaians, even some whose business takes them to city hall, could not tell you where The Executive Office and Executive Council are located. Many don't know they exist. These offices are rarely discussed in the press. They've got no facilities for the public, no ombudsmen, no accessible press spokespeople. Dubai Inc., after all, is an autocracy.

State Affairs

Most people associate state-owned businesses with socialism-inspired factories you might see in Iraq or the former Soviet bloc. These places bear names like the State Enterprise for Soap and Cleaning Products. Years ago, governments sought self-sufficiency and jobs by making their own soap, rather than importing it. But most state companies needed subsidies to survive, and their products were too bland to be exported. The experience was so dismal that economists generally agreed that governments shouldn't be producing private goods and services.

Now comes Dubai to turn the model on its head. While the rest of the world was privatizing state business, Dubai was launching a new breed. Dubai created these companies by calving them off from the government. It hired top managers, usually expatriates, to run them.

Dubai's portfolio of businesses is huge. Dubai World is one such group, with its profitable port operator DP World and glamor developer Nakheel, responsible for the Palm islands. Emirates airline and Dubai Aluminum are 100 percent state-owned, as are investment funds Istithmar and Dubai International Capital, a slew of property developers, banks, and several others. Each is run along conventional corporate lines, financing investments with debt or earnings.

The companies aren't subject to civil service hiring rules. They get special access to the ruler and bypass the bureaucracy. Sheikh Mohammed asked them all to develop internationally, and several are dominated by foreign investments, especially DP World, property developer Sama Dubai, and increasingly Emaar, partly state-owned and building neighborhoods in more than a dozen countries. Sheikh Mohammed's own Dubai Holding Group, with its Jumeirah hotel brand, operates the same way.

These state companies are central to Dubai's growth strategy. Sheikh Mohammed directs them to take the risk of breaking open sectors targeted in the city's strategic plan, and private companies sweep in behind them, perceiving their investments protected by the government. The cluster zones like Internet and Media cities are examples. Dubai International Airport and Emirates work in tandem, and the Nasdaq Dubai stock exchange gets backing from state firms, like DP World, that offer shares there.

Dubai's state-owned corporations challenge the conventional wisdom about public sector inefficiency. The rest of the Gulf has scrambled to follow along. Qatar's developer Qatari Diar, launched in 2005, looks like Emaar. Emirates has spawned copycats in Abu Dhabi's Etihad Airways and Qatar Airways. But by the crash of 2009, Dubai-owned businesses were among those in the biggest trouble. Their easy access to capital meant they carried most of the city's debt, worth tens of billions of dollars. There was talk of merging some of them.

Dubai Ports World: The Lynching

In February 2006, American news outlets began running an alarming story. It centered on Dubai, a place many Americans were hearing about for the first time. The story said that cargo operations in several major ports—including New York, New Jersey, Philadelphia, Baltimore, New Orleans, and Miami—had been purchased by the Arab government of Dubai. Reporters described Dubai as a logistics center for the September 11 terrorists, and pointed out that it sits in a country that was the birthplace of two of those hijackers. Soon, they alleged, the security of America's ports would rest in the hands of Arabs: the Dubai-owned port operator DP World.

New York Senator Charles Schumer led the charge against Dubai. Just after the story broke, Schumer called a press conference with families of the September 11 terror victims. He demanded that President Bush reconsider a deal he had approved.

"A lot of families are incensed by this, because you're talking about the safety of the country," said William Doyle, whose son Joseph died at the World Trade Center. "We have a problem already in our ports because all of our containers aren't checked, but now they want to add this unknown? It's not right."[4]

Soon, Schumer's Senate partner from New York, Hillary Clinton—now the U.S. secretary of state—added her voice to the uproar. New York Congressman Peter King said he opposed the deal because Dubai had not explained how it would prevent al-Qaida from infiltrating its ports company, and, it can be assumed, attacking America. This furor was, in the words of *The New York Times* columnist Nicholas Kristof, an episode of "quasi-racist scaremongering" of the sort that hadn't been seen since the World War II internment camps.

Foreigners had been running U.S. ports long before Dubai got into the business. In fact, foreigners were already managing the U.S. ports in question, through Britain's Peninsular and Oriental Steam Navigation Company, known as P&O. Dubai acquired the U.S. operations—as well as those in sixteen other ports around the world—when it bought P&O

for $6.8 billion. No one cared that a British-owned firm had operated U.S. ports. But when the owners of that firm became Arabs, it became a national security crisis.

Otherwise reputable Americans tarnished their names by joining the Dubai bashing. Even the Anti-Defamation League took its turn at defamation. Dubai's investor-technocrats, used to operating behind closed doors, were shocked to find themselves at the center of a storm of xenophobic hysteria. And they weren't sure why.

Dubai and the UAE remained among America's closest Arab counterterror allies, even though the U.S. government has problems with Dubai's freewheeling trade with Iran. UAE authorities had handed over terror suspects and allowed U.S investigators to monitor its banking sector for suspicious transactions. U.S. spy planes and refuelers fly out of Abu Dhabi. Dubai is the U.S. Navy's biggest overseas port. The fact that two UAE nationals[5] had attacked America was a distraction to an otherwise solid friendship.

There was no question that America's port operations would stay in foreign hands. Consolidation in the industry had forced most U.S. companies out. Eighty percent of container terminals at big U.S. ports were operated by foreign firms like Denmark's Maersk and Japan's Yusen Kaisha. Dubai's only bidding rival for P&O was Singapore's PSA International, another government-owned operator.

DP World didn't lurch blindly into the U.S. ports business. Sultan bin Sulayem, the head of Dubai's port authority, began acquiring foreign port operations in 1999 when he invested in Beirut. Soon after, Dubai bought long-term contracts to run Jeddah, Saudi Arabia's big Red Sea port; as well as Djibouti, on the Horn of Africa. DP World deepened and renovated these ports, upgraded warehousing and cranes, increasing their capacity and thereby boosting trade and the company's revenue. In 2003, bin Sulayem converted the port authority into a profit-seeking corporation that continued to buy foreign port operations. It was less constrained by ties to the government, although it remained a state asset. The company was called Dubai Ports World, or DP World.

By the time Americans heard about it, DP World was the world's fourth-largest port manager by tonnage—carrying nearly 10 percent of global shipping—but held the greatest number of port management contracts, with forty-three container terminals in twenty-two countries.[6] In 2005, DP World made its first major acquisition, buying the ports arm of America's railroad giant, CSX Corp., for $1.15 billion. CSX operated ports in Asia that went to Dubai. In Asia, there had been no outcry over Americans operating ports, or the subsequent Arab takeover.

Before making an offer for P&O, DP World did its homework. In 2005, it hired a pair of Washington lawyers to approach the U.S. Committee on Foreign Investment in the United States, known as CFIUS. By November, the lawyers learned that members of the twelve-agency panel would not oppose U.S. port management moving from Britain to Dubai.[7]

But a small Florida company did mind: Eller & Co., a joint venture partner with P&O. A Florida newspaper cited Eller's fears: its customers would refuse to use its Miami terminal if an Arab company bought it; or perhaps the port owner might cancel its lease.[8] In 2008, two years later, Eller lawyer Michael Kreitzer said the company's chief reason for opposing the deal was its fear that DP World might have motives other than profit in mind, because it is owned by the Dubai government.[9]

The company hired a semiretired lobbyist living on a Maryland horse farm, Joe Muldoon, to persuade Congress to block the deal. Muldoon drove to Washington day after day, with his laptop and binder of documents, meeting with one lawmaker after another. Muldoon struck out until he found Schumer, whose pro-Israel credentials made him a likely pitchman for a plan that would stoke fear of an Arab government.[10] Schumer had another asset: a talent for grandstanding. His attention-seeking efforts had spawned a joke: What's the most dangerous place in Washington? The space between Chuck Schumer and a microphone.

Schumer was in a position to influence the Dubai deal. He had a seat on the powerful Senate Banking Committee and Dubai's takeover of New York's operations fell within his district. Schumer's press conference with the 9/11 families triggered a media frenzy. Democrats found a convenient way to burnish their national security credentials, so they piled on. Republicans, sensing that Americans were behind the Democrats, began deserting President Bush, who had threatened to veto any congressional move to block the deal.

Schumer cleverly pulled strings that launched a wave of xenophobia. "It was just cheap political theater for him and he worked it, he played it. I think he was genuinely hostile towards the Arab world," says David Stockwell, a former U.S. consul in Dubai. Stockwell stayed in Dubai after retiring from the State Department and now runs the local office of Rudy Giuliani's law firm.

CNN sent its anchor Wolf Blitzer to Dubai to interview UAE leaders. Emiratis were dismayed by Blitzer's aggressive questioning, especially of Economy Minister Sheikha Lubna al-Qassimi, a member of the Sharjah royal family. The feeling grew stronger that Americans simply didn't trust or respect Arabs.

Dubai felt blindsided by a storm that made no sense on rational grounds. Dubai is the most American place in the Arab world, a haven of fast food and Disney, with buzz-cut American sailors thronging the malls. Its brash capitalism and antitax attitudes would make Grover Norquist dance a jig. Even the pro-Israel angle fell flat. Israeli shipper Zim stood up for Dubai, its chief Idan Ofer sending letters to congressional leaders to say it was satisfied with the security in Dubai's ports.

"We knew there would be sensitivities and some PR flak," says DP World chief executive Jamal Majid bin Thaniah, a big, slow-talking man in an office decorated with models of ships. "But we thought this would be manageable. I thought it would stop one day."

The political agenda of those feeding the controversy was so bald-faced that former President Bill Clinton and his wife, Hillary, found themselves on opposite sides of the issue. While Hillary worked to de-rail the deal, Bill, a confidant of Sheikh Mohammed, was trying to usher it through. He convinced DP World to agree to a forty-five-day delay to allow U.S. investigators to reexamine the purchase.[11]

At the time, bin Thaniah was negotiating with the U.S. Navy about its continued use of the Jebel Ali port. Those negotiations went a lot smoother. "For a moment we thought we had very good relations," bin Thaniah says, shaking his head. "From one side you're opening the door and from the other side you're closing it. They wanted friends and they started to create enemies."

The U.S. terminals would have connected exports from DP World's container ports in China to the massive U.S. consumer market. Dubai hung on as long as it could, hiring lobbyists to press its case, assuring the U.S. Congress that American agencies would still control port security. The flood of opposition was too strong. It became clear that President Bush himself couldn't rescue Dubai's investment. In Abu Dhabi, the na-tional president, Sheikh Khalifa, got tired of seeing his country's name dragged through the mud. He told Sheikh Mohammed that the deal wasn't worth all the bad publicity.[12]

In March 2006, bin Sulayem decided to sell DP World's U.S. operations and pull out. Sheikh Mohammed's team of American-educated advisers was too small and inexperienced to fight a political battle in the United States.

Dubai's departure met a sudden silence. Schumer, Hillary Clinton, and the talk radio set looked like a pack of schoolyard bullies who'd beaten up a Boy Scout. They'd chased away a major foreign investor while the United States was sinking into deficit and economic hardship.

"There's no sense in sugarcoating what is becoming clearer with each passing day: Killing the deal, at its core, was an act of racism," wrote op-ed columnist Rick Martinez in the Raleigh, North Carolina, *News & Observer*. "Is it so hard to understand that when it comes to international trade, we're going to have to deal with foreigners?"

Soon after, Eller & Co., the company that kicked off the furor, showed its hand. It offered to buy DP World's U.S. port operations. "We think we are one of the companies (that could buy it). We have been in the business for 70 years. We could do it," Kreitzer told the *Miami Herald*.[13]

Eller's initial motivation for blocking the deal wasn't because it wanted P&O's half of the Port of Miami, Kreitzer said in 2008. But soon after, it figured that, if DP World were forced to sell, it could pick up Dubai's Miami operations, and perhaps others. "There is a linkage between them," says Kreitzer. "It was all happening at the same time. We made multiple offers."

Eller didn't get the prize. In 2007, Dubai finally sold its U.S. port operations, but not to a shipping firm. The buyer was the American International Group insurance company, which would soon require a gargantuan government bailout. Negotiations into a U.S.-UAE trade pact fell apart around the same time, victim to the ports implosion. It made little sense to try to sell a trade deal to a hostile Congress.

Sheikh Mohammed must have been furious but kept his composure throughout. After the sell-off, he published a sober op-ed in the *Wall Street Journal* admitting that Dubai had been naïve by not preparing the political landscape. "The DP World experience taught us to approach international investment in a much more holistic manner. We now take the time to analyze the social, political and economic landscape, identify the stakeholders and then carefully prepare the way by ensuring that the concerns of all parties are properly addressed."[14]

While the Bush administration was alienating Arabs with its wars and hard-core support for Israel, Congress managed to do one better, insulting one of America's most valuable Arab friends. Gulf leaders publicly questioned whether America was a suitable place for its burgeoning investment funds. Many began to turn to China and the rest of Asia, saying the political risk was lower.

Stockwell visited Washington after Dubai's pullout and the air was thick with shame. "It was sort of like a lynching where the mob got all fired up and lynched an innocent guy. In the morning they looked at their work and said 'Oh, this is terrible! How did this happen?' People felt genuinely embarrassed," Stockwell says. "In the end, America was the one hurt by this foolishness, not the UAE or Dubai."

Some good did come of the episode. Suddenly, Americans, heretofore oblivious to Dubai's emergence, knew about the place. The size of the controversy accorded Dubai far more clout than it merited. People thought tiny Dubai was as powerful as China.

"I hope Americans have come to learn what a big friend the UAE is to them," says Paul Bagatelas, who heads the Dubai headquarters of the Carlyle Group, a politically connected buyout firm based in Washington. "This is a very important relationship—my God—terribly important for the United States. We need to cultivate this relationship and treat our friends better."

Quietly, some in Congress repented. A Dubai-based U.S. diplomat said that a number of them visited Dubai and told bin Sulayem and Gergawi that they were embarrassed by the affair. "We even had someone who came and said, 'I voted for the measure and I am ashamed,'" the diplomat said. Many of the visiting congressmen also stopped by the Carlyle Group's office for briefings. "They've all been over here. Many of them have been to our offices and they have a much different attitude now," says Bagatelas. "Every single one has a positive view of Dubai now."

Bin Thaniah says he'd received a few apologies as well. But those don't mean much. The representatives who expressed remorse didn't do it in public and didn't repeat their statements when they got home.[15]

The UAE has also implicitly admitted its own mistakes by moving to shore up its next investment drives. Abu Dhabi's Mubadala group reached out far more methodically to the Washington elite when it bought a 7.5 percent share of the sensitive Carlyle Group in 2008. The UAE government also launched the UAE-U.S. Business Council as an avenue for the 750 American companies doing business in the country to use their influence in Washington.

Two of the UAE's most powerful women, Sheikha Lubna and diplomat Reem al-Hashimy, also sought to improve the UAE's image in America. They embarked on whistle-stop tours of the American heartland, giving talks and answering questions—many of which were dismayingly naïve. Al-Hashimy, now a federal minister, says she was shocked by Americans' scant understanding of her part of the planet. She found herself dumbing down her talks so audiences could grasp them, even in sophsticated cities like Chicago. "She had to start with the basics, like: 'The UAE is about the size of Maine, our population is around five million.'"

The World's Next Financial Capital

In 2007 a colleague and I pay a visit to the Dubai International Financial Centre for a chat with its chairman Omar bin Sulaiman. Before we can leave, bin Sulaiman says he's got small gifts for us. It's a Dubai tradition, these business handouts. "We've got rosaries for you guys," he says. My colleague, Jim Calderwood, shoots me a look that says "What the hell?" He's a Northern Irish Protestant.

Bin Sulaiman hands us lacquered wooden boxes. I flip mine open and there's a set of Muslim prayer beads, with a card describing the Emirati artist who made them. At first I think it's mildly amusing that, being a Catholic, I'm told I'm going to be given a rosary and then am handed a set of Muslim prayer beads. Then I take a closer look. The beads come to a confluence where the cross would hang on a rosary. But instead of a cross, there is a metal bead shaped in the diamond logo of the Dubai International Financial Centre. "These guys want us to pray for money!" I tell Calderwood, who laughs. Dubai is truly unabashed.

Sheikh Mohammed wants Dubai to rule the financial world. He doesn't envision it as a scrappy challenger to the world's centers of finance. In his book *My Vision* he declares that he wants Dubai to be "on a par with the world's most prestigious financial centers, including London and New York."[16] It's a goal that his aides don't usually mention, because it sounds either unrealistic or overly aggressive.

In 2002, Sheikh Mohammed recycled his free zone model again, launching a new district called Dubai International Financial Centre. This time he handed over prime real estate in the city center, and approved a much grander plan. It called for a Vatican-like enclave of stark modern architecture, where the U.S. dollar is the official currency and the financial code of the City of London holds sway, not the civil law of the UAE.

The centerpiece of the financial center is The Gate, a blocky Arc de Triomphe in gray granite and glass. Sleek Germanic office buildings surround the arch, and the whole place basks in a hushed atmosphere of understated wealth. On one level, the financial district has done exceedingly well—by luring major international banks to Dubai.

In 2005, the *Financial Times*'s front page declared that U.S. investment bank Morgan Stanley would open an office in Dubai. The story triggered a mad dash for space in the district as Morgan moved more than one hundred people to Dubai. Prior to that announcement, most investment banks had decided not to send permanent staff to Dubai. They were content to send Middle East specialists from New York or London to the Gulf, where they'd spend a few weeks working from their hotel rooms. Morgan's move changed the rules.

"We don't open offices lightly," says Georges Makhoul, who heads the Dubai office. "So the others went back to their drawing boards and said 'Let's see, did we make the right decision? What is it that these guys see that we didn't see?'"

By 2008, more than 450 member companies had opened offices in the district, including the world's biggest banks and brokerages: Goldman Sachs, Merrill Lynch, UBS, Citibank, Credit Suisse, and Deutsche Bank. Lehman Brothers came as well, and then shut down in September 2008 when the bank failed. The center cemented Dubai as the financial services hub of the Middle East, which, in turn, won recognition as the latest of the world's major emerging markets. "Game Over. As far as business and economy in the region are concerned, it's done," Makhoul says. "It's another Southeast Asia, another Eastern Europe, another China. That's where it's going."

Dubai wants far more than leadership of a new emerging market. It is angling to become the financial capital to an underserved central swath of Planet Earth, home to two billion people. This region stretches from Morocco to China and from South Africa to Turkey. At the moment, it's got no financial metropole. You can see this on CNN. When the trading day begins in Hong Kong and Singapore there's a gap of several hours before Frankfurt and London wake up and start trading. Dubai aims to fill that blank space.

Until the financial crisis clipped his wings, Sheikh Mohammed's goal of ruling the financial world had begun to look slightly less far-fetched. In 2008, London hired the management consultancy McKinsey to help it compete against upstarts like Dubai. That followed a McKinsey warning that New York could lose its status as world financial center in a decade, without changes in regulation and policy. New York also named Dubai as a challenger. Earlier that year, Dubai's commodities exchange fired a warning shot by launching trading in an oil futures contract previously only handled in London and New York.

But the Dubai International Financial Centre has struggled in other ways. The debut of its stock exchange, known as the Nasdaq Dubai, was badly timed, coinciding with the end of a two-year bull run on the local market that saw values rise more than 200 percent. When the floor gave way, the index plummeted by around 50 percent in 2006. Few people were in the mood to test the waters at the new international exchange. And as individual investors, they couldn't. Trading was restricted to brokers and wholesalers.

In contrast to the local exchange, with its leather couches and screens that invite day traders to hang out, the international exchange has no public face. This was a mistake, says Essa Kazim, chief executive of Borse Dubai, the government authority that operates both exchanges. "It's an unsuccessful business model," Kazim says. "You need the retail market to drive your sales. Institutions take most of the sales, but we can't trade among ourselves all the time."

Dubai may be the financial center of the Middle East, but the Nasdaq Dubai can't seem to attract listings. More than two years after it opened, the market lists just sixteen companies. City fathers hoped it would get a kick when it hosted the initial public offering of 20 percent of DP World in November 2007. The offering launched with hoopla at $1.30 a share and raised nearly $5 billion, after being fifteen times oversubscribed. It was the Middle East's largest IPO. But instead of rocketing in value, as was the custom on the local exchange, DP World's shares fell from the get-go. By January 2009, in the credit crunch sell-off, they were worth just 25 cents.

The Nasdaq Dubai has since pegged its hopes on its tie-up with the Nasdaq in New York. In 2007, the Dubai exchange's parent, Borse Dubai, sold a 33 percent stake to Nasdaq-OMX. In return, it acquired a 20 percent stake in the Nasdaq. This time, Washington's security review triggered no major opposition from Congress. Kazim wants Nasdaq Dubai to serve as a bridge connecting U.S. and European stock markets with the Middle East. If it works, Dubai would serve as a link in a chain of exchanges allowing twenty-four-hour trading on Nasdaq's platform. Companies wanting to tap the liquidity of the Middle East—nothing to sneeze at in the wake of the global financial meltdown—could list on the Nasdaq and sell shares in Dubai.

"Dubai can play the role of a market that can connect markets," Kazim says. "If Nasdaq-OMX becomes one of the biggest globally, we're now part of it. We own a big chunk of it."

8

SPREADING OUT
AND GOING UP

Building Islands

WHO WAS THE twentieth-century artist with the greatest impact? Was it Pablo Picasso or Henri Matisse, with their modernist paintings? Edward Hopper and his scenes of America? The pop artist Andy Warhol? Hard to say.

In terms of physical impact, the greatest twentieth-century artist is Warren Pickering, a chunky fifty-nine-year-old from Christchurch, New Zealand. Pickering's masterpiece is a 1997 untitled work with colored pens and airbrush on a piece of art board. The picture, never seen in public, depicts a stylized island in the shape of a date palm.

Pickering's painting is the basis for a man-made island that is three and a half miles wide and three and a half miles long. It's a city neighborhood built at sea for more than 100,000 residents and workers. From space, it's clearly recognizable as a Pickering original. That's more impact than even Christo can claim from ringing islands with pink polypropylene.

Astronauts peering down on Earth might ponder another Pickering masterpiece a few miles away: an array of hundreds of islands shaped like a map of the world. In fact, the Gulf off Dubai is becoming a gallery of Pickerings. He's had a hand in designing two more man-made archipelagoes that are either finished or under construction.

The tale of Dubai's island building dates to the mid-1990s. Even then, Dubai's forty miles of beachfront was being eaten up by developers. Sheikh Mohammed wanted to raise his tourism venture to a new level, but the valuable coastline was too short for his ambitions.

At some point, the legend goes, he told ports boss Sultan bin Sulayem to build some more beach. It wasn't as audacious as it sounded. Bin Sulayem, who had just overseen dredging and expansion of the Jebel Ali port, was Dubai's expert on reconfiguring the coastline. And Sheikh Mohammed had done some reclaiming himself. A small picnic island lies in the sea off his beach palace.

Bin Sulayem must have had artificial islands on his mind when he and his family arrived in the Australian resort town of Surfers Paradise in 1997. Pickering happened to be living in the beach town on the Queensland coast, running a concept design business out of his modest bungalow. One day, he opened his front door and got his first glance at bin Sulayem's mustachioed face.

Warren Pickering is a plainspoken man with a shock of gray hair, built like a rugby player. He speaks with the broad, flat accent of New Zealand, pronouncing "car park" as "cah paak." He'd look more at home in a pub than an art gallery. It was in Pickering's drawing studio that bin Sulayem divulged what he wanted: a concept drawing of an artificial atoll with a lagoon and beach. Pickering sketched a crescent-shaped island that looked a bit like two cashew nuts lined up end to end. "That's exactly what I want," bin Sulayem said, warning Pickering to keep it secret.[1]

Bin Sulayem took the drawing back to Dubai and showed it to Sheikh Mohammed. The crown prince liked the idea but not the shape. He wanted a design that maximized beachfront. And there were a few other requests. "We want it tied to the land," bin Sulayem told Pickering, asking him to draw in a causeway. "And our national symbol is the date palm," bin Sulayem said. "Keep that in mind."

Pickering got right to work. He drew ten islands, each on the palm tree theme. There were double palms, quadruple palms, a palm in reverse—with a water cutout in the center shaped like the tree—and even a palm at sea mirrored by another dug as channels from shore. But one of the drawings he sent bin Sulayem was a single stylized palm tree with seventeen curving fronds and a crescent-shaped breakwall protecting it from the open sea.

"That's the one," Sheikh Mohammed said when he saw the simple, strong drawing.[2]

Pickering focused on that design. He drew in hotels and homes and roads. The palm's original "trunk"—the island's main spine—was much narrower than it was built five years later. And the crescent breakwall was just wide enough to walk on. Pickering later widened it so that it could hold dozens of hotels.

Back in 1997, he could never have imagined that thousands of men would toil for years—a few would even die—to raise his concept from the sea. A hundred miles away, men would blast mountains into Volkswagen-sized boulders, load them in an endless convoy of dump trucks, and drop them in their thousands on the sea floor, until they rose above the surface. And they would dredge up square miles of the sea bottom and pile it and sculpt it until a landmass emerged as an exact match of Pickering's airbrushed form. The Palm Jumeirah would give Dubai forty-eight miles of new shoreline, including thirty-eight miles of beach.

One day Pickering and bin Sulayem flew along the beach in a helicopter, trying to find the best place to plunk down an island. Peering down at the open sea, it was tough to imagine the island's scale. Bin Sulayem figured the best site would be roughly in the center of Dubai's coast, just beyond the Burj Al Arab construction site.

In 2000, Sheikh Mohammed launched a new company to build the island. He lopped it off the government's department of ports and customs, and it eventually became known as Nakheel—palms, in Arabic. Bin Sulayem took the helm. The planners commissioned dozens of studies on the island. At least one of the consultants had a warning: Don't try it. This told the ports chairman that he was on to something.

"If a consultant says, 'Don't do it,' that's great. It's an opportunity for us," says Robert Lee, who became Nakheel's investment director after his stint at Emaar. "That tells us there are going to be barriers to entry for that market. If we can crack into it, we're going to have a leadership position. That goes to the core of Dubai. We're always encouraged to do what's seemingly not possible."

On April 22, 2001, four years after he'd done his drawing, Pickering

got called back to Dubai. Sheikh Mohammed had given the secret project the green light. It was time to start building. "It was a dream project,"
he says. "The biggest thing anyone could've imagined."

The selling of the Palm Jumeirah has to rank as one of history's weirdest
real estate pitches. In May 2001, Dubai hosted the Arabian Travel Market trade show. There, among tourism industry executives from around
the world, the city made a rather bizarre announcement: It would build
an island in the Gulf in the shape of a palm tree. Oh, and by the way, if
you had a checkbook or credit card handy, you could buy a piece of that
palm—a mansion or an apartment or a building plot.

Bin Sulayem found himself at a disadvantage. Although he had models of the island and architects' renderings of the homes he was selling,
he couldn't drive investors to see the land, so they could get an idea of the
positioning of the homes and streets. There was no land. The site was
open sea.

But bin Sulayem wasn't going to let that get in his way. When a potential buyer turned up, bin Sulayem, an elegant man with a perfectly
clipped mustache and an ingrained politeness, fired up his speedboat.
He'd zoom investors a mile and a half out to sea, where the sail-shaped
Burj Al Arab could be seen above the swells. Then he'd cut the motor.

"This is where your villa's going to be," bin Sulayem would tell his
client, as they bobbed in the Gulf. "Now give me a deposit."[3]

When it came to marketing, Dubai cast off its inhibitions. Its market-
ers convinced the English soccer team to stop in Dubai on its way to the
World Cup in South Korea. The British tabloids screamed. How could
Dubai real estate trump the World Cup? With the players in their clutches,
Dubai's salesmen went to work. "Somebody took David Beckham and
said, 'You know what? We would like to give you the most expensive
house on the Palm. You'll have your own beach,'" says government adviser Yasar Jarrar. "Based on the fact that David Beckham had a house,
all of the English football team bought. And his wife, Victoria Beckham,
she also came. Dubai and the Palm were on the front page of all the British newspapers all week. You cannot buy that kind of advertising. The
Palm was sold out in three days."

Beckham wasn't the only one who made out. Sheikh Mohammed
underpriced everything, figuring that a fast sell-out would further Dubai's

long-term goals, even if it cut profits. He wasn't building the island for the sake of having an island. It was a cog in the plan to make Dubai a great city. Bin Sulayem banked the deposits and used them to fund construction. Over the coming months and years, speculators bought and resold villas over and over, driving prices through the roof while the home sites were still open sea. "They sold it cheap and people made fortunes," says Ryan Mahoney of Better Homes. "It created excitement and hype overnight. 'Dubai is where you can make your fortune!' "

At that time, the Palm's initial 2,000 mansions were selling for around $1.3 million. It was a decent price for a brand-new six-bedroom villa with a pool. The best thing was, every single one of them would sit right on the beach. You could slide open the back door and plunge into the warm sea before your morning coffee. At their peak valuations in late 2008 those villas sold for as much as $9.5 million.

In fact, just about *all* the buildings on the Palm sit on the beach. It was Dubai at its most cunning. Since seafront properties are the most valuable, why not build a development that has nothing but seafront?

You couldn't build a palm-shaped island from sand in most places. If currents are too strong or the sea too deep, it wouldn't work. But conditions in the Gulf are perfect. Gulf tides are mild, as are the currents. There are few storms. The sea deepens gradually. At the Palm's furthest end, three and a half miles out to sea, the water is just thirty feet deep. The sea floor is a mirror image of the land: gently undulating and pale sand. "That made it very easy to pick up the sand and redistribute it," says Lee. "It's like sand play. You scoop the sand and put it in the middle. Voilà."

Nakheel's executives like to say the sea was devoid of creatures as well. "There was absolutely no sea life whatsoever," Lee says. That may be true now, but it wasn't at the start of construction. The sea bottom had grasses and algae and crabs, worms, oysters, and fish. The organisms that didn't flee got dredged up and buried.

Unlike Dubai Internet City, the Palm Jumeirah was far too outlandish to attract financing from a bank. Dubai had to pay up front, using investors' cash. The dredging costs alone were $275 million, a huge outlay, but a good price given the scope of the work. Ships with giant hoses sucked up the sandy seabed and sprayed it in brown rainbows onto the rising island.

Niggling construction delays plagued the Palm. Nakheel promised villa buyers that they'd get their mansions in 2005, an unrealistic deadline

given that no one in Dubai, or the world for that matter, had ever reclaimed a palm-shaped island. Buyers got their keys two years later.
Many of the island's amenities won't be finished for years. The centerpiece, the gigantic pink 1,539-room Atlantis resort, opened in September
2008.

One problem that cropped up was that the new land settled and
sank. It caused a year's delay. The company wound up hiring a contractor to use a new technique called vibro-compacting to tamp down the
land.

Several workers died building the Palm islands. Once, a group of
them were swept out to sea and lost when a big swell crashed over the
crescent. Another time, bin Sulayem himself had a close call. One night
he was inspecting progress when his boat ran aground. The land buildup
had progressed further than he'd realized. He only just managed to get
unstuck before the very place he was mired was inundated by umpteen
tons of sand from the sea bottom, hurled through the air by a dredging
ship. Bin Sulayem and his boat could have been buried on the island
without anyone seeing him again.[4]

The accomplishment of bin Sulayem and Sheikh Mohammed is undeniable. They created an asset worth around $25 billion by piling rocks
and sand on the sea floor. But the Palm is more than an asset. It's Dubai's
newest neighborhood, with thousands of residents and owners from
seventy-five different countries. Those who bought mansions in 2001 may
have grumbled a bit about delays, and about the jamming of these
homes a lot closer in reality than they appeared on sales brochures. But
most were assuaged by the quintupling of values. They were among the
hottest properties in the city until values, like those across Dubai, started
to slip in 2009. They cause endless consternation for those who had the
means to buy one at launch but they were too scared. "I wish I'd had the
balls and the pocket to have gotten in on the beginning at the Palm,"
says Anthony Harris, the former British ambassador.

Driving onto the Palm is a curious experience. There is no sea view.
The reclaimed land is so valuable that every inch is built upon. A
broad highway lined with apartment towers bisects the Palm's trunk.
The island's residential fronds—each one lined by blocky mansions
with red-tiled roofs—spread out on either side. Each frond is a separate gated community. At the treetop, the road dives into a tunnel and
emerges on the outer crescent, where most of the hotels are rising. Two

dozen five-star hotels are under contract or under construction on the island, among a total of thirty-two planned. Dubai will have fourteen thousand additional hotel rooms when the construction finishes by 2013.

Donald Trump was erecting his latest hotel on the stem, a sixty-one-story horseshoe in steel and glass. Trump said Gotham City would never countenance such a structure. "New York is at a huge disadvantage to Dubai," he told the *New York Post*. "If this project were ever proposed for New York, it would be a ten-year review process at the end of which you'd receive a 'No' vote by the community board for being too high, too dramatic, too beautiful or whatever." In this case, Trump's No vote came from the global financial meltdown, which caused him to halt construction in late 2008.

To give an idea of the magnitude of the Palm Jumeirah, compare it with the $8.6 billion CityCenter Las Vegas project, the largest privately funded development in America. CityCenter is seventy-six acres of casinos, hotels, and condominiums. It would sit nicely in one little corner of the Palm. Anyhow, Dubai's got a piece of that action. Nakheel's parent company, Dubai World, has partnered with MGM Mirage to develop CityCenter. The partnership makes Dubai's government a major investor in the gambling industry, which, depending on your view, either showcases Dubai's tolerance and pragmatism, or runs counter to its citizens' Muslim sensibilities.

Of course, Dubai is as satisfied with one palm-shaped island as it was with one cluster zone. The Palm Jumeirah is the smallest of three planned palm islands, as well as a plethora of other fanciful island groups that are being strewn offshore from one end of Dubai to the other.

The second palm, the Palm Jebel Ali, is 50 percent bigger than the Palm Jumeirah. Dubai plunked it atop its only marine protected area, a reserve that once held a giant coral reef. Where fish once thrived, American resorts will rise. They include Sea World and Busch Gardens, which planned to open theme parks on an island shaped like Sea World's killer whale Shamu. In 2008, workers were building the Palm Jebel Ali's seventy-eight-mile road network, installing sewer and water infrastructure and erecting bridges to the mainland. But the downturn elbowed in. Busch Gardens and Sea World announced they'd postponed plans to open in Dubai.

The third palm, the Palm Deira, is planned with as much surface area as Manhattan. It looks more like a pineapple than a palm tree, and won't be finished for at least twenty years, if at all. Reclamation was about half done when it was halted by the credit crunch in 2008.

A few years ago, bin Sulayem asked Pickering to do another quick sketch. This was to be a concept known as the Pearl Islands. "Warren, I have to show this to Sheikh Mohammed tonight. It has to be quick," bin Sulayem said.

The New Zealander sketched as fast as he could: a few roundish pearls on the sea, and a few islands shaped as shells. He noticed that, on his perspective drawing showing the islands from an angle, one looked like Australia and another like New Zealand.

Bin Sulayem liked the rendering. "That's exactly what I want," he said.

"Thanks for letting me put Australia and New Zealand in there," Pickering joked. When bin Sulayem asked what he was talking about, Pickering jabbed his finger at the drawing. "There's New Zealand there. And there's Australia there." Bin Sulayem recognized the shapes.

"Right," bin Sulayem said, a brainstorm gathering. "Let's download the rest of the world."

Pickering found a map online and sketched the nations of the world as separate islands. He landscaped them and drew trees and the roofs of resorts. It was much more interesting than the Pearl Islands. Sheikh Mohammed liked it. "That's how we came up with The World," Pickering said.

The three hundred-island archipelago is now a fixture in the sea a few miles off Jumeirah Beach. If it ended there, Pickering could be satisfied with a lifetime accomplishment far beyond the dreams of any artist. But his palm island concept got used again, two more times.

"It just needed to be photocopied," the New Zealander says. The Palm Jebel Ali has subtle differences in the trunk and crescent. And the Palm Deira is similar but larger, with height restrictions because it lies in the approach for Dubai International Airport.

The palms are part of a dense thicket of islands that Nakheel wants to reclaim as far as twelve miles offshore over the next three decades. One group, The Waterfront, looks like the blade of a scythe. Another, The Universe, looks like a spider or a squid, but is said to be a sun that will wrap around The World. If they ever get built, the islands will double Dubai's landmass and population, housing as many as three million people on brand-new land, says Lee.

"That's crazy!" I respond.

"Bold," says Lee.

The Burj Dubai

Dubai gets a lot of comparisons to Las Vegas. And it's no wonder. Both cities are awash in mass-market kitsch that residents take too seriously. Dubai also resembles 1850s San Francisco, a male-dominated immigrant city that serviced the gold rush, just as male-dominated Dubai services the oil boom.

But in speed of construction, the place it resembles most is Shenzhen, the Chinese boomtown. Like Dubai, Shenzhen mushroomed from a dirt-poor pearl diving and fishing village. It burst into a city in the years after 1979, when Chinese premier Deng Xiaoping declared it a special economic zone, China's first major experiment with capitalism.

Shenzhen's tallest building is the 1,260-foot Shun Hing Square, a turquoise office and apartment complex. It sandwiches what looks like a typical housing block between a pair of glassy silos. From its upper stories, you can gaze over the dense forest of high-rises to gentle rice paddy and forested hills just across the Pearl River.

One of the project managers on Shun Hing Square was a New Zealand civil engineer of Chinese ancestry named Greg Sang. Sang left New Zealand in the 1980s to work in Hong Kong's booming construction sector, gravitating to the tall buildings that typify the city. The chance to build Shun Hing Square took him just across the border into China, where he got his first look at a true boomtown. In the 1990s, Shenzhen was described as a city building a high-rise a day and a new boulevard every three days. The city swelled beyond four million, as villagers flooded in from the Chinese countryside following dreams of riches. "The pace," says Sang, "was frantic."

"They don't get caught up with a lot of planning issues you get in the West," he says. "You could see the growth in the economy. GDP was sky-rocketing. A lot of people were making a lot of money."

When the turquoise tower topped out, Sang crossed back into Hong

Kong. In 1997, he was tapped to manage construction of 2 International Financial Centre, a tapering square skyscraper that was even taller than the Shenzhen tower. It was to stretch 1,335 feet above Hong Kong harbor. The eighty-eight-story 2IFC, completed in 2003, was the tallest of Hong Kong's portfolio of skyscrapers and the world's eighth tallest building. It was a tough project to beat. Sang was getting a reputation as a guy who could raise super-tall skyscrapers in a hurry. But just as 2IFC opened, the SARS epidemic hit, sending Hong Kong's economy into a skid. For a skyscraper man, it looked like tough times.

Sang was wondering what to do with himself when the phone rang. A guy named Essam Galadari was on the line, calling from Dubai. Galadari said he worked for a company called Emaar. The firm wanted to get into tall building construction, but nobody in Dubai had experience. His offer was an arresting one: Come and build the tallest building in the world.

Sang, forty-two, is not a man who gushes prose. He talks in monosyllables gummed over by his Kiwi drawl. He looks like Spiderman's city editor J. Jonah Jameson, with the wrinkled white dress shirt, sleeves rolled up, tie askew. He's even got Jameson's flat-top buzz cut. Instead of chomping cigars, Sang parks a Marlboro in the corner of his mouth. If Galadari's invitation jazzed his soul, he didn't let it show. "Sure," he told the Dubaian. "Why not? Give it a go."

Sang flew to Dubai to meet Galadari. The two men eyed each other up and down and seemed to get along. The skyscraper man was back in his element.

The Burj Dubai came about as the showpiece of a master plan for a new downtown. When the crown prince merged the Dubai Defence Force with the federal army in 1997, the emirate's troops abandoned their base. It sat at a highway interchange known as Defence Roundabout. Ten years earlier, the base was too far out of town to be valuable. But the city's expansion left the 416-acre plot in a prime location, right next to the new financial center.

Sheikh Mohammed wasn't going to build a trailer park there. In 2002, he handed the plot to Emaar. The conditions were tough. Emaar's chairman, Mohammed Alabbar, had to build a downtown that would command the world's attention.

Alabbar, who directed the city's Department of Economic Development, launched Emaar five years earlier, seeding his start-up with backing from the Dubai government and $50 million borrowed from associates and savings.[5] The company listed on the Dubai Financial Market in 2000 and shot off like a bottle rocket, amassing a market capitalization of $25 billion by June 2005, when it was declared the world's largest developer by value.[6] (It tanked soon after and in early 2009 languished in the penny stock realm.) At the time, Alabbar was Dubai's golden boy. *Financial Times* magazine declared him Middle East Personality of the Year in 2006. And he was offered Donald Trump's role in a Middle East version of the TV show *The Apprentice*. After a splashy launch, Alabbar quit. Many in Dubai thought the developer bowed out so as not to overshadow his own boss, Sheikh Mohammed.[7]

Emaar hired Los Angeles-based master planner David Klages to lay out the new downtown district. Klages had just finished the design for a new city center in Kuala Lumpur, Malaysia, where the trophy was the Petronas Twin Towers, the world's tallest buildings between 1998 and 2004. Alabbar asked him for something similar in Dubai.

But Sheikh Mohammed was unimpressed with Alabbar's initial design for the Burj Dubai. When he scanned the selection of architectural renderings of potential skyscrapers in 2002, he found they lacked a certain something: height. The Dubai crown prince asked for details of the world's tallest building, a tower in Taiwan called Taipei 101: "Why is it taller? Are people there smarter than you?"[8]

When the Emaar chairman returned with a new rendering depicting the Burj Dubai—a pointed spire that rises in stair-stepped cylinders—it was the world's tallest, but not by much. Sheikh Mohammed's response was brief: "Go a lot taller."[9] The idea was to intimidate potential challengers into giving up. That's why Alabbar needed Greg Sang.

When Sang moved to Dubai in late 2004, Alabbar's rush-rush design competition had produced a winning entry: the silver spike of architect Adrian Smith of Chicago's Skidmore, Owings & Merrill. The Burj Dubai looks like a 1950s sci-fi depiction of a Mars rocket, a glossy creation with a needle tip and a cluster of booster engines at its base.

Alabbar chose Smith's design because it was as good-looking as it was practical. Its concrete structure looked relatively simple and well proportioned. The building steps back as it rises, leaving external terraces that provided mounting spaces for cranes and staging points for construction material. It would cost $1 billion to erect.

There was another reason Smith's design won. Super-tall buildings are susceptible to high winds. Earthquakes aren't a big danger, Sang says, because their shaking usually ends before major damage occurs. And an airliner strike of the sort that brought down the steel-frame World Trade Center wouldn't topple the Burj, Sang believes. "Concrete can withstand impact better than steel. And it doesn't burn." But gusts are another matter. The building has to resist incredible wind loads that shove it from the side. Wind can even apply a dangerous twisting pressure.

"A strong gale trying to push the building over, that's one of the things you need to design for," Sang says.

The Burj Dubai is built to wave gently in the wind, like a reed bending slightly. In high winds, the top of the building sways ten feet back and forth in slow motion. A hazardous phenomenon called vortex shedding can take advantage of that waving cycle. Blasts of wind ricocheting off the structure can morph into tornadolike vortices that then peel around the building, pushing against one side, then the other. These swirling winds can generate a violent pulsing force that, if it matches the tower's natural bending cycle, can cause a tower to rock back and forth in an ever-larger arc. "It's like someone's on a swing and you just give them a little push at the right time and they'll swing higher and higher."

Most vulnerable are towers that retain the same footprint from bottom to top, Sang says. Smith's stair-stepped design defends well against vortex shedding. There's a new shape presented to the wind at different levels, so the vortices can't pulse simultaneously at different heights.

I first met Sang a few months after he arrived in Dubai. The Burj was then just a concrete pad surrounded by trucks and debris. Sang took me in a construction elevator to the thirty-seventh floor of a neighboring framework that would become an apartment block. It was a disorienting experience. There was no barrier between us and the abyss. We looked down at the Burj's base and Sang spoke confidently of how the tower would rise in stages, growing so tall that its swaying motion would necessitate special dampeners to keep the elevator cables from whiplashing in their shafts.[10]

It was hard to imagine. But three years later, the tower has risen just as he'd predicted. Sang has ridden herd on his chief contractor, South Korea's Samsung, which brought several members of its team that built the Petronas Towers. How's it possible to build so fast?

"It's a matter of throwing some design together, feeling reasonably comfortable with it, getting some foundations in the ground, and building the superstructure," he says. "We're designing and building at the same time. You can walk it if you want. But why walk it? We want to run it."

As Sang spoke in October 2008, the world's tallest building rose just a quarter mile behind him. It was a year from completion, with scaffolding still covering its highest tip, where clambering men could barely be seen by the naked eye. "Our construction right now is over seven hundred meters tall. And we're still going up."

Sang makes it sound simple. But he's had several knotty challenges to sort through. One dealt with the concrete mix that forms the Burj's structural core. No one has ever done concrete work anywhere close to such heights. Taipei 101 held the previous record for vertical pumping of concrete, just under 1,500 feet. The Burj's concrete superstructure is nearly 2,000 feet tall. The pump would have to push twenty-five tons of wet concrete up a tube far into the sky. Sang and his men found it flowed better when they halved the size of the gravel in the mix, using stones no bigger than half an inch.

Concrete is usually a simple mixture of four ingredients: Portland cement, sand, gravel, and water. The concrete that went into the Burj Dubai uses twenty-five ingredients. In summer, with temperatures over 110 degrees, crushed ice replaced some of the water. "It was like a concrete Slushie," Sang says. The idea was to keep the mix from overheating. If wet concrete hits 160 degrees Fahrenheit, it weakens dramatically.

Samsung built the superstructure with an innovative self-climbing "form," the mold in which concrete slabs are poured for each floor. The form used 230 hydraulic jacks to push itself up from each new slab just twelve hours after the concrete was poured. The system allowed Samsung to add a story every three days. But it called for a very special mixture of concrete.

"We want it to stay wet and sloppy while we're pumping it up all that way, but when it gets there, we want it to get hard fast. Those are contradictory requirements," Sang says. To cope, they used a range of plasticizers and hardeners.

The Burj's concrete core rises 156 stories into the sky, skinned in silver glass. Beyond that, the tower's framework is of riveted steel girders. Those upper floors are tiny, too small for offices or apartments. They're there for prestige' sake, holding mechanical and communications gear.

The Burj is the tallest man-made structure on the planet, with 5,000 workmen swarming over its every corner. In July 2007, it surpassed Taipei 101's 1,670 feet. Two months later, it climbed past Toronto's CN Tower, the world's tallest freestanding structure. In April 2008, it stepped above the KVLY-TV antenna in North Dakota, the last remaining structure to challenge it. Two months later, Emaar announced that it would increase the Burj's finished height. It reached 170 stories in November 2008, and the structure was more than 2,400 feet tall. In January 2009, an antenna appeared atop the Burj and newspapers declared it had topped out at 2,684 feet. Emaar had yet to announce the final height. Either way, that's a half-mile-tall skyscraper, twice as high as the Empire State Building.

That kind of height allows for unique experiences. You can watch the sunset at ground level and then ride the elevator to the top and watch it again. If Dubai's steamy skies ever clear, Emaar suggests you could see Iran, ninety miles across the Gulf, from the upper stories. More often, those near the top will be unable to see the ground.

The world's tallest structure, for most of recorded history, has resided in the Middle East. Egypt's Great Pyramid of Giza held the record for 3,900 years. It was only surpassed in 1311 by Lincoln Cathedral in England, when tall buildings went to the West. In the 1990s, Asia embarked on its tall building spree, and the trophy went there. Now the Middle East has reclaimed the distinction.

Alabbar knows that the Burj Dubai won't always be tallest. Nakheel in 2008 announced a one-kilometer-tall skyscraper in Dubai—and then canceled the project a few months later. Developers in Saudi Arabia and Kuwait have also kicked around plans for kilometer-plus towers.

The Burj's main tenant is an ultraluxury hotel operated by Giorgio Armani. It sits next to the gargantuan Dubai Mall, with 1,200 shops; and is surrounded by nineteen apartment buildings, several hotels, and the Disneyesque Old Town, an apartment complex with wooden balconies and ocher domes evoking old Arabia.

The project has had its problems. In November 2007, Burj laborers joined a surprise general strike that swept Dubai, with 40,000 men refusing to work until they won a 25 percent pay raise. The strike took out Arabtec, the Burj's concrete contractor, for a week.

Power demand is another headache. The downside of record height means everything must be hoisted a half mile into the sky. The Burj's electrical load has been listed as anywhere from 45 to 150 megawatts of power, enough to run a small city. The Burj is one reason Dubai is dangerously short of electricity.

Three men died building the Burj Dubai thus far. The first was an Indian laborer erecting scaffolding. He stepped on a plank that was cantilevered over dead space. The board gave and he fell to his death. The second victim was an Indian concrete crewman who fell from the 138th story. Workers found his body thirty stories below on one of the upper terraces. Sang says no one is sure how he fell. The climbing form is hung with safety netting. "We suspect he was trying to take a shortcut, climbing somewhere he wasn't supposed to be." The third man to die was crushed when a giant panel of aluminum and glass, a piece of the building's exterior cladding, tipped and fell on him.

There is a notion that the Burj Dubai is too tall for the sensibilities of most people. The upper floors in a swaying, needlelike building might be uncomfortable places to live or work. "If you don't like high places, this isn't the building you should be living and working in," Sang says. "The views are going to be fantastic. The design is first class. But if you're afraid of heights, you're afraid of heights. Nothing we can do about that."

When I was a teenager, my dad put me to work painting the gutters on his apartment building in Cleveland. I climbed up a forty-foot extension ladder to get there, a bit over three stories high. It was scary. I got used to it. But I've never been comfortable up high. I understand how people get acrophobia, the irrational fear of heights. So I was worried when my request to visit the top of the Burj Dubai was approved in the summer of 2007. The tower had just hit 141 stories, but it was a concrete skeleton, open on all sides. I phoned the guy at Emaar who was supposed to escort me to the summit.

"You're not afraid of heights, by any chance?" he asks. He's got a thick New York accent.

"I've never been that high so I can't guarantee it," I tell him. "Why? Have you had problems?"

"Oh yeah," he tells me. "Saturday we had an incident. Some people just can't help themselves when they get up that high. They feel like throwing themselves off. They get these thoughts in their heads, like 'I'm going to end it right now!' And they're otherwise normal people."

He tells me how he grappled with a woman visitor who, soon after reaching the top, tried to leap to her death. "It was a real struggle to get her down."

"I think they call it vertigo," I said.

"So tell me," he says. "Are you a big guy? Reason I ask is because I could chain you to me. That way, if you get a crazy idea, I can bring you back."

"I'm about six foot one," I tell him.

"Oh, forget it," he shouts. "You'd take me with you!"

He mumbles something about checking on permits for my visit and hangs up. Thankfully, I never hear from him again. My visit to the exposed top of the Burj Dubai never happens. Maybe it's a good thing.

9

DIAMONDS, DUBAI, AND ISRAEL

The Dubai Cut

THE ISRAELI TAKES the stage and the Dubai diamond conference springs to life. He's a blocky man in a pinstripe suit with tufty gray hair on a very large head. His name is Chaim Even-Zohar. He kicks off with a recession joke in his thick Hebrew accent. For a moment I'm in the Borscht Belt.

"Yesterday one of the dealers said to me, 'You know, Chaim, we always believed that diamonds were rare. But today there is one other product that is rarer than rare.'"

"'What's that?' I said."

Even-Zohar wags his eyes back and forth in a campy gesture suggesting a great truth about to be revealed.

"Money!"

He pumps his fist and yells it again in case anyone didn't hear: "Money!"

The Saudis, Emiratis, and Chinese in the audience sit unmoved. They're wearing headphones, listening to simultaneous translations into Arabic, Cantonese, and Mandarin. A few seconds later, when the interpreters finish, they erupt in guffaws.

Even-Zohar is one of the world's foremost experts on the diamond trade and he's a jolt of caffeine to an otherwise staid show. He squats and leaps to emphasize his points. He throws his arms wide and shouts, "Look at this!" and flicks his green laser pointer at a graph on his Power-Point slide.

"We saw *history* being made this week," he booms. "Forty percent of De Beers product offer was left on the table! That's never happened before. A hundred years of the cartel structure is over!"

In the front row is young Ahmed bin Sulayem, the top diamond official in Dubai. Bin Sulayem, in his *kandoura* and *gutra*, is a big fan. He once gave me a copy of Even-Zohar's book.

The Jewish presence in Dubai got a lift with the opening of Sol Kerzner's mammoth hotel, Atlantis, The Palm, the diamond conference's venue. It's managed by a guy named Alan Liebman, and it's where Israeli tycoon Lev Leviev operates one of Dubai's four high-end Levant jewelry outlets. There's a smattering of guttural Hebrew amid the Arabic, English, Turkish, and Chinese conversation. But there was to have been much more. Some 250 Israelis had registered for the conference, which focused on hot new diamond markets in the Middle East and China. But most couldn't get visas.

It's one of those things. When the planets line up, Israelis get UAE visas, even though the UAE and Israel have no relations. But often the stars don't align. Israelis who thought they could spend a few days in Dubai are locked out. Israeli tennis player Shahar Peer, refused entry in 2009, is the most prominent among them.

"If they want you in, they get you in. It's that simple," Even-Zohar explains over lunch at the Atlantis's Asian-themed buffet.

From virtually nothing in 2002, Dubai has clambered up the ranks of global diamond capitals. In 2007, Dubai was the world's fifth largest overall diamond center and the number four handler of rough diamonds, with $5 billion in trade. Dubai's share of rough diamonds is catching up with the big centers: Mumbai (number two) and Tel Aviv (number three) handle around $9 billion each. Antwerp, number one in the world, traded $19 billion that year.[1]

Dubai's splashy entry into diamonds has created some fascinating geopolitical juxtapositions. The ancient diamond trade has been the purview of Jewish craftsmen and traders for hundreds of years. Tel Aviv—the Middle East's chief diamond center—controls a large portion of it. Dubai cannot get into the sector without dealing with Jews in general and Israel in particular. Tel Aviv is a vital supplier of rough and polished stones, a cutting and polishing center, and a hub of global companies that handle the trade. When it comes to diamonds, Israel is a fact of life.

But Israel has a problem. It has no formal relations with the Arab countries that now form the world's fastest growing jewelry market. The oil-rich Middle East commands 14 percent of global jewelry sales.[2] Diamond sales jumped by 20 percent in Saudi Arabia alone in 2007.[3] For Tel Aviv's diamond merchants, Dubai's Diamond Exchange is a godsend. It's their only plausible gateway to a market that lusts after jewelry. It's also one of the few platforms for Arab-Jewish cooperation.

If it were any other country, the business relationship wouldn't be worth noting. But the UAE and Israel have no diplomatic ties. Dubai, massive air hub that it is, offers no direct flights to Israel. You cannot phone one country from the other. Israeli freighters call at Jebel Ali port, but Dubai has no direct air cargo connection to Tel Aviv that diamond merchants can trust. The UAE honors the Arab League boycott and says it won't normalize relations with Israel until the Palestinians do.

Despite these hurdles, the trade flourishes. The world's largest diamond companies maintain offices in Dubai and Tel Aviv, as well as in Antwerp and Bombay and other jewelry capitals. Dubai and Tel Aviv's bourses are members of the same associations. When a dealer in Tel Aviv sends stones to Dubai, he ships them through Switzerland. Many Israeli traders have dual citizenship and use second-country passports to get into the UAE. Those who only carry Israel's blue passport are subject to the UAE's good graces.

"Israeli traders fought their way into the market," says Youri Steverlynck, CEO of the Dubai Diamond Exchange. Steverlynck, a former Antwerp diamond official, says business relations between the two countries are a lot smoother than political ones. Maybe it's the way forward. "The best way to solve problems is through business," he says.

Problem is, trade with Israel goes against UAE foreign policy. Dubai plays up its Arab credentials to avoid a political backlash—even a terrorist attack—and keeps quiet about facts that go against the grain, like U.S. bases and ties with Israel. "There is more Israeli business here than you think and the less that is said about it the better," Even-Zohar says. "It's in the interest of Dubai not to talk about it. Dubai is worried about the reaction from the rest of the Arab world."

Israel is cautious, too. In 2008, I sought an interview with Ran Gidor, an Israeli diplomat at the country's embassy in London. Gidor agreed to discuss Israel-Dubai ties until he informed his higher-ups in Jerusalem, who batted it down. His e-mail was apologetic. "I've been instructed in the most unambiguous terms to avoid making any reference to Dubai," he wrote, adding that he hadn't "the faintest idea why it is deemed so sensitive."

Dubai-Israel ties are sensitive because they are substantive. Stanley Fischer, Israel's central bank governor and former Citibank vice-chairman, mentioned the relationship at a 2008 press briefing in London. An audience member asked Fischer whether Dubai's success was coming at Israel's expense, as some U.S.-based Israel backers were saying.[4] Fischer said the reverse was true: Dubai was more interested in trade than deepening the boycott. "Various business contacts are taking place between Israel and the Gulf, without wishing to identify the parties since both sides want to keep it quiet," Fischer said. "Both sides know what they're doing."[5]

Dubai and Israel share a "very good informal relationship," says Even-Zohar. "Dubai doesn't hurt Israel at all," he says between spoonfuls of vanilla ice cream. "My first contact with Dubai came because our Israeli foreign ministry suggested that I call somebody here."

The lack of formality greases the skids. Qatar was, until recently, the only Gulf state with diplomatic ties. It hosted an Israeli trade mission until January 2009, when it closed it in protest of Israel's assault on Gaza. But Qatar dealt far less with Israel than the UAE does.[6]

Some Israeli concern is warranted. Dubai's entry into the diamond business is a long-term challenge to Tel Aviv's status as the Middle East's diamond capital. But in the short term Dubai's tax-free and lightly regulated sector is a bigger challenge to Antwerp and a boon for Israeli dealers who can serve the Gulf's fast expanding markets.

"We are indeed challenging existing positions," says Peter Meeus, CEO of Dubai-based International Diamond Laboratories. "Publicly we always say we are complementary. This is also true. With the business growing so fast in the Mideast, people who want polished stones come here instead of going somewhere else."

Dubai has capitalized on important shifts in the sector. The diamond business is drifting away from Europe and the mighty De Beers cartel. New trade centers are rising in Africa and India. Markets are growing in the Middle East and Asia. Europe and America are still the most important, but they are slowing.

Dubai is better placed than Tel Aviv and Antwerp to serve the Arab market, and the emirate is fast deepening ties with China and Africa. Dubai's long relationship with India allows it to capitalize on the explosion of the diamond business there. In short, Dubai sits at the center of the revamped trade matrix. This realization caused Meeus, a native Belgian, to dump Antwerp and move to Dubai.

Meeus, a buzz-cut man with a fireplug physique, said he'd been stifled in clannish Antwerp. In 2005, the board governing the Belgian diamond sector told Meeus to halt his plans to expand the city's operations into Bombay and New York. At the time he directed Antwerp's Diamond High Council. Meeus reckoned that Flemish fortunes were fading. He accepted an offer from Ahmed bin Sulayem to open the Arab world's first diamond exchange.

When Meeus defected, Belgian newspapers plastered it on page one. The Antwerp chapter of the World Diamond Council stripped him of his leadership post. But not everyone was scandalized. Meeus was able to poach another fifteen Antwerp experts. One by one they followed him to his headquarters near the Jebel Ali port, an area the gem industry press now calls Little Antwerp. Meeus is a man rejuvenated. He's jettisoned Belgium's stolid traditions and regulatory morass for a new place that seethes with dynamism.

"What pushed me away was the lack of vision and ambition," he says. "I'm a very ambitious guy. I want to build. And Dubai gives me that environment. We take risks. Okay, sometimes it doesn't work, but at least we do things. That mentality is missing in Europe."

Meeus's stewardship partly explains Dubai's astonishing rise. Sheikh Mohammed invited him to an *iftar* dinner at Zabeel Palace during Ramadan. The Dubai leader asked him two questions: "How will you internationalize your business? Where are you going to expand?" Meeus told him Dubai needed to move into markets in Russia, Europe, and India. Sheikh Mohammed didn't say much in response. Meeus got the feeling he was unimpressed.

For Meeus, however, the sheikh's attitude was sweet music. His global ambitions had been shot down by the gray men of Antwerp. In Dubai, his ambitions needed beefing up.

Dubai's nearly instant success in diamonds isn't completely on the up-and-up. The zone's tax-free status makes it a convenient transfer center for dealers looking to launder profits and avoid taxes in their home markets.

Even-Zohar explains how it works in his book *From Mine to Mistress*. Exporters send diamonds to Dubai with paperwork listing them at a fraction of their value. The stones are then transshipped elsewhere, often unopened, at marked-up values. African exporters send stones through Dubai to avoid paying heavy export taxes. Europeans and Israelis use Dubai to manipulate profit figures and reduce income taxes or, like the Africans, to avoid export tax. The scheme costs those governments revenue, and it fills the wallets of their corrupt bureaucrats and merchants. In short, Dubai makes money on crimes committed elsewhere. It's another reason Dubai's diamond exchange has grown so fast.[7]

"They're thriving on the greed of others," Even-Zohar says. "It's cheating other countries' tax systems. It's not sustainable."

A U.S. State Department money laundering report cited the practice and Belgian authorities have begun cracking down.[8] But so-called transfer pricing has slowed in recent years as Dubai's more legitimate business has grown. Local regulators have worked with global money laundering authorities to stem the manipulations, even though no criminal activity takes place on UAE soil. Steverlynck, the Dubai exchange boss, says he has no desire for Dubai to be labeled a repricing center.

Meeus believes Arabs previously avoided the diamond business because of its Jewish flavor. That attitude, and Dubai's willingness to circumvent it, has turned the city into something of a cultural bridge. In 2004, Dubai hosted the World Diamond Council's annual conference, where Sheikh Mohammed personally welcomed prominent Jews including De Beers chief Nicky Oppenheimer and diamond council chairman Eli Izhakoff. Sheikh Mohammed sat in the audience between the two men.

The Dubai leader must have known this might be seen as risqué in Arab capitals. But Sheikh Mohammed's dream for Dubai is to emulate tenth-century Córdoba, a Muslim city where Jews held important roles in business and academia. If that is the case, the city has a ways to go to build up its Jewish population.

But it wasn't Arabs who initially fought Dubai's foray into diamonds. It was the Jewish diamond establishment. Dubai faced prickly opposition in 2004, when it tried to join the World Federation of Diamond Bourses in New York, even though the city was already trading more diamonds than several of the federation's weaker members. Meeus, who was Antwerp's representative at the time, said Belgian kingpins tried to block Dubai's entry. There were complaints that Israeli members could be prohibited from traveling to the UAE because it doesn't recognize Israel. In the end, the opposition failed and the federation accepted its first Arab member, with Israel voting in favor.[9] In 2006, in what seemed like atonement, the largely Jewish New York Diamond Dealers Club on Manhattan's Fifth Avenue threw a party at the Rainbow Room for Ahmed bin Sulayem, probably the first Arab to be feted by the club.

While bin Sulayem mingled with Jewish diamond dons, Dubai moved to add a Muslim flavor to the business. The bourse announced that it had created a unique new stone: the Dubai Cut diamond. It's a dazzling rectangle with ninety-nine separate facets. Each represents one of the holy names of Allah.

Israeli Inroads

Israel's quiet openings in the Gulf tend to dry up in times of conflict. Oman shut Israel's trade mission in 2000 after the outbreak of the second intifada. Relations plunged again after the 2006 Israeli onslaught on Lebanon that killed more than a thousand people. In 2008, Israel's threats to bomb Iran's nuclear sites got in the way, and the Jewish State's subsequent killing of hundreds of civilians in Gaza triggered war crimes accusations from the UAE government.

Even so, America's Israel lobby has pleaded Israel's case in the UAE, while trying to persuade Dubai to take a tougher line with Iran. The American Jewish Committee has sent four delegations to Dubai since 2006. The Anti-Defamation League sent one. The pro-Israel Washington Institute for Near East Policy also sent a group to high-level meetings with Emirati officials, including at a mixer at the home of U.S. Consul Paul Sutphin. A person who attended the gathering said the anti-Iran rhetoric made little headway among Dubai leaders, many of them descended from Iranian migrants. (In Abu Dhabi, however, the U.S.-Israeli position on Iran gains more traction.)

Still, the UAE is more receptive to Jewish concerns than most of the Gulf. The AJC wangled meetings with Gergawi and other top officials. It threw a Shabbat dinner in October 2007 in the Jumeirah Emirates Towers Hotel. Most of the guests were Israelis in town for a dental conference.[10] "There's a reason we keep going to the UAE. There is a sense of openness. Every time we go, it gets easier," says the American Jewish Committee's Carmiel Arbit. "It'd be great to see the Jewish community organizing comfortably in Dubai."

Israel's inroads aren't always so surreptitious. Israeli jeweler Lev Leviev, who operates the Levant diamond shops, triggered an uproar when he sent press releases announcing the opening of new stores in Dubai. A flurry of newspaper articles documented Leviev's support for Israeli settlers in the occupied West Bank. Dubai's *Gulf News* reported that UNICEF halted its partnership with Leviev after learning that his companies were building four Jewish outposts on seized Arab land.[11] Leviev's Dubai shops opened anyway. One operates in Sheikh Mohammed's Al Qasr Hotel, another in his Mina A'Salaam Hotel.

No such outcry has emerged over a joint venture between Dubai-owned port operator DP World and Israel's chief shipper, Zim Integrated Shipping. In June 2008, the two firms announced a joint purchase of Spain's port operator Contarsa, which runs the Spanish port of Tarragona. The deal handed DP World a 60 percent share and Zim the remaining 40 percent. Dubai ports chairman Sultan bin Sulayem is known to be a friend of Zim president Idan Ofer, who stood up for Dubai during the furor in Washington.

"Idan is a very good businessman, very decent. These people don't mix business with politics," says Jamal Majid bin Thaniah, CEO of DP World's shipping group. "When you're operating in a global marketplace, you can't pick and choose. You're bound by international business practices to deal with companies like Zim. We'll continue to conduct business on an unbiased basis."

Dubai also owns a 20 percent slice of the Nasdaq, which lists more than seventy Israeli stocks, its largest foreign contingent. Dubai exchanges are linking operations with the Nasdaq. When that is complete, Nasdaq listings, including Israeli ones, could be bought and sold in Dubai.[12]

In July 2008, Gregg Rickman, the U.S. State Department envoy who documents global anti-Semitism, stopped in Dubai. I met him and a colleague during their visit to the Dubai School of Government, where they was escorted by Susan Unruh, the political and economic officer at the U.S. Consulate in Dubai.

As yet, Dubai has no synagogue. Rickman asked whether Sheikh Mohammed would allow one. Unruh said she thought he would; if not allowing a synagogue to be purpose-built, at least he wouldn't object to one being allowed to open quietly, like the Mormon temple that operates in a Dubai villa.

"I can't believe they wouldn't tolerate it. It would be out of their nature," said Unruh, who, like the envoy, is Jewish. "Their brand image of tolerance is incredibly important to them."

The intricacies of Jewish travel to Dubai is a popular topic on the online discussion group FlyerTalk. The forum's "Kosher Food in Dubai" thread has Dubai's Jewish residents and frequent visitors giving advice to newcomers.

> Mar 23, 07, 5:13 am
> I've been to Dubai a few times and I can tell you from firsthand experience they don't care about your religion. My son's name is Israel Moshe on his passport (and in real life) and the woman at passport control looked at him, smiled, and said, "Welcome." Many Israelis do business in Dubai and even have offices there.

> Apr 13, 08, 1:04 pm
> Anyone have experience traveling to Dubai as a gay Jewish couple? I know of a few Jews who have gone and said it's no problem, but I am still concerned to go there with my partner.

> Mar 9, 07, 12:45 am
> I have been to Dubai as an Orthodox Jew. You can buy quite a few [Kosher] products in the supermarket. I have heard that people have asked in the BBQ fish restaurants for a kosher fish

to be double-wrapped in foil and barbequed. The staff were quite familiar with the request.

Dubai's don't ask, don't tell policies aren't going to bring peace to the wilds of the Middle East. But the city's spirit of tolerance and its willingness to compromise for the sake of commerce are steps in that direction, and stand as examples to others.

10

SHEIKH MOHAMMED: BORN TO RULE

The Six-Million-Dirham Man

ON MARCH 30, 2008, students at Zayed University got a civics lesson, Dubai style.

That day, Sheikh Mohammed turned up at the women-only campus to hear two of his daughters recite poetry. But when he arrived, Sheikh Mohammed appeared less interested in poetry than with a marketplace erected in the campus's soaring central atrium. There, hundreds of students—all of them young local women dressed in black *abayas* and *shayla* headscarves—staffed flea-market booths. They flogged necklaces, earrings, clothes, and even Krispy Kreme donuts. Sheikh Mohammed, who has long struggled to kindle a spirit of entrepreneurship in Dubaians, was excited by what he saw.

A student named Amna al-Akraf escorted the Dubai leader and fielded his questions. "Who financed this?" he asked. "Where did the idea come from? Where do the profits go?" Before he left, Sheikh Mohammed asked for al-Akraf's phone number.

The next day, she got a call from the ruler's *diwan* asking for a list of the students involved. Not long afterward, men from the diwan arrived on campus with several briefcases. Each was crammed with cash. The men handed the briefcases to the incredulous American administrators of the university. One told them: This money is a gift from Sheikh Mohammed. Divide it among the Emirati girls who ran booths at the crafts fair.[1] It took administrators a few days to count it: 6.2 million dirhams, or $1.7 million, to be split among the 300-odd students who'd operated booths. It worked out to just over $5,300 each.

The ruler's handouts left students giddy. But administrators and teachers, mainly Americans, were aghast. "What kind of message does that send?" one teacher asked over lunch in the cafeteria. Another groused that the students had probably ordered their maids to craft the jewelry for them. The teachers felt that the cash would've been better spent on new computers. I wasn't so sure. Sheikh Mohammed was keeping up his end of the tribal ruling bargain with these handouts, of course. But he had also been trying to inculcate entrepreneurship among Emiratis. I asked a student named Shayma, a tall and slender young woman in a plain black *abaya*, what lesson she took away from her handout.

"We should start a business and we will earn money," Shayma said with a smile. The ruler would've been proud.

Sheikh Mohammed, the muscular, blunt-spoken, sixty-year-old monarch, is Dubai's chief architect. He is a man's man, with the entrepreneurship bravado of Richard Branson, the city-building prowess of Robert Moses, and the social engineering ambition of Ataturk.

Paul Bagatelas, who directs the Carlyle Group's Dubai headquarters, likens him to a cross between Teddy Roosevelt, the big game-hunter who represented emerging America, and Bill Gates, the entrepreneur whose personality is inseparable from his empire.

Sheikh Mohammed is simultaneously raising a city from the sand, creating business opportunities to power it, and preparing a population of desert dwellers to rise to the task of running it. His ideas are so stamped on the landscape that two of his poems are being written on the sea as a group of islands.

Sheikh Mohammed is not an eloquent speaker, at least not in English, in which he seems to have difficulty expressing himself. Interviews are rare. When he does them, his answers are abrupt and simplistic, but allude to a grand outlook, akin to America's manifest destiny. His manner is serious, his voice gruff. He is not a man of jokes and chitchat. He is a public figure, but distant and difficult to know. He prefers to express himself through deeds.

"Am I a good leader? I don't know and I guess no one else does," he writes in *My Vision*. "The people, the future and history will stand judge and I'll accept their judgement no matter what it might be. Nevertheless, I'm fully convinced that I'm leading my people not only on the right path but on the only one available."

Sheikh Mohammed says in his book that he never wanted to rule Dubai. He was happy with his job in the security forces and ports. But his elder brother, the ruler Sheikh Maktoum, asked him several times to accept the title of crown prince. Each time, Mohammed said he asked to be excused. Finally, in 1995, Maktoum ordered him to take it.

"What's important for me is to always do what I consider is my duty, to God, my conscience, my homeland, my people and my leader," he writes. "I'm therefore working today as if I will die tomorrow and working for tomorrow as if I'm going to live forever."

He's trained as a fighter pilot, drinks green tea, jogs on the beach, and drives in Dubai's cutthroat traffic in a boxy white Mercedes G-class SUV. His Dubai license plate carries the single digit 1. Sheikh Mohammed fishes for marlin in the Arabian Sea and hunts game in Africa and Pakistan. He's a champion racer of endurance horses and the world's largest owner of thoroughbreds. And the ruler is an astute investor, one of the planet's richest men, and sole owner of a global portfolio worth billions of dollars. *Forbes* magazine ranks him in the modest number five slot on the world's richest royals list, with an $18 billion fortune—behind his cousin, UAE ruler Sheikh Khalifa, at $23 billion. Despite his riches, he cultivates the persona of a minimalist.

"I need little from my world," he writes. "My prayer mat and water container are in my car wherever I go, together with my work documents and my vision."

Sheikh Mohammed's Zabeel Palace overlooks central Dubai from atop a dune, its marbled halls gilded to the baseboards and bathed in the glow of hundreds of chandeliers. The gargantuan palace resembles an American high school, its grounds crammed with fountains and strutting peacocks. Spreading out before it is a royal family domain containing a palace that looks like Versailles and another that resembles the White House. There is the lush Zabeel Club, the royal family's manicured private recreation haunt. The family's Zabeel Stables sits next to the club, with racetracks, barns, and horse rings, along with a spa and swimming pool for its million-dollar steeds. Every morning, as the sunrise gilds surrounding skyscrapers, stable hands take the horses for a stroll.

In October 2006, I sat in Zabeel Palace with Sheikh Mohammed as he broke his Ramadan fast with his staff. The men building the world's most futuristic city ate with their fingers, like Bedouin, grabbing hunks of lamb—including the eyes and brains—from greasy carcasses, wadding it with rice and thumbing it into their mouths. After dinner, manservants appeared with incense burners gushing gorgeously fragrant *oudh* smoke. The men washed their hands in the smoke and let it flow under their headscarves to perfume their hair.

Sheikh Mohammed's upbringing was decidedly less grand. He grew up in the Maktoum family compound known as Sheikh Saeed's house, kicking a ball around a sandy courtyard that overlooked the creek. His father, Rashid, his mother, Latifa, and his siblings occupied one of the home's smaller wings. It consisted of four small, interconnected rooms with thick coral walls, fifteen-foot ceilings, low doorways, and tiny windows. The house had no electricity during Mohammed's early years. There was little privacy. The only room with a door was the bathroom. It held a toilet—a hole in the floor leading to a pit—and a bath. The royal family washed by drawing water from a clay urn and ladling it over themselves. It was a rare privilege. Most Dubaians washed in the sea.

"In those days it wasn't like today, where every child gets their own room," says Abdulla al-Mutairy, forty-nine, director of the museum that now occupies the house. "Sometimes at night they all slept together in one room with a fan."

In summer, the royals slept in rooms on the rooftop, overlooking the clamor of the creek through carved wooden *mushrabiyah* screens.

When Sheikh Mohammed was a boy, a hundred people or more lived in his family compound, including guards, slaves, and the families of his grandfather Sheikh Saeed, and those of his great-uncles Juma and Hasher. In the giant kitchen, slaves cooked pots of *machbous* and *salouna* on fires built of scraps of wood and charcoal. A big set of doors swung onto the courtyard, where handlers would lead camels that bellowed as they kneeled under their loads. Cats and dogs wandered the home. And in the evenings, falconers brought out their birds.[2]

Pictures in the home depict the hard life in pre-electric Dubai. Sheikh Mohammed comes across as a tough little boy. In one photo, young Mohammed sits on his father's lap wearing a skullcap and a serious look while his father reads from the Iraq Petroleum Company yearbook. In another, Mohammed appears about eight years old wearing a filthy *kandoura* and a beat-up suit jacket. He's got a falcon clamped to his wrist. An old man appears to be teaching him to train the bird.

Young Mohammed lived in Sheikh Saeed's old house until he was nearly ten, moving out after his grandfather died in 1958 and his father became ruler. Sheikh Mohammed still visits his boyhood home. He takes visitors on tours, pointing out the places where he played and the pictures of his relatives. President Bush got the guided tour in 2007.[3]

Sheikh Rashid often took Mohammed for walks along the creek, pointing out locations where his city of the future would rise. Rashid was said to be impressed by young Mohammed's intelligence and decisiveness. Early on he steeped his third son in the details of running Dubai. He sent him to Sandhurst to beef up his leadership skills and to improve his English.

By the age of twenty, the young sheikh was in charge of Dubai's police and security forces. Sheikh Mohammed has enjoyed a remarkable run since then, managing to preserve the city's safety despite its overwhelming social changes and the conflicts in countries nearby.

At the age of twenty-two, when the UAE emerged as an independent state, Sheikh Mohammed became the country's minister of defense, the world's youngest. But it wasn't until 1997 that he agreed to integrate Dubai's own troops—which he led—with those of the other emirates. Only after the UAE received defense guarantees from Washington, Britain, and France was he convinced the merged forces would be better able to stand up to neighborhood bullies like Iran and Iraq.[4]

Sheikh Rashid seems to have outlined a succession scheme after his 1980 stroke that would eventually put Mohammed in charge. By 1985, his serious-minded son controlled several levers of power, enjoying the support of a growing posse of powerful backers. When Sheikh Rashid died in 1990, the Dubai leadership role passed to Mohammed's eldest brother, Maktoum, a horse enthusiast known for the kind heart and mild manner, which made him a natural diplomat. The second-eldest, Hamdan, became deputy ruler and UAE finance minister. But Mohammed gradually took control of the emirate, plunging his hands into every aspect of the city's growth, sculpting the landscape and tinkering with the economy. By 1995, when Maktoum appointed him crown prince, Sheikh Mohammed emerged as the city's key decision maker, his Executive Office the center of power.[5]

Sheikh Maktoum remained ruler of Dubai and federal prime minister and vice president until January 3, 2006. On that day, Maktoum died of an apparent heart attack while vacationing in Australia. He was only sixty-two. Maktoum's three brothers buried him next to Sheikh Rashid, and, with barely a hiccup, Sheikh Mohammed assumed his brother's titles.

Running into Sheikh Mohammed can be akin to meeting a leprechaun. For Mohammed Saleh Khamis al-Kaabi, the oldest man in the remote Wadi Al Qoor, that's exactly how it was. Al-Kaabi, who guesses he is a hundred years old (he looks more like seventy), was sitting in his crumbling house one day when Sheikh Mohammed's entourage rumbled into his village.[6]

The Dubai ruler happened to be touring the area, assessing its housing needs, which in the UAE means giving housing grants. He came across al-Kaabi and sat with him on a carpet. "Do you know me? I am Mohammed bin Rashid," the sheikh told the old man. "Give me an order, father. Whatever you want, just name it."

He asked the old man, with cropped gray hair and an unkempt beard, what was lacking in his life. He addressed al-Kaabi's wife respectfully as "my aunt."

Al-Kaabi leaned over and grasped Sheikh Mohammed's hands and the two men rubbed noses, their foreheads touching in traditional greeting. Al-Kaabi spoke of losing four of his seven sons, three of whom died in car crashes. The wife and children of one of his dead sons scratched out a tough existence in the *wadi*. Sheikh Mohammed, in a khaki *kandoura* and olive headscarf, saw the cracks in the walls and understood that the old man's life could be more comfortable. Still, al-Kaabi asked for nothing. He told the Dubai leader that he'd vowed never to leave the house that Sheikh Rashid gave him thirty years ago, despite its deterioration from lack of maintenance.

"We owe the Maktoum family many favors," al-Kaabi said. "They provided me and my family with housing all our lives."

On the spot, Sheikh Mohammed ordered a new house built for al-Kaabi as well as for the family of one of his dead sons. Days later, crews turned up in the lonely *wadi* to start work. A year later, al-Kaabi had a six-bedroom house that would have made Martha Stewart proud, with wooden beams, palm-thatch porticos, lanterns hanging on the walls, and heavy wooden doors. The house was furnished right down to the boxes of Kleenex and fresh fruit. It spoke of style and luxury, worth at least a million dollars.

Al-Kaabi's wife Aliba, in a metallic burqa mask worn by Gulf women, was flushed. "God created this man to look after his people. We never imagined we'd see him in this remote area."

Her husband said: "Sheikh Mohammed can fulfill anyone's dreams. It only requires meeting him once. He looks you in the eye and then looks around you. He can easily find out what you want without you asking for it."

Giving houses is part of a tribal leader's bargain with his people. But it doesn't usually happen with such a personal touch. Sheikh Mohammed's housing charity recently gave away 260 five-bedroom villas—with free utilities, schools, and a clinic—in the mountain town of Hatta. Each cost $220,000 to build.[7]

Around the World on a Jet Ski

When I was at Sheikh Mohammed's Ramadan *iftar* for journalists in 2006, he avoided the dozen or so Western reporters he'd invited. A few Emirati women journalists were the only ones to chat with him. At dinner, I tried to strike up a conversation with his aides. All I could coax out of them were monosyllabic grunts. Finally, one of them looked at me and said, "We've been told to watch what we say around you journalists."

It was against the odds, then, when in 2007, the American TV show *60 Minutes* persuaded Sheikh Mohammed to grant an interview. CBS sent a crew of seven to spend a few days with the Dubai leader. The crew interviewed him several times and filmed his wanderings around the city, chatting with him as he drove his Mercedes 4x4. What followed was a fawning portrayal of the Dubai leader and his accomplishments—a rare event for a program dedicated to investigative reporting.

When filming was finished, Sheikh Mohammed's three top lieutenants—Mohammed al-Gergawi, Mohammed Alabbar, and Sultan bin Sulayem—threw the CBS crew a going-away party. Representatives from the *diwan* handed each crew member a bathing suit and led them to a speedboat, which whisked them two miles out to sea. Nakheel's archipelago, The World, rose in front of them. The boat beached on the only inhabited island, home to a mansion belonging to Sheikh Mohammed's second wife, Princess Haya. The CBS crew swam in the infinity pool and lounged on the beach, with a view over the neighboring islands.

A row of twenty brand-new Jet Skis sat parked on the beach. Bin Sulayem, Alabbar, and Gergawi hopped aboard and told the crew members to follow. Mike Charlton, a Dubai-based cameraman, was one of the CBS crew that day. The forty-year-old Australian jumped on one of the craft and roared after the three billionaires. It was an unbelievable opportunity. It wasn't just spending simultaneous time with the three busiest men in town—getting an interview with one of them is difficult enough—but the fact that they'd tossed aside their responsibilities to horse around with a camera crew.

The men sped around the three-mile by five-mile archipelago. The three hundred islands are separated by narrow, curving passages of water, making it difficult to see far ahead. Charlton, a Jet Ski novice, found it exhilarating—and dangerous. A few times, he'd slash out of a narrow channel to find the boyish Alabbar bearing down on him, in what looked to be a head-on collision. At the last moment, the Emaar chairman, with a devilish grin, would jerk the handlebars to the side and send his craft swooshing in a long skid, launching a giant wave over Charlton and nearly knocking him over. Then he would speed off.

"Boy, can those guys Jet Ski," Charlton says. "They tag-team you. You don't know where you're going because they just sprayed you with water and they're gone."

The men chased each other around The World, juddering around the tip of South America, circling Australia, and darting through the channels separating the European countries. After a while, a helicopter passed overhead and landed on the island. The Jet Skiers followed. Sheikh

Mohammed stepped out, dressed in a short red wetsuit. The Dubai leader said hello to the CBS crew, then he, too, peeled away, skittering over the sea faster than any of them.

"He just shot off around the islands. Man, was he fast! You'd chase him and every now and then you'd see him, just shooting past," Charlton says. "I gave up trying to catch him. He was just flying."

It wasn't the most salubrious activity for a head of state. Charlton, a daredevil cameraman inured to the front lines of the globe's war zones, was worried he was going to crash, either into an island or into one of his Jet Skiing companions. The chance of taking out Sheikh Mohammed was an alarming possibility.

"You have to pay attention. These things are moving maybe fifty miles per hour, which is why it was so exhilarating. You're going in and out of these islands, and some of them only have a sandbar between them. Three or four inches of water. And you've got to make a really quick decision. Can I make it?"

"In terms of my life experiences, it was right up there," Charlton says. "I was thinking to myself, '*This is the business*. I'll remember this until the day I die.'"

At the end, the exhausted group sat around and swapped stories with the boss and his lieutenants. When it was time to go, *60 Minutes* correspondent Steve Kroft gave the sheikh a CBS baseball cap as a parting memento. Without missing a beat, Sheikh Mohammed took off his own cap, a boxy military hat, olive drab with a UAE flag on its face. "Then you shall have mine," he says, handing it to Kroft.

Knocking Heads

In a region where people speak in elliptical platitudes, Sheikh Mohammed is a rare straight shooter. He's an incredibly energetic man who disdains the laziness that envelops many of his countrymen. He understands that a cushy life is part of the tradeoff that keeps him in power, but the excesses tick him off.

His favorite targets are "ministers," a broad term for bureaucrats. He hates hiring quotas, smoking, and the attitude that says service jobs are beneath Emirati stature. He reminds his countrymen that comforts are useless without work.

In Dubai, Sheikh Mohammed launched a deep reorganization of government, replacing the old department structure with a new order, based on authorities and subordinate agencies. For instance, the Dubai Roads and Transport Authority sets policy for the Public Transport Agency, the Traffic Agency, and the Dubai Taxi Agency.

The structure encourages the liberation of businesses stuck inside the bureaucracy, allowing them to turn a profit that can be recycled back into the municipal budget. It's an institutionalizing of the moves that created DP World, the global ports operator. The scheme, led by the Executive Council, was stalled in early 2009 by opposition from the *diwan*. But Dubai is so steeped in change—and Sheikh Mohammed's critical eye—that the reforms didn't cause a big stir.

Abu Dhabi and the rest of the UAE are different. In 2006, when Sheikh Mohammed assumed his new role as federal vice president and prime minister, he was suddenly in charge of a bureaucracy he'd publicly disdained. He'd described ministers as lazy and accused them of allowing their underlings to wallow in monotony. His takeover would cause major trauma.

He toured the sixteen antiquated ministries and twenty-two authorities, often dropping in by surprise. At some point, he and UAE head of state Sheikh Khalifa agreed that the federal government needed a total overhaul. Sheikh Khalifa agreed that the Dubai leader, with his teams of consultants and advisers, would handle it.

In 2007, Sheikh Mohammed traveled to the $3 billion Emirates Palace Hotel[8] in Abu Dhabi to address the largest audience of UAE luminaries since independence in 1971. Sheikh Khalifa sat at front, with his Federal Supreme Council—the rulers of each emirate—and their crown princes, the twenty-one federal ministers, and assorted deputies, royals, and various VIPs from every corner of the country.

What followed was a speech of unprecedented bluntness, with deep criticism of the federal government and harsh personal critiques leveled at several ministers. The effect was similar to Senator Joseph McCarthy's personal attacks on congressmen in the 1950s, except Sheikh Mohammed focused on incompetence, not politics. His speech, carried on TV, stunned the nation.

Viewers saw Sheikh Mohammed sitting at a dais in a cream-colored *kandoura*, with gold-trimmed black gown and eyeglasses. He scanned the room and opened with a prescient joke: "It looks like the guys at the back are more nervous than me." The camera panned to a chuckling Sheikh Khalifa and the silent crowd of royals and dignitaries behind him. The laughs didn't last.

Sheikh Mohammed first turned to the minister of education, Hanif Hassan Ali, and minister of higher education, Sheikh Nahyan bin Mubarak al-Nahyan, and put them on notice that they'd better stop wasting students' lives—or else. UAE high schools, he said, are so substandard that graduates must study a further two years in a support program before they can be admitted to a university. "I demand that the ministers of education and higher education resolve the issue of the support programs . . . within the next three years," he told the men, who sat in front of him. "There is no room for compromises on education."

He told Health Minister Humaid Mohammed Obeid al-Qattami that modern hospital equipment and buildings were no replacement for skilled doctors and nurses. He demanded better training and standards.

He lobbed a rare broadside at Emirati families, lambasting their reliance on foreign maids, valets, gardeners, drivers, and the sundry domestic helpers who keep order in their homes. "Domestic help accounts for 10 percent of the labor force in the UAE, a very high figure for which society in general and UAE nationals in particular are responsible. Domestic help in some homes exceeds the size of the family." Get rid of some of them, he told his countrymen.

Then he skewered Labor Minister Ali al-Kaabi for forcing companies to hire a quota of Emirati secretaries. "I appreciate his dedication and enthusiasm, but his decisions were not successful because they ignored reality as well as the nation's priorities," Sheikh Mohammed told his audience. Al-Kaabi's mistake was twofold: He'd set up a quota, forcing companies to hire less productive and more expensive Emiratis, which was bad enough. But he'd also targeted the lowly job of secretary. This, for a leader working his heart out to turn Emiratis into "lions," as he calls his leaders-in-training, was inexcusable. "We need to have UAE nationals in more important roles and responsibilities," he said. Al-Kaabi soon lost his job.

Justice Minister Mohammed Nukheira al-Dhahiri was next in line. He must have been bracing himself, because he'd known about the boss's fury when he found the ministry using paper ledgers and other anachronisms that went out with the typewriter. Mohammed told the audience of his "utmost dissatisfaction" at the state of the ministry's caseload and backwardness, and said he would give al-Dhahiri "the chance" to clean things up.

"We will not allow this to continue," he said. "We will not accept that people's cases and rights get stuck in courts for long sequences of useless procedures."

All this was a warmup for a broader announcement. Sheikh Mohammed ordered the ministers to develop strategies to revamp their workplaces and thus the entire federal government. He gave them a year to do it, and promised to follow up personally. When it came time to judge their reorganizations, Sheikh Mohammed said he would measure them against the world's best governments: Singapore, New Zealand, Australia, and Canada. The ministers could keep their jobs if they managed to climb international rankings in competitiveness, transparency, and efficiency.

"It's not good enough to be first in the Arab world. We want to be the first globally," Sheikh Mohammed said. "Each ministry shall work within its area of expertise to improve the ranking of the UAE. The evaluation of each ministry will depend on the ranking of the UAE a year from now."

Not all of them made it. The Dubai leader reshuffled the federal cabinet in 2008 and brought in several new faces, most of them can-do technocrats from Dubai. The revamping of government is still under way.

The Motivator

Sheikh Mohammed runs Dubai by motivating people to excel. He prefers to use his celebrity status and personal attention to get things moving, rather than ordering people around. Every other month, he hosts a palace dinner for business leaders. If it's bankers in January, it might be airline executives in March and hotel owners in May. The boss's management consultant Yasar Jarrar, who'd previously advised Jordan's government, attends these dinners. Jarrar says the sheikh's personal attention works wonders.

"How many presidents or prime ministers do you see having lunch with the hotel owners and managers because they think tourism is important? A hotel manager would be lucky to see the minister of tourism after crying and begging for six months," Jarrar says. "By doing that he sends a very strong message to his director of tourism, who realizes he has to be on a first name basis with all these guys."[9]

Another time, Jarrar was with a team of consultants reporting on the performance of Dubai's government. The assessors graded departments with traffic lights: green for good, yellow for so-so, and red for bad. One department—Jarrar didn't say which—had nothing but red lights for all their key indicators.

"What's the problem with this department?" Sheikh Mohammed asked.

Jarrar explained that they'd slipped behind on deadlines and their managers' skills were lacking, and a few other issues.

"Next time you bring me these reports, put the mobile phone number for the department head at the bottom of each page," the boss told him. Sure enough, the next few presentations, more red lights appeared. This time there were mobile numbers for the leaders of the offending departments. Sheikh Mohammed reached into the pocket of his *kandoura* and pulled out his Nokia.

"Twice I saw him calling the head of government departments," Jarrar says. "If you're a department head and you get a call from the ruler on your mobile, that's scary enough. But when he's asking you why you're not performing, that's serious punishment."

A few years ago, Jarrar was awakened by a phone call at midnight. An aide from The Executive Office was on the line. She said Sheikh Mohammed wanted to see his Delivery Unit—the team that pushes people to "deliver" on their promises—at Dubai International Airport.

Jarrar, a fast talker who favors tweed jackets and jeans, drove to the airport and the boss was there, taking a surprise tour. He looked in a mood to start cracking heads. Surly travelers waited in interminable lines at immigration and again at the baggage carousels. Sheikh Mohammed had met one arriving flight and walked alongside a passenger—who probably had no idea who he was—to time his journey through customs, to the baggage claim, and out the exit. At the end of his tour, he addressed his staff.

"First of all, it's one in the morning. This is our peak hour. I don't see any managers here," he said. Managers, it turned out, worked the 9:00 a.m. to 6:00 p.m. shift, a calmer time at the airport.

Then he pointed to the crowds. He told his advisers that there was no reason for arriving visitors—Dubai's economic lifeblood—to be left waiting so long. Many of them were vacationers, and the airport's inefficiencies were giving them a disastrous first impression.

"In six months I will come back," he said, bidding them good night.

After that, the Delivery Unit spent its nights tracking passengers at the airport. Managers worked night shifts. The airport added a baggage carousel and streamlined immigration checks. They installed biometric immigration booths, allowing frequent travelers to come and go using a chip-embedded ID card. The airport was still overcrowded and operating far beyond capacity, but the improvements boosted efficiency.

He Is Electrifying

Sheikh Mohammed is not a man to be messed with. Even his uncle says so. "He is pushy. He is aggressive," says Sheikh Ahmed bin Saeed al-Maktoum, who heads Emirates airline. Sheikh Ahmed, by rights, has a claim on the Dubai ruler's job. But he has no qualms about letting his nephew be the boss.

"He is the main driver behind pushing everybody," Ahmed says of his nephew. "He wants things to happen yesterday if you decide today. But at the same time he gives you all the support you need. He will push you to do things but he will always be there to support you."[10]

Reem al-Hashimy, a federal minister and a top aide of the Dubai leader, says meeting Sheikh Mohammed is an opportunity not to be missed. "He is electrifying."

I ask everyone to tell me their best Sheikh Mohammed stories. Most people dodge the question. Sometimes I get a look of horror, as if I've asked someone to drink poison. People are afraid to discuss him. Good anecdotes and criticisms are tough to come by. To some degree, everyone in Dubai depends on his good graces for their livelihood.

"Sheikh Mohammed? Most people find him very direct. He has terrific energy. You see an article in the paper saying he's just ridden in some endurance race in Spain and then he's here. It's amazing what he manages to do," says Anthony Harris, the former British ambassador. "He has the ability to lead. People are motivated by him and very loyal. I never heard anybody, I don't think, say a cross word about him. I'm not saying he's a man without fault. He spends enormous sums on horses, but I don't even hear people criticizing him for that. He has very high popularity for a ruler, by any standards."

Georges Makhoul, who heads Morgan Stanley's Dubai operations, ascribes him with the ability to understand complex detail at a glance, like a great hitter sees the stitching on a fastball before knocking it out of the park. "He's a deep, deep guy," Makhoul says. "You have to stretch your imagination to see what he has in mind. I know he sees it all in his mind. It's not just some abstract vision."

Others, not wanting to be named publicly, describe him as a megalomaniac who is turning a pleasant city into a bloated megalopolis. The giant projects, the constant striving to be number one, to surpass New York and London, to drag the Arab world into a renaissance, to recreate the cosmopolitan tolerance of tenth-century Córdoba—these are the dreams of a desert sheikh deluded by acolytes. Others say he understands these goals aren't realistic, but he uses grand language as a motivational tool.

"The standard response is, 'We're dealing with someone who's got a kind of Napoleon complex.' I don't see him in those terms," says Eddie O'Sullivan, author of a book on the Gulf, and the former editor of the *Middle East Economic Digest*. "I see him as a man in a hurry. Not only does he know what he wants to do, he wants to do it faster than other people. He's using language to get people going. 'If I don't do it now, who will?' It's a great burden of responsibility that he feels. And it's not yet clear whether any of his children are up to the task."

Sheikh Mohammed is as much a tribal sheikh as he is a twenty-first-century politician. He's as comfortable rubbing noses with the men at a traditional wedding as he is in haranguing Bill Gates or Warren Buffett for investments. He can be charming and understated, and a ruthless manager. He hires slick public relations companies, consultants, and lobbyists to work behind the scenes, but he gets his message across through personal charisma that stems from unrivaled power. He is a master of gesture and style, always in control.

Sheikh Mohammed is unique in the world, someone with the confidence, energy, and money to create. He's secure enough to ignore his critics and unafraid of borrowing ideas. Tom Wright, the Burj Al Arab architect, believes Sheikh Mohammed is the greatest builder alive, akin to the great kings who built Barcelona and Rome, or the temples of India and Egypt. Others hold him responsible for covering the desert in Disni-fied chintz, more appropriate for a bygone era when energy was cheap and global warming wasn't understood.

"Who else has done it?" Wright asks. "Other places, like Saudi Arabia and Libya, they have loads of money but they haven't got the vision."

Family Matters

Unlike royals elsewhere, Sheikh Mohammed manages to keep his private life private. The tame UAE news media know that his wives and children are off-limits except on rare occasions. It is widely held that discussing the antics of Sheikh Mohammed's children is not the way to get ahead in Dubai. My questions on the topic were nearly always rebuffed.

What is known is that the Dubai leader has not followed in his fa-ther's more modest footsteps of taking just one wife. He is a polygamist who has fathered nineteen children, give or take, by at least two women.[11] His first marriage, to Sheikha Hind bint Maktoum al-Maktoum, was an arranged one and the dominant relationship responsible for most of his children. Sheikha Hind is the ruling family's chief matriarch who lives with her brood in Zabeel Palace.

In 2004, Sheikh Mohammed married again. His bride was the Jorda-nian Princess Haya bint al-Hussein, the half-sister of Jordan's King Ab-dullah. Princess Haya is Sheikh Mohammed's public wife. Haya, a beautiful former Olympic show jumper with sun-streaked auburn hair, maintains an office in Dubai's Convention Tower and practices her horsewomanship in a pair of rings at the Zabeel Stables across the street. She travels frequently with Sheikh Mohammed, and the two are pictured together buying horses in Kentucky or cheering on their steeds at Ascot. When he has time, Sheikh Mohammed collects Haya at work, riding her private elevator to the ground floor and then walking her hand-in-hand to his Mercedes.

The two wives lead separate existences. Hind, whose photograph has never been shown publicly, oversees the upbringing of her children and a smattering of orphans she has adopted in the name of charity.

Sheikh Mohammed's children range from one-year-old Aljalila, born in 2007, Haya's only child as of this writing, to Manal, probably the oldest, in her late twenties or early thirties. A few bear mention.

Rashid, the eldest son of Sheikha Hind, has a difficult relationship with the family. As the oldest son born into wedlock, he was a natural candidate to take over for his father as Dubai's crown prince.[12] Like his father, Rashid is a champion endurance rider and racehorse owner. But Sheikh Mohammed passed over his first son in 2008 and gave the crown prince title to the younger Hamdan. Neither was Rashid named deputy ruler, a title that went to the Dubai leader's third son, Maktoum. Sheikh Mohammed's decree naming his number two and three sons did not mention his first son, and the reasons behind Rashid's fall from favor are unclear. His father in the past had lavished him with public praise, once writing a poem in his honor titled, "Became, Oh Rashid, of the People a Leader." But Sheikh Mohammed's hopes for his son appear to have dimmed. In May 2008, young Rashid's home, a palatial villa in a walled compound in the city's Umm Suqeim section, was demolished without explanation. The trees, bushes, and driveway were torn up, the swimming pool filled in; the Japanese pagoda and garden bulldozed. One evening in June, I drove past the empty lot. Wires and pipes poked out of the groomed rubble where the mansion once stood. An Indian man who told me he once worked on the grounds said Sheikh Rashid's home had been razed because of a "royal family matter."

"Something bad happened?" I asked.

"Something bad happened," he said. He declined to elaborate. Rashid appeared to be spending the summer of 2008 in England. His personal Web site said he'd been given leadership of the UAE's Olympic committee.

Sheikh Hamdan bin Mohammed, the twenty-seven-year-old crown prince, is a simpler topic. In February 2008, his father named him Dubai's crown prince, the emirate's next ruler. Immediately, the family began to create a personality cult around the young prince. Hamdan's round face, with prominent ears and five-o'clock shadow, popped up on billboards around the city, a red-checked scarf wrapped around his head in the youthful style. His eyes stare skyward in the manner of Barack Obama. The signs carry no messages other than his moniker Fazza', and his Web address, www.fazza3.com. A smattering of Hamdan videos appear on YouTube, including one of the crown prince being mobbed in a Saudi shopping mall. The bemused prince, dressed in a knotted headscarf and brown robe, is surrounded, practically held captive, by a pack of squealing girls in black *abayas*. Perhaps they'd heard *Forbes* magazine ranked him number six among the world's Hottest Young Royals. Hamdan's female escort, sheathed totally in black except for a slit showing her eyes, glues herself to the crown prince's side and screams "Please get away from him!"

Another YouTube clip purports to display Hamdan's car collection. The jerky video rolls past a fleet of Rolls-Royces, a metallic blue Hummer, and a dozen of the world's rarest sports cars, each with single- and double-digit Dubai license plates that point to royal ownership.

Whatever the hype, Sheikh Hamdan is already taking on leadership duties. The twenty-seven-year-old sits at the head of the Executive Council, his father's cabinet. And he has begun making speeches on Sheikh Mohammed's behalf. Like his father, Hamdan graduated from Sandhurst. He then went on to study at the prestigious London School of Economics. He has agreed to head the alumni association at the Dubai School of Government, where the first master's degrees will be awarded in 2010.

Less is known about Maktoum bin Mohammed, named Dubai's deputy ruler. Maktoum, twenty-five, earned a bachelor's degree in business administration from the lackluster American University in Dubai, and went on to take leadership seminars offered by Harvard University and the Dubai School of Government. He's the ceremonial head of the governing body of Media City and Internet City.

Sheikh Mohammed's best-known daughter is Sheikha Maitha, a twenty-eight-year-old world tae kwon do champion who won a gold medal at the Asia Games in 2007. Maitha is still the most public of the children, comfortable giving interviews and being photographed by the press. In 2007, she traveled to southern Sudan as part of the Dubai Cares charity. Local papers ran front-page pictures of the young princess amid a swarm of Sudanese schoolchildren. Her arms were bared in a short-sleeved polo shirt, her olive face and black hair uncovered. *Forbes* magazine chose her as number seventeen of the world's twenty Hottest Young Royals.

Let Him Try

Maryam Behnam is an eighty-seven-year old Iranian woman, a diplomat under the shah. She fled Iran in 1979 and resettled in Dubai, landing UAE citizenship. She's written several books about her adventures. But she's never stopped thanking Sheikh Mohammed for his family's kindness in her hour of need. She prays that the ruler might attain his dreams for the city.

"How can you find someone with more love and passion for his country? He wants a cultured country. He wants to be a precious stone in a vicious ring, in the Middle East," Behnam says in an elegant voice soaked with pathos. "He's putting his entire life on this dream. Let him try. If you aim for the moon, you know, you may get some stars."

III

BLOWBACK: THE DOWNSIDE

11

LABOR PAINS

Melting Candles

THE CHILDREN OF Mother India form the largest and most important ethnic group in Dubai. As many as 1.9 million Indians live in the UAE[1]—about twice as many as the roughly 1 million Emiratis. Roughly half of those Indians live in Dubai, where they outnumber Emiratis by around seven to one.

India supplies much of Dubai's brainpower: many of the accountants who balance Dubai's books, the engineers who design its structures, and the chief financial officers who crunch the numbers. Indian doctors wield the scalpels and deliver the babies. Indian bankers and brokers count the cash and manage the portfolios. Indians own eleven thousand UAE businesses, more than any other group beside Emiratis.[2] They've controlled a wide swath of Dubai's retail sector since the 1940s.

India also supplies the largest portion of the UAE's 1.5 million construction workers. Their muscle is the lever that has raised Dubai up from the sands.

The word "hero" gets bandied around too often these days, especially in America. But these laborers are some of the most impressive people anywhere. They toil in difficult and dangerous conditions, but not for personal benefit. They live like ascetics in a city that claims ostentation as its brand. The scraps of cash they squeeze from their employers are immediately dispatched home. To their families, at least, they are heroes.

Dubai isn't kind to these men. It gives them no recognition. Their feats of construction don't mean they share the wealth their projects generate. Instead, Dubai hides them from view. Most eat and sleep in hardscrabble labor camps in the desert, with a distant view of the skyline that they've sacrificed so much to build.

The laborers who build Dubai aren't just Indian. They come from Pakistan, Nepal, Bangladesh, China, Sri Lanka, North Korea, and a few other places. They earn salaries measured against those in their home markets, just enough to entice a man to leave his wife and children to toil sixty-hour weeks in the world's fiercest heat.

"They are like candles burning and melting to light others," says K.V. Shamsudeen, a counselor who deals with the financial problems of Dubai's Indian workers. "Love becomes money for their families. They say, 'My life is gone. Let them live in comfort.'"

The City of Gold

Dubai's biggest cluster of labor camps is labeled on maps as Al Muhaisnah 2. Everyone calls it Sonapur, the City of Gold in the Hindi language. Sonapur is Dubai's poorest neighborhood but, in a triumph of irony, its most important. The hundred thousand or so laborers who sleep in the hundreds of company camps are the men who make Dubai run. They are the construction workers building bridges and skyscrapers. They are the cooks and cleaners, the men who maintain Dubai's elevators and air-conditioning systems, who tidy offices and polish floors. They drive the trucks that deliver the food and goods the city consumes. They fix cars. They guard the gated communities and troll for shoplifters at the mall. They are the slaughterhouse men who kill sheep, cattle, and chickens, and they're the supermarket butchers who cleave those carcasses into steaks and chops. If Sonapur were to shut down—if its residents went on strike or some cataclysm befell it—Dubai would cease to function.

Sonapur lies in a far corner of Dubai reserved for refuse. Its northern border is hemmed by the city dump's hills of garbage, which give it a satirical mountain backdrop. At the very heart of the square-mile district is an old cemetery with thousands of graves marked only by bricks standing on end. To Americans, Sonapur might resemble the shanty-towns that ring the *maquiladora* plants on the Mexican side of the U.S. border.

The term labor camp, as it is used in Dubai, comes from the days when laborers lived in tents and trailers in the desert. Back then, the men rode to work packed like livestock in the back of trucks. Sheikh Moham-med personally banned the practice. These days, most camps are clusters of three-story buildings arranged around a central courtyard. They look like scruffy college dorms, with tin roofs, laundry lines draped with cov-eralls, and portable air conditioners poking from the walls. Toilets, kitch-ens, and bedrooms are communal. Men sleep in narrow bunks, four to eight in a room that would comfortably sleep two.

Sonapur is filthy. Most streets are unpaved. Talcum-like moon dust covers the ground. Every evening, when the cavalcade of labor buses roars back into the neighborhood, all of Sonapur is engulfed in a dust storm. The buses lurch over the hummocked dirt roads, headlights stabbing through the murk, delivering exhausted workers to showers, supper, and sleep.

Sonapur, like the rest of Dubai, has a sewage problem. The city pro-duces more sewage than it can process. But Sonapur lacks the clout to do anything about it, so the black sludge flows in the streets and camps. At mealtimes, the pungent aroma of curry vies with the stench of human waste. In October 2008, I photographed a sewage-inundated camp run by the ETA Ascon Group, a conglomerate jointly owned by Dubai's al-Ghurair Group and Hong Kong-based Amana Investments. Fetid sewage boiled up from an overflowing septic tank and formed an algae-fringed pond in the camp courtyard. The black waters lapped at the very door-steps of hundreds of residents, just inches from the shoes they'd left outside.

Standards of living vary greatly from camp to camp, as do pay rates and benefits. The Al Bakhit General Contracting camp is small by Sonapur standards: just two low-slung concrete bunkhouses with cor-rugated asbestos roofing. It looks like a seedy Route 66 motel court. Each eight-foot by eight-foot room sleeps four to six of Al Bakhit's la-borers, electricians, and masons—about two hundred in all. The camp lies in smelling distance of a sewage lake, but feels salubrious. There is a shade tree, and the clean-swept brick courtyard is sprayed with water to keep the dust down. It's not one of the better camps in Sonapur—there is no recreation hall or staff canteen—but it's less crowded than the giant camps and a short walk from the grocery store.

Rajesh is a twenty-four-year-old native of the southern Indian state of Kerala who's been living at the camp since he was nineteen. He's well built and fastidious, with coffee skin and a neat mustache. He's also shy and doesn't want his last name used. Rajesh lives with three others in a tidy room with a lumpy linoleum floor and a window privacy-pasted with Arabic newspaper. The yellowed newsprint mutes the sunlight to a pleasant apricot hue. When I enter, Rajesh picks up an orange juice bottle filled with water and offers me a drink.

"My father came to Dubai more than thirty years ago. He worked here for twenty-three years," he says. He died of a heart attack when Rajesh was sixteen. That meant Rajesh, the oldest son, would take his father's role in Dubai. His first job paid just $160 a month, or $1.30 per hour, in a country where the average wage is $2,100 a month. But that's the basic salary for Al Bakhit's laborers and helpers. This rises to as much as $275 for an experienced electrician. The salary comes with accommodation at the Al Bakhit camp, but not meals. A stack of cooking pots sits in Rajesh's room, with a forty-pound sack of rice.

A short stroll away lies the labor hostel run by Japan's Taisei Corporation. The difference is immediately apparent. The five hundred men building roads, overpasses, and roundabouts in some of Dubai's most prestigious projects—the Palm Jebel Ali and Dubailand included—live in a solid complex with new windows and large, high-ceilinged rooms. They still sleep four or five to a room—bed space is at a premium in Sonapur—but the lowest-paid laborer gets $190 per month. The salary includes three meals a day. As soon as the workers are done eating breakfast and bussed to their jobs, cooks prepare lunch in the camp cafeteria and Taisei delivers it to sites across Dubai. Dinner is served when the men stream back after dark.

Taisei's hostel is one of the better ones. But since Sheikh Mohammed's 2006 tour of Sonapur, when he shuttered more than a hundred camps that the Dubai government described as rife with vermin and unfit for humans, there's been a flurry of building activity. The grimmest blocks have been demolished. Others are being renovated, with workers fitting new windows and doors. New hostels look like college campuses, with a dozen or more apartment blocks linked by shaded walkways. One boasted ornamental cupolas with red tiled roofs and even a few date palms.

Friday is the only day off for 98 percent of Sonapur residents. It also happens to be the day the city all but halts bus service to the neighborhood. Residents believe the transportation cutoff is a move to prevent laborers, known in the UAE as bachelors, from spoiling the atmosphere in Dubai. The few Friday buses are overfilled before they reach Sonapur's center. They pass through without stopping. Sonapur's laborers are unable to visit the tourist and shopping destinations they built.

"They don't want bachelors in Dubai," Rajesh says. He likes to visit his uncle's room in Deira, but it takes too much energy to get there. He spends Fridays washing, ironing, and watching Indian movies.

Most laborers only see Dubai's marvels as they barrel to work in their white Ashok Leyland buses. Rajesh says he's glimpsed the Burj Al Arab from the highway. The man sitting on the bunk next to him, a forty-six-year-old named Hanuman, says he's never laid eyes on the Burj. That's like a Parisian saying he's never seen the Eiffel Tower.

"I never leave the camp. Why should I go out? My life is here," the pockmarked man says with a smile. "I only leave Sonapur when I go to the airport to go back to India." He's the camp cleaner.

Rajesh is the point man for an Indian family striving to rise into the middle class. He sends his widowed mother $250 per month, with which she manages family expenses. Rajesh paid for his brother Radeesh to graduate with an MBA from Calicut University. And he pays tuition for his brother Ranju, who just entered university. Rajesh will never attend college himself. He won't leave Dubai until his two brothers find jobs and the family is stable. That's why, when he does spend a Friday wandering the city, he goes window-shopping. "I don't want to spend money here," he says. "My brothers are studying. They need this money."

Rajesh, like most laborers, gets two months' paid leave every two years. But the workaholic Keralite stayed in Dubai last summer, spending his vacation pay learning how to drive. By summer's end, he'd landed a commercial driving license and a job with a German firm that installs high-end flooring. He's raised his salary to $680 a month. Rajesh plans to pay his brother's university fees and still sock away a nest egg for when he returns to India, perhaps in three years.

Rajesh's story isn't typical. He speaks English, which allowed me to interview him easily and increases his salary. And he got invaluable help from his uncle, who has lived in Dubai for thirty years and handled his visa paperwork. Rajesh was able to circumvent the labor recruitment sharks who typically charge $4,000 to place Indians in Dubai jobs.

More typical is the story of Hanuman, named for the Hindu monkey god. Hanuman's skin is nearly black, his wavy hair streaked gray. He wears an open-necked blue cotton shirt that has been sun-bleached nearly white. A purple-and-green checked *lunghi* wraps his waist. Hanuman has toiled in the Gulf for sixteen years: five in Saudi Arabia, six in Oman, five in Dubai. He spent his early years repaying the Indian labor agent who recruited him. His next years' earnings bankrolled the weddings of his brother and sister. Only then was he able to return to his native Hyderabad and take a wife. Hanuman now has two daughters and a son. He supports the family, but they're not likely to rise from poverty. Despite his experience Hanuman earns just $260 a month, including overtime. But he must feed himself on that salary, and inflation has cut into his earnings. In Saudi Arabia, where his company provided food and accommodation, he sent his family nearly $200 a month. A decade later he sends his wife and children only $100.

Hanuman hasn't saved a single rupee. Everything goes to the wife and children he barely knows. While his earning power has dropped, salaries have risen in India. He says he could probably earn as much at home. Many Indians are leaving Dubai to find work in India. "Why don't you go home and live with your family?" I ask.

"In India I can't guarantee I'll work every day. One day I might work as a cleaner, another day as a plumber. Here I have guaranteed work every day. I need to take care of my children. That's why I stay."

He smiles as he talks and his white teeth flash, but his message isn't cheerful. "I'm not happy here, but what can I do? Soon I'll have to pay for my daughters' weddings." Hanuman won't go home unless Dubai forces him, it is clear. He's at a loss for words. He looks at the man next to him, who articulates his thoughts: "We're giving our lives for their happiness."

Labor of Love

C. P. Mathew is a social worker who deals with the men Dubai grinds up and spits out. He volunteers for a charity called Valley of Love. It's not a well-funded outfit. His office is on the third floor of a grubby commercial building in Dubai's blue-collar Al Ghusais neighborhood, above a restaurant called Public Cook.

Mathew, a baby-faced man with the serene manner of a priest, sits at a glass-top table with a laptop computer. He scrolls through a series of snapshots and tells a story about each man.

Here is Raneesh Raj, a thirty-two-year-old electrician, who, like Mathew and many Dubaians, hails from Kerala. The picture shows Raj sitting in his hospital bed. He's a burly, dark-skinned man with white teeth and a brushy mustache, and a healthy mop of wavy black hair. But he's only got one leg.

Six months earlier, Raj was winching a giant spool of electrical wire to the twenty-third story of a half-built skyscraper. The cable hauling the spool couldn't handle the weight. It snapped and somehow wrapped around Raj's left leg. The falling spool yanked his leg off. Raj told friends that he watched his limb being dragged away.

When Mathew visited Raj in the hospital, the electrician had recovered from the wound but was a panicked man. "He was losing his job. He couldn't support his family. He didn't know what the future would bring."

Raj's company did the right thing. It gave the electrician a $30,000 disability payment, even though it didn't have to, by law. The Valley of Love arranged for the cash to be deposited in an Indian bank account paying a high fixed interest rate. Raj was able to buy a house, and he and his family will be able to live off the settlement. In October 2008, he was in Jaipur, India, being fitted for a prosthetic leg.

Mathew taps his finger and another picture fills his laptop screen: four plywood coffins holding corpses for shipment to India. One of them belongs to a laborer who killed himself. He's going to Lucknow. The other three are headed for Hyderabad. Mathew says at least one was killed in a road accident. He's not sure about the other two.

Click. Here is the face of a dazed man. His blank eyes are wide, and his jaw hangs open, a patch of spittle in the corner. A plastic tube runs into a hole in his neck. "He's in a vegetable state," says Mathew. "His company isn't cooperating, so we will sue them on behalf of the family."

"I get a lot of these," he says.

The man's name is Bhawarlal Mulla Ram. He's fifty and worked as a mason for a Dubai-based construction firm named Sun Engineering. He was helping pour a second-story concrete slab in January 2007 when the framework holding it aloft collapsed. Bhawarlal fell with it. Another man was killed but Bhawarlal survived—in a manner of speaking. His injuries include severe brain damage.

Bhawarlal had lain in Rashid Hospital for nearly two years when I found him in the long-term neurology ward. The ward is crammed with a dozen contorted men, nearly all with feeding tubes protruding from their throats or noses, and bags of urine hanging on their bedsides. Just one of the patients can speak, and only a few slurred words. These men were healthy when they were either struck by vehicles or hurt while building Dubai. All but two are Indian.

Bhawarlal did not look comfortable in his hospital bed. He lay with his head turned to the wall, panting. Sweat covered his cheeks and matted his hair. His eyes darted. He appeared to be under nonstop stress. "Hello, Bhawarlal," I said. He clenched his fists and cocked his wrists, both arms pressed so tightly to his chest that nurses keep them wrapped with towels. Every now and then his mouth released a gurgling sound.

Mathew shows pictures of Bhawarlal's family in Rajasthan, India. Here is his wife, grandmother, and mother, each with a sad face, sitting in colorful saris in front of a concrete shack in a dirt yard. Bhawarlal's teen son stands to the side, in shirt and trousers. Since his father stopped sending checks, the boy has left school to work.

The family is too poor to provide the constant care he'll need for the rest of his life. Mathew says it's worthwhile to send him home, if there is money for support. A family's affection sometimes brings a person out of a coma. But Sun Engineering hasn't given a thing to its shattered mason or his family.

"They've got no more remittance, no more support," Mathew says.

"The company refuses to pay anything?" I ask.

"There is no law," Mathew explains. "No one can force them to pay a dirham."

So he's stuck in the neurology ward. Sun Engineering's personnel manager, T. V. Ismayil, told me that Sun has made no disability payment to the family to compensate the loss of its breadwinner. Ismayil says there is a limit to what the company can provide. He would agree to pay $6,000 for treatment in India, but he feels Bhawarlal is better off in Dubai, where the company's medical insurance covers his treatment. "We cannot pay his wife or son. We don't know who his legal heir is," Ismayil says. "The company cannot take responsibility for a family for their whole lives."

Mathew says he's been reduced to visiting the grimy Sun Engineering labor camp in Sonapur to collect donations from Bhawarlal's co-workers, among the most impoverished men in Dubai.

Falling to Death

Construction work is dangerous. Especially in Dubai. The city has six thousand building sites and just sixteen inspectors.[3] That leaves safety precautions up to individual companies. Standards range from sensible to negligent, reflecting the practices of contractors' home countries.

Hundreds of workers die on the job each year, but the exact numbers are unclear. In 2004, *Construction Week* magazine reported 880 workers died in the UAE, most of them in Dubai.[4] The Dubai government reported just thirty-four site deaths that year.[5]

A construction safety trainer told me that some eight hundred workers fell to their deaths in the UAE in 2007, more than twice as many as in the United States. He described falls as the city's chief on-the-job killer. Sixty percent of the UAE's falling deaths happen despite victims wearing safety harnesses. The laborers perish while dangling from a rope. The safety expert, who asked that his name not be used, says Dubai's rescue services aren't skilled or quick enough to reach the dangling men before they die from what is called suspension trauma. Blood pools in their legs and keeps oxygen from reaching the brain. They lose consciousness, and they're dead in under an hour. It's the condition that killed Jesus on the cross.

The lack of training extends to the laborers themselves. The men erecting skyscrapers tend to come from farming villages in India's poorest corners, places where the chief pursuits are raising goats and rice. "The sad fact here is that workers are expendable," the expert said. "These are really unskilled guys and they get into really stupid accidents."

Another problem for Indian laborers is kidney failure. Working in the Dubai heat is punishing enough, but workers don't drink enough water. Their kidneys bear the consequences. Mathew cites a survey of Gulf returnees to his home state of Kerala that says 70 percent come home with kidney problems. Kidney failure is especially frequent among skyscraper crews, because toilets are far away on the ground level. Those toiling on the upper stories don't want to take time to go all the way down to urinate, so they don't drink enough.

The Debt Trap

The AM radio show is called *Lifeline*. The host is fast-talking K.V. Shamsudheen, a sixty-one-year-old investment manager, who speaks in a blur of South Indian Malayalam peppered with English. Shamsudheen's studio guest today is yet another Indian immigrant in trouble. The man says he and his wife are grappling with $35,000 in debt on a combined income of $2,300 a month.

"He has six credit cards! His wife has seven! They're not going to be in a position to repay this—ever," Shamsudheen says.

The man appeals for kind souls in Radioland to help him repay his debts and keep him from the Dubai jail. Then Shamsudheen hands his countryman a pair of scissors. Still on the air, the debtor slices each of his credit cards in half and promises to buy only with cash.

This is talk radio, Dubai style.

Shamsudheen is a small man with gold-rimmed glasses and neat hair. His smile is persistent, his manner precise. He's a campaigner against debt, especially the predatory lending he holds responsible for sending so many Indians to the Dubai jail. More than 40 percent of Dubai's prisoners are debtors.[6]

Dubai's economic boom has enriched huge numbers of Indians, but not those in the lower echelons. Many have also seen their financial status fall over the past decade. Shamsudheen blames the ease with which one could borrow money and get credit cards. He uses his broadcasts to extol his micro-savings plans, telling workers to set aside 50 dirhams— $14—a month and invest it in Indian mutual funds available from his investment company.

The debt trap starts in India, where, as mentioned earlier, recruiting agents charge up to $4,000 to place men in Dubai jobs. The agents often exaggerate the salary, which encourages emigrants to borrow their recruiting fees from usurious lenders. Once they arrive in Dubai, reality sets in. They're locked in debt bondage at half the salary they expected.

"They've taken a loan that's growing daily," Shamsudheen says.

"They can't go back to India. They can't repay the loan. They can't even pay a substantial amount."

Low-paid workers without company housing pack themselves into plywood cubicles inside illegally subdivided homes. In August 2008, a fire broke out in one of these houses in Deira. Authorities sorting through the wreckage found at least five hundred men living in a house built for a single family. It was a warren of makeshift rooms, each of which housed as many as twenty-five men. Firemen pulled eleven corpses from the smoking ruin, those of a Bangladeshi and ten Indians. Afterward, the Dubai government banned multiple families from sharing houses, and inspectors chased "bachelors" from homes across the city.

By the time the economic boom petered out at the end of 2008, Dubai was becoming untenable for anyone who wasn't rich. For many, the one-house, one-family law made it impossible to stay. A typical one-bedroom apartment rented for $1,400 per month. That's an outrageous amount in a city where the minimum monthly salary is just over $100.

Shamsudheen advises Indians to go home. It's easy to get $150-a-month jobs in India now. Housing is cheaper, the standard of living better for a low-wage worker. "Why come here? Before you leave India, think about it. Make sure you get a better income."

Damaged Relations

Migrant workers have formed a majority of the UAE population since the 1960s. After the country hit oil, the thriving economy allowed citizens to coast into high-pay, low-effort government jobs, while hiring immigrants to do just about everything else.

Emiratis have since seen their numbers diluted in a sea of migrants. The foreign workforce now scares people. Emiratis worry that laborers will organize unions and make political demands, even form terror cells. Construction laborers since 2005 have held dozens of short strikes over unpaid wages or bad living conditions. As noted earlier, in November 2007, a strike by forty thousand construction workers halted work for more than a week at the city's most prestigious sites, including the new airport terminal and the Burj Dubai.

The strikes led Dubai Police Chief Dhahi Khalfan and others to describe migrant workers as a national security threat. In 2008, the UAE began mulling over a six-year visa limit that would help it control the country's demographic makeup. The law would reduce the dominance of Indians while forcing a rotation in the workforce to prevent immigrants from settling long-term or organizing political groups.

All this has damaged Indians' once-close relations with their Emirati hosts. Indians' status has slipped since the death of Sheikh Rashid, who openly courted Indian traders, seeking their advice and friendship. The archives of Pakistani photographer Noor Ali Rashid show Sheikh Rashid, Sheikh Maktoum, and other royals visiting homes of prominent Indians to wish them well on the Hindu festival of Diwali. That tradition has ended, the goodwill evaporated. Sheikh Mohammed seems keen to court expatriate Arabs, and these newcomers now lord it over longtime Indians in Dubai's stratified society.

Indians' contributions aren't recognized. Workers' rights and welfare are ignored, says Venu Rajamony, the Indian consul in Dubai.

Rajamony rejects suggestions that the labor strikes have anything to do with political demands. The UAE could halt them by instituting a decent minimum wage rather than the market minimum of just over $100 a month, or about 55 U.S. cents an hour. Rajamony says it should be around $300, the minimum monthly salary the Indian government has set for its housemaids working in the UAE.

"Workers deserve a much better deal. Whenever there is cost cutting, what is sacrificed is wages of workers and their welfare," Rajamony says. "Allowance is always given to rises in the price of steel and cement. The wages of the labor force is probably the smallest component of the overall bill of any contractor or developer. Wages can be easily increased without too much burden."

Dubai's leadership has been deeply embarrassed by the coverage of its labor camps and working conditions. Among the city's policy makers there is recognition that government has failed to come up with a workable policy on labor, but no one will discuss it openly. Sheikh Mohammed is said to be concerned about laborers' well-being, but he and his advisory team are averse to bad publicity. They don't address the problem because they don't want to be seen as responding to outside pressure.

At one point, Sheikh Mohammed was going to tour labor camps and publicly thank migrants for their role in building Dubai. But the boss's advisers feared the gesture would backfire in the press. In 2006, the American news show *20/20* skewered Sheikh Mohammed for treating his horses better than the workers building his city. The criticism stung. Negative coverage also damages Dubai's reputation as a tourist destination, thereby taking a direct toll on the economy. So the Dubai leadership decided to proceed carefully, by making improvements first.

Wages haven't budged, but conditions in many camps have been upgraded. Dubai is building a slew of labor hostels on its southwest side, near the new airport. The Labor Ministry is forcing companies to pay salaries electronically, and workers are beginning to withdraw funds with ATM cards. Health insurance will soon be mandatory. For the past few years, outdoor work in the searing July and August afternoons has been banned, although many companies disregard those restrictions.[7] The Labor Ministry has also banned—but not effectively halted—the standard practice of withholding passports, which holds workers in virtual bondage.

But labor policy remains a muddle. Officially, the Labor Ministry takes the lead. But other ministries also get involved, as does the Dubai government. The parties don't agree. In 2008 Sheikh Mohammed replaced the labor minister in his cabinet reshuffle.

U.S. and EU free trade negotiators have pressed the UAE to bring its labor laws up to international standards and drop its ban on trade unions. And New York-based Human Rights Watch issued several damning reports on labor conditions in the UAE. Its 2006 report "Building Towers, Cheating Workers" described labor conditions as verging on slavery. "The UAE has abdicated almost entirely from its responsibility to protect workers' rights," the report said. There was no serious response in the report from the UAE or Dubai authorities.

The head of Human Rights Watch's Middle East reporting, Sarah Leah Whitson, lambasted the government in a public press conference in a Dubai hotel. Still Dubai authorities said nothing, although federal officials responded by describing the improvements mentioned above. Inside the Dubai government, however, the report divided those who said Dubai should meet with Human Rights Watch and lay out its improvement plans and those who said it should not. The rights group made it clear that its report would be balanced if it contained Dubai's response. Again Sheikh Mohammed's advisers decided not to talk. It was seen as bowing to foreign pressure. The issue continues to fester.

In 1990, the Dubai-Abu Dhabi highway, later renamed Sheikh Zayed Road, cut a lonely swath through the desert in central Dubai. This shot, taken from the top of the World Trade Centre, shows the Hilton Apartments and three other buildings that stood alone amid camel grazing land. *Dubai Municipality*

The same view in 2009 shows the desert covered in twin walls of skyscrapers lining the ten-lane Sheikh Zayed Road. The old Hilton Apartments are still there, now with a Dubai Metro stop in front. The Emirates Towers rise behind it, with the needle-like spire of the Burj Dubai in the background. *Kamran Jebreili*

When George Chapman took this photo of the Dubai creek in the 1950s, the town bore no trace of modernity. While other countries in the region shot rockets into space or made films, Dubai was electricity-less, its ships sailing under wind power. Homes were cooled by breezes funneled indoors by the ubiquitous square wind towers seen rising above the mud-and-coral houses. *George Chapman*

An aerial shot of Dubai circa 1955. Prior to the 1960 dredging, the creek was a shallow tidal wash choked with silt and difficult to navigate. This photo clearly shows the town's three original neighborhoods: Shindagha in the foreground on the beachfront, site of the ancestral Maktoum homes; the Iranian-themed Bastakiya on the right-hand side; and Deira, the bustling commercial district, across the creek. *Media Prima, Dubai*

In 2007, neighborhoods along the bustling Dubai creek remained the city's most traditional, with wind towers and minarets still crowding the skyline. The Dubai dhow port still sheltered ships trading with Iran, India and East Africa, just as it had for more than a century. But in 2009, Dubai said it would move the freewheeling dhow trade outside the creek for security reasons. *Kamran Jebreili*

Sheikh Rashid bin Saeed al-Maktoum in his ceremonial robes, traditional *khanjar* dagger at his waist, circa 1960. Rashid was a determined man, driven to make Dubai the envy of the world. *Media Prima, Dubai*

Sheikh Rashid's tolerance of other faiths was a key part of Dubai's pragmatism. To this day, Dubai welcomes non-Muslims to live and work—and worship—in its confines. Here, Sheikh Rashid greets local Christian leaders. *Media Prima, Dubai*

Sheikh Zayed bin Sultan al-Nahyan overthrew his brother in 1966 and took control of Abu Dhabi. Upon UAE independence in 1971, he governed the federation of seven sheikhdoms until his death in 2004. Zayed was a true Bedouin chief who achieved legendary status long before he died, overseeing Abu Dhabi's rise to wealth and distributing much of it to his subjects. *Emirates News Agency, WAM*

Sheikh Zayed (right) takes coffee with Dubai's Sheikh Maktoum bin Rashid al-Maktoum, in this 1979 photo. Both men sit barefoot on the floor in the Bedouin fashion. Sheikh Maktoum held formal leadership of Dubai from the 1990 death of his father, Sheikh Rashid, until his own death in 2006. Sheikh Maktoum was a mild-mannered horse enthusiast who had little passion for governance. He left most of the affairs of state to his ambitious younger brother Mohammed. *Emirates News Agency, WAM*

Sheikh Mohammed bin Rashid al-Maktoum gets ready for takeoff in a trainer aircraft, during military schooling in Italy in the 1980s. The third of Sheikh Rashid's four sons, Sheikh Mohammed is most like his father. He acted as Dubai's de facto ruler for more than a decade before taking formal leadership in 2006. *Media Prima, Dubai*

Sheikh Mohammed is a helicopter pilot, a poet, a big game fisherman and hunter, and one of the world's most prolific buyers of thoroughbreds. He rides his horses in grueling endurance races, as seen here. *Emirates News Agency, WAM*

Sheikh Mohammed closed Dubai's roads in 2007 so he could lure President George W. Bush to his boyhood home in Shindagha. Here, the two men are greeted by Emirati girls bearing *oud* incense, just before Bush declared Dubai was "a model" for the region and Sheikh Mohammed "an inspiration." *Emirates News Agency, WAM*

The Burj Dubai, at 2,684 feet (818 meters) is the tallest structure ever erected by mankind, nearly twice as high as the Empire State Building. The half-mile-tall skyscraper sways like a reed in high winds and burns as much electricity as a small city. *Kamran Jebreili*

The arch-shaped Gate Building is the centerpiece of the Dubai International Financial Centre, home to the Nasdaq Dubai stock exchange and most of the international banks and brokerages that have flocked to the city. The financial district is governed by laws modeled on those in the City of London. *Kamran Jebreili*

Emiratis look over the latest Rolls-Royce at the 2007 Dubai Auto Show. The UAE is one of the world's most lucrative markets for makers of the most expensive cars. Auto sales are spurred by the intense car culture in Dubai, as well as the high rate of crashes. *Kamran Jebreili*

The Dubai Marina was an empty patch of low-lying coastal desert in 2002. Seven years later it looked more like Hong Kong than the Middle East, jammed with apartment towers and hotels catering to the global jet set. (The buildings on the left in the bottom photo are part of the Jumeirah Beach Residence, the world's largest single-phase housing complex, with thirty-six towers built simultaneously.) *Kamran Jebreili*

The man-made Palm Jumeirah's seventeen fronds are crammed cheek-to-jowl with mansions, each with a swimming pool and stretch of private beach. The construction of the Palm, seen in this 2007 photo, kicked off one of the world's most fanciful real estate binges. It added an asset worth tens of billions of dollars to Dubai's economy, while altering Gulf currents and fogging the waters. *Nakheel*

The Burj Al Arab's iconic sail shape stems from architect Tom Wright's design criterion: "If you can draw it in five seconds and everyone recognizes it." *Mike Charlton*

Dubai's luxury apartment towers—and everything else in the city—are built by anonymous workers, mainly from India, who get no credit and little pay for their efforts. Laborers such as these work in some of the harshest conditions imaginable. At the end of their shifts they crowd onto buses that ferry them to their quarters in crowded desert camps. *Kamran Jebreili*

A laborer toils on a Dubai skyscraper using simple hand tools. *John Hollingsworth*

Police and towtrucks clear away some of the 250 wrecked vehicles that crashed in heavy fog on March 11, 2008. Hundreds were injured and at least four killed in the series of crashes, caused by speeding and reckless driving in low visibility. The pileup was a boon for car dealers, who reported a surge in sales. The National *newspaper, Abu Dhabi*

12

SEX AND SLAVERY

$400, Your Place or Mine

WEDNESDAY NIGHT AT the Rattle Snake and the bar is jumping. A Filipino cover band is romping through "Georgia on My Mind," the lead singer bending backward and roaring like Otis Redding. At the worn mahogany bar, men trade pink chits for bottles of Sol beer. The décor is Old West, a hangman's noose next to a façade labeled Court House—perhaps useful for the temporary marriages Islam allows.

There will be many temporary marriages tonight. A hundred women are on parade. The Rattle Snake, as its name implies, is a whorehouse.

Here is Elena, the pouty Romanian. Her curving figure is packed into matching white jeans and jacket, platinum-blond hair yanked back in a ponytail. She leans against the wall, smoking a thin cigarette with exaggerated impatience. Her clothes, including her silver Playboy bunny belt buckle, glow bright purple in the bar's black light. Next to her stands Lana, twenty-four, a slinky Ukrainian in a black top of gossamer gauze. Lana sips Red Bull from a straw and flicks stray locks of hair from her face. Her overdaubed lipstick hides a cold sore. Lana is enthusiastic and blunt. "You want sex? I am ready!" Perhaps it's because she's only in Dubai for two weeks on a tourist visa. Or maybe it's the Red Bull talking. She says it'll cost me 1,500 dirhams, $400, her place or mine. When I beg off, she says, "Why not take two girls?" and tilts her head at the Romanian, who shoots me a look of disgust.

Here is Aisulu from Kyrgyzstan. Her round face with its smiling almond eyes speaks of nomads, yurts, and snowcapped mountains. She wears a black turtleneck that highlights small breasts and a tidy figure. Every speck of lint on her sweater glows in the black light, as does her pendant of the Sanskrit letter Om. When I point it out, she tilts her head alluringly, clasps her hands in Buddhist prayer and hums, "Ohmmm" and then erupts in laughs. "Like yoga," she says, laughing some more. Aisulu has no day job. She watches TV in an apartment in Deira, waiting for sunset. She became a prostitute after her husband died in a car crash. She supports a twelve-year-old daughter back in Bishkek.

Marketing methods vary at the Rattle Snake. Here is a young woman in a green top stretched over a push-up bra. She circles the bar over and over, gazing at men from under the mop of brown hair hiding her eyes. After fifteen minutes watching her parade, a group of beery British men waves her over. She slithers her arm along the back of one of the men, rises on her toes, and plants a kiss on his ear. Soon they are holding hands.

The Rattle Snake is part of the Metropolitan Hotel, one of the city's oldest. When the low-rise complex opened in 1979, it was surrounded by camels grazing in the scrub. Now the Metropolitan sits in the shadow of the skyscrapers of the Business Bay district. It's owned by Dubai's Al Habtoor Group, a family business. The company Web site lists the VIPs who've spent the night, including U.S. President George H. W. Bush, Britain's Princess Anne, actors Jean-Claude Van Damme and Omar Sharif, golfer Greg Norman, and singer La Toya Jackson. The site invites hotel guests to "dance the night away with our live entertainment at the Rattle Snake."

Tonight's live entertainment includes a woman with shoulder-length blond hair who struts in a skimpy black dress that looks painted on, her neckline plunging to reveal a quarter of her rounded breasts. As she jiggles past, heads turn to watch her bare back. The lateral muscles pulse as she walks. She catches my eye and turns on a dime. In a flash her greenish eyes, set a bit too far apart above her big hawk's nose, are staring into mine. She squeezes my forearm.

"An American! Oh, wow! I love Americans," she gushes. Her face shines with delight. She whispers something into my ear that the band drowns out.

"How's life?" I ask. "Do you like your work?"

"I enjoy it! Yes. Why not? It's fun," she says.

Her name is Rasha and she is from Iran. Not just anywhere in Iran but the Shiite holy city of Isfahan, the Paradise of Mosques, where the skyline revels in enchanting blue-green domes. Rasha has strayed further from social acceptability than anyone else in the bar. Iranian hookers are in high demand because they've got close cultural ties to Dubai, including their Muslim faith. "I come only for business," she says, wagging her finger. "I stay six months, then I go home."

She'll have to make a few changes in her appearance before returning to Isfahan. She'll don a modest *manteau* dress and, when the plane lands, draw her headscarf. She may even dye her hair back from its platinum blond.

I ask what she charges. "Depends," she says. "If you are a very nice man, pay me two thousand. Otherwise, pay me fifteen hundred—four hundred dollars."

For the past few years, the U.S. State Department labeled the UAE as one of the most lax places on earth when it comes to combating trafficking of women for prostitution, or the abuse of workers trapped in slave-like conditions.

The State Department estimated in 2006 that Dubai held some ten thousand victims of human trafficking. Women from Asia, Eastern Europe, and Africa sign contracts to work as maids, waitresses, and hairdressers. But when some of them arrive, employers seize their passports and force them to work, usually as prostitutes. Their suffering and exploitation hasn't been taken seriously by the government, at least not until recently. In 2006, the UAE passed an antitrafficking law, the first in the Middle East. It named an antitrafficking czar, Minister of State for Foreign Affairs Anwar Gargash, who has sworn to fight the abuses. I ask the women at the Rattle Snake about this.

Janet, a Russian woman in a baggy T-shirt and tights, is as sweet as can be—until I tell her I'm a journalist who wants to know about trafficking. She undergoes a drastic mood swing. "Every woman who has slept with more than two men is a prostitute," she says venomously. "So what do you want?"

When I reply, "Actually, some women are forced into this," she practically spits.

"That is a fairy tale. It's not true. No one is that naïve," she says. Her friend cautions her in Russian and Janet calms down. "Okay, a few years ago, people didn't understand. Now they do."

Janet then explains that she works in a travel agency on Sheikh Zayed Road, not far away. She comes to the bar to moonlight for extra cash. No pimp controls her movement or shares her earnings. She pays the same thirteen-dollar cover charge that I did, and she often buys her own beer. If she doesn't get picked up within an hour or two, she shrugs and goes home. She can't stay late because she's got to get up for work.

She waves her hand at the women pouring through the bar's front door in all manner of outlandish costumes. "None of us would be here if we didn't want to be," she says.

Shattered Lives

I met a pair of trafficked women in Dubai at a private shelter called City of Hope. Both refused to be interviewed, but through volunteers at the shelter and its Emirati-American director, Sharla Musabih, I heard their stories.

The shelter is a hard-luck place, home to broken women doing their best to get over traumatic abuse. At the same time, they struggle to navigate the slow and complex Dubai legal system, seeking permission to leave the country. The two dozen women at the shelter come from Eastern Europe, Iran, India, Britain, and former Soviet Central Asia. Most come from Ethiopia. Few of the Ethiopians speak anything other than Amharic, and, until coming to Dubai, they knew little beyond rural subsistence. People from such uneducated backgrounds are easily manipulated.

One Ethiopian woman at the shelter signed on for a three-year stint as a Dubai housemaid. She wound up enslaved on a farm in the desert. The woman escaped after seven months of brutal work, for which she went unpaid.[1]

A nineteen-year-old Moldovan woman named Ivana came to Dubai in 2004 with a group of young women who signed on for waitressing jobs.[2] On arrival, the women were driven to Sharjah and locked in an apartment, their passports confiscated. There Ivana reported that a Russian man and a Turkish woman confronted them with slaps on the face and a threatening lecture. The two were pimps. The pimps told the Moldovans they were being dragooned to work as hookers until they'd repaid the debts they'd amassed.

"We've just paid for your airline tickets. You'd better pay us back," the Turkish woman threatened.[3] The prostitution ring sent them to three-star hotels in Dubai and Sharjah, where the Moldovans had sex with customers who'd made arrangements. Ivana described a special fear of Arab clients. Many raped her with cruelty that seemed to stem from hatred. It's a common complaint. After a year, Ivana ran off with one of her customers and escaped the ring. She moved in with the man for a while, but he got deported. She took up with another man, who brutalized her, then disappeared. She gave birth to two children along the way. With nowhere else to turn, Ivana moved into the shelter in 2007.

Musabih has a long list of such cases. There are the two young Uzbeks who dashed out of the brothel where they were held captive, bounding down the street in leopard-print halter tops and gold disco boots. They hailed a cab to the airport, where security bundled them into black *abayas* and called City of Hope. There is the nineteen-year-old from Belarus, enslaved in a Dubai brothel for four years by a Russian man, who forced her to perform sex on hundreds of men—even while pregnant. In 2007, after giving birth to a son, the Belarusian managed to weaken the bars on her window and escape. She spent four months at the shelter before returning home.

The Indian consulate in Dubai also operates a shelter. Its location is secret. It receives as many as forty women a month, many of them trafficked prostitutes. Victims who turn up are sometimes dropped off by a sympathetic John, or they escape by leaping out a window. Women have been known to turn up with sprained ankles and other injuries from their leaps to freedom.

The circumstances described by trafficking victims have a similar ring. Gangs operating in home countries lure women and girls as young as fifteen to Dubai on false pretenses. A pimp or madam meets them at the airport, seizes their passports, locks them away in a brothel, and forces them to recoup a debt, up to $10,000 each. Once they've earned enough, the women might win freedom, or they might be sold like slaves to another pimp or two until finally running away.

The State Department report quotes a twenty-three-year-old Kyrgyz woman named Alexia: "I answered a newspaper advertisement for a Russian-speaking waitress in the United Arab Emirates. When my plane landed, a man took me to an apartment where I met a dozen other women. I asked them if they all worked at the restaurant as waitresses. They laughed and one said: 'Restaurant? You're not going to work at a restaurant! You'll find out tonight where you are working!' I was held in Dubai for six months and prostituted by the traffickers. I met a man from Moscow who helped me to escape to the Kyrgyz Embassy."

The report says women from Uzbekistan, Kyrgyzstan, Ukraine, Russia, Kazakhstan, Armenia, Azerbaijan, Ethiopia, Somalia, Uganda, India, Pakistan, China, the Philippines, Iraq, Iran, and Morocco are trafficked to the UAE on false pretenses and prostituted. The UAE did not demonstrate vigorous law enforcement or victim protection efforts, the State Department says.

Fighting such crimes is tough in the UAE. Diplomats prefer to place escaped victims at shelters rather than involving the police, because the lawmen—most of them imported from conservative Sudan and Yemen—usually jail them as criminals. "The police just don't get it," Musabih says. "They take these poor women and stack them in police headquarters."

Investigators face problems of jurisdiction and a lack of will to prosecute UAE citizens. When a foreign embassy reports the arrival of a trafficked woman to Dubai police, an investigator may find that the Emirati citizen who sponsored her work visa lives in the emirate of Ajman.[4] The Dubai authorities tell the diplomat to pursue the case there. But in Ajman, police send the diplomat back to Dubai, saying that's where the crime took place. The Emirati accomplice, who may be using his sponsorship quota to bring women into the country, evades prosecution by denying knowledge of the crime, usually reporting that the women ran away.

The victims don't usually speak English or Arabic and rarely care to spend months in the UAE to cooperate with investigators who treat them as criminals. Prosecution is rare.

The trafficking crackdown that Gargash has promised has not dented the number of abused women turning up at shelters, Musabih and others say. There is a clear path to the culprits that is being ignored. The key to unraveling trafficking gangs, observers say, is to arrest the victim's sponsor, often an Emirati citizen, who may have sold work visas to a trafficking ring.

The Trafficking Czar

Anwar Gargash is one of the busiest men in the country, with two ministerial portfolios. He heads Gargash Enterprises, a family business with an exclusive import license for Mercedes. He also chairs the UAE's anti–human trafficking committee. It sounds like an incompatible role, but Gargash is a can-do sort, with a Cambridge University PhD that qualifies him to speak with authority and sensitivity on issues of potential embarrassment to the government.

Gargash is shorter than he appears in news photos. He is dressed in a white *kandoura* and toys with his headscarf as he speaks. He's got a Kenny Rogers beard and smiles broadly at any hint of humor. His mobile phone interrupts, but Gargash never takes his calls, just glances at the screen.[5]

Gargash agrees that investigators need to target visa sponsors. But, he says, prosecution under the UAE's tough trafficking law requires strident burdens of proof.

There are other measures the UAE is taking, including training police and prosecutors to take a more inquisitive view of the prostitutes they arrest. Rather than locking up hookers as simple morality criminals, the cops need to probe the gangs behind them. "Is this a simple case of prostitution? Or is this a case where the prostitute is a victim who's been trafficked? Maybe the person in front of them is a victim, not a culprit," he says.

Since the 2006 trafficking law took effect, a few cases have filtered into Dubai's courts. Those on trial didn't appear to be linchpins of the trade. An Indian housemaid and driver were charged with trafficking in 2007 after trying to sell an Indonesian woman to a policeman for $1,200. They'd already forced her into prostitution. In another case, police arrested a pair of Indian men trying to sell two maids, one Indian and one Bangladeshi, for $1,250 each. They, too, had already forced the two women into the sex industry.[6] But in December 2008, authorities arrested eight Emiratis, some of whom worked as undercover policemen, and charged them under the trafficking law. The suspects had been taking payments from brothels, apparently where trafficked women had been forced to work.[7]

Gargash defends the small number of prosecutions as a good start, since the cases are so hard to assemble. "We want to get to twenty or thirty a year, which under the trafficking law is quite a respectable number."

The UAE's 2007 report on human trafficking says "at least 10" trafficking cases had been registered, five of which resulted in convictions. Nearly four hundred prostitutes were arrested in 2007 and two brothels shuttered. And "several others are under constant surveillance for any trace of illegal activity." The report gives no information on convicted traffickers.

Overall, Gargash seems less concerned with ending human tragedies than improving the UAE's ranking in the State Department's reports, and thereby its image. "I don't think it's negative on us that we have a human trafficking problem. It'd be negative if we didn't do anything about it," he says. "Is our strategy ending the problem? No, it's not. But our strategy is impacting positively."

Why is Dubai the Middle East's capital of prostitution? One reason is sheer demand: There aren't enough women to go around. The city is more than 75 percent male. "The way the city is structured provides the basis and condition for prostitution," says Dubai sociologist Rima Sabban. "There is a huge market for it. I don't know how much the government can do."

Dubai is also a business and convention hub. The multiethnic smorgasbord of prostitutes gives the city's nightlife a bit of added excitement. A Google search turns up chat sites describing Dubai's sex tourism sector: the best brothels and hooker bars, with sex prices listed by ethnicity.

Prostitution is also an unspoken part of Dubai's atmosphere of tolerance, which the city uses to lure skilled expatriates. The sex business may offend Muslim sensibilities, but it's part of a policy that underpins the economy. The authorities put up with it. "There must be some level of tolerance," Sabban says. "But how far can you stretch tolerance?"

Every few years when the sex market spills into full view, the police crack down and it slinks back into the dark. This happened in 2007 when Dubai's biggest brothel, the infamous Cyclone, closed down. The Cyclone had been getting too big an international reputation, appearing in a *Vanity Fair* article and then, after it closed, featuring in the 2008 movie *Body of Lies*, with Russell Crowe and Leonardo DiCaprio. Once I unwisely uttered the word "cyclone" in a taxi. I was speaking about the impending arrival of the 2007 storm Cyclone Gonu, but the cab driver slammed on the brakes and started into a U-turn. "You want to go to Cyclone?" he asked.

Vice cleanups have been a Dubai staple for generations. There was a crackdown on hookers in Deira in 1936, when Sheikh Saeed's *wali* forced them to get married or leave town.[8] In the 1950s and 1960s, Iranian prostitutes worked under two madams, one who controlled business in Bur Dubai and another who ran the Deira red-light district around Nasser Square, now Baniyas Square. One old-timer who asked to remain anonymous remembers that things got so bad that Sheikh Rashid ordered hookers rounded up and deported. The crackdown triggered a run on the local bank.

"The British bank nearly went bust," he says with a windy guffaw. "They didn't have the money to pay all the girls off when they came for their savings."

13

THE AIR-CONDITIONED
NIGHTMARE

Repeating the Mistakes of the West

DUBAI'S NEW WEALTH has transformed the city, extended lives, erased illiteracy and malnutrition. It's also trashed the environment. In the 1950s, Dubaians lived below their ecological means, using virtually no energy, practicing sustainable fishing, and emitting hardly a trace of carbon dioxide. Since then, their ecological footprint has grown alongside their wealth.

By 2006, UAE residents, with their indoor ski slope, monster 4×4s, and chilled swimming pools, had become the world's most rapacious consumers of energy and producers of greenhouse gas, burning through even more of the earth's resources than the average American.

Energy consumption in the Emirates runs high for many of the same reasons found in the United States: a feeling that the good life requires huge air-conditioned houses and cars, and disdain for public transportation. The UAE produces next to nothing, so food and other staples have to be shipped in. The world has recognized that America's way of life can't be supported much longer. But somehow Dubai didn't get the message.

In 2008, the Worldwide Fund for Nature's Living Planet Report pegged the UAE's ecological footprint at 9.5 global hectares per person, number one in the world. That was higher than America's 9.4 hectares (number two), and more than triple the global average of 2.7.[1] Britain's footprint was 5.3 hectares. Nearby Yemen, a poor country with little oil, used less than a tenth of the UAE's resources. Yemen's footprint was 0.9 hectares per person.

The report suggests that if every person in the world devoured as much as those in the UAE and the United States, four and a half planets would be needed to provide the resources. The WWF warned that the UAE could be one of the worst hit by its own contributions to global warming. Rising seas are a stark thought given the low-lying islands Dubai just built.

Residents of the UAE and Dubai consume more water and electricity and produce more waste per capita than nearly anyone on the planet.[2] Water use is particularly galling. The UAE's consumption, at 145 gallons per person, per day, is the highest in the world—beating America's 128 daily gallons and Canada's 112. But those countries have water. The UAE's supplies are among the world's lowest. By contrast, the average person in nearby Jordan uses 22 gallons per day.[3]

The fact that Dubaians squander so much water means the ozone layer takes a big hit. Some 80 percent of the city's water is desalinated, made by boiling seawater and separating steam from briny waste. This process burns prodigious amounts of carbon-spewing fossil fuel. The brine gets dumped back into the Gulf, further upping the salinity of one of the world's saltiest seas. Dubai encourages overuse by giving the water away, or selling it below cost.

"Environmental awareness in all Gulf countries is very low. That's especially true in Dubai," says David Aubrey, the fifty-eight-year-old chairman of the Woods Hole Group, a Massachusetts-based consultancy on the aquatic environment. Aubrey has done some work in Dubai, but more often was told that his expertise wasn't needed.[4]

When Dubai took off in the late 1990s, no one stood up for the environment. Aubrey believes that a deliberate policy at the highest level favored development at all costs, with no consideration for sustainability. Developers saw that Sheikh Mohammed's personal projects took no notice of the environment, so theirs didn't either. "When the top guy in the country is a major investor and major player, people get away with a lot in his name," Aubrey says.

Every aspect of Dubai's development is contributing to its world-beating carbon footprint: building design, choice of materials, neighbor-hood layout, and city planning. All of it is based on cheap energy and government-subsidized electricity. Energy demand is out of control, bizarrely outstripping supply in a producer country.

"They are repeating the stupid mistakes of the West," says Eckart Woertz, a German economist at the Dubai-based Gulf Research Center. "You could argue that you shouldn't build a city for five million people in the desert. You could say, 'Okay, they could build solar power stations.' But there is the thinking that, 'No, we want it this way.' It's like the whole Kyoto debate. 'It's our right to waste energy like there's no tomorrow. You did it yesterday.' "[5]

In 2007, Aubrey tried to interest Dubai in a sustainability master plan. The plan would crunch numbers and follow trends to paint a picture of where the city was headed. That way, city fathers could examine options for reining in pollution and energy use. But the authorities Aubrey visited at Dubai Municipality and The Executive Office saw his scheme as damning the city they'd already built.

"I was immediately told, 'That's not going to happen,' " he said. "They said 'What's wrong with what we've done? Everything we've done is fine.' I started to mention the adverse impacts of some of their projects and the interview was over. It was very clear that I was not to talk about those things. If a sustainability road map would imply there's anything less than perfection in the development so far, then it would get nowhere."

It didn't have to be this way. Dubai came of age after 2002, by which time it was clear that burning fossil fuel was warming the earth and the era of cheap oil was ending. With a bit of forethought, Dubai could have built a sustainable city, that would have boosted property values and prestige.

Mathis Wackernagel is the Swiss engineer who created the concept of the ecological footprint in his PhD dissertation. He now heads the Global Footprint Network in Oakland, California, a nonprofit that tallies the carbon emissions of most countries. His reports show exactly who is living furthest beyond the biosphere's means of supporting them.

Wackernagel calls Dubai's shimmering skyscrapers "monuments to the past." Their rapacious electricity needs will be outmoded by rising energy costs. "Those will be abandoned pretty soon," he says. He, too, is advising the UAE government on cutting its world-beating carbon footprint. Thus far, it's not working.

Dubai's haste to build and sell has combined two wasteful traits. First are the suburbs of big, energy-inefficient houses that can only be reached by private cars. Second are the dense districts of high-rise apartment towers. The glassed-in towers are passive collectors of solar energy. If Dubai was a cool place, the free heat would be welcome. Here it means residents need to crank up the air-conditioning. In summer, as much as 85 percent of Dubai's power generation is used for air-conditioning, the actual cost of which is shrouded in subsidies.[6] Towers waste energy in other ways. "You need to pump water half a mile into the sky to flush a toilet," Wackernagel says. "And they don't even have shading in front of the windows. Totally weird."[7]

If you split the difference between Dubai's glass towers and its concrete McMansions, you get an urban scale that needs much less energy. Wackernagel points to Paris as an efficient cityscape. It's got five-story walkups that don't need elevators or water pumps. Buildings use less heating and cooling because there is little surface compared with volume. Population density allows for local shopping districts and effective public transportation, so people don't need cars. France's ecological footprint is 4.9 hectares per person.

Less hurried Abu Dhabi contrasts with Dubai. Residents in the UAE capital probably pollute as much as Dubaians. But their leaders have put thought to the future, seeking ways to cut their emissions. The city plans to produce 7 percent of its power from renewable sources—mainly solar—by 2020.[8]

It is Abu Dhabi's Masdar initiative that has gotten the most attention. Masdar is a $22 billion city that will rely entirely on renewable power. Masdar's designers, led by the Massachusetts Institute of Technology, say the city's 50,000 residents and the 40,000 workers in its 1,500 businesses will produce zero waste or carbon emissions. The businesses, in fact, will focus on green technology. Cars will be replaced by "personal rapid transit" pods. Even the treadmills at the gyms are supposed to generate energy rather than burn it. If it comes true, Wackernagel believes a home in Masdar City will hold its value longer than one in a Dubai tower.

Abu Dhabi's investments aren't just good publicity. Rather than lavishing energy on air-conditioning, it can sell it to foreigners. By contrast, Dubai is partying like it's 1999. The city's electricity consumption nearly doubled between 2002 and 2007. Dubai will need to spend nearly $10 billion to keep up with demand expected to rise 16 percent a year until 2015.[9] Power consumption in tiny Dubai could reach half the level of Florida's in twelve years.[10] Crazy as it sounds, the world's most energy-rich region is short of power.

"Dubai's got a mountain to climb. I see it as a key risk," says Philipp Lotter, who heads the Dubai office of rating agency Moody's, which analyzed the power sector. "Everyone's obsessed about the real estate crash. But if there's a single risk to sustainable growth, it's the energy risk."

The UAE energy shortage is already crimping the housing supply. Finished apartments in Dubai sat empty in 2008 because the utility lacked capacity to connect them to the grid.[11] North of Dubai, in Ajman, Umm Al-Quwain, and Ras Al-Khaimah, apartments, malls, and half-built gated communities sit in the dark because there is no energy to light them. Incredibly, Ajman plans to build a huge $2 billion coal-fired power plant.[12] Coal, the dirtiest fuel, is the one fossil fuel that Arabia lacks. The closest mines are in India and South Africa, countries accustomed to being on the receiving end of the UAE's energy trade.

Abu Dhabi does have huge gas reserves. But much of it is toxic and requires expensive scrubbing before it can be burned. The emirate is just getting started on the investments needed to make the gas usable. Long term, the UAE plans to meet its needs with nuclear power, but Moody's says that's more than ten years away.

The UAE has one thing going for it in this respect: money. If Dubai needs to retrofit all its buildings with window shading and high-efficiency cooling, or if it must build solar energy farms in the desert, it can. "Being wealthy, they can afford more stupidity," Wackernagel says. "You can do crazy things and get away with them."

Getting It Right

In the flat wastes of Dubai's southwest outskirts sits a green glass building. It's a simple horseshoe facing the highway with a red-lit sign reading PACIFIC CONTROLS. Inside, the atmosphere at midday is a soothing twilight. Windows are shaded with sun-blocking curtains. Hallway lights spring to life when you approach and dim as you pass. Occupied offices are cool and bright. Empty ones are warm and dark.

The business of Pacific Controls is controls—software that allows buildings to be managed remotely, from a computer. The programs govern thermostats, alarms, sewage disposal, telephones, lights, and everything else. The company manages power use at Dubai International Airport and apartment towers in the Dubai Marina, and it monitors fire and burglar alarms for Dubai Civil Defence authorities.

But the most impressive thing about Pacific Controls is the message carried on a plaque in the lobby. This is the first building in the Middle East given a platinum rating under the Leadership in Energy and Environmental Design, the U.S. green buildings standard known as LEED. In 2007, the Pacific Controls building became the sixteenth building in the world to achieve platinum status, the LEED's highest rating. In a city that prizes superlatives like no other, that kind of recognition was enough to bring Sheikh Mohammed's right-hand man, Mohammed al-Gergawi, to the building's inauguration in 2007.

Dilip Rahulan, the Indian-born Australian who founded Pacific Controls, gave Gergawi a tour.[13] One array of solar panels on the roof—technically illegal under Dubai's outdated utilities code—produces electricity for the building's lighting. A second array powers a quarter of the building's air-conditioning. The air-conditioning chiller uses the evaporative cooling method used in old kerosene refrigerators, applying heat to produce cold. The building's dark glass blocks the sun's heat, and its software tweaks lighting and temperature. Everything is calibrated to save energy. The stairs are prominent and central, and with just five stories, the elevator is a convenience. The building uses 35 percent less power than a comparable structure.

Gergawi was impressed. A day later he phoned Rahulan to tell him that Sheikh Mohammed appreciated his initiative. "Stay tuned," Gergawi said.[14]

Later that day, Sheikh Mohammed made a dramatic announcement: Starting January 1, 2008, every new building launched in Dubai would have to comply with environmental standards. Until Dubai developed its own, the basic LEED standard would be the minimum. Rahulan believes the directive is among the toughest sustainability laws on any city's books.

Sheikh Mohammed made the directive in October, less than three months before it would take effect. It required architects and engineers to scramble to rework designs to comply. A rule change like that would take years to push through in the European Union or the United States.

Of course, rules are only as good as their enforcement. And the UAE has a notoriously difficult time implementing its laws, especially those requiring inspections. If Sheikh Mohammed's directive is followed, future buildings will be at least 12 percent more energy efficient than those built before 2008.

Pacific Controls believes it can make money this way. A more realistic tariff rate by the Dubai utility might bring the chance to retrofit buildings with efficient switches. Many buildings could cut consumption by 30 percent right now, just by turning off the lights and air-conditioning at night.[15]

Dubai has made a few strides as of late. Besides Sheikh Mohammed's green buildings directive, the emirate in October 2008 announced it was considering mandating the use of solar power to produce hot water and perhaps electricity. There has also been discussion about creating an environmental agency with enforcement powers, like the U.S. Environmental Protection Agency. Abu Dhabi already has one. At the time of writing, Dubai's EPA hadn't been decided upon. Environmental issues were just starting to gain attention in Sheikh Mohammed's Executive Office. "We definitely will have to do something about it," says Nabil al-Yousuf.

Burying the Reef

The Gulf's development rampage may be enriching humans, but it's been a disaster for wildlife. The once-pristine UAE coast has been inundated with Florida-style sprawl that is knocking out species one by one. Neighboring Oman, too, a country so untrammeled it was like a national park, is now coming under the developer's bulldozer. The white-collared kingfisher, an extremely rare subspecies that exists only in mangrove swamps in the UAE and Oman, is down to about fifty nesting pairs. The Arabian tahr, a mountain goat, and the Arabian leopard are nearing extinction in the UAE.[16] The Arabian oryx, a large antelope, is already extinct in the wild. In Oman, a luxury hotel was built on a beach used as a nesting site for the critically endangered hawksbill turtle. Other developments have taken habitat from the rare Socotra cormorant and the dugong, or sea cow, a marine mammal akin to the manatee.

A mangrove and flamingo sanctuary in Dubai was handed over for a luxury development dubbed The Lagoons. And a giant mangrove flat at nearby Umm Al-Quwain, vital habitat for migratory birds, is being developed by Emaar as a marina and resort. Scuba divers have fled Dubai for the clearer waters off the east coast.

"We try to be positive. But sometimes for your own sanity you block out what's going on," says Habiba al-Marashi, chairwoman of the Emirates Environmental Group. "In the end I can only do so much."[17]

Dubai's contribution to the environmental mess isn't just emissions. The Palm Islands, which brought the city fame, are among its worst offenders. The Palm Jebel Ali got dropped into a protected wildlife zone, burying much of a coral reef. Bits of the reef remain uncovered and Nakheel wants to revive it, but the damage is done. Other man-made archipelagoes have buried oyster and sea grass beds. Dredging, which could continue for another decade or two, has left the sea a silty fog, killing algae, plants, oysters—basically everything that can't get up and swim away.

The Palms have also altered the Gulf's offshore currents, probably forever.[18] Sand used to drift with the prevailing northeast currents along the shore from Abu Dhabi, past Dubai and into Sharjah. The new islands have blocked those replenishing flows. Sand is piling up on the southwest side of town, while the altered currents now scoop away Dubai's beaches. The city is stuck replenishing its beaches by dumptruck.

Brats Tossing Butts

Dubai's build first, ask questions later ethic isn't the type of setting that encourages environmentalists. Bucking the odds is Habiba al-Marashi, a forty-five-year-old former government official, who now spends her days lecturing and hectoring, trying to get Emiratis and the two hundred other nationalities in Dubai to consider the resources they waste.

Al-Marashi wears the black *abaya* of a local woman, with her *shayla* wrapped tightly around her face, so that no wisps of hair stray out. She has the disarming habit of laughing when she discusses dire issues.

Al-Marashi is resigned to struggling in a country destined to remain among the world's worst polluters, because the barren UAE can never soak up the carbon dioxide its spews. "This is a fact. We'll always be in the top ten. We have to desalinate water or we will die," she says. "But the culprit isn't that we're desalinating water. It's that our consumption is wasteful. People live excessively here."

She focuses on the things she can change, starting with behavior. Al-Marashi is a born activist. She has no training in environmental science. She didn't grow up as a Bedouin in the desert. But her parents taught her that national pride meant caring for the land. Islam says the same thing. Every day she finds herself yelling at litterers and spitters, those cramming paper in the recycling bin meant for plastic. Smokers tossing butts are a favorite target. "Excuse me, can you pick that up? There's a garbage bin right there," she tells them. "Don't do it next time."

Problem is, environmentalists find themselves bumping into the sheikhs' ruling bargain. People fritter away electricity and water because it is subsidized and cheap—nearly free, if you're an Emirati. Royal families trade these subsidies for the popular mandate that keeps them in power. Al-Marashi, a mother of four, says the policy has spoiled the country's residents.

"The UAE acts like a spoiled child. It's like these brat children. They go into the playroom and mess it up. You have to go clean up after them. And they go back in and mess it up again," she says. "There's lots of apathy. If you're using more than your fair share, you should pay more."

14

THE LAWLESS ROADS

The Dubai driver's a special breed
Low on charm, but high on speed.
He overtakes on either side,
And slips through any gap he spies.

He sits up high in his four-wheel drive,
Phone in hand and driving blind.
Riding a meter from your rear,
And flashing lights to make you fear.[1]

The 250-Car Pileup

THE FOG HAD rolled in off the Gulf and lay thick and woolly when twenty-six-year-old Matthias Seifert left for work on March 11, 2008. He set off in his sporty red Peugeot 307 hatchback for the hour-and-a-half drive. It'd be dangerous for a while, but once he was off Abu Dhabi island, the fog would probably thin. Seifert, a German who manages seaplane flights at the five-star Jebel Ali resort, had a full day's work ahead and didn't want to delay. Anyway, he was used to fog.

He crossed the Maqta Bridge to the mainland and started up the highway toward Dubai. Seifert drove straight past the Adnoc gas station. Its brightly lit blue trim is normally visible a half mile away. But he didn't see it until he was past it. He thought, "Okay, I'll stop at the next one." But Seifert breezed past the second Adnoc as well. He couldn't see from one light pole to the next, but he kept driving anyway.

Reckless driving is a part of life in the Gulf. There are mentalities at play that make the roads among the world's most dangerous. One is a self-important "me first" attitude; the second is the belief that safety is in God's hands. Seifert knew this. But he chose to drive in the treacherous fast lane, despite the fog. He kept his speed under seventy-five miles an hour, rather than his usual eighty-five. Even in the heavy fog, cars cruising at a hundred pulled up to his rear bumper, flashing their headlights and forcing him over to pass. The only precaution most drivers took was putting on their emergency flashers.

Seifert figured that he was safer coping with the sharks in the fast lane than the trucks and laborers' buses in the slow lanes. Overloaded trucks typically creep along while the buses barrel at high speed. If he was going to be rear-ended, he would prefer a Toyota Land Cruiser to a bus. It turned out to be his only wise decision.

"I thought about pulling over. But I just decided to go for it," Seifert says. "It was like flying blind."

About 7:45 a.m., Seifert was nearing the overpass for Ghantoot, a beach resort near Abu Dhabi's border with Dubai. A car materialized out of the fog directly in front of him. The car was turned slightly to the right. He didn't have time to realize the car was stopped. He couldn't see that its front end was smashed into the car in front of it, or that that car was also smashed into the preceding car. In fact, the entire highway was blocked by dozens of smashed cars hidden under the fog. Seifert had no chance. Just as his reflexes were telling him to brake, his Peugeot 307 buried its nose full force into the stopped car. The effect was like a bomb detonating. First the impact, then Seifert's air bag slammed him back into his seat, wrenching his head. The front end ripped open. The car caromed and spun. When it stopped, the young German flailed at the air bag, batting it away from his face so he could see. His car had spun 180 degrees. He was still in the fast lane, but now facing oncoming traffic.

The fog that swirled around him was darkening with arabesques of smoke. In the next lane, a driver climbed out of his wreck and ran, head down, for the roadside. Seifert peered into the fog. He was next in line for a smashing. Should he climb out and run? No chance. The white headlights and yellow flashers bore down on him. There was a brief scream of tires. He clenched. The head-on smash fisted him, throwing his little car back into the wreck he'd just hit. Glass and debris geysered into the sky and rained down on his car, which was now turned to the side, a flank still exposed to the road. Then it came: Slam! Another wrenching crush pounded his new Peugeot. Again he was thrown back. Now he was hemmed in by wrecks on all sides. He could see drivers going through the same experience he'd just had. Then a car walloped the rear of the first car that hit him, whiplashing his neck a fourth time. Seifert groped for the latch, kicked the door open, and ran for his life. He leaped over the guardrail and crouched like a fugitive behind a lamppost.

The surreal horrors continued. Every few seconds, a blind-driven car or bus added itself to the pileup. He could hear the moans of the injured, the screams of the terrified, and the screeching, thundering crashes. The air was thick with burning rubber and roasting paint. Ash and debris showered from the sky. After a while it was quiet. The German looked at his hands and then ran them over his head and body and then looked at them again. He checked every inch of himself for blood or broken bones. Each time he looked at his hands they were clean. He found his cigarettes, took one out, and lit it. He was fine.

Others weren't. Seifert wandered from car to car. He saw mashed wrecks, twisted chassis, vans aflame. There was a car like his crushed into a cube between two buses. Some he couldn't identify. They'd been pummeled into crullers of scrap, with a wheel poking out here, a tailpipe there. He saw wounded people and corpses. Men were breaking car and bus windows to rescue those trapped. A group gathered on the pavement looking at the ground. A man lay there, his limbs crushed under a bus. Mercifully, he was dead.

Seifert was glad he'd driven in the fast lane. The buses, notorious for their reckless drivers, had caused the most damage. The buses had ripped open like cracker boxes. But the cars they'd rear-ended were the worst off. Many were aflame.

As the fog lifted, the mile-long pileup materialized like a Polaroid photograph. About 80 cars, trucks, and buses lay strewn together, some of them on fire, some of them already burnt husks, some with emergency flashers blinking inanely. All told, 250 vehicles crashed on their way from Abu Dhabi to Dubai that day. There were several pockets of wrecks along the road. The pileup at the Ghantoot bridge was the biggest. The first police car arrived on the scene half an hour after Seifert crashed. The officer stepped out of his car, glanced around, then got back in and drove off.

The walking wounded were a slice of cosmopolitan Dubai: Emirati nationals in blood-spattered *kandouras*, limping Filipino and Indian laborers in blue coveralls, Western managers in dress shirts and ties. Police put the official death toll at four. Hospitals reported 8. Seifert thinks initial news estimates of twenty-five to thirty dead are closer to the truth. Nearly 350 people suffered injuries.

A second police officer arrived, telling milling laborers to get away from the wrecked cars. The officer warned that looters were combing the wrecks. Seifert checked his car for valuables. Nearby, two men linked arms and carried a wounded Indian man, his head and bare foot wrapped in gauze, and put him in the back seat of a police cruiser.

Emergency crews had their hands full sorting out the biggest road disaster in UAE history, a situation they'd never prepared for, nor one that could've been imagined a few years earlier. Seifert was stuck on the highway for seven hours. He walked up to the source of the pileup. There, he saw a white Toyota van without major damage to its front end. It had been rear-ended by a white Mercedes. Was this the crash that started it? Seifert thought his assessment was more thorough than that of the police. They simply pushed the battered vehicles to the roadside without trying to sort out the cause.

Why did it happen? UAE officials were quick to blame the weather. One absurd headline in the progovernment *Gulf News* summed up the initial reaction: "Need to Tackle the Fog Problem." Gregor McClenaghan, a British reporter with the Abu Dhabi newspaper *The National*, offered a more realistic assessment. "The reason it happened is because people here drive like fucking idiots."

McClenaghan, too, commutes every day between Dubai and Abu Dhabi. Lucky for him, he drives the other way. He saw the crash spooling past his window, with laborers at the roadside waving rags to warn him. He saw the smoke and then the walls of flame roasting the fronds of the date palms on the median. "I started talking to myself. 'This is insane. I should get off the road.'"

Bill Spindle, *The National*'s business editor, also drove to Dubai that day. He left at 9:00 a.m., as the fog lifted, and gawked at the carnage that stretched for miles. Spindle, a forty-six-year-old American, counted five separate pileups as he wove through the burnt-out husks and the roadside triage, the sirens, the stumbling victims, the highway covered in oil and glass and, at one point, pickles. The pickles had dumped from an overturned van and workers were sluicing thousands of them to the roadside with a board. It was worse than anything he'd seen in Baghdad. It was the grimmest disaster he'd seen, in fact, since the day he watched a 747 plow into the World Trade Center.

Road Wars

Driving in Dubai and the rest of the UAE is blood sport for some young men. A crash happens, on average, every two minutes.[2] The rate of fatalities is among the world's highest. Each day three people die in UAE traffic wrecks,[3] two of them killed by reckless drivers. The carnage is a public health crisis on par with a serious outbreak of plague or smallpox. Crashes are responsible for about 15 percent of all deaths in Dubai and the rest of the Gulf region, the biggest killer after heart disease.[4] In neighboring Abu Dhabi, where driving is arguably worse than Dubai, road wrecks are already the leading cause of death.[5] All told, more than 1,000 people died in UAE car crashes in 2007, an increase of nearly 200 over 2006.

It's amazing the death toll isn't higher. Cars pinball across six-lane highways at 100 miles per hour. When drivers lose control, their vehicles might tumble end over end, spewing wheels and bits of taillight and windshield. Sometimes they mount the highway's median barrier and take out cars in the oncoming lane. The authorities have stepped up fines for reckless driving, but the pace of infrastructure expansion and Dubai's 12 percent yearly growth in vehicle numbers have overwhelmed their efforts. In April 2008, a spate of accidents killed 21 people in 72 hours.[6]

For fresh arrivals, especially those accustomed to the tame American and European roads, driving is a shock. Shirley Morrison, a forty-year-old South African who heads Executive Expatriate Relocations, helps the newly arrived get used to it. Some companies, like British oil firm BP, insist that staff take defensive driving courses.

"I advise people to get into a car as soon as possible and start to drive," says Morrison. "The longer you leave it the harder it is, especially for women. When you leave it too long, you see what it's like on the roads, and then you fear it more."

At Dubai's Gulf Traffic Convention in 2005, a video showed dozens of children orphaned by traffic wrecks marching in Abu Dhabi. The children wore black mourning robes, and some carried banners reading, "They were killed by speed."

"We lost our fathers," the children chanted. "Why didn't he go slowly?"

Young Emirati men, known for aggressive driving, appear to be among the chief culprits—and victims. Across the UAE, more Emirati men are killed in road accidents than by any other cause.[7] It's common to hear Emiratis speak of sons or relatives lost in crashes. Jonathan Somcio, a thirty-three-year-old Dubai police paramedic who makes a living extracting the dead and injured from their vehicles, says most of the people he tends to are Emirati and Arab men in their twenties and early thirties, along with those driving labor buses and vans, generally Indian and Pakistani men.[8]

Many more would be dying if it weren't for air bags and improved safety equipment. In Somcio's homeland of the Philippines, most folks drive older cars. People die from crashes that Dubaians walk away from. "Sometimes we find the driver standing at the side of the road, still able to walk. It's surprising," he says.

The UAE's plague of high-risk driving is a by-product of a traditional culture beset by breakneck modernization. In a society that frowns on dating and, ironically, drinking alcohol, young men seek arousal from driving fast. The huge number of 4x4s and trucks on the roads contributes to the high death rate, since bigger vehicles cause bigger injuries. In a study of crashes in the city of Al Ain, Emiratis made up more than 60 percent of those hospitalized, despite forming around 20 percent of the population. More than 75 percent were male.[9]

"Young people use their cars for competition and passing time in late afternoon and evenings, which, incidentally, is the time when most of the casualties occur," write public health researchers Abdulbari Bener and David Crundall. In the United Arab Emirates, there are 116 deaths per 100,000 vehicles, six times the U.S. rate and ten times that of Britain, according to the pair's research at the University of Nottingham in England.[10]

Bad driving is a knotty problem. There is little road enforcement beyond cameras that monitor the fast lane. Worse, reckless driving is a matter of pride. "Drift" racing is one scourge of the roadway, with young men racing each other to destinations around the city, sometimes videotaping their careening runs through heavy traffic. Type "Dubai accident" or "Dubai drift" on YouTube and scores of clips turn up, including a couple of horrific crashes in Dubai's tunnels. One shows a policeman getting run down while investigating a disabled car. Another shows a speeding car trying to zoom between two slower vehicles without the space to do it. The speeder's car and those of his two victims spin and slam into the tunnel walls.

Young men speak of their crashes with pride, bragging about the number of cars they've "canceled." Ignoring seat belts is also a badge of honor, common in Arab countries. One afternoon, I send my Emirati assistant, a woman in her twenties, on an errand to buy some books. "Drive carefully," I tell her.

"*Inshallah*," she says, which means "God willing."

A colleague tells her: "Wear your seat belt."

She replies in a noncommittal singsong. "I'm a *Mowatina*"—a local—"I don't wear the seat belt. I pray that I will get there safely."

This exchange might be funny, except that the young woman lost four aunts in a single accident.

Enforcement of the law in Dubai depends on who is breaking it. Here is how Dubai FAQs, an unofficial Web site for newly arrived expatriates, explains traffic law:

> There is some flexibility in applying road rules in Dubai. Many expats learn about *wasta* through a driving experience. In simple terms, the more *wasta* someone has, the less likely they are to cop a fine or be blamed if there's an accident. Nationality will make a difference to how much *wasta* you have. So can having the name and phone number of somebody with a lot of *wasta*. It can result in some unusual situations. For example, green lights were actually red when you went through them because the person who crashed into you had enough *wasta* to change the color retroactively. You'll find it easier to enjoy Dubai if you get used to that rather than try to fight it.[11]

The Wacky Races

Remember the 1960s cartoon the *Wacky Races*, where drivers in souped-up sports cars and homespun contraptions competed for rally victories? Dubai is the Wacky Races, day in, day out. There may be no place on earth with such a variety of vehicles on its roads. Backhoes compete for lane space with Lamborghinis. Gasoline tankers rumble among ATV quad bikes. There are scurrying minibuses crammed with waitresses, juggernaut dump trucks piled with boulders, and flimsy Chinese hatchbacks tailgated by hulking Hummers.

General Motors has carefully studied this vehicular cornucopia. GM's managing director of its Middle East operations, Terry Johnsson, says ninety separate vehicle brands share Dubai's roads—twice as many as in most countries.

"You have a consumers' paradise. Every possible brand is here: all the Chinese, all the Indian, all the European, Asian, and American brands," Johnsson says in a very slight Scandinavian lilt. "A lot of markets say they're competitive. There is no market with Dubai's number of brands."

The UAE is one of the world's biggest luxury car markets. The tiny country is the number one destination for the world's most expensive car, the $1.5 million Bugatti Veyron. Only around three hundred Veyrons have been built. UAE drivers bought twenty-seven brand-new ones in 2006 and 2007, says Stephanie Vigier, a Paris-based auto market analyst for the research firm Global Insight.

The UAE is the world number two market for Hummer, second only to the United States, and the world's number three market for Bentleys. The UAE is a vital market for Lamborghini, Range Rover, the sumptuous Maybach limousine, and the $95,000 Porsche Cayenne SUV. The UAE is the world's fourth-largest buyer of Cayennes, behind only Germany, China, and Russia. There are so many Porsches on Dubai's roads that they've become mundane. Hence the demand for Veyrons.

Cars are practically driving themselves out of the showrooms. Rolls-Royce sales tripled in Abu Dhabi between 2006 and 2007. Ferrari purchases jumped 60 percent that year.[12] Sales of new cars rise 20 percent a year in the UAE.

An Emirati household may own up to a dozen vehicles, each with a distinct purpose, whether it's going out in the desert, dropping the kids at school, shopping, or nightclubbing.

In the United States, where gas rose above $4 in mid-2008, GM's penchant for big cars was a liability. In the UAE, subsidized fuel is less than $2 per gallon. Big SUVs are the rage. GM sells its biggest 4x4s as fast as it can ship them in. Sales of Chevy Tahoes and Suburbans and GMC Yukons are growing at 100 percent a year. In the Gulf, people want V8 engines, as much air-conditioning and on-board electronics as possible. GM's dire sales would be even worse if it weren't for the Gulf.

"Call it four-dollar gas, call it American competitiveness, call it the weak dollar, but all that has done nothing but focus our attention on the opportunities over here," Johnsson says, in his office near the top of the World Trade Centre. "You definitely want to be investing where you can generate cash."

Johnsson doesn't look like a typical GM man. He carries himself with Euro-intellectual poise, with a shaved head, square black plastic-framed glasses, and a sharp blue suit. Instead of a tie, a checkered hankie juts from his breast pocket.

Over the next decade, Johnsson expects the Gulf to be such a large car market that its preferences will start shaping the way American vehicles are designed. "If you were to go into the design studio in the U.S. for a look at the next-generation Chevrolet Tahoe, and you asked them, 'Where's the coolbox in the center console for the Middle Eastern consumer?' they'd show you," says Johnsson. "They have a whole list of things they're doing for the Middle East market."

Crashes and Profit

One reason the UAE is such a profitable car market is because the driving is so bad.

Rajan Jacob is the showroom manager at the Al Tayer Motors Ford dealership in Dubai. Al Tayer is the world's tenth largest Ford dealer and the top seller of Ford Mustangs outside North America. It also happens to be the world's number one dealer of Jaguars and Land Rovers, and one of the biggest sellers of Maseratis.[13] Al Tayer's showroom, with Ferraris, Maseratis, Range Rovers, and Jaguars poised in the windows, is a major source of rubbernecking on the adjacent Sheikh Zayed Road. (The al-Tayer family also happens to be tribal cousins to the ruling Maktoums, with roots in the Liwa Oasis.)[14]

The 250-car pileup in March 2008 might have been bad for those involved, but it was great for car dealers. Most of the victims, once they got out of the hospital, needed new wheels. Some of them came to Al Tayer and a few looked over the new Fords. Rajan Jacob was lucky enough to outfit four crash victims with Ford Explorers and Ford Focuses.

"A lot of people who got out of Fords in that crash, they came to us again and bought another Ford, because they weren't injured," Jacob says. "A lot of people who crashed their Japanese cars also bought Fords. They opted for something safer. Safety is a big factor."

At rival General Motors, Terry Johnsson hasn't examined the link between crashes and sales, but he knows it's there. "It will drive sales. It has to. There will be a replaced car, there'll be replaced parts. I can't put a number to it," Johnsson says. "For an individual dealer, it could make a significant difference."

Cars and Identity

In the West, establishing your identity is a simple matter. You wear a T-shirt with a slogan, you let your hair grow long and shaggy, or you shave it off. Or you stumble into a tattoo parlor and have ink injected under your skin. Or you don't do any of it, and that says something, too.

In the Gulf, Arab men generally wear plain all-enveloping white robes, plain white headdresses, or perhaps a red-checked headscarf, and a black band or two that fixes the scarf to the head. There are no brand names, no fancy embroidery, no stripes or plaids.

Women have a bit more room for adventure in their black *abaya*, some of which bear patterns in sequins or crystal and can be sheer, even see-through (with clothes worn underneath). Their headscarves might be turquoise or saffron, not always black.

It's difficult, especially for a man, to make a big personality statement with his clothing. You can glean hints from a man's sandals or shoes, perhaps noting that his toes are manicured or not, and the type of pen clipped to his pocket, his cufflinks or the brand of watch on his wrist. If he wears a long beard, okay, he's religious. But those are small details compared to the booming personality statements made when the man climbs into his car. Is it a white Range Rover Sport? That signals understated wealth. Is it a red Ferrari or Maserati? That's an attention-craving rebel with cash to burn. A Bentley? An old-money identity. A boxy Mercedes G-Series 4x4? That's an admirer of Sheikh Mohammed. A Mercedes or BMW sedan? That's for the gray man who disdains attention. A Toyota or Nissan sedan? That's sensible frugality, which says, "I am poor."

Terry Johnsson got a briefing on local preferences at the U.S. embassy just after arriving in 2004. Then ambassador Michelle Sison told him that influential Gulf nationals, especially members of the royal families, care deeply about three things. "First, oil and gas. Number two, airplanes. And number three, cars," Johnsson says. "The rest of their business relationships might be important, but none carry the same level of passion."

Gridlock, Confusion, and Loss

Dubai's road network is a puzzle. On the one hand, streets are modern and well lit. Ample signs in Arabic and English point the way. On the other hand, Dubai's streetscape is anonymous. The roads are often unnamed, or given names like Street 14b or Road 363 that nobody uses. Worse, names are repeated from neighborhood to neighborhood. There are probably a dozen named Street 14b, for example. They meander in curlicues and culs-de-sac that only residents can fathom. There are no house addresses. Since there is no mail delivery, the municipality never introduced them. Everyone in Dubai gets mail in a post office box.

All this makes navigation difficult. Directions are given by proximity to landmarks. In the old days, this worked. But in a city of two million spilling over the desert, navigation is akin to Sudoku.

On January 9, 2004, the confusing street grid was part of the reason Paul Johnson, General Motors's top executive in the Middle East and Africa, died. Johnson was a tall man with dark hair and a baby-faced friendliness. He was fifty, but looked more like forty. His colleagues at GM called him P. J.

Paul Johnson was Terry Johnsson's predecessor. The two are unrelated. Johnson was a longtime GM man, starting with Pontiac in 1978 and then working his way up through the Saturn division and to Vaux-hall, GM's British make. In 1999, GM sent him to run the carmaker's Middle East operations. He and his wife, Jane, and their three sons, settled in a comfortable villa in Umm Suqeim, near Jumeirah Beach.

Johnson's last moments alive were spent at his home. His eldest son had returned on winter break from college in the States and Johnson grilled steaks in his backyard to celebrate. At dinner, however, Johnson began choking. A piece of steak lodged in his windpipe and he couldn't dislodge it. Jane and the boys tried to help but nothing seemed to work. Jane called an ambulance. In her distress, she did her best to describe where she lived. But Johnson's wife spoke English and the emergency dispatcher did not understand it well. He sent an ambulance but the crew couldn't find the home. For the next forty minutes, paramedics meandered in search of the choking man. The GM executive's condition grew grave. Without air, Johnson lost consciousness. He was close to death when the paramedics finally found him. They rushed him to the American Hospital, another twenty minutes across town, but Johnson never regained consciousness. Soon he was dead.[15]

Johnson's death jolted Dubai's authorities. A memorial service at the World Trade Centre drew two thousand mourners. Sheikh Mohammed phoned his condolences to Jane, and city authorities began straightening up the emergency response system. The roads department began giving streets names and numbers.

"He should never have passed away," Johnsson says.

Dubai's relentless growth has stretched roads beyond capacity. More than a million vehicles pack the streets, with 135 new cars registered every day in 2008. Entire neighborhoods are built and populated with no expansion of the surrounding streets, which descend into gridlock as buildings fill with tenants. The congestion costs Dubai $1.2 billion in yearly economic losses.[16]

A survey of Middle East commuters declared Dubai's streets the most congested in the Arab world, surpassing even the infamous gridlock of Cairo. The average Dubai commuter spends an hour and forty-five minutes on the roads, twelve minutes longer than the average Cairene.[17]

Dubai is a city of incongruities. The roads are modern but the network is incoherent. The cars are advanced but driving is anarchic. Malls are rife but there is no art museum. The airport is world class, but education is substandard. An optimist would say that's the essence of an emerging market, the reason Dubai crackles with opportunity. A realist would point to a government that preferred impulsive decisions to level-headed planning.

One reason that Dubai's urban fabric is so incomprehensible is the fact that until 1995, the city had no functioning master plan to guide its growth. In 1993, Egyptian urban planner Hamed Hattal was hired to bring order to Dubai's hurtling sprawl. When Hattal arrived from Saudi Arabia, he was stunned to find that Dubai had no database of land ownership, no zoning laws, no planning standards or building regulations. The city's Land Department, which registers property ownership, had barely discovered computers. The department was infamous for its bureaucratic depths, and as a hangout for Emirati falconers who would swill coffee and stroke their birds.

"Dubai was growing without boundaries, without standards," says Hattal, a slim man with a shock of gray hair and the technocrat's white shirt and tie. "The government didn't know what land it had available. There was no information about the population. And we had no idea which pieces of land had been allocated for what."

The city relied on a 1985 master plan, the Dubai Comprehensive Plan, which the government never approved, perhaps because it vastly underestimated the pace of expansion. The 1985 plan, drawn up during the doldrums of the Iran-Iraq war, projected Dubai's population would reach 500,000 by 2005. But as the war wound down, Dubai took off on a growth tear. The city reached half a million by 1990, fifteen years earlier than predicted. Hattal says planners understood the document's deficiencies, but still used it as a rough guide, for lack of another.

The acute misjudgments of the Dubai Comprehensive Plan are partly responsible for the grinding traffic jams that locked down the roads in later years. One oversight was the lack of bridges over the creek. After the 1976 completion of the Garhoud Bridge, no creek crossings got built for thirty years, until the 2007 opening of Business Bay Bridge. All traffic from one side of the eight-mile creek to the other funneled into two bridges and a tunnel that were bunched near the seashore. Crosstown traffic flowed through the heart of the city and local drivers had to jam onto the highways simply to cross the creek. These were major bottlenecks before a spate of new bridges started opening in 2007.

Now Dubai is in the midst of building a $4.2 billion light rail system. It's a hugely ambitious project, with forty-five miles of underground and raised track coursing through town like giant strips of linguine, rising up and over bridges and burrowing beneath Bur Dubai and Deira. At the time of writing, the city was testing trains on its Red Line, set to open by the end of 2009.

It'll be a godsend when the trains start running. With an alternative in place, city fathers say they'll tackle the vehicle fleet: hiking gasoline prices and parking fees and installing more toll gates. The idea, says planning director Abdulredha al-Hassan, is to "make it harder for people to use private cars."[18]

But the Metro, too, has seen coordination problems. In 2004, Dubai announced its latest palm-shaped island, the Palm Deira. It was to be enormous: the size of Manhattan with more than a million residents. It would rise offshore of densely populated Deira. The Roads and Transport Authority had just finished designing the Dubai Metro, and the route went nowhere near this significant future neighborhood. One planner told me he had no idea it was coming. The route had to be redrawn. This incident seems to have triggered a willingness to share Dubai's project plans not just among developers and the ruler's office but with municipal planners.

"Sheikh Mohammed now coordinates these projects with us," Hattal says.

Dubai wouldn't be what it is if Sheikh Mohammed was one to sweat the small stuff. In his book, he says, "if anyone asks me how Dubai achieved so much at such a record speed, I'll simply say that it's because we never drowned ourselves in detail. The key to a true and effective development process is a vision that doesn't allow small details to cloud its basic goals."

Dubai is nimble because the city-state is an autocracy, governed by one man. If projects had to be approved by a series of public committees, the public would know what to expect. Growth would be more coherent. It would also take a lot longer.

"Here the sheikh simply says, 'That flyover isn't big enough. Knock it down and double it,' which is great," says Anthony Harris. "They opened thirty-one new lanes over the creek in two years. That's bloody quick time. In Britain, the planning committee would discover that some rare bat is living in a tree nearby and the whole thing would be scrapped and it would take ten years to figure out what to do."

Walking the Line

Right up until the 1970s, Dubai was a walking city. It had a compact center and pedestrian souks. Its alleys were too narrow for cars. But Dubai embraced modernity and the automobile. Cars make sense. When it's hot, you drive in cool comfort. But Dubai's car fetish necessitated an urban redesign. Other ways of getting around, like walking or cycling, were tossed out.

Dubai's streetscape is now actively hostile to walkers and cyclists. Most streets have no sidewalks. There is no custom of driver courtesy to pedestrians, even where there are marked crosswalks. One especially deadly design is the mile-long wall of skyscrapers on either side of the twelve-lane Sheikh Zayed Road. At the time of writing there was one pedestrian underpass. Fourteen people died in horrible fashion on that stretch in 2006 alone, trying to dash across. Pedestrians are cut down by cars far too often in Dubai.

Rashidi Sayfulin, a young man from Samarkand, Uzbekistan, is one of them. On December 5, 2005, he and his brother ran across a street in Deira. His brother didn't make it. A car flattened him. When Sayfulin dashed back to help him, he, too, was struck down, his skull bashed open. Sayfulin's brother recovered enough to return home. But Rashidi has spent the past two and a half years lying in the neurological ward at Rashid Hospital with severe brain damage. He's fed through a tube in his nose, or when he gets visiting volunteers, someone squirts yogurt into his mouth with a syringe. Sayfulin struggles to say a few garbled words. He rubs his hands in frustration over his eyes and tilts his lopsided head to squint at his visitors. When I visited, a pair of volunteers from the Valley of Love charity helped him sit up in his bed and placed him into a wheelchair for a quick tour of the hospital lobby. He's better off than the others in the ward, most of whom are in a vegetative state.

Dubai could be a great biking city. It's flat and the weather is nice most of the year. But cyclists have to cope with highway overpasses and jutting curbs that force them into traffic. Few take the chance. In 2007, I attended a convention for traffic planners. An engineer showed me how he'd redesigned a roundabout in Al Ain to a four-way intersection with a traffic light. It could now handle more vehicles and was better for pedestrians, who could wait for the light, and walk across.

"What about cyclists? Why not put in bike lanes?" I asked him.

His face darkened. "The locals won't allow it. They don't cycle. They say, 'Indians are the ones who ride bicycles. Why should we pay for something that they use?' It's a backward mentality," he says. The engineer pointed out that Indians and every other frustrated cyclist wind up driving and making traffic worse for everybody.

The man charged with designing a way out of the mess is Abdulla al-Nedhar, an Emirati who studied planning at Georgia State and had a hand in revitalizing downtown Atlanta. Back in Dubai he worked his way up from city hall until becoming the chief of strategy and planning for Sheikh Mohammed's Executive Office. He runs a new outfit called the Dubai Center for Research and Urban Innovation.

Al-Nedhar carries himself with a can-do spirit, the sleeves of his *kandoura* rolled up and long sideburns poking from under his white *gutra* headscarf. He is a thoughtful man who watches over a busy patch of Dubai from his Aeron chair on the forty-third floor of the Emirates Office Tower.

Al-Nedhar travels a lot. He studies cities with an eye to bringing positive aspects home to Dubai. Asked which cities he likes best, he answers indirectly. "We look at all the cities in the world as models."

Vancouver offers the best example for a mix of cars, bikes, and walkers. South London is doing interesting things for pedestrians, with its walkway along the south bank of the Thames. Copenhagen's driverless Metro is an obvious inspiration. But those places are aspirations. For now, al-Nedhar compares Dubai with cities in his league: emerging behemoths in China and the former Soviet Union, and, of course, Singapore.

Now that Dubai has been given over to the automobile, al-Nedhar wants to take bits of it back. His team has drawn up a master plan called "Dubai: The Human Environment," which seeks pedestrian spaces and lanes for cyclists. One idea calls for a bike-only space beneath the raised Metro platform. The scheme carries a number of advantages. One, cars can't get near it. Two, it's shaded.

"We see how important the human is in relation to vehicles and machines. We have to meet in the middle," he says. "It's very difficult to get people out of their cars. But there are a lot of advantages. It's good for your health and the environment. We're trying to see how we can get people to stop making short car trips and to start walking or biking."

Al-Nedhar's goal is to use design to lower the city's stress levels. He wants a calm city that respects the needs of business without destroying the comfort and safety of families, children, vacationers—and those crossing the road.

"I have a dream that Dubai will be sustainable, that it will be livable and healthy for me and my kids," he says, leaning forward, arms on his desk. "The important thing is that we keep going toward excellence. Martin Luther King said, 'I have a dream.' He innovated that, right? He said that if you don't have a dream you won't get what you want."

IV

DUBAI'S CHALLENGE

15

DANGER AHEAD

Demographic Insanity

WHEN AMERICANS THINK of immigration run amok, Miami comes to mind. More than 60 percent of Miamians were born outside the United States, mainly in Latin America. No other major U.S. city comes close. Foreign-born residents make up just over 40 percent of Los Angeles and 36 percent of New York and San Francisco, census figures show.[1]

Compared to Dubai, Miami is a bastion of nativity. Ninety-five percent of Dubaians are foreigners, and they come from 200 countries. There are only about 100,000 citizens among the city's 2 million inhabitants.[2] Dubai is probably the world's most cosmopolitan city.[3]

In one way of looking at it, Dubai's welcome to foreigners gives the city a competitive advantage over its resource-rich neighbors. Foreigners have started businesses and taken management jobs and the city's workforce has benefited from their expertise.

But swarming immigration now extends beyond Dubai, and has left Emirati citizens a minority in every one of the UAE's seven emirates. The million or so UAE citizens make up about 15 percent of the country's total population of around 6 million.[4]

The Gulf Arab and Persian culture that once radiated from the creekside alleys has been overwhelmed by a thorough globalization. The dominant culture is South Asian, and the city's streets are lined with neon-lit curry houses and tailor shops. Sidewalks teem with brown faces and slick black hair. Also conspicuous is the Western golf and yachting lifestyle of America and Australia, with its malls and gated communities. Arab fashion and staccato pop music streams in from Beirut and Cairo, coloring the street scenes. Urban Iran makes a stand: the soft Farsi chatter, the smoky outdoor kebab houses, and the Jackie O lookalikes in their Gucci headscarves and Tehran-chic *manteaus*. There are Ethiopians and Ghanaians parking cars and hustling fake watches, Filipinos strolling in shorts and tank tops, and a rising force of Chinese laborers and prostitutes.

The only people absent, it seems, are locals. Emiratis have retreated into walled mansions on the city's outskirts. Once renowned for their gregarious hospitality, they've become clannish. Their simple meat-and-rice cuisine, drum-heavy music and male line dancing, and their guttural, tough-sounding dialect are difficult to find nowadays. It's gotten to the point where citizens stick out, even attracting stares. Most Dubai expatriates have never held a meaningful conversation with a UAE citizen. Understanding of their historic struggle is almost nil.

"Every day when I roam the town I ask myself, 'Where are my people? Where are the local citizens of my own country? Where are they? I can't find them,'" Ebtisam al-Kitbi, a university professor, said on a radio talk show in May 2008.

Dubai isn't just packed with foreigners, it's also crammed with men. A recent census found that women make up less than a quarter of the population and just 14 percent of the workforce. "There is just too much male energy here," says Rima Sabban, the sociologist. Most migrant men come from male-dominated places like India and Pakistan and bring conservative views toward women. There is no more macho city on the planet. Dubai clearly needs a woman's touch. "We don't just need to reduce the percentage of foreigners, we need a feminization policy," Sabban says.

The demographic imbalance is the hottest topic in the UAE, or it was until the economy began to sink. In a country where political opposition is stifled and complaints about society are made in private, the "foreigner problem" has spawned a bold national debate and an anti-immigration backlash. Citizens are starting to blame the crisis on their rulers, even if they rarely mention them by name.

Immigration is a talk radio staple, just like in the United States and Britain, except the banter in the UAE carries an edge of desperation. Americans and Britons typically oppose immigration on economic grounds, however spurious. In the UAE, where immigration clearly undergirds the economy, Emiratis call it a national security crisis. Dubai's police chief, Gen. Dhahi Khalfan, says the swelling foreign population endangers the reign of UAE royal families. If not curbed, Emiratis will lose control of their country.

"I'm afraid we are building towers but losing the Emirates," Khalfan said at a national identity conference in April 2008. "We are at a crossroads. Unless drastic action is taken we will disappear in the waves of foreign workers."

In the United States, the government defuses any security threat by granting immigrants citizenship. In the UAE, citizenship is guarded like a vault of nuclear fuel rods. It's impossible to get near it. Nationality is passed down the male blood line, from Emirati men to their children. If an Emirati woman marries a foreign husband, even a man from her own tribe who happens to be a citizen of, say, Oman, neither the husband nor the couple's children receive UAE citizenship. They can live in the country their entire lives, speak Gulf Arabic, pray at the mosque five times a day. They'll always be foreigners. Many other residents who never took nationality in the UAE after 1971 have no citizenship at all. They and their offspring are the *bidoun*—the "withouts"—those with no nationality.[5]

Most people born in the UAE take citizenship in their parents' countries, even if they've never lived in those countries. My son Jay is one. He holds a U.S. passport like mine and a British passport like my wife's, but he was born and is being raised in Dubai. He's got no chance of getting citizenship in the country of his birth. Indians and Pakistanis make up the greatest number of UAE-born foreigners, with multiple generations born and raised in the UAE, often with no connection to the land of their ancestors.[6]

Anti-immigrant activists in the UAE believe this situation could soon change. When Sheikh Mohammed allowed foreigners to buy property in 2002, he may have unwittingly given them additional rights under international law. Many properties sold in Dubai came with permanent residency visas. Now, academics believe foreigners can argue—successfully—in an international court that those privileges give them rights of citizenship. One successful test case could swing the balance, at least in the eyes of the international community, says Mohammed al-Roken, a lawyer and dissident in Dubai who favors shipping foreigners home before this happens.

Al-Roken, forty-four, is a big man with a charismatic smile and a forceful personality. He was once the head of the UAE Jurists' Association, akin to the bar. Al-Roken taught constitutional law at UAE University and wrote a column for the newspaper *Al Khaleej* until 2000, when the government forced him to stop. He is one of the few Emirati professionals who doesn't keep portraits of the ruling sheikhs on his office wall.

"Foreigners living here have built the country. Some have been here two or three generations. They have no ties whatsoever to their mother countries," al-Roken says. "It's against their human rights to deprive them of citizenship."

If Washington or the United Nations—or another international organization—pressures the UAE to recognize second-class residents as citizens, al-Roken doesn't think the UAE government could resist for long. Naturalizing hundreds of thousands of foreigners would topple the country's Arab heritage. The UAE would become a multiethnic state like Afghanistan or Iran. Foreigners could take control of Dubai, perhaps declaring it an independent city-state. It's not far-fetched. Singapore seceded from Malaysia in 1965 under similar circumstances. Chinese and Indian immigrants overwhelmed the local Malays and then declared independence. Malays now form less than 15 percent of Singapore's population. That's a high percentage compared to Dubai. Al-Roken believes Dubai could go the way of Singapore within a decade.

Let's Get Lost

Dubai's locals exhibit a strange combination of comfort and uncertainty. Emiratis marvel at the lush life that envelops them, but they gape as foreigners pour into a city they no longer recognize: skyscrapers thrusting up from the sand, and colossal highways seething with BMWs and sewage tankers. Few have a clue where they're being dragged. But they stay quiet and the payoff keeps coming. Each new immigrant notches a slight boost to the value of Emirati citizenship. As Dubai gives itself to migrants, locals reap ever-higher subsidies and access to education and high-salary jobs in the city-state's power structure. Citizenship is increasingly a badge of privilege.

Umm Hussain is a thirty-nine-year-old housewife in Dubai's Al Twar section. She lives with her husband and three of her children, her disabled mother, and a staff of maids and a gardener. The house is modest by Dubai standards, with tasseled couches, chiffon curtains, and slipcovered tables lined with dishes of homemade Arabic sweets. Umm Hussain is an *Ajam*, an Arab of Iranian ancestry. She grew up in a narrow house on a crowded *sikka*, or alley, in the Dubai Gold Souk, a neighborhood now packed with Pakistani and Nigerian men. She doesn't know what to think of Dubai these days. On the one hand, she's proud of the name Dubai is making for itself. She felt like a celebrity, being showered with compliments on a recent trip to Germany by people fascinated with Dubai. Her daughter lives in Australia, where she, too, hears admiration for Sheikh Mohammed's creations.

On the other hand, she can't find her way around town anymore. With the traffic and what she sees as aggressive foreigners, Umm Hussain prefers to stay home. On the day I stopped by, she wore a modest rose-print gown and a gold-trimmed black headscarf that accentuated a friendly face with a ready smile. She pressed me with glasses of watermelon juice and sweets, bustled me on a tour of the house, and spoke wistfully of happy times in the *sikka*, when neighbors would spend the afternoon chatting.

In those days, Umm Hussain's mother and grandmother baked bread in a clay oven in the courtyard. Sometimes they'd split open a fish, rub it with spices, and roast it on a flat stone. If someone came home with a tuna, they would pack layers of raw fish in a clay jar, covering each layer with salt. After a month or two, the salted tuna, known as *maleh*, was ready to eat.

"We played hopscotch and hide-and-seek. There were so many children. Arabs, Indians, Pakistanis, Iranians, *Ajam*. We played with boys, too, and went swimming in the creek," she says, slapping her knees. But life in Dubai has grown more complex. Children spend long hours in school and study when they come home. New Islamic strictures separate boys and girls. Houses are big and far apart. Work hours are longer. Everything, it seems, conspires to keep people apart. These days, pleasure comes from shopping, not visiting neighbors. Umm Hussain tells her children about the life they've missed by growing up in the new Dubai.

"Before, life had a taste," she says, rubbing her fingers as if crumbling a cracker. "Now nothing makes you happy. Before, you could buy one mobile phone and you are happy. Now you buy five mobiles in a year and you're not happy. There is nothing making people happy now. Children have so many things in the house, but they are bored."

Umm Hussain was raised by immigrant parents who took Emirati citizenship before it became valuable. She is a grateful and proud Emirati, but she wonders what the future holds. The trends don't make her comfortable.

"We are afraid that one day we're going to lose our country. We don't say our sheikhs are doing something wrong. But we don't know what they are planning for us. We are opening the door for everybody.

"The people coming here are buying houses and they're buying everything. We don't know who they are. If you were in my place you wouldn't be afraid? This is too much. They must stop giving visas to everybody. The Indians, before they were not like this. Now they make problems. They stop the work, they sit in the road, they kick the police.

"How do you control all these people? It's very dangerous. You're paying for this growth. You may pay with your life. We see a big, big accident coming. The bad luck is coming to us. When you make something beautiful, everyone comes to look at it. You're afraid of the evil eye. This is what we are saying: Stop building. Leave what we have. There's too much building, building, building. It's like someone sleeping on your chest. There's no air."

Seven months later, Umm Hussain's wishes, and some of her fears, were realized. A big accident did come: Dubai succumbed to the global contagion. And that brought building and immigration nearly to a standstill.

We Did This to Ourselves

In May 2008, Sharjah Radio host Mohammed Khalaf dedicated a week of his daily talk show to this debate. The program aired blistering criticism of the UAE's leaders and shocked listeners with alarming predictions for the country's future. Ebtisam al-Kitbi, the UAE university professor, was one of his guests. One day, Khalaf started the show by asking al-Kitbi whether she thought Emiratis might disappear.

"Is this an exaggeration or is it reality?" Khalaf asked.

"It is reality," al-Kitbi replied in a defiant tone. "Today we face an invasion of millions of people coming to us from abroad to stay. They have no intention of leaving this country. As a result, our existence is threatened."

Al-Kitbi spoke angrily, dismissing callers who suggested she was exaggerating. She insisted that the sheikhs were leading the country in the wrong direction. She beseeched listeners to take up the cause. "Today the locals can't find plots of land to build their houses, while you are selling entire areas to foreigners," she shouted. "The person responsible for this should be punished. No matter how high-ranking they are, these people should be punished."

"I totally agree," said Khalaf's second guest that day, Jamal al-Bah, president of the Arab Family Organization, a group that pushes traditional values. "We have too many foreigners competing with us for work, education, even marriage. Our girls are finding it difficult to get married because of the expatriate girls. We are like a ship lost at sea. This ship was sailed by his highness Sheikh Zayed, may God bless his soul. Now we want to know where we're heading. We need to do something before it's too late."

"We are pushing ourselves into a dark tunnel from which we'll never emerge," al-Bah said. "We sold our lands, we brought the foreigners here and gave them power over us. We built the skyscrapers and asked them to live in them. We did this to ourselves."

The host, Khalaf, suggested the country's leaders were more responsible than average citizens. But he steered around naming them. "We're not the decision makers. But, I want to ask, isn't our decision maker afraid of this? There has to come a day when he is affected by these decisions. Doesn't he think about this matter and the seriousness of it?"

"No," al-Kitbi blurted. "He is not aware of anything whatsoever."

It's unclear whether Khalaf and al-Kitbi referred to UAE president Sheikh Khalifa or Dubai leader and UAE vice president Sheikh Mohammed.

Khalaf lamented that Emiratis have no tradition of public dissent. They are outmaneuvered by foreigners, for whom speaking up is natural. Indian laborers take to the streets, marching for better wages and housing. Emiratis can't, or won't, do the same. Al-Kitbi said Emiratis need to start taking action to get the government's attention.

"In one of the emirates, someone decided to build in front of a complex that was occupied by foreigners. The proposed building would block their sea view. So the foreigners decided to take action and stop this building. They succeeded, by obtaining twenty thousand signatures. Why did they get what they wanted? Because they come from countries that respect their opinions. Their leaders listen and act accordingly. We don't have this in our culture. Our civil society is weak. We don't have groups that defend the rights of the citizen. There is a gap between you and the decision maker."

"I want to say this to the decision maker: You might have to pay a price for your acts tomorrow. The people will not allow this to continue," al-Kitbi said in a challenging tone. "I hereby state that God is my witness. I have spoken up. I was not quiet about this."

She suggested that the UAE's rulers are allowing unlimited immigration to further their personal businesses. This, she said, is a conflict of interest. "You have to choose between being a ruler or a merchant. You cannot make money for yourself while you issue decrees."

Khalaf announces that listeners are barraging his mobile phone with text messages. He reads one: "I am surprised that the host has not been arrested!"

Al-Kitbi is incensed. "We haven't said anything yet! Let them arrest us. We're not afraid because we're speaking the truth. If the reward of someone speaking the truth is jail, let them put us in jail. I'm not afraid at all. God is there, I am only afraid of Him."

Khalaf takes a call from an agitated Emirati man. "You are pouring salt into our wounds. You're making us cry. I am telling you that if this situation does not change, I will leave the country in the next three years and I vow never to return." The caller starts weeping and hangs up.

Khalaf takes another call. "I just want to tell you what an Indian man said the other day when he heard a UAE national complaining about the number of Indians here. His reply to the local was: 'No Indian, no UAE!'" Khalaf and his guests share a few dark chuckles.

Khalaf's final caller suggests they are cowards. "People say one thing to the faces of our sheikhs and they say another thing behind their backs. Stop being hypocrites! If you have anything to say, say it to our rulers' faces. We can't deny that our hotels are the best, our streets are clean, everything is beautiful. Let's not forget what our rulers have done for us."

Backlash Against Westerners

On a Friday in July 2008, thirty-six-year-old Michelle Palmer, a sales manager for a Dubai publisher, went to a champagne brunch at the Le Méridien hotel, near the airport. Friday brunches are a Western expat staple. While Muslims head to the mosque for the sermon, Dubai's hotels offer buffets crammed with every delicacy imaginable: Maine lobster and raw oysters, roasts on the bone, hearts of palm, tiramisu, and all-you-can drink booze.

The brunches brim with Roman-style excess. I've been to a few. I usually ask a friend, by way of a joke, to direct me to the vomitorium, so I can gorge some more. Sometimes Friday brunches descend even deeper into the moral mire. The Double Decker, a British-themed bar and restaurant in the Murooj Rotana hotel, is the favorite of blue-collar Brits whose composure tends to melt when the booze arrives.

"It's unlimited drink so people tend to get a bit loud and sometimes there's fighting, but we have a lot of bouncers who take care of these things," said Julio Rodriguez, a supervisor at the Double Decker. "Sometimes the police get involved. We would call them if there was a big fight with blood all over the place, or if property was being destroyed."[7]

The afternoon Palmer went to brunch, she and her friends began guzzling $100-a-bottle Bollinger champagne. She met a British businessman, thirty-four-year-old Vincent Acors, who'd been in Dubai just a few days. Palmer, with a round fleshy face and black hair, told friends that she'd gotten extremely drunk and lost her sense of judgment. She and Acors departed on a Dubai pub crawl that took them to Jumeirah beach at sunset. Palmer took off her Jimmy Choo high heels and clasped them in her hand as she and Acors strolled the strand. When the police spotted them, the pair were writhing in the sand, clamped together at the hip. Britain's *Sun* tabloid quoted a policeman as saying Palmer had straddled the prone Acors and was "moving up and down."

The police accosted the sweaty pair. Probably because they were Europeans, the linchpin of Dubai's tourism sector, the police let Palmer and Acors off with a warning. They told the couple to uncouple and left them on the beach. When the officers returned, they found they'd only briefly interrupted their lovemaking. Palmer and Acors were back at it. They strode up and forcefully told the drunken Brits to stop. This time

Palmer lashed out with a high-heeled pump at one of the cops. The police immediately arrested the pair. They woke up in jail with cracking hangovers, facing six years in prison. A few months later, a judge sentenced them both to three months in jail, followed by deportation.

The press picked up the story and it boomeranged between the UAE and England. UAE papers focused on a clampdown on carnal post-brunch behavior. Police combing the beaches arrested more than seventy people for lewd acts. British tabloids veered toward outrage at Dubai for subjecting paying tourists to Muslim-style punishments over a harmless tryst. As the story picked up steam, the pair seemed to lose sympathy at home. Most observers seemed to think it was funny. A few Britons were quoted saying they wished their English bobbies had the nerve to clamp down on such behavior.

It wasn't the first time Dubai's amorous beachgoers got themselves arrested. A couple months earlier, police arrested a Lebanese woman and her lesbian lover, a Bulgarian woman, after beachgoers at Mamzar Park dialed 911. "The Lebanese woman was lying atop the Bulgarian and the two were cuddling and kissing each other in front of us," a witness told police. The two women got a month's jail and deportation.[8]

Drunken tourists having public sex was not what Sheikh Mohammed had in mind in 1985 when he proposed that Dubai build a tourism industry. These stories give Emiratis the feeling that their country has been overrun by foreigners with whom they have little in common. They also stoke opposition to the Maktoums' development choices that fuel immigration. Just before the beach romp, an e-mail circulating in the UAE pleaded with Western women to dress more modestly. The message, titled "Modesty=Respect," described offensive scenarios including Emirati men emerging from prayer at the Jumeirah mosque to encounter bikini-clad women walking to the beach. The e-mail urged women to wear midlength skirts and cover their "chest, bosom, back, thighs and knees." The author also warned that Westerners shouldn't misjudge Arab women as backward because of their modest dress.

"One of the effects of sun-and-sand tourism is that it starts bringing in the kind of excessive behavior that we're seeing," says government adviser Yasar Jarrar. The city learned that it can't pick the tourists who visit, but rather it is they who pick Dubai. "When you open the gates to a sector like tourism, you get a lot of side effects."

Emiratis are liberal by Gulf standards, but sex before marriage is against the law and the rules of society. Marriages are typically brokered by the mother and sisters of a young man, who approach the parents of an eligible bride, usually without the girl's knowledge. In more liberal families, typically those of the Persian *Ajam*, there may be courtship between the man and the target of his affection. But many Dubai couples meet for the first time just before their wedding. There is no kissing, no hand-holding. Premarital meetings are monitored by parents. The only kissing done in public is by men, who give each other pecks on the cheek or, even more traditionally, rub noses. Even married couples don't kiss in public.

Many locals feel that European women are deliberately insulting them by romping in malls with bulging cleavage and bare legs. "Some of it has to be deliberate. The skirt is so short you can see their underwear," says Hamda bin Demaithan, a twenty-one-year-old Emirati who usually wears the conservative *niqab*, a piece of black cloth covering her face. "There are limits to how much we can take. Because of this a lot of old people don't go to the mall anymore."

The British beach frolic turned out to be a milestone. It turned up Muslim heat up against Western excess. But it also delivered a message that the Dubai expatriate gravy train is too good to allow a few degenerates to spoil. There was a call for self-control.

"What happened on the beach is the tip of an iceberg of contempt. It's jeopardizing the tolerance of the UAE and the Muslim community," says Eddie O'Sullivan, who heads the Dubai office of the *Middle East Economic Digest*. "It's tarred everyone here. It isn't the police or the government that needs to deal with it. It's got to be the British community saying, 'I'm not going to have this scum.'"

Balancing the Imbalance

Law professor Mohammed al-Roken has been lecturing for sixteen years about the dangers of expatriate domination. Since he began, the proportion of Emiratis in the UAE has slipped by 10 percentage points. Al-Roken thinks tolerance has run dry. It isn't normal for passive Emiratis to give their rulers a verbal lashing on the radio. Criticism is usually done in the privacy of the ruler's *majlis*. Even so, he says, the leadership isn't ready to roll back the country's liberal immigration policies.

"They don't give a damn about the imbalance," he says.

At Sheikh Mohammed's Executive Office, however, advisers are devising policy to turn around the imbalance without savaging the economy. Nabil al-Yousuf, the office's director, says the shrinking proportion of locals is Dubai's single most pressing problem. "It's dangerous," he says. Then again, skilled foreigners are vital to Dubai's bid to become a global capital. It's a problem requiring a deft policy hand.

"Economic growth cannot be sustained by the local population. We will always need expatriates. But the balance is, we don't want to be a complete minority in our own country and lose control," al-Yousuf says. "There are ways to achieve both."

The first step is to diversify foreign residents. Police chief Khalfan has publicly stated that no single ethnic group should hold a majority. The government is taking steps in this direction. Emiratis might be a minority, but as long as the other groups are also minorities, there is less danger that one will take over. In practice this means replacing Indian and Pakistani laborers with Chinese, Nepalese, Bangladeshis, and North Koreans, as well as bringing in more Arabs.

Another obvious solution is to be generous with citizenship. The UAE is studying naturalization standards in Japan, Canada, and Australia with the aim of creating qualifications and a transparent application process. Citizenship would still be tightly controlled, but open to longtime Arab residents and perhaps Iranians, Pakistanis, and others who fit. Foreign husbands and children of Emirati women are another easy source of new citizens. Also under consideration are those with valuable skills or degrees, or those with thirty or more years in the country.[9]

But naturalization is a taboo subject. Many Emiratis, especially those with deep tribal roots in southeastern Arabia, are against it. No one wants privileges eroded so foreigners can be granted citizenship.

What is an Emirati? Hamda bin Demaithan grew up in a Bedouin family. Her ancestors roamed the deserts around Dubai for thousands of years. Her elders still talk of the ways of the nomad, the edible plants, the intricacies of hunting, weaving tent fabric from goat and camel hair, and the ancient rituals of Bedouin hospitality. Bin Demaithan is deeply patriotic in the sense that she feels attached to the *land* of the UAE, rather than to the privilege of being a daughter of Dubai. How can a foreigner understand this?

"Citizenship is identity. That's what I'm worried about," she says, her green eyes shining with intensity. "What if they don't love this land as much as we do? I would want to live here even if there was nothing, like my ancestors did. Life was harsh. Still they stayed. It wasn't about the economy."

Problem is, immigration is outpacing even a sensible naturalization policy. Without democracy, there is no effective way for citizens to influence policy. "It's a one-man show," al-Roken says. "People need to have a say in the future of their country. That might put a brake on what's going on. We'll understand it's our future, too, and we'll plan accordingly."

The breakneck development pace has sent cracks ripping across the city's façade. Inflation is one of them. Dissent is another. Traffic overpowers every effort to contain it. Foreign domination is nearly total. Energy is running low. And greenhouse gas emissions are the world's highest. Is Dubai sustainable?

Al-Roken looks out his office window. *Abras* jammed with passengers chug across the creek, as they have for a century. His mobile phone rings. He ignores it.

"No, it is not," he says.

Can the lifestyle be maintained?

"No, it cannot."

Sheikh Mohammed has said he could stop immigration tomorrow. That would prevent foreigners from investing and block skilled managers and technicians from filling job openings. The economy would be crushed. The boss appears to prefer to let things run their course. At the time of writing, Dubai was slowing. In an environment wracked by triple-digit real estate gains, things usually go into reverse for a while. The immigration problem was starting to fix itself. As the building boom tapered off, thousands of foreigners were leaving. The city's strategic plan calls for further cuts in labor-intensive industries, and an emphasis on high-skill sectors. But beyond that, foreigners will always handle Dubai's maintenance and middle management jobs, while training Emiratis to take the commanding heights.

My friend Jim and I step into the taxi after a night at the bar. Our driver is a fastidious man. He wears pressed Western clothes, a dress shirt tucked into his trousers. His gray hair is cropped and neat. His face is clean-shaven. His glasses are spotless, as is his English. He reminds me of a favorite uncle. As we get under way, I notice that his driving is as competent as his looks. He flicks his turn signal, he keeps his distance from cars ahead of us, and he carefully overtakes other vehicles on the left. And he knows Dubai's streets! It's practically a miracle. Who is this guy?

I start asking questions. Quizzing cabbies became a favorite pastime since I heard a rumor that Sheikh Mohammed pays cabdrivers to report suspicious customers. I've yet to find one who confirms this rumor. The driver, whom I'll call Anwar, is from Pakistan. He says he took up taxi driving three years ago after the collapse of his export business.

"I had to do the same thing once," I tell him. It's true. I briefly drove a cab in Brooklyn when I couldn't find another job. Anwar, it turns out, also has a degree in political science. "So do I," I tell him. He says he's been living in Dubai for twenty-five years. "Twenty-five years!" I exclaim. "That makes you an old-timer. I bet you've seen a few things."

Then it starts to flow. Dubai has gone way downhill since Sheikh Mohammed started his building program. "This place is such a mess now. I really can't stand to live here anymore," he says.

I'm startled. It's not something you usually hear. He grumbles something about Arabs.

"Do you feel discriminated against?" I ask.

"These Arab motherfuckers. They think they're civilized because they put on a suit. They are ruining this place. You watch. In five or six years they will fuck this place up just like they fucked up their own countries."

Anwar says he comes from a cultivated background. His father and grandfather served in Britain's Indian Army. Both were decorated for bravery. They lived by strict moral standards. "They were gentlemen. They knew how to behave. They treated people with respect. Not like these motherfuckers here."

Anwar's driving is starting to get erratic. He cranes his neck to look at Jim and me in the backseat as he rants. He nearly rams someone. I ask him to be careful. But he's just getting warmed up. He moves on to the locals, to Emiratis, who, he says, pull rank on him anytime there is a dispute. They refuse to discuss it. No matter what the circumstances of their encounter—a traffic accident, a place in a theater queue, stepping into an elevator—he is forced to defer to them. "They say, 'I'm a national. You are in my country. I am right.' They treat us like shit."

I ask whether he speaks Arabic. "I am a Muslim and I refuse to speak that fucking language. I don't want to speak to Arabs. I understand it but I refuse to speak it."

I tell Anwar that he is on the wrong side of a government policy that seeks to increase the number of Arab expatriates at the expense of Indians and Pakistanis. The aim is social cohesion, since Arab foreigners have more in common with Emiratis than do South Asians. Anwar listens carefully. He says this policy is ruining Dubai.

Jim chimes in: "What do you think of Sheikh Mohammed?"

I've been in Dubai for three years at this point and I've never heard anyone criticize Sheikh Mohammed by name, not even Westerners. There is a long silence.

Anwar returns to his earlier theme: Dubai is discriminating against the people who built the city, the laborers and Indians and Pakistanis who fill the ranks of midlevel professionals. They're being systematically marginalized, he says, due to ethnic favoritism.

Eventually the anger burns itself out. He drops Jim off, then it's just the two of us. I ask whether he's planning to return to Pakistan. He's silent. We reach my block and I direct him to stop. I step into the street and pay the fare. He turns to take it and I look at his face. He's utterly deflated. I wish him good night and shut the door.

The Flip Side: Privileged Locals

There are many facets of the immigration debate. Another is the $55,000 yearly subsidy given to the average male Emirati. It's no wonder the country needs to import foreign workers. Emiratis get free land, cheap electricity, and free water. Health care is free. Food and gasoline are subsidized. Education is free, often including graduate degrees in Europe and America. When they marry, Emirati men are eligible for no-interest loans to build houses. The state gives them $19,000 toward their wedding costs. Many earn windfall salaries for sponsoring foreign businesses. And there is no income or property tax.

"What else do you need money for? Suppose someone gave you $55,000 a year, would you be inclined to work?" asks Nico Vellinga, a Dutch economist who coauthored a Zayed University study that examined the subsidies. "People aren't interested in working when you take away the incentive. The sheikh wants to be good to people, even spoil them. But there is a tradeoff."

These are big subsidies, even by Gulf standards, and they're part of the unwritten tribal bargain that has kept royals in power decade after decade. Handouts don't make for a competitive workforce. Privileged attitudes and a lack of skills have already excluded Emiratis from the private sector. British scholar Christopher Davidson describes the quandary as "one of the hidden costs of political stability." The payments keep people happy, but they've destroyed the relationship between work and income.

The UAE grapples with a citizen unemployment rate near 20 percent[10] in an economy that creates tens of thousands of jobs a year. Fewer than 10 percent of the Emirati workforce toils in private companies, where 99 percent of employees are expatriates. Eighty percent of Emirati workers hold government jobs and most of the rest work for state-owned companies like Emirates airline and Dubai Properties.[11] Of the few in the private sector, many—especially those in banking—owe their jobs to government quotas.

The CEOs at the top of UAE companies are Emiratis. But these men are often figureheads. When it comes to the skilled jobs, Emiratis are absent. In 2007, Bloomberg News reported that just one of the twenty-eight companies on the Dubai stock exchange's main index had an Emirati chief financial officer.

Vellinga echoes the words of Sheikh Mohammed. The educational system needs to prepare students for the jobs that exist: management, trade, engineering, information technology, accounting. But two-thirds of citizens get degrees in arts, education, and religion.

Vellinga spoke in a Zayed University coffee shop, surrounded by young Emirati women giggling over milky lattes. The students wore high-fashion *abayas* and pecked away at laptops trimmed with fake leopard skin and feather boa ruffs. The all-female university with its American professors is an egalitarian place. Sheikh Mohammed's daughters take classes alongside poorer girls from Umm Al-Quwain and Sharjah in a stunning campus where buildings of glass and fabric are mirrored in rectangular pools. But like the UAE's work culture, Zayed University isn't a bastion of feverish study. Emirati girls glide through the halls at their glacial walking pace, back straight, head high. At 5:00 p.m. most days the campus—including the library—shuts down and the students' brothers or fathers collect them from the curb. There is none of the frantic studying, the all-nighters in the library, or the activism that typifies universities in the West. It was an appropriate place to illustrate the effect of subsidies.

But women are the bright spot in the UAE education picture. They are more inclined to finish university and take education seriously. "We're more bookish," says Hamda bin Demaithan, herself a Zayed graduate.

Women make up 70 percent of university graduates and nearly 80 percent of the student body at the coed national university in Al Ain. Female graduates have swept into new jobs in government, starting at the entry level and working their way up. The youngest staffers in three of Sheikh Mohammed's top policymaking bodies, The Executive Office, the Executive Council, and the prime minister's office, are mainly women. The Executive Council, on the thirty-seventh floor of the Emirates Office Tower, is awash in black *abayas*. One employee said 70 percent of the council's staff were women.[12] Sheikh Mohammed predicts that women will someday take most leadership posts below the royal family.

Increasingly, the pool of unskilled locals is made up of Emirati men. Education has never been a particularly respected pursuit in male society. Many are content to finish high school and take high-salary, low-skill jobs in the police and military. This attitude is one of Sheikh Mohammed's biggest headaches. He harangues his subjects to take private sector jobs, warning them that efficiency drives are trimming the government workforce and increasing its skills. In 2006, he extended civil servants' seven-hour workday to eight hours. Now and again, the sheikh pops up for photo opportunities in the malls, shaking the hands of Emirati "pioneers" who work as checkout cashiers or supermarket butchers.

Rolling back the state subsidies causing the rot cannot be done. Any sheikh who tried would probably be ousted. "People don't see it as the government giving them something. They see it as a right," says Anwar Gargash, the state minister for foreign affairs.

Subsidies can be revamped to pull Emiratis into the private sector. It's a variant on Sheikh Rashid's approach to land grants. Instead of simply handing citizens money, Vellinga reckons the subsidies should be directed toward Emiratis who take low-paying jobs outside government.

But Emiratis may not cooperate. Young Emiratis have never known the poverty of their parents. For most, prosperity is a given. Incremental increases in the wealth of an already rich person don't mean much.

Quality of life becomes more important. People may agitate for a voice in their country's affairs, and, like Umm Hussain, they may wish to brake the construction and immigration that is transforming their society. At some point, Sheikh Mohammed's grand plan for Dubai may be incompatible with the wishes of his subjects.

16

DEMOCRACY AND TERRORISM

Elections Are in Fashion

DUBAI AND THE UAE are among the world's least democratic places. Like China, Dubai has embraced unbridled capitalism without political freedom. Most people here prefer it that way. Sheikh Mohammed's maneuverability in planning and execution depends on acting fast. The city is not going to surpass Hong Kong and Singapore if the boss has to sell his ideas to parliament. He doesn't want to put everything on hold every few years to run for reelection.

Therefore it's no surprise that the UAE sits in the cellar when it comes to democracy rankings. The advocacy group Freedom House rated the UAE as "not free" in 2008. The Economist Intelligence Unit in 2006 ranked the UAE 150th out of 167 countries, saying it was less democratic than Zimbabwe or Congo. The UAE got the Economist Intelligence Unit's lowest possible score—zero—on its electoral process and pluralism. The only reason it's not dead last is that researchers also measured variables such as a functioning government, civil liberties, and political culture, on which the UAE scores better. Saudi Arabia, despite holding men-only elections for municipal government, ranked below the UAE.

After thirty-five years of independence, the UAE held its first-ever election in 2006. It was the last of the laggard Gulf states to allow some form of voting. Some 450 candidates, including sixty-five women, ran for twenty seats on forty-member panel called the Federal National Council.

In power-sharing terms, the election was nearly meaningless. It hasn't been repeated. "It's not really democracy yet," concedes candidate Sheikha al-Mulla, a female psychologist who ran for one of eight seats in Dubai. The government hedged against revolutionary change by handpicking an electorate of 6,700 Emirati voters. It offset the panel's twenty elected members with twenty appointed by the royals in each emirate. And the council has no formal power. It acts as an advisory body whose advice is often discarded.

The election wasn't triggered by internal dissent. By and large, Emiratis believe their government is doing a good job, and the rise in living standards is evidence. The government organized elections more because they are global fashion. "It was getting awkward so they had to address it," says Abdulkhaleq Abdulla, the UAE University political science professor and democracy advocate. "From a historical perspective, it's a step forward. But this is also for outside consumption."[1]

Democracy isn't seen in the same idealistic light as it is in the West. In the Middle East, democracy means chaos. Anwar Gargash, the thoughtful minister who organized the voting, said he was moving cautiously. Elections in Bahrain, Kuwait, Lebanon, Israel, Iraq, Iran, and the Palestinian territories have either deepened sectarian divisions or brought extremists to power. "We see elections as divisive and breaking up the social fabric," Gargash said ahead of the 2006 vote. "We'd rather be safe than sorry. That's why we're moving forward in this measured way."

The lack of democracy had become an embarrassment in a country that boasts one of the world's highest levels of education and personal income. "I'm in my mid-forties. I have a PhD, and I've never taken part in an election," Gargash said ahead of the 2006 balloting. I spoke to him again in October 2008. He'd voted for the first time in 2006. "It felt good," he said with a broad smile.

Changes to the political structure will come in tiny increments. Gargash is mulling an extension of the Federal National Council's term from two to four years. And he's considering allowing more than 6,700 Emiratis to cast ballots. "For someone looking in from the outside, these are modest steps. We're fine with that," Gargash says.

Democracy follies in Kuwait are a favorite argument against elections. UAE papers have ridiculed the Kuwait parliament's thirteen-year dithering on whether or not to allow in foreign oil companies. And they blasted the 2008 walkout by Islamist parliamentarians who refused to attend the swearing-in of female ministers who declined to wear headscarves.

"One of the hallmarks of the Kuwaiti parliament has been its habit of continuous quarrelling, of vitriolic grilling of ministers, and its propensity to throw the political system into turmoil," wrote political analyst Khalid Salem al-Yabhouni in Abu Dhabi's *The National*. Yabhouni said the Kuwait model "has proved to be one that we should not emulate."

The popular view is that democracy is stifling development in once-mighty Kuwait. While Kuwaiti politicians waste their time discussing the finer points of headscarves, the UAE is building skyscrapers and an urban rail system. "Look at Kuwait. We can see how politics made the country stagnant. We have, *Hamdulillah*, been able to overtake the country that used to be the richest in the Gulf," Sharjah-based political columnist Sultan al-Qassimi boasted during a forum in May 2008 at the Dubai School of Government.

Not so fast. Kuwait's foibles with free speech may not be lathering the country in concrete, but democracy itself also counts as advancement. "Democratizing leads to a decrease in government efficiency and performance," responded Amr Hamzawy, a political analyst with Washington's Carnegie Endowment for International Peace. "It can even lead to a severe economic crisis. But democracy creates more vibrant institutions."

By sidelining citizens' voices, Emirati sheikhs are deepening the chasm between the UAE's economy and social fabric on one hand, and the immature political sphere on the other. The country can't sustain the imbalance indefinitely.

For instance, at the Harvard-affiliated Dubai School of Government, one can discuss economics and social topics as openly as students in Boston. But start talking about the legitimacy of Sheikh Mohammed's rule, and the discussion, as Hamzawy puts it, "falls off a cliff." Dubai may feel like it's racing ahead of competitors like Kuwait, but by locking its citizens out of the decision-making process, it is falling behind.

The UAE may not have much in the way of elections, but vestiges of the old "tribal democracy" remain. Citizens can meet ruling sheikhs and get a hearing on their issues. Sheikh Mohammed's decisions aren't his alone but stem from discussion with advisers, consultants, and important families. The Dubai leader mingles with the public more than the average head of state. His mobile phone number is said to be programmed into about half the locals' phones. When someone has an urgent problem, he sends a text message to the boss.

"If you're the head of an important local family, you can probably get to a sheikh quite quickly. Why would you want elections? Only three to four percent of the total population could vote. It's kind of crazy, don't you think?" asked Anthony Harris, the former British ambassador to the UAE. "I think tribalism is here to stay."

The majority population, expatriates, won't be allowed to vote under any circumstances. In my conversations, I haven't found a single expat who thinks democracy is a good idea. No one thinks Emiratis would vote in their best interests.

Security and Terrorism

In 2005 I asked my friend Mike, a longtime resident of Dubai, whether he planned to buy a home. The housing market was as hot as a gas flare and everyone was weighing the same decision. Mike wasn't having any of it. "If you buy a house here, you're betting that bin Laden is a nice guy. I'm not going to make that bet," he drawled in his Australian accent.

Mike's logic was that Dubai's housing values hinged on the fact that terrorists had not bombed the city. Once the bombs started popping, prices would do the same. Since that conversation, Dubai house prices have quadrupled. The only thing nudging them down in late 2008 was the financial meltdown. Bin Laden, it turns out, is a nice guy—so far.

In matters of terrorism, Dubai finds itself in a strange position. On one hand, American pundits regularly blame Dubai as an enabler of terrorism. They point to the September 11 attackers' use of Dubai's banks and airport as evidence that the city is a logistics center for al-Qaida. It doesn't help that two of the attackers held Emirati citizenship. But Dubai also sits on the other side of the terrorism equation. It is a potential target. People point to its social freedoms, its boozy brothels, and its welcome for U.S. warships as red flags that could trigger an attack.

As of this writing, neither of these characterizations is fully accurate. Al-Qaida certainly used Dubai as a logistics center—and doubtless still does—for no reason beyond the fact that it's where the banks, flights, and business opportunities lie, where visas are issued on arrival, and where, until recently, there was little scrutiny of financial transactions.

But, as one UAE government official told me, Al-Qaida also wires money through Western Union in the United States and flies on American Airlines. That, he said, also makes America a logistics center for terrorism.

Dubai's hedonistic excess has offended Muslims for years. It has yet to attract a major al-Qaida suicide campaign. The idea that terrorists "hate us because of our freedoms," the preferred explanation offered in America, has never been correct. Al-Qaida says it attacked the United States because of the presence of U.S. troops in Arabia and America's lopsided support for Israel.[2] In short, Muslim terrorists base their attacks on specific U.S. policies. America hasn't taken the lesson to heart. But the UAE has. Its pro-Arab foreign policy pays careful heed to Muslim causes. That's why Dubai can offer broad social freedoms without, thus far, stoking a backlash.

Nabil al-Yousuf of The Executive Office goes a step further. He believes Dubai's policy of openness and tolerance acts as a protective measure, rather than a risk factor. Give people freedom to do what they please and they're more likely to start businesses or jazz combos, not take up radical philosophies that call for attacking the state. "I very much doubt that there would be a sustained series of terrorist attacks. That usually happens when a country has a political stance and it is being attacked for its stance," al-Yousuf says. "The UAE doesn't have that. We're neutral. What might happen is that someone goes for a specific target."

Dubai, like anywhere else, could find itself victimized by a one-off assault. This happened in Qatar in 2005. An Egyptian man drove a car bomb into a theater full of Westerners, killing himself and a British man and wounding twelve others. Investigators concluded the attacker wasn't part of any organized plot. He was said to be a pissed-off guy of the same ilk that open fire in American post offices. Dubai's nightclubs and restaurants are just as vulnerable.[3] But a protracted campaign of terror, such as those seen in Saudi Arabia and Israel, is unlikely.

That leaves the issue of about 1,300 U.S. troops on UAE soil, which goes against al-Qaida's stated demands. The UAE hosts the Americans as quietly as it can. There is almost no local coverage of the U.S. Air Force operations in Abu Dhabi, nor of the navy port visits in Dubai, although sunburned U.S. sailors, in their crew cuts and polo shirts, are easy to spot in Dubai's malls and bars. The U.S. military presence in the UAE and three other Gulf states triggered a 2006 videotape warning from al-Qaida number two Ayman al-Zawahiri to get them out—or else. "You should worry about your presence in the Gulf," al-Zawahiri said, wagging his finger at Americans watching him on CNN.

A 2005 warning posted on the Internet by a previously unknown group, "Al-Qaida in the Emirates and Oman," demanded the dismantling of U.S. bases within ten days, failing which "the ruling families would endure the fist of the *mujahedeen* in their faces."[4]

Al-Qaida has demonstrated an ability to shut U.S. bases. Its bomb-punctuated offensive in Saudi Arabia forced the kingdom to end the U.S. military presence in 2003. U.S. troops shifted across the border to two huge bases in Qatar. Neighboring Kuwait and Bahrain also host big American bases. The U.S. presence in the UAE is far smaller. But it remains grounds for an al-Qaida attack.

In a region where political violence is a fact of life, Dubai hasn't been immune. Its worst assault came in 1961, as mentioned, when Omani rebels detonated bombs in the passenger steamship *Dara,* killing 236. In 1983, a bomb blew Gulf Air flight 771 out of the sky just after it took off from Abu Dhabi en route to Karachi. All 117 people aboard died when the plane crashed in Jebel Ali. The Palestinian terrorist Abu Nidal was said to have authored the attack to convince Saudi Arabia and other Gulf states to pay protection money, which Kuwait and the UAE did, according to some.[5] In 1981, Dubai's Hyatt Regency was bombed after the hotel's bar broke an unwritten local code by serving alcohol to Emiratis wearing their white *kandoura* cloaks. And, in 1999, Dubai authorities discovered explosives in the Deira City Center shopping mall.[6]

Most alarmingly, in October 2002, UAE authorities arrested a man considered one of the most dangerous in the region: Abd al-Rahim al-Nashiri, a Saudi described as the head of al-Qaida's Gulf wing and mastermind of the 2000 bombing of the USS *Cole* in Yemen. In 2002, Dubai airport authorities spotted the young Saudi arriving on a flight from Yemen and grabbed him.

Press reports said al-Nashiri was planning an attack on a UAE oil installation, perhaps by turning an oil tanker into an enormous suicide bomb.[7] Dubai handed the Saudi to the CIA, which flew him to its interrogation camp in Jordan and tortured a confession from him.[8] CIA Director Michael Hayden said al-Nashiri was one of three people his organization had waterboarded, which simulates drowning. In 2009, the Obama administration dropped the terror charges against the young Saudi, who remained locked away in Guantánamo Bay. Al-Nashiri denied the charges, saying he made a false confession to get the CIA to stop torturing him.[9]

In early 2001, Dubai authorities detained Lebanese al-Qaida member Ziad Jarrah and offered him to the CIA, a UAE government official said. Tragically, Dubai released Jarrah after the CIA said it didn't want him. The CIA disputes this version of events. Either way, Jarrah continued to the United States, where he died on September 11, 2001, at the controls of United Flight 93, which crashed in Pennsylvania.[10]

Authorities have also handed traveling terrorists to Egypt and Pakistan.[11]

Thus far, warnings like al-Zawahiri's have come to nothing. "They look credible initially but these attacks never materialize," says Mustafa Alani, a security expert at the Dubai-based Gulf Research Center. "We never discover a cell, never find a plot. These warnings are losing credibility."

Still, it is legitimate to ask: Why has Dubai escaped major terror blows since the 1961 bombing of the *Dara*?

One reason, as al-Yousuf pointed out, is that the UAE lacks the marginalized population that normally carries out these attacks. Another is that security is tight and out of sight. Dubai, with only seven policemen in 1955, now employs tens of thousands of them, many undercover. A U.S. diplomat once told me that street sweepers and roadside gardeners would greet him by name in English as he went for his morning jog. The diplomat assumed his admirers were Sheikh Mohammed's undercover security men.

Radicals are drummed out. Islamists, even those with mild views who would be allowed on the air in Qatar and Kuwait, are frozen out of public debate. The Ministry of Education fired eighty-three teachers in 2007 for mild Islamist beliefs, transferring them to menial government jobs. In October 2008, heavily armed security forces raided several homes in and around the east coast city of Khor Fakkan, arresting dozens of young men and boys, presumed Islamists. At the time of writing, the government hadn't acknowledged the arrests.[12]

The government is on the lookout for any form of radical expression, whether it's Saudi Wahhabism, Salafism, or radical Shiite theology from Iraq and Iran. The UAE chapter of the Muslim Brotherhood cannot operate openly. Most imams are paid directly by the government, which gives them guidance on sermons and monitors their speech for political content.[13]

"We don't have radicalism," al-Yousuf says. "It has been contained."

Dubai is one of the world's safest big cities, despite being one of its most cosmopolitan. There is no electronic privacy law and authorities are widely believed to monitor e-mail and phone calls.[14] Visas are tied to employment. Lose your job and you're out. Commit a crime and you're out—after you've served time. Everyone who gets deported has his irises scanned. The scans are stored in the UAE's Iris Expellee Tracking System, described as the world's largest such database. When deportees try to return—as thousands do every year—they're caught and sent out on the next plane. In 2008, the UAE was on target to expel nine thousand returnees.[15] U.S. Homeland Security official Bob Mocny said after viewing the iris database that he wished he could build a similar system in America, but couldn't because people balk at allowing their eyeballs to be scanned.

UAE authorities see their biggest security threat in the groups of Indians, Iranians, and Pakistanis who outnumber Emirati citizens. Most won't risk their jobs by organizing political parties or unions.[16] But a more sinister specter is the presence of foreign agents and activists thought to be prepared to act against UAE interests. Top worries in this category are Islamic terror groups and Iranian cells that could retaliate against U.S. interests in the event of an American or Israeli attack on Iran. The UAE's periodic arrests and roundups of illegal immigrants—a 2007 amnesty deported around 185,000—have these threats in mind.

Another theory of Dubai's resistance to terror is more spurious: Rulers pay off al-Qaida to prevent attacks. This is a frequent allegation, even made by diplomats. The rumor seems to stem from an apparent willingness to submit to terrorist demands. The UAE may have paid off the Abu Nidal organization in the 1980s, as alleged. The country seems to have given in to kidnappers' demands in 2006 when an official in its Baghdad embassy, Naji Rashid al-Nuaimi, was held in Iraq. Al-Nuaimi was released after the UAE sent its staff home and shuttered its embassy.[17]

In 1999, several Abu Dhabi royals apparently spent time with bin Laden in Afghanistan. The CIA monitored a C-130 planeload of Emirati sheikhs who went on a hunting trip to Afghanistan, where they built a luxurious tent city. Lawrence Wright describes the scene vividly in his book *The Looming Tower*. Each time bin Laden visited the camp, a CIA mole in the UAE secret service reported the terrorist kingpin's arrival. The Pentagon readied a cruise missile strike. The CIA's top terrorism man, Michael Scheuer, saw it as his best chance to assassinate bin Laden. But the Clinton administration terrorism czar, Dick Clarke, rejected the strike. As many as three hundred people might have died, with dozens of UAE royals among them. And the CIA couldn't guarantee that bin Laden was actually in the camp.[18] But that happened before September 11. These days the UAE has special forces in Afghanistan. It is doubtful that al-Qaida would want them to get in touch. Ironically, Clarke's security firm, Good Harbor Consulting, has landed several contracts from the Abu Dhabi government and operates an office in the UAE capital. It's possible that the same royals he saved are now his clients.[19]

Yet another theory says Dubai doesn't get attacked because it's too useful to terrorists and smugglers. An attack would tighten security and stop the party of lightly regulated banking and freewheeling ports. "I don't think any terrorist organization will conduct any huge operation in Dubai or in the UAE, because it's like shooting yourself in the foot," says Rabih Fayad, Middle East intelligence manager for security firm International SOS.[20]

After the revelations of pre-September 11 al-Qaida money transfers, the U.S. Treasury Department and the UAE set up a joint unit that watches for terrorist funds and those connected to Iran's nuclear program.[21] Terrorists use UAE services at their own risk.

Smuggling Gets Serious

The UAE may not welcome terrorists, but it certainly hosted smugglers. After independence in 1971, Dubai and Sharjah emerged as supply bases for mercenaries and bloody regimes like Charles Taylor's Liberia and others blocked from the international weapons market. The arms trader Victor Bout, a former KGB man, operated Sharjah's biggest air cargo company, arming African rebels and dictators as well as the Taliban.[22] The UAE finally deported him in 2001 under pressure from Washington.[23] UAE-based smugglers weren't operating just one way to Afghanistan. Dubai acted as a conduit for Taliban and al-Qaida gold smuggled out of Afghanistan and into Sudan. Bout's planes handled some of those shipments.[24]

A U.S. counter-narcotics official in Afghanistan told me in 2006 that Dubai was the chief destination for the profits of Afghani and Iranian opium traffickers. He said drug gangs laundered profits by buying Dubai apartments and earning legitimate rental income.

Dubai was also a center of the nuclear black market, a key base for a smuggling network led by Pakistani scientist A. Q. Khan. Until his group was wrapped up in 2004, Khan and Pakistan exported millions of centrifuge parts via Dubai to secret nuclear programs in Iran, Libya, and elsewhere. Shipments that passed through Dubai's free port include high-strength aluminum, high-tech lathes, aluminum tubes, and finished centrifuges. Khan's network was able to thrive in the city's no-questions-asked business and trade environment, which allowed him to set up shell companies—some of which were little more than letter drops—and meet with potential buyers. At one point, Pakistan shipped twenty used centrifuges to Libya's nuclear program through Dubai, along with a container of spare parts for two hundred more. Khan made dozens of visits to Dubai, hosted meetings and dinners, even getting a vasectomy in the city. Eventually the operation became such a well-known target for Western and Israeli intelligence that Pakistan's military told Khan to move elsewhere. UAE authorities caught and imprisoned some of his accomplices and closed down his businesses. In 2009, Khan was released from five years' house arrest in Pakistan.[25]

Dubai's wealthy and trusting environment is also attracting organized crime, especially East European syndicates, which have committed gory murders and audacious robberies in the city's tourist spots. In 2007, a gang of Serbian jewel thieves raided the Egyptian-themed Wafi City mall, roaring into an outdoor café pavilion in a pair of Audi A8 sports cars. They robbed the ultra-expensive Graff jewelry shop of $4 million in stones and then raced off. "It was the wildest thing I had ever seen in my life," says Rick Carraway, an American architect who witnessed the crime. "There was a deafening crash and these cars sped into the mall. Shoppers were screaming, panicking and running away."[26] Onlookers filmed the heist with camera phones and then uploaded clips to YouTube.

Even the sail-shaped Burj Al Arab has hosted a bloody crime scene. In 2006, suspected Russian mobsters murdered a Syrian diamond dealer and stole his wares in one of the Burj's suites. And in 2008, Lebanese pop singer Suzan Tamim was stabbed to death in her Dubai apartment, victim of an apparent hit by an Egyptian tycoon.

These days, the crime headlines tend toward the financial variety. In 2008, the government placed under investigation more than a dozen bankers and corporate leaders, and two former federal ministers[27] in a broad-ranging crackdown on corruption. Suspects have been arrested and held for months, usually on allegations of bribery or embezzlement, while the crackdown continues. Sheikh Mohammed's *diwan*, leading the investigation, warned that "there will be no tolerance shown to anybody who tries to exploit his position to make illegal profits." None of those arrested had been charged at the time of writing, including executives at Dubai's biggest state corporations, nor Zack Shahin, a U.S. citizen and former chief executive of the developer Deyaar, whose arrest in March 2008 kicked off the probe.

Dubai's outlaw legacy is a spin-off of its openness and laissez-faire capitalist ways. But nowadays the stain on its reputation causes problems. Western banks aren't eager to plow investments into a shady locale. So Dubai regulators say their cleanups have gone further than otherwise necessary to reassure investors. Still, as long as Dubai remains a duty-free port and travel hub, it'll be useful to smugglers.

High Stakes in the New Dubai

Dubai is strict when it comes to security because the stakes are so high. Stability is the keystone of the economy and a chief reason Dubai diversified away from oil. But Dubai's new ventures depend on volatile foreign investment, which tends to die when the chips are down. More than ever, the economy requires foreigners to vacation, invest, and live in Dubai. If they take the money and run, the Dubai model implodes. This was starting to happen in 2009 as the credit crunch swept in. An attack would only worsen matters.

"It's skating on ice. You get a bomb in the Burj Al Arab or a major terrorism attack and everybody starts to lose money. Less people coming to the hotels, less people buying into the Dubai property market," says Peter Hellyer of the National Media Council in Abu Dhabi. "Anything that tarnishes the image can affect the flow of investment."

Tourism, responsible for nearly a quarter of Dubai's economy, remained vulnerable, as did the already foundering real estate market. And the city's financial sector is run by foreign bankers and fund managers, many of whom were among the UAE's two hundred thousand European, North American, and other "first-world" nationals.[28] Some were already leaving after losing jobs as the economy slowed in 2009. An attack would hasten the exodus. In this case, Dubai's stinginess with citizenship works against it. Skilled professionals who underpin the private sector would be less likely to leave if they had a sense of belonging.

Al-Yousuf disagrees. "We've been through this. It's not as if investments will evaporate if there's an attack. Even if Iran gets attacked, we might get hurt in the short and medium term, but not in the long run," he says. "Companies are more rooted now. When Dubai was still developing, people had liquid investments that they could easily take out. Now people own houses and investment properties."

It doesn't pay to worry in Dubai. Warfare has dogged the neighborhood for decades. Old-timers are jaded about the danger. The city has watched the raging of three wars since the 1980s and wound up turning a profit when it came time to rebuild. Saddam Hussein's misadventures made millionaires in Dubai. In 1980, the Iraqi president's invasion of Iran triggered an exodus of educated Iranians and their businesses to Dubai. In 1990, when he attacked Kuwait, the same thing happened.

"We've never had sustainable periods of peace and tranquility in the region. But Dubai's still here and we're growing. So what's the worst that can happen?" asks Essa Kazim, the stock exchange chairman. "I agree, certain sectors are vulnerable. They might be affected for a short time. But every time we've had a problem in the past we came out of it much stronger."

17

STUCK BETWEEN AMERICA AND IRAN

Dueling for Dubai's Loyalty

THE FIVE THOUSAND Iranians had waited for hours on May 13, 2007. They'd finished the last crumbs of their picnics and hung their homemade banners. They killed time by practicing their chants: "Down, down USA!" and "Nuclear energy is our right!" And they sat through a speech by a Shiite imam who promised: "You're in for an unforgettable night!"

The hardships melted away when their man finally strode onstage: the bearded leader with his infectiously humble charisma and trademark workingman's jacket. They rose cheering to greet him. They frantically waved their tiny green, white, and red flags. The camera flashes and klieg lights danced on him, as he raised both arms and waved, graciously reflecting back their adulation.

President Mahmoud Ahmadinejad was the first Iranian president since the 1979 revolution to visit the UAE, and this would be his first public speech. For the Emiratis present in the soccer stadium at Dubai's Iranian Club, it was a rare spectacle: a political rally in a country where politics are illegal.

Ahmadinejad's speech was a masterstroke of timing. The high-octane Iranian blew into the UAE just hours after the departure of U.S. Vice President Dick Cheney. The contrast between the two visits could not have been deeper. The dour Cheney, with his characteristic disdain for the public eye, hunkered out of view in the Emirates Palace Hotel in Abu Dhabi. His entreaties to his hosts to back the aggressive U.S. line on Iran got no play in the media.

Ahmadinejad was another matter. The UAE pulled out all the stops for the Iranian president, giving him a red-carpet welcome at the Abu Dhabi airport from the president, Sheikh Khalifa, and Dubai leader Sheikh Mohammed. It seemed as if the UAE let him issue its response to Cheney. Ahmadinejad made three public speeches during his visit, taking questions from the press, touting his country's controversial nuclear development, and glad-handing the crowds.

By the time he arrived at the Dubai soccer stadium, the place had been gussied up with huge posters of his grinning face. Ahmadinejad spoke to the crowd in the style of an American evangelical preacher, dividing the world into beauty and ugliness. He linked beauty with God and his believers, and the ugly things with the unbelievers.

"A man who believes in God respects everyone. Look at history," he said, when the crowd had finally settled. "The wars, the suffering, the racism; it's the product of selfish people who don't believe in God, people with Satanic beliefs."

A few energetic men at the back waved a black banner demanding nuclear rights. In an ominous parallel to suspicions about Iran's ambitions, their banner carried the yellow nuclear fallout symbol, rather than the usual three orbiting atoms of atomic energy.

"Look at Iraq. These people destroyed Iraq," Ahmadinejad continued. "They sent millions fleeing their homes. They said they came to save Iraq. That's a big lie. They came to control the region, to control the oil!"

He soon honed in on the U.S. embargo that stifles his nation. "They have industrial and medical improvements, but they keep them for themselves," Ahmadinejad railed. "They want to control other nations, to keep others dependent on them. They're not against nuclear weapons, they're against Iran's growth. The nation of Iran, a young nation with faith in God, will have this energy!"

At this point the restless crowd erupted and Ahmadinejad stood back to listen. "Nuclear energy is our right!" they shouted. He stooped to receive an admirer's gift of a bouquet of roses.

When he stepped back to the microphone, Ahmadinejad spoke of the mighty bond between Iran and the Arab countries across the Gulf. He said the unbelievers wanted to force these natural allies apart. The aim? To start a war that allows them to control the wealth. He turned and addressed the unbelievers directly.

"We're telling you to leave the region!" Ahmadinejad yelled, pointing into the air. The crowd stirred into applause. "The nations of this region can no longer take your forcing yourself on them. We know better how to bring peace and security to our region. What is it that you've done in this world, that every time your names are mentioned, hatred swells up? This is Iran's advice to you: Leave the region!"

A few months later, President Bush's motorcade roared into Dubai. It was a rare gray drizzly afternoon. To locals who cherish the rain, it was a good omen. But to most folks, it looked like the black cloud shrouding the Bush administration had followed the U.S. president to Dubai.

To be safe, Sheikh Mohammed gave Dubaians a mandatory holiday. Businesses were shuttered and the main roads blocked. The titanic Sheikh Zayed Road sat unused all day, except for a single American motorcade traveling in tight formation. Sheikh Mohammed's precautions probably stemmed from the real chance that something could happen to the U.S. President on Dubai's anarchic roads and the thought of all the bad press that would ensue. Clearing them solved the matter. It also minimized distractions so that Bush got a full view of Dubai's architectural marvels. The motorcade took the president through the forests of skyscrapers in the Dubai Marina, past the imitation Chrysler Buildings of Dubai Internet City, near the Burj Al Arab and the nearly finished Burj Dubai, and through the shimmering skyscraper corridor approaching the city center. By the time Bush reached Sheikh Mohammed's ancestral home on the creek, the American president's perceptions of the Middle East were soundly shaken.

"He was in awe of what Dubai had accomplished," says Tarik Yousef, the forty-one-year-old dean of the Dubai School of Government, who was waiting in the home to greet the arriving president. "He didn't expect it to be this developed. You could see that he was blown away."

It was clear that Dubai's creations couldn't have been managed without stability and good governance. It was as if Bush's focus on Iraq and terrorism had blinded him to the progress transforming other parts of the region, and that these changes had come with little or no effort from

Washington. "Dubai is a model," Bush gushed to his hosts. "The sheikh is an inspiration. There is hope for the Middle East."[1]

Bush took a seat in the old coral house and fielded questions from School of Government students. The questions had been prepared in advance and were easy softballs, eliciting feel-good responses. Sheikh Mohammed was annoyed. He wanted to put this controversial leader on the hot seat. He leaned over to Tarik Yousef and gave him an order: "*Inta es'aal!*"—You ask a question! Yousef whispered back that he hadn't prepared anything. "Come up with something," the Dubai leader demanded.

The Libyan American cleared his throat and piped up. "What's your legacy going to be, Mr. President? It seems like you've spread yourself too thin. You're not really going to accomplish anything. It's all controversial and bloody in this region."

"I don't care about legacy," Bush shot back. "I've always believed that a man's best deeds will be talked about in the future, long after he's gone."

That's exactly my point, Yousef thought to himself.

Dubai and Iran

Dubai's ties with Iran are warmer than those of any other of the Arab sheikhdoms. Dubai has capitalized on those ties, and Iran's missteps, since at least 1900, when Sheikh Maktoum bin Hasher coaxed away the merchants of Bandar Lengeh.

The last Iranian shah, Reza Pahlavi, was a Dubai admirer, haranguing his engineers to build ports like Sheikh Rashid's. In those days, people on the Arab side of the Gulf crossed to Iran for boozing and carousing. After the Islamic revolution that ousted the shah in 1979, the flow reversed. Iranians fled the stifling atmosphere in Tehran to let their hair down in Dubai.

"For Iranians, Dubai is the symbol of a well-balanced Islamic society," says Saeed Leylaz, the editor of *Sarmayeh*, Tehran's financial newspaper, and a leading commentator. "It's an Islamic country, but nobody is forced to be Islamic."

Dubai didn't join Saudi Arabia, Iraq, and others who agitated against the ayatollahs. Sheikh Rashid and his sons still saw Iran as a lucrative trade partner. That won them Tehran's respect. The little city-state across the Gulf came out a winner in the Iranian revolution. Nowadays, with around four hundred thousand Iranian residents, Dubai is Iran's lifeline to the world. American politicians like to bray about Iran's ties to Syria, Iraq, and Lebanon's Hezbollah, but it is Dubai that keeps the ostracized nation functioning.

"Dubai is the most important city on earth to the Islamic Republic of Iran, with the exception of Tehran," says Leylaz.

Iran also keeps Dubai afloat. Iran is Dubai International Airport's top destination, with more than three hundred flights per week. The UAE is Iran's largest trading partner, responsible for about one-seventh of Iran's $100 billion international trade.[2] Dubai is also the main destination for capital flight from Iran, much of which has been plowed into real estate.

"You cannot imagine the number of ads for apartments in Dubai on the Persian satellite channels," Leylaz says. "There is a constant stream of money flying from Tehran to Dubai."

The price of Dubai's friendship is high. Billions of dollars a year flow out of Iran and into Dubai. This is not a relationship that Dubai wants to halt, even at Washington's request.

Dubai and America

At the same time, Dubai is a key U.S. ally, a crucial Middle East base where American companies are extending their reach into the Arab world, central Asia, and Africa. Dubai has become so useful that in 2006, U.S. oil services giant Halliburton moved its CEO, Dave Lesar, to Dubai.

Ironically, Washington sees the UAE as the anti-Iran, says Afshin Molavi, a fellow at the New America Foundation in Washington. America and the UAE have signed agreements allowing U.S. companies to provide nuclear energy technology. The idea is to help the UAE get generating plants running quickly, demonstrating to Tehran that there is a right way to pursue nukes—and a wrong way.

Dubai is also an example of religious tolerance, clean government, capitalist success, and progressive attitudes toward women that the United States likes to tout to the Arab world. American diplomats say bluntly that Dubai is their model for a new Baghdad.

But the UAE also needs America, even more than it needs Iran. The country's defense ties with America are nothing short of existential.

Without a protector, the UAE, with its oil riches and tiny native population, might be a tasty morsel to a larger neighbor. Cooperation with Washington comes readily. The UAE was the first Middle East country to adopt U.S. port security measures. UAE special forces work alongside NATO in Afghanistan. And Jebel Ali is the only Gulf port that can berth a carrier, and the only Middle East stop where U.S. sailors can take shore leave.

Dubai Intelligence City

Dubai is also a U.S. spy center. America hasn't had an embassy in Tehran since 1979. Dubai, with several hundred thousand Iranians, is the next best thing.

Picking up details on Iran is easy. Day after day, Iranians line up to spill their secrets to the U.S. government. How is this possible? Dubai and Abu Dhabi are the closest places that Iranians can apply for U.S. visas. The visa windows at the U.S. consulate and embassy are lucrative intelligence collection points. So lucrative, in fact, that the Central Intelligence Agency stepped in to save the Dubai consulate from closure. The State Department tried more than once to shutter the consulate, mainly for budget reasons. But with hundreds of Iranians coming every day to be monitored, interrogated, and, sometimes, recruited into spying on their own government, the CIA argued that cuts needed to come elsewhere.[3]

Iranians seeking U.S. visas are interviewed by Iran specialists, some of whom speak fluent Farsi. Those with interesting backgrounds find themselves in a long process. U.S. interviewers ask them to return time and again, pressing them to collect more and deeper details, and all the while holding out the possibility of a U.S. visa. In the 1980s, one of the more colorful spies working the rich fishing grounds in Dubai was none other than Gary Schroen, the veteran CIA operations officer later tapped to lead the first U.S. team inside Afghanistan after the September 11 attacks.[4]

The once tiny U.S. consulate—with just six American staffers—expanded, taking over multiple floors in the Dubai World Trade Centre. Intelligence collection became a priority.[5] Washington sought to monitor Iranian banking, business, and trade. Besides the CIA, U.S. Customs monitored trade, and the U.S. Treasury sent people to watch for money laundering and suspicious cash flows. The U.S. military sent liaison officers as well, including navy investigators whose job it is to collar drunken sailors in whorehouses and get them back on their ships.

In 2006 the State Department opened a new office in the consulate dealing solely with Iran: the Iran Regional Presence Office. It became the first U.S. diplomatic mission aimed at Iran since 1979, when revolutionaries seized control of the U.S. embassy in Tehran. The half dozen U.S. diplomats at the low-profile office appear to focus on the softer side of relations, attending cultural events in the Iranian community and leaving the nuclear confrontation to Washington.[6]

Washington isn't the only government that spies in the rich grounds of Dubai. Iran also runs covert agents, many of whom operate Dubai branches of state-owned companies, including those owned by the hardline Revolutionary Guard Corps and the Iranian ministries of defense and intelligence.[7] The Iranians aren't in Dubai to collect information on the United States. There aren't enough Americans to make that worthwhile. They're there because even state-run companies find business easier in Dubai than in sanctions-hobbled Iran. Some state firms have used their Dubai offices to transfer to Iran nuclear technology banned under the UN and U.S. embargoes.

Working for the Clampdown

The Iranian presence in Dubai has brought heavy U.S. government pressure on the UAE. Even American Jewish groups have harangued the sheikhs to trim relations with Iran.

When the Clinton administration enacted U.S. sanctions in 1995—under pressure from the Israel lobby—the UAE initially ignored them. It was, in effect, like Spain asking Texas to cut ties with Mexico. U.S. laws don't apply in the UAE, of course, and Dubai's merchant families—who still speak Farsi and stay in touch with relatives in Iran—weren't about to shrink their businesses on a foreign government's say-so. Trade with Iran is one of the key underpinnings of Dubai's prosperity. Cutting it off is shooting yourself in the leg.

But over the years, the UAE's resolve buckled somewhat. The UN began levying sanctions in 2006 after Ahmadinejad revived Iran's nuclear enrichment program. The UAE observed the UN's mild sanctions, as it must under its treaty obligations. By this time, U.S. pressure had grown so intense that the UAE quietly began cutting its thousand-year ties with Iran.

The UAE imposed export restrictions in 2007, and customs authorities stepped up inspections of Iran-bound cargo. Shipments that used to get turned around within hours now sit for days or weeks. Suspicious cargoes are impounded, even seized, as was a 530-pound shipment of zirconium—a metal used in nuclear reactors—found in 2007 on an Iran-bound ship at Jebel Ali. That shipment violated UN sanctions, but UAE officials went beyond the UN mandate by shuttering forty Iranian companies.

The government effectively froze the growth of Dubai's Iranian community at the behest of the United States. Iranians now find it more difficult to travel to Dubai. Newly arriving Iranian businessmen find themselves unable to open UAE branches of their firms. Dubai-based companies can no longer get visas to bring in new employees from Iran. Dubai branches of international banks like HSBC, StandardChartered, and Citibank have asked Iranian customers to withdraw their deposits because their accounts were being closed.[8] These actions appear driven by U.S. sanctions, not the UN's. Dubai's vaunted neutrality is slipping.

The clampdown is blatant discrimination, says Nasser Hashempour, the deputy director of the Dubai-based Iranian Business Council. Expatriate Iranians with no ties to Iran's nuclear program found themselves in U.S. crosshairs, and now Dubai's. Business is suffering. Hashempour, like many Iranians, once held the United States in great esteem. In the 1980s, he and two friends made a glorious two-week road trip from Los Angeles to New York. That esteem evaporated as Washington began to thwart his livelihood. And now Dubai, a city practically built by Iranians, is doing the work of America and Israel.

"Why should they make life hard for Iranians? We helped this place develop from the very beginning," he says. "If they pressure Iranians, a lot of Iranians will take their assets to a country where we're welcome. A lot of non-Iranians will lose confidence in Dubai."

The tip of the American spear is a guy named Stuart Levey, the U.S. undersecretary for terrorism and financial intelligence. Levey is a fixture at international business conferences, where he tells people to stop dealing with Iran. His logic is effective: If the United States finds you've traded, even unknowingly, with an Iranian government entity—even if disguised as a shell company—you'll be hit by the full force of U.S. law.

The upshot is that companies must choose between doing business in Iran or America. Given the size of the U.S. market, most heed Levey's advice. His talks have cast a chill of paranoia over Dubai's banks and exporters.

"The world's top financial institutions and corporations are reevaluating their business with Iran because they are worried about the risk and their reputations," Levey told two hundred bankers gathering in Dubai. "You should worry too. Be especially cautious when it comes to doing business with Iran."[9]

Hashempour finds it galling. Iran and Dubai have hundreds of years of ties, through marriage, shared cuisine, traditions, and religion. The Arabic spoken in Dubai has a Persian inflection. Neighborhoods and families are named after towns in Iran. And a minor functionary from halfway around the world tells people to break those ties—at great personal cost—and they do what he says.

Not all the U.S. inroads in Dubai have harmed Iran. American firms, says Hashempour, have quietly courted the Iranian Business Council. With Obama in the White House, Iranians feel that a warming is due. Iran's 70 million consumers make an alluring market. In October, there was a good sign: Citibank sponsored the business council's monthly luncheon. "They are thinking of the future and of Iranian assets," Hashempour says with a chuckle.

Cyrus Kheirabadi runs a company that imports spare parts for Chinese-made Komatsu bulldozers and cranes and reexports them to Iran. It used to be possible to run such a business from Iran. The equipment could be purchased in China with a letter of credit in dollars from, say, Bank Saderat Iran, and imported directly. When the Bush administration blocked Iranian banks from using dollars, Iranian firms switched to letters of credit denominated in euros. But then corresponding banks—even those in China—stopped dealing with Iranian banks. So Kheirabadi, like thousands of other Iranian businessmen, opened an office in Dubai. In Dubai he can usually get a letter of credit from an international bank and import goods to Dubai. Then he reexports them to Iran. Is it a hassle?

"Yes. It makes things costly for us. Credit lines are closed. Some banks don't deal with us. We have to work with cash," says Kheirabadi, the director of Prime Apex General Trading. "The end user winds up paying more. The sanctions don't do anything to the Iranian government. The ones who get hurt are the poor people."

When America tightened its embargo against Iran around 2003, there were fewer than 3,000 Iranian-run businesses in Dubai. In 2008 there were nearly 10,000.

Charley Kestenbaum moved to Dubai in 1984, just three years after Iranian radicals finally released the fifty-two U.S. hostages they'd held in the U.S. embassy in Tehran for 444 days. The U.S. quarrel with Iran had a clear rationale and Kestenbaum, as the American commercial attaché, was Washington's man to monitor trade with the Islamic Republic. For the next fifteen years, he was a familiar sight in Dubai's trading souks and wharves. He oversaw the local implementation of Bill Clinton's sanctions.

U.S. policy, as he describes it, is the economic strangulation of Iran. Washington means to put pressure on the Iranian regime in every possible way short of dropping bombs. That means blocking capital, technology, and investment, and sabotaging commerce.

"Part of sanctions enforcement against Iran was simply to make things more expensive for Iran and to bleed their economy over long periods of time," Kestenbaum says. "Every dollar spent above normal market price was a dollar unavailable for other procurement."

Dubai, as Iran's main window, has long been targeted as the main hole in the embargo. Congress viewed the city's merchants as working at cross-purposes to its wishes. That attitude was reinforced when, not long after the U.S. sanctions were announced, Dubai's GE distributor told the press that he had no intention of complying, since U.S. law doesn't hold sway in Dubai. Compliance meant giving up as much as 60 percent of his business.

"GE had to backpedal and shut that guy up quick," says Kestenbaum. To this day products from Kodak and GE and everyone else are being loaded onto dhows and freighters in Dubai and Sharjah, and going to Iran. "There's very limited control. Someone can say, 'Okay, we're not shipping to Iran. We're shipping to Tanzania.' The boat goes out and instead of turning south it runs east toward Iran. Who knows?"

These days subsidized Iranian gasoline—which sells in Iran for forty cents a gallon—gets exchanged in the UAE for all manner of goods blocked by the U.S. embargo or thwarted by Iran's import restrictions, from cases of Jack Daniel's and cartons of Marlboros to microchips, software, computers, and cell phones.

The blatant embargo-busting makes Dubai a more sensitive destination for all sorts of U.S. goods, on the premise that sending them to Dubai is as good as sending them to Iran. One day Kestenbaum got a call from Washington asking him to track a shipment of bacterial culture, a precursor used in the manufacture of yogurt that might also be useful in biological warfare.

"We checked it out," says Kestenbaum. "It was going to a yogurt factory in Dubai."

Things in Iran would be a lot worse if it weren't for Dubai. Dubai's willingness to protect most of its trade in the face of Washington's pressure is a great insulator, allowing Tehran a freer foreign policy hand while decreasing American harm to the country's stability.

"Dubai is a very wide window that allows us to bypass the sanctions and our tough relations with the world," says Saeed Leylaz.

Dubai's leaders are justified in resisting pressure from Washington, says David Stockwell, the U.S. consul in Dubai in the mid-eighties. American and Emirati interests are not identical. The United States risks overplaying its hand. The UAE is a reliable oil producer, a huge purchaser of Boeing jets and U.S. military hardware, and a major ally.

"They have no reason to have to comply with U.S. wishes on this," says Stockwell, "With all due respect to the U.S., the reality is that the UAE has to live in this neighborhood. If the U.S. pushes too hard, they defeat themselves. They don't want to turn friends into enemies."

Torn Between Two Lovers

The simultaneous presidencies of Bush and Ahmadinejad were a nightmare for Dubai. The specter of yet another Gulf war looked frighteningly close. Worse, this war might've dragged in the UAE, since it hosts U.S. bases that would be likely Iranian targets.

In the neutral atmosphere of Dubai, Bush and Ahmadinejad looked like angry men who shared philosophies and methods. Both hail from the extreme right wing of their nation's political sphere, both leaned on support from religious fundamentalists and rural bases; both used simple language with anti-intellectual overtones; both required external enemies—in this case, each other—to legitimize their grip on power. Neither had much use for diplomacy.

"Both of them are being jerks," said twenty-one-year-old Hamda bin Demaithan. "They should just leave us out of it."

How did Dubai manage to navigate the treacherous shoals between sworn enemies? By being pragmatic and staying out of politics. This is the central plank of Dubai's diplomacy.

"It's like the song: 'Torn between two lovers, feeling like a fool.' We have to satisfy them both. And it's no easy task," Abdulkhaleq Abdulla says with a smile. "When these two start going at each other you really need to be careful."

Sheikh Mohammed was a confidant of both presidents. He enjoyed good rapport with President Bush at Camp David in June 2008. And he's also spent time in Iran with President Ahmadinejad. Dubai presents itself as the essential neutral point, where all sides interact. "It's a complex and dangerous situation but they've finessed it brilliantly all along," Kestenbaum says.

No War, Please, We're Working

America is central to the UAE's survival. The two countries signed a defense cooperation agreement in the mid-1990s that was triggered by the shock of Saddam's 1990 invasion of Kuwait. The agreement's contents are secret, but the gist is that the U.S. military will respond to an attack on the UAE in exchange for use of air and sea bases.

With Saddam out of the picture, the UAE sees Iran as its chief military threat, especially given Iran's nuclear program and its arsenal of ballistic missiles. The UAE's defense strategy means sustaining a first strike and praying for allies—the United States, France, and Britain—to arrive.

In one sense, the United States is both the cure and the sickness. The most plausible reason Iran would assault the UAE would be in retaliation for a U.S. or Israeli strike on its territory. This possibility led UAE president Sheikh Khalifa to publicly forbid the United States from using UAE territory to attack Iran. He also banned the U.S. military from using its Abu Dhabi-based spy planes to conduct intelligence missions over Iran.[10]

At the same time, the UAE has spent vast amounts on American military hardware, including $6.4 billion for 80 F-16 fighter jets in 2004. Americans train Emirati F-16 pilots at Al-Dhafra Air Base near Abu Dhabi. The UAE bought Raytheon's Hawk missile defense system in the 1980s and since integrated it with the U.S. military, so the two countries can respond jointly in the event of an attack.[11] The Hawk batteries can be seen scattered in the desert and along the coast. In 2007, the UAE notified Congress that it also wanted $9 billion worth of Raytheon's longer-range Patriot defense missiles.

And, perhaps to show the Americans that their aggressive posture toward Iran isn't appreciated, in 2007 the UAE invited France to open an air base. The UAE wants to further diversify its defense relationships away from America, which is seen as too favorable to Israel, a potential enemy. UAE fliers also pilot French Mirage jets, and their ground forces operate French tanks and Russian armored personnel carriers. But everyone knows that only the United States can protect them if there is real trouble. "When the sheikhs dial 911, it doesn't ring in Paris," Kestenbaum says.

Losing Touch with America

In the long run, Iran is bound to win the tussle over the UAE's loyalty, if only by dint of its location. While the UAE's long-term plans call for diluting reliance on America, Iran, with its young population and huge reserves of oil and gas, is in the ascendancy.

And Dubaians can't help but notice that Americans don't really like them. There is a knee-jerk hostility in the States, as seen in the Dubai Ports furor. Partly this is because Dubai sits inside the UAE, the homeland of two September 11 hijackers. But mostly it's because Dubai lies in the Arab world, and America's view of Arabs is a dim one.

Relations with America are drifting. America tightened visa requirements for Emiratis, an understandable move after 9/11, but one that wound up diverting Emirati college students to Australia and Europe. Stories of Emiratis detained and humiliated by U.S. airport security are rife in the local press. At the moment, most of Sheikh Mohammed's team of advisers is U.S.-educated. They have a natural proclivity to follow the American style in business and government. But that will change as the new crop of leaders takes over. Crown Prince Hamdan studied at the London School of Economics.

The Bush administration's vehement support for Israel and its wars in the region caused huge damage to its reputation.

"People in this region have moved on. They think, 'These guys just hate us, pure and simple,'" says Hafed al-Ghwell, a World Bank official seconded to the Dubai School of Government. "The view is that Americans are not interested in discussion or truth. They're going to do whatever they want because of internal American politics and whatever prejudices they have."

Relations with Washington could go either way under the Obama administration. President Bush's stark unpopularity in the Arab world masked a good working relationship with the UAE. Cheney, with his Big Oil ties, has long been a familiar figure in the Gulf. Obama, with his calls for a "new way forward with the Muslim world," is far more acceptable to the masses, but his actions haven't proven friendly. Obama joined the Democrats who came out against Dubai when DP World acquired the U.S. ports. His secretary of state, Hillary Clinton, was, as noted earlier, a chief orchestrator of the anti-Dubai hysteria. She will have some crow to eat before she is welcome in the UAE.

But Obama's pledge to lessen tensions will bring relief to Iran-dependent Dubai. Ironically, any direct U.S. dialogue with Iran could also wind up sidelining Dubai as a key go-between. An end to the U.S. embargo would drastically cut Dubai's reexport trade and make much Iranian foreign investment unnecessary.

Of course, it's not just up to Obama to assuage the wounds. Relations also depend on another electorate. The voters of Iran were to go to the polls in June 2009.

18

THE MEANING OF DUBAI

The Big Comedown

BY 2008, DUBAI was bloated, with as much property under development as Shanghai, which has thirteen times the population.[1] The city was like a runaway train full of champagne drinkers barreling down a mountain track. One way or another, the party was going to end.

Housing demand remained incandescent as the year wore on. In May, a mob turned up at the launch of a thousand waterfront apartments in Nakheel's Badrah development. The units sold in a few hours and most of the potential buyers had to be turned away.[2] It was a scene that had grown common. Emaar avoided these frenzies by using a lottery system to pick lucky buyers for its property launches. At Abu Dhabi's Cityscape property show, investors in Russia and the United States booked off-plan properties on the Internet and then flew in to make their down payments. When they arrived they found their apartments had been sold to others at higher prices. Demand was so intense that developers raised prices by the hour. Investors at the show flipped homes within hours, raking in instant profits. The wild speculation alarmed governments in Dubai and Abu Dhabi, and the authorities announced restrictions on quick resales. The buyers, roughly a third from the West, were driven by an unsubstantiated belief that the government would prop up the market if prices slipped.

That year Dubai reached the limit of its capacity to build. The labor force could work no faster and there wasn't housing enough to import more. Steel and concrete supply could not meet demand. And it seemed there were no more idle cranes to be found anywhere on earth. It was physically impossible to simultaneously build the entire supply of projects that had been launched.[3]

This realization gave contractors leverage to demand higher rates. Homes that had been sold off-plan years earlier, when costs were lower, were no longer economically feasible to build. A few developers tried to cancel projects and refund buyers' deposits. At first, authorities forced them to follow through, lest the city's reputation be harmed.

Meanwhile, America's subprime mortgage crisis was morphing into the global credit crunch. For a while, Dubai continued its surge. Investors rationalized the ongoing party by saying Gulf economies had decoupled from developed markets. This dubious theory proved correct for about three months.

In October 2008, the credit crunch sneaked into Dubai like a Trojan horse. No one believed that the Gulf, its banks sloshing with surplus oil revenue, could ever find itself short of cash or unwilling to lend. Oil revenues had recently been running seven times their medium-term average. Inflation was the problem. Banks were looking for creative ways of unloading their stockpiles of banknotes. Then the lights went out. Suddenly, banks had no cash.

Where did the money go? Essentially, it ran back to the home countries of the investors who'd sent it. First, currency speculators unwound their bets on the dirham's revaluation and pulled $55 billion out of the UAE. Then foreign investors sold off their shares and took tens of billions more out in a matter of weeks.[4] People woke up one morning and lending had stopped. The liquidity squeeze that gripped the UAE and the rest of the Gulf came as a complete surprise in a region that hadn't experienced a financial shock for more than three decades. Banks lost their trust in each other and in people asking for mortgages. The UAE Central Bank pumped cash into them so they could keep funds flowing to projects. But banks cut way back on mortgage lending. The real estate market slammed to a halt.

The fall Dubai Cityscape property show opened amid this unfolding backdrop. The show saw plenty of the usual glitter-glazed launches, including Nakheel's one-kilometer-tall skyscraper. But analysts canvassing attendees found that no one was buying. Dubai's excess suddenly looked excessive.

Morgan Stanley was the first to articulate the looming gloom. The bank forecast a modest 10 percent drop in property prices for 2009, because of overbuilding. But, it said, things could also get much worse. Dubai might follow the pattern of Singapore in the late 1990s, when values dropped 80 percent in eighteen months. "We expect oversupply to hit Dubai in 2009, leading to a period of price declines," Morgan Stanley's research note said.

The city's financial base was starting to resemble the foundation holding up its towers: sand. Earlier, or Dubai's skyscrapers aren't fixed on bedrock. Friction is the only thing holding their pilings in place. In the buildings' case, it's said to be safe. In October, Moody's Investors Service said Dubai's financial underpinnings were caving. Debt had swollen beyond GDP. If things went south, the government lacked the resources to pay it off. The emirate had borrowed not just to finance its signature projects—man-made islands and the Burj Dubai—but also to purchase stakes in overseas companies whose values had crashed.

Dubai's strategy worked while its assets were bringing in money. But by the fall, the debt overhang was deepening faster than its investments were generating returns. Sheikh Mohammed faced the humiliating prospect of selling stakes in state-run companies to Abu Dhabi. The list of injured companies included those under the Dubai World umbrella and the sheikh's own Dubai Holding. All found themselves grasping shaky assets. The go-go expansion of Emirates airline, with 177 planes on order worth more than $58 billion, was another worry. The airline is the key to the ruler's plan to double yearly tourists to fifteen million by 2015. But vacationers in recession-gripped lands would be hard-pressed to cooperate. Orders might have to be canceled.

Cocky investors who'd crowed about "decoupling" saw their theory unwind. Dubai's stock index was down more than 70 percent by year's end, with some property developers losing 80 percent of their value. The wastage of Dubai's overseas assets has been equally impressive. In 2007, Dubai World paid about $5.1 billion for almost 10 percent of MGM Mirage. A year later MGM's $84 share price had shrunk below $20. Ports operator DP World, the company that spent a whopping $6.8 billion for Britain's P&O shipping, saw its value wither away.[5]

With the credit market frozen, real estate prices fell back at last in late 2008, the first drop since foreigners got permission to buy in 2002. Prices on unfinished apartments got hit hardest, dropping as much as 50 percent. As his emirate wobbled, Sheikh Mohammed took the stage at a World Economic Forum event in Dubai. It was the perfect venue to unveil the response to his first major leadership crisis. The sheikh made perhaps the worst speech of his life. First, he boasted that he'd predicted the crisis. This left audience members wondering why Dubai, with more advance notice than anyone, hadn't prepared for the downturn. Then he pooh-poohed the jagged plunge in the Dubai stock index. His talk spooled past the bankers and economists like a catalog of non sequiturs.

"A few of my friends were wondering what's happening in stock markets, where some shares were dropping," the Dubai leader said. "I told them it didn't matter. Since these shares rose from what they originally started from, technically we are still ahead. Unfortunately, people tend to be pessimistic and focus on losses and forget their gains. Investors should always keep in mind that, in trading, you may lose and you may win."[6]

The leader's unpreparedness didn't inject confidence into the economy. Dubai's shares plumbed new lows, with some nearing their original launch values, as if mocking the sheikh's message. A few weeks later, Dubai issued a more coherent response. It merged its two crumbling state-owned mortgage lenders and put the new entity under the Department of Finance. Dubai's big three developers—Emaar, Nakheel, and Dubai Holding—together responsible for 70 percent of the city's construction, stopped competing and started cooperating. Sheikh Mohammed deputized Mohammed Alabbar to lead a nine-man economic advisory council. A sober Alabbar told a bankers conference that his committee would decide where to hold the line: which projects would stay funded until they get built, and which would be choked off. "These are tough realities that we are going through," Alabbar said. "We are rationalizing our expenditures and consolidating our activities. Times are changing."

Alabbar wisely clarified his city's murky financial position, revealing that Dubai's sovereign debt was $10 billion, plus another $70 billion owed by state-run companies. This, he said, was more than covered by assets worth $260 billion. The city's debt was greater than its entire economic output in 2007 of $54 billion. That's higher in relative terms than the burden in neighboring countries, but far smaller than debt loads of

America and some European countries. And Alabbar dropped a hint where the city would turn if it needed help. He mentioned Dubai's "proud identity as part of the UAE," which, in go-it-alone Dubai, means that rich uncle Abu Dhabi would be asked to clean up the mess.

Time to Rest

Hard times in Dubai is a relative term. Financial conferences invited bankers to blather about the crisis between bites of chocolate mousse. And nobody says a global crash means you can't party. Sol Kerzner certainly never said that. He threw a giant bash at the grand opening of his $1.5 billion hotel Atlantis, The Palm. The seventy-three-year-old magnate flew in Robert De Niro, Charlize Theron, and Wesley Snipes and paid Kylie Minogue $4 million to sing to them. He served up two tons of lobster and dropped another $4 million on fireworks that, in the best Dubai style, blasted up simultaneously from every frond and islet on the Palm Jumeirah. If you'd been lucky enough to be in outer space, you'd have seen a palm-shaped fireworks display. From the ground it looked like shock and awe over Baghdad.

When the party ended, the global age of excess was over. Dubai was the era's poster child. While the rest of the world appraised the party as a foolish overindulgence, Dubaians considered it a justified celebration of six years of wild growth that put the city, at long last, on the map. Downturn or no, Dubai's accomplishments are undeniable. In six years, the city quadrupled in size and doubled in population. It became a frenzied tourist destination and the financial center and air hub for a quarter of the globe. It had produced the world's most fanciful construction boom, sprouting islands and skyscraper pinnacles as far as the eye could see. The bubble may have burst, but it left behind an amazing physical legacy. Sheikh Rashid's prayers had been answered. Eighteen years after his death, everyone on earth had learned of Dubai.

With so much under its belt, some Dubaians saw the coming recession in the manner that a fattened bear views a cozy cave at first snowfall. It was time for reflection and a long snooze until, at some future date, it would reemerge lean and hungry. A few years of slow growth might also readjust the woeful demographic imbalance, giving foreigners reason to leave and the local population a chance to make some babies.

"Slowing down is a blessing for this city. We're headed for a situation where the locals might soon make up zero percent of the population," Abdulkhaleq Abdulla says. "Sheikh Mohammed's legacy is secure. He doesn't need to prove anything else. He has enough to his credit."

Dubai, of course, has been through recessions before. This one was unstoppable. Dubai's vaunted diversification, which was supposed to save it from oil shocks, could do nothing to prevent infection. The global contagion kneecapped Dubai's economic pillars one by one: tourism, real estate, shipping, financial services. Strive as it might, Dubai's fortunes remain linked to the oil price.

Big Dreams

In 1999, Sheikh Mohammed told his advisers that he wanted Dubai to become the world's finest center for finance, investment, and tourism in the twenty-first century. He said the goal of displacing New York and London as the world's financial capital is a difficult one, but not impossible. If it isn't impossible, then it must be possible. If it's possible, he told his staff, draw up a plan to get us there.

By this way of thinking, Dubai's growth trajectory has been so steep that, if it simply keeps up the pace, the city will eventually surpass the global capitals of commerce. It's unlikely. Before the crisis hit, Dubai had expected its financial services sector to contribute $16 billion a year to the economy by 2015, quadrupling 2006 levels of $3.7 billion. Even if it reaches that level—not likely with the business in ruins—Dubai's financial output will be worth less than a tenth of what London, the world's largest, produced in 2005.[7]

Dubai will have to surpass forty-three cities to reach number one. MasterCard ranked the city as the forty-fourth largest global center of commerce in 2008. But Dubai managed to rank as the planet's number five business center, based on travel, shipping, and hotel amenities, in which it outranked New York and Tokyo.[8]

That's pretty good for a town that wasn't electrified until the 1960s. However improbable its leader's goals, Dubai has undergone perhaps the fastest rise to wealth from underdevelopment in the history of the world. Men born into hand-to-mouth subsistence now live in greater splendor than the tycoons of Beverly Hills and Long Island. Dubai's rise was so improbable that it makes sense for Sheikh Mohammed to think big when he triangulates where the city will go in the current century.

Observers should be careful not to dismiss Dubai as an Arab Monaco or Las Vegas that has fizzed out. It's more than a playground. It's the most stable and comfortable city in a fast-growing and volatile region of 1.5 billion people. It's the natural place for the region's wealthy to invest, take their companies public, set up distribution centers, and buy second homes. As the wealth of the Middle East and South Asia increases, it will percolate into Dubai. It may not beat London or New York, but the city is well placed to keep expanding.

I Know You Got Soul

Given everything I've written about this fascinating place, one must understand that Dubai is not a genuine city. Yet. It's still an unfinished collection of buildings where the atmosphere is transitory, like an airport or hotel. The population consists of flows of people rather than permanent residents. Life is superficial. Ninety-five percent of its inhabitants are temporary, with no chance at legal permanence. Whether they stay a week or forty years, they'll never fully belong. Dubai's expatriates are like nannies raising a rich kid. They're responsible for his well-being and accomplishments, but they'll never get ownership. Like nannies, they're cast aside when their usefulness ends.

The city's physical structure is constantly evolving. Streets and neighborhoods are torn up and moved. Several clusters of buildings vie for the title of city center. Dubai is environmentally rapacious, overwhelmingly male, and socially stratified, with men earning a few dollars a day living across the road from billionaires. "It's difficult to imagine a less sustainable city," says Jeremy Kelly of property consultancy Jones Lang LaSalle.

Dubai is also a city without a city mentality. It's governed by rural people. The elite are descended from Bedouin and small-town traders. Their urban roots go back just one generation.

Sharjah-based architect George Katodrytis's critiques are perhaps the most imaginative. Dubai, he says, is the urban equivalent of a fractal, a constantly subdividing and repeating pattern. "The city has ceased to be a site. Instead it has become a condition," Katodrytis writes. "It tends to be everywhere and nowhere. It is more like a diagram, a system of staged scenery and mechanisms of good time."[9]

Dubai privatizes public spaces. Instead of parks, it builds themed malls where it can weed out low-wage expatriates and tranquilize consumers from reality. It's make-believe Arabia, with fancy boutiques.[10] Dubai is modern yet obsolete. Profit-seeking has scarred the skyline with unimaginative towers built by unskilled men using cheap materials. These are unsuitable for the environment, making the city dangerously dependent on cheap energy. Many find Sheikh Mohammed's creations tacky.

"He's building a large Disney city," says Tom Wright, the Burj Al Arab architect.

"I think it's a flattering statement," responds Nakheel's Robert Lee. His assistant chimes in: "Everyone wants to go to Disneyland."

People who lived in Dubai before the post-2002 explosion lament the bathing of the city in concrete. Quiet pockets have been lost. The One & Only Royal Mirage hotel was one such place. It resembled a Moroccan village on an empty shore. Diners sat on a shaded deck and looked out to sea. It's now surrounded by skyscrapers and hemmed in by flyovers bringing dump trucks to the Palm Jumeirah. The sea offshore is a twenty-four-hour construction site.

"That typifies for me where Dubai can go off the rails," says Anthony Harris. "Can you build another row of shoreline apartments in front of the ones you just built? Of course you can! Let's have another row of shoreline apartments in front of the shoreline apartments."

Some of the rush to judgment is unfair. Dubai may have lapsed into overexuberance, but the city isn't finished. Lebanese intellectual Rami Khouri says Dubai is halfway to matching the great cities of the world, like London, Istanbul, New York, or Delhi. It has conquered the physical realm. But it's nowhere close to becoming a contributor to civilization and the arts. Maturity requires attending to music, art, literature, journalism, and research, along with political pluralism.

"They haven't yet produced anything useful for the human condition," Khouri says. "But it's too early to judge them. It'd be like judging New York in 1782. They're still physically building the place."

Of its major missing elements, political life will be the most difficult to create, being mostly illegal. Dubai's not much for intellectual life, either. Its universities are the equivalent of the so-called party schools in America, places where serious study isn't possible. That is changing. Michigan State and Harvard Medical School are opening campuses and the Harvard-affiliated Dubai School of Government is offering master's degrees in public policy. Abu Dhabi has stepped forward with branches of New York University and Paris's Sorbonne.

Dubai's cultural side is in its infancy. Most impressive is the spontaneous art scene centered in the Al Quoz warehouse district. The artists are foreign, mainly from Egypt, Iran, and Syria. They ship their works to Dubai galleries to find buyers. Dubai has precious little in the way of theater, museums, or music. There is no garage culture of rock bands, nothing in the way of neighborhood theaters, no modern dance, no writers' hangouts.

Dubai, like the rest of the Gulf, does maintain a tradition of poetry. Recitals are popular with young Emirati men, and they can get raucous, with shouting audience members trading spontaneous verse. Poetry events often get sponsored by Sheikh Mohammed, who, as a teen, sent verses to local newspapers under the penname Sulait. But these events are used to buttress the national identity among Emirati males. Interlopers are unwelcome.

This critique notwithstanding, Dubai's global appeal is the pride of Arabs everywhere. There is excitement, incredulity: Look at what those Bedouin have done! That's why intellectuals like Khouri point out the deficiencies, to help Dubai along. The Arab world has seen leaders aspire to greatness before, especially Egypt's Gamal Abdel Nasser. Each one saw his project collapse in humiliation. Lebanon, Egypt, Syria, and Iraq found free-flowing ideas cut short by strife and security men. Dubai is the next Arab hope.

"You can feel the soul of a city emerging," says Hafed al-Ghwell, a former World Bank official now at the Dubai School of Government. "The skeleton is built. Now the challenge is to encourage the soft side. It's not the tallest building in the world that's going to sustain this place. You need to invest in institutions that can accumulate knowledge and pass it on."

The Dubai Mix

In a wide-open city like Dubai, a homegrown culture is bound to emerge. The early hints are fascinating. An example is my neighbor, a forty-year-old Iranian who goes by the name Pierre Ravan. He's a nightclub DJ and music producer. He runs a perfume business. And he's a meditation guru.

Ravan is an intense man with a shaved head and the hard muscles of a fitness buff. He also manages to exude inner peace, which seems incongruous with his intensity and especially with his Porsche Cayenne. When I see him, he shouts, "How you doing, bro?" from his car window, then roars down the road.

Ravan studied mechanical engineering in Tehran and took a job calculating stress loads on oil pipelines. He served two years in the Iranian air force, maintaining American F-14 jets that the Pentagon had sold the shah.

But Ravan was more interested in music, especially the ancient drumming and primal twang of Iranian Sufi mystics. He journeyed into the mountains to record their spiritual sounds on his reel-to-reel tape machine. He mixed them with hip-hop and electronic house beats. Ravan's strange mixes became the rage in Tehran's underground party scene.

But Iran under the ayatollahs isn't the best environment for an aspiring DJ. Ravan moved to Prague and then to San Francisco, honing the uplifting and hypnotic music he called "spiritual house." In the late 1990s, he tested his mix at a club in San Francisco. "We started playing the sounds of these big Persian Sufi drums and people started jumping into the air," Ravan says. "An American guy ran up to me and said, 'Bro, what is this drum? It takes me high!'"

Ravan spun his records in dance clubs from Moscow to Ibiza. But it wasn't until his work brought him to Dubai that he felt at home. He found a budding club scene right across from his native Iran. The combination of Persian culture and pumping nightlife hit home. Ravan settled permanently in 2000. He quickly became the city's top resident DJ, gigging under the moniker Body and Soul: "You bring the body, we provide the soul." The fashion industry discovered Ravan's trippy music and stylized looks and he began spinning for catwalk shows.

Since then, Dubai's dance scene has grown into a destination in its own right. Ravan plays wild all-night gigs like the Coma Festival on Al

Maya Island in Abu Dhabi, a royal resort where gazelles wander among bikini-clad women twirling in the sunshine. Dubai's air hub allows Ravan to jet off to DJ gigs in Miami, Greece, Beirut, and Spain. He hops over to Iran all the time.

During all of this, Ravan became devoted to Sahaj Marg yoga meditation, studying it until he knew enough to open his own school. It's not the kind of thing you can do in Iran or Saudi Arabia or a lot of other places in the Gulf. But in Dubai, no problem. Ravan's meditation group has six hundred adherents—Arabs, Europeans, Indians, Chinese. The spirituality is also key to his club image. Ravan's Web site pictures him in the lotus position with a candelabra backdrop.

"Everything in life needs balance, bro," he says over a cup of green tea in his orange-painted living room. "I can be in a party jumping up and down. And I can be in a calm place and meditate. This for me is Dubai. That's why I'm bound here. All angles of my life are satisfied: spiritual, financial, artistic."

Learn from Us

In the stagnant and conflict-prone Arab world, Dubai is an obvious development model. Copycats have seized many of its ideas. But Dubai's economy can't be picked up and replicated. It leveraged unique characteristics: a small native population, proximity to oil, and an enlightened ruling class. Its model wouldn't apply in Iraq or Egypt, with their large pools of unemployed. Most states wouldn't countenance importing so many foreigners. Besides, Dubai's already won first-mover advantage in many sectors.

But Dubai offers vivid lessons for the region and the world. First among them is a superb cultural model, one that shatters the assumptions that Muslims, Christians, Jews, Hindus, Buddhists, and others can't live and work together. Dubai puts the lie to propaganda that says Muslims are intolerant.

Dubai is simultaneously the planet's most cosmopolitan and tolerant city, a beacon of peace and prosperity where all of mankind is welcome—as long as you work. This is the city's greatest achievement. And, amazingly, this model of social harmony sits in the Arab world.

"The way Islamic and Western values and cultures are being merged is wonderful," Bill Clinton said in a 2005 speech in Dubai.

Also worthy of imitation are Dubai's innovations in government, its efficient airport, and its intolerance for corruption. The emirate's legal system inspires confidence enough for Western firms to invest. And Sheikh Mohammed's use of strategic planning has been deft and successful. Dubai conceives daring new developments, like Internet City, and then it builds them exactly as promised. It's a new concept in the Middle East. Emulators have taken note.

It used to be that reformers looked to America for inspiration. As America has grown discredited in the Arab world, Dubai has taken over that role. It's a more convincing example because it's right next door. Sheikh Mohammed's reforms can't be dismissed as the product of an alien culture. His success stands as an embarrassment to backward regimes, even as Dubai's top-down model is appealing because it doesn't involve democracy.

Sometimes it's the small things that impress the most. A few years ago, Dubai took a step toward reducing lines at the airport by launching the e-Gate card for frequent travelers. A chip on the card stores biometric data and allows arriving and departing travelers to skip immigration and pass through an automated booth. It's a huge time-saver. But to people from surrounding countries, it's a marvel. To them, the card says the Dubai government trusts people enough not to interrogate them when they want to leave the country.

"It reflects a new mentality in a region that is controlled by police states," says Sulaiman al-Hattlan, a TV talk show host and former editor of *Forbes* magazine's Arabic edition. "It shows efficiency and trust in the system. And it shows political security."

Al-Hattlan, in his white *kandoura* and red-checked headscarf, is a Saudi, one of many who prefer the social freedoms in Dubai to the enforced Islamism across the border. Saudis and Iranians, especially, find a refreshing dignity in Dubai, a respect for their ability to make the right choice. Their governments are keeping a close eye on Dubai's lifestyle freedoms. It's not yet a model, but many would like it to be.

"Friday you can pray, but Thursday night you might want to go to the bar," al-Hattlan says. "It's up to you."

Dubai has shown its neighbors that political stability comes from a solid economy and a government that serves its people, rather than the other way around. Absent is the Arab obsession with politics, the syndrome of feeling slighted by the West, which favors Israel and works to divide and weaken Arabs. Al-Hattlan believes that obsession is based in unemployment.

Dubai offers itself as a new option to Arab professionals, reversing the age-old brain drain that saw dissatisfied Arabs leaving for Europe and America, where their contributions did nothing for their homeland. "Sheikh Mohammed is calling the bluff of Arabs in America and Europe," says al-Ghwell. "Instead of sitting in Washington and London complaining about the Arab world, he's asking us to help him build a new Arab city. 'Why don't you come and help out instead of whining?'"

Al-Ghwell, a Libyan, did just that. He left his post at the World Bank in Washington to take a job at the Dubai School of Government. "After 9/11 Arabs in America were subject to racism. I know enough Arab women wearing the *hijab* who were insulted in public, even attacked. That was the impetus for some of us to say, 'I'm a stranger here. Maybe I should go.' Moving to Dubai is like coming home."

Dubai has opened a window of creativity for the Middle East. Arabs and Iranians take its ideas home, spreading the seeds of reform. Washington has begun to understand this. It started paying more attention to Dubai after the crash of the ports deal. Since then, U.S. congressmen have filed into the city, touring the power centers and malls to study this powerhouse of Arab investment and reform. U.S. policy now calls for expanding Dubai's moderating influence on the Middle East. It does this quietly. A public embrace from Washington is counterproductive.

Fool's Gold

Leaders across the Middle East also point to Dubai as an example of what *not* to do. You don't build a city of glass-skinned high-rises in the desert, because it wastes energy. You don't hitch your economy to sun-and-sand tourism because you get overrun by drunken Westerners having sex in public. And you don't turn your city into an air and trade hub, or a center of international finance, because Dubai has beaten you to it.

There are areas where nations emulate Dubai to their detriment. Mostly this means real estate. Across the Middle East, from Morocco to Iran, developers are bulldozing the countryside to erect American-style gated communities. Dubai developers, especially Emaar, are behind many of these. Beirut, Cairo, Amman, Tunis, Damascus, and Marrakech are seeing districts rebuilt or sprawling deeper into their hinterlands. Bahrain and Qatar have dredged up Dubai-style islands. Saudi Arabia has launched a handful of entirely new cities, taking Dubai's cluster zone model to new heights. Most tragically, pristine Oman has taken bits of its breathtaking coast away from sea turtles and handed it to resort builders.

Economists tend to downplay real estate as a development tool. What the seller wins, the buyer loses. There's no gain for the wider economy or society. In Dubai's case this isn't strictly true. The city built artificial islands and peopled them, creating assets from nothing. And since Dubai's real estate is developed locally but sold internationally, its winnings come as other economies' losses, via capital flight. But no economy can rely on real estate for very long. It's an unproductive investment, as Dubai was learning in 2009.

"We have to be careful and honest about what Dubai has done that is pioneering and what has been reckless," Rami Khouri says. "These speculative developments have been the main export. They're not sustainable."

Head East

Dubai's emergence is a manifestation of a shift in the Middle East's center of gravity. This is happening in broader fashion globally, as America and Europe see their powers drifting to China and India. The old capitals on the Mediterranean, Cairo and Beirut—even Tel Aviv, to an extent—are seeing themselves eclipsed by the wealthy Gulf. Banking decamped from Alexandria to Beirut in the 1950s, then fled to Bahrain in the 1970s. Now Dubai is the banking center.

The Gulf is also the Middle East capital of cash. Abu Dhabi is home to the world's biggest sovereign wealth fund, and there are similar funds in Saudi Arabia and Kuwait. The UAE government has bought chunks of Citibank, the Nasdaq, and the Carlyle Group and real estate on New York's Central Park. No Arab state has done that before, perhaps because no region on earth ever reeled in so much wealth in such a short period.

The Gulf states are also taking the lead in Arab politics. The old lands of Egypt, Syria, and Lebanon seem to have surrendered their role to Saudi Arabia and Qatar.[11]

Cairo, Beirut, and Damascus still produce far more books, art, and music. They're still the cities of the Arab soul. But cultural leadership is starting to migrate to the Gulf. By 2012, Abu Dhabi will hold opening ceremonies for Frank Gehry's massive Guggenheim Museum and the first-ever outpost of the Louvre. Film festivals in Dubai, Abu Dhabi, and Doha are getting massive support. Dubai's golf, tennis, and horse racing tournaments have captured international attention.

"There was a tendency five or ten years ago to laugh. 'Dubai's building the world's biggest this or longest that.' People would laugh and say, 'That's Dubai!' Well, nobody's laughing now," says Harris. "Dubai's a worldwide brand. Whether it's horseracing, architecture, wealth creation, or development, this city has an influence far beyond its size. That's an astonishing feat in such a short time."

These accomplishments are just a foreshadowing of what Sheikh Mohammed has in mind.

A New Golden Age

In the tenth century, Córdoba in Arab-ruled Spain was Europe's largest and most enlightened city, with dozens of libraries stocked with hundreds of thousands of books. It published more titles then than Spain produces now. Córdoba's universities cradled deep research traditions, where Muslims, Jews, and Christians delved into philosophy, mathematics, and astronomy. The city's Arab rulers commissioned some of the world's most sublime architecture, some of which survives today. Its merchants traded with cities as far away as China. Córdoba remains the pinnacle of Arab achievement. When it fell apart after 1031, the Arab world sank into a long and debilitating decline. It has never regained its greatness.

Córdoba is Sheikh Mohammed's archetype for Dubai. He wants to recreate this ancient spirit of learning and tolerance. But his ambitions go beyond that. He views Dubai as the engine that will drag the Arab world into a renaissance. Not an economic engine, per se, but a model of effective governance and self-reliance. He sees the Arabs' salvation not in the traditional way, as something that can only be achieved when Washington and the great powers change their policies. He's calling for internal rejuvenation, by spreading management skills, knowledge, and entrepreneurship. And he's backing those calls with cash, by investing in key sectors.

It's a stirring goal, requiring a revamped society and a city that can accommodate the world's dreamers and inspired people. He's partway there. The economic portion of the new Córdoba is done. Dubai is a global trade hub and business center.

Sheikh Mohammed's next step is to support learning and the arts, as the Medici family in Florence did during the Renaissance. He's started by inviting universities and by funding culture through a foundation that seeks to incubate books, film, and painting. One of its tranches funds the translation of books into Arabic, a perennial deficiency. Another backs budding authors with Ivy League scholarships. Another bankrolls the biennial Arab Strategy Forum, a platform for serious debate that has long been missing in the Arab world. The 2006 forum brought together Google CEO Eric Schmidt, Iran's nuclear boss Ali Larijani, and U.S. general Wesley Clark, among others.

Sheikh Mohammed's experiment is working. Arab states are sending officials to the Dubai School of Government to learn public policy. Entrepreneurs are pouring in. Dubai is working on an art policy that will give artists residency and stipends to produce important works.[12]

"I think he can get there. This is already a center for discourse, a marketplace," says Georges Makhoul of Morgan Stanley. "He's almost there."

But his own people show signs of tiring of his lofty ambitions. He wants to groom Dubai's citizens as the leaders of the leaders; "lions," as he calls them. But many prefer to sit back and be pampered. Others oppose Sheikh Mohammed's great project because it is forcing their numbers into insignificance.

The sheikh's ultimate success could reduce his family's governing role. The human spirit he seeks to liberate will fly into politics. The new Córdoba cannot bloom without more freedoms of speech and press, so that thinkers can challenge their leader's decisions. It doesn't mean Dubai must adopt democracy, but it calls for institutions where people can debate and criticize.

And Dubai can't emulate Córdoba without a more permanent and respectable role for expatriates. It'll never become a global capital with locals alone exercising power and identity. Noncitizens have legitimate interests that go beyond serving a ruling class. (This might resemble Córdoba in one sense, however: Its Muslims had more privileges than non-Muslims.) For now, rights of noncitizens is a radioactive topic. No one will address it publicly.

"The Córdoba model is definitely something we should aspire to," says Rami Khouri. "It's noble to aim that high. But does he have the courage to go all the way? Córdoba needed creative and scientific talent. People were allowed to discuss ideas, do research, engage in debates. It's not yet clear whether the leadership in Dubai is prepared to open the system to full use of intellectual and cultural talent."

For now, most folks are content to leave decisions to the Maktoums and their deputies. Even fewer raise their voices against the city's environmental depredations or the mistreatment of its poorest workers. Few protest the censorship of newspapers and banning of books and politics. The old ruling bargain has allowed many to grow rich without much risk or effort.

Despite the unanswered questions, Sheikh Mohammed's investments into education are bound to alter society. When the pressures for openness come, so will the day of reckoning, when the Córdoba aspirations will be put to the test.

Arab thinkers like Khouri are urging Sheikh Mohammed to stick to his goal, saying the city can climb far higher. The boss would say something similar. He says just 10 percent of his plans have been realized. "What you see now is nothing compared to our vision. It's just a tiny part of what lies ahead," he writes.

Dubai's come a long way since 1961, when Sheikh Rashid started it all by dredging the creek. The city entered the modern age and then blew right past it. It's now somewhere out in the future, with Sheikh Mohammed at the controls. He knows that building roads and skyscrapers was the easy part. Incubating an enlightened society will be harder.

"We must be prepared to face the most delicate, toughest and complicated challenges that lie ahead," he writes. "If moving to this stage necessitates crossing yet another bridge, we must be ready to cross it at the right time and as quickly as possible. If later stages require more, we must be ready to cross several bridges at the same time. We must prepare to overcome the impossible."[13]

Not long ago, the story was one of poverty and isolation. Dubai had managed a tenuous toehold on the edge of the world. The village had better odds of melting back into the sands than rising as a city. It took an incredible run to place this metropolis before us.

Those of us watching it sprout and stretch have undergone challenges to our sense of what we thought achievable. Dubai forces us to think beyond the rational, to ponder the outer borders of the possible, right where they brush up against the limits of physics. The city's accomplishments are difficult to believe, even as you watch them materialize. It's a place that mercilessly taunts the pessimist. As Georges Makhoul says, "You have to stretch your imagination to absorb the reality."

How far will Dubai go? Hard to say. But it'll be fun to watch.

EPILOGUE
DUBAI, FEBRUARY 2009

AS THIS BOOK went to press, Dubai was lapsing into recession. The end of the six-year boom made a handy place to finish our story, but for Dubaians, the dream of capitalism had become a calamity.

Dubai's fundamentals looked bleak in 2009. With the oil price below $50 at the time of writing, the surplus in neighboring states that funded Dubai's investment-driven economy was gone. That left the city-state exposed to the ravages of the global recession. Its tourism and luxury retail sectors were starting to suffer, since vacations and pricey trinkets are dropped—like pearls—in hard times. Air travel was slumping, as were the ports. The West wasn't buying and China wasn't producing, so DP World had little to ship. The bleeding was even more copious in real estate and financial services.

Predictions of the recession's effects on Dubai ranged widely. A few pointed to the possibility of a total crash—the biggest white elephant in world history. But most observers swung the other way. Dubai looked set to languish in recession for 2009, and perhaps some of 2010. The UAE as a whole could eke out a bit of growth on the back of Abu Dhabi's oil earnings but there, too, recession was possible. Dubai looked set to languish in recession for 2009 and some of 2010. The UAE as a whole could eke out a bit of growth on the back of Abu Dhabi's oil earnings, but there, too, recession looked likely. The $80 billion in oil revenues Abu Dhabi earned in 2008 would drop sharply, probably to less than $30 billion in 2009. The national economy was predicted to shrink by as much as 2 percent.[1] By 2010, Dubai was expected to be in recovery and the UAE's economic growth was to return to a reasonable rate, around 4 percent.[2]

City fathers said they would spend their way through the recession. In 2009 Dubai announced a huge expansion on public infrastructure. Sheikh Rashid would have been proud. As for the private sector, the opposite was happening. One tally found that nearly half the city's major construction projects had halted. Foreign workers were being furloughed and sent home, including some of my neighbors. Population was expected to drop by as much as 10 percent. Banks were said to have a nine-fold increase in "skips," where debtors have fled personal loans. The city was rife with rumors of laid-off expatriates abandoning cars at the airport and fleeing without settling their debts. Credit agencies downgraded most of Dubai's big companies.

Aspects of the slowdown showed promise. Dubai finally had the opportunity to assess the stunning hodgepodge of assets it built, and plan a coherent city around them. There were many blanks to fill: cultural life, bike paths, street addresses, sewage treatment, recycling, and a Persian Gulf less fogged by silt.

With the right policy moves, Dubai would emerge virile and ready to sprint in a year or two. "I'm still convinced by the Dubai business model," Simon Williams, HSBC's chief economist for the Middle East, said in January. "When we return to more normal times this place will fly."

Slamming on the brakes after a decade of hurtling economic growth was always going to be painful. Especially since so many thought they'd bypass the recession. Exacerbating the embarrassment are conservative neighbors who could finally gloat at seeing ritzy Dubai eating humble pie.

"A lot of people are pointing at Dubai right now and saying 'I knew it was going to happen. They were flying too close to the sun.' That's wrong," Williams says. "There is a real economy here that may see some of its expression through the construction of the world's tallest building, but it's actually about a lot more. It's about being a service hub for a region, the outlook for which is extremely positive. Dubai does that better than anyone else in the region."

By New Year 2009, thousands had been laid off, including five hundred at Nakheel, which mothballed most of its projects, including the kilometer-high skyscraper and the zanier of its offshore islands. The emptying and demolition of Satwa—sadly, already under way—looked set to pause. Other developers and real estate stalwarts cut staff, as did banks. Morgan Stanley cut 15 percent of its workforce. Goldman Sachs and Credit Suisse scaled back their Dubai operations, and three smaller investment firms closed their offices entirely.[3]

The overbuilt retail sector, dependent on free-spending tourists and expatriates, was suffering. The specter of failure hung over entire shopping malls. Few in Dubai even noticed the November 2008 opening of Emaar's humongous Dubai Mall, one of the world's largest. The mall sat nearly empty at the time of writing. By year's end, city retailers were reporting a 20 percent drop in sales.[4]

Sheikh Mohammed and his government said little in public, leaving Dubaians guessing about his policy prescriptions. He shuffled his phalanx of top advisers, with Mohammed al-Shaibani, director of the *diwan*, taking a more prominent role, while demoting his admired finance director Nasser al-Shaikh, whose department had been moved out of the municipal government and integrated directly into the *diwan*. Nabil al-Yousuf left The Executive Office to start a consulting firm, and the institution that devised Dubai's rise was emptying out. The official silence led investors and the public to give credence to worst-case scenarios and rumors, which pushed share prices to nearly worthless levels.

Dubai's treasured autonomy might also slip, as it cozies up to Abu Dhabi to make good on some $20 billion in debt that will come due by 2010. Abu Dhabi's leaders pledged to help Dubai, and the Central Bank did just that by buying up $10 billion in bonds that Dubai issued. The price for such assistance was unclear. The most feared scenario was for the capital's upstart airline Etihad to demand control of Emirates, the Maktoums' crown jewel, although UAE President Sheikh Khalifa declared that Abu Dhabi had no such designs on Dubai's assets.

In a global context, Dubai's troubles didn't look so bad. If you were in America or Europe, the go-go Gulf was thought to be one of the better locales to ride out a global recession. Many Dubai expats, given the choice of going home to an even more dismal economy, tried to stick it out. If not in Dubai, there were jobs in Abu Dhabi, Muscat, and Doha.

Meanwhile, the economic damage was paying dividends in quality of life. Suddenly the airport was manageable. Traffic thinned. Free tables materialized in restaurants. Flagging a taxi at rush hour was again possible.

Inflation was trending down, as were rents and home prices, giving the middle and lower classes a break. Groceries got cheaper. As foreigners began leaving, the demographic imbalance was showing signs of slowing.

And finally, even the driving habits seemed to improve. Maybe it was the sobering times, or the new high-tech speed traps, but the road warriors bore signs of weariness with their wayward ways. It could be a temporary phenomenon. After all, they don't call it the world's fastest city for nothing.

ACKNOWLEDGMENTS

I DIDN'T LABOR in a mountain retreat to write this book. I burned a lot of gasoline and wore out a pair of shoes and a lot of welcomes. I became a fixture on the Dubai conference circuit. I bought many rounds of drinks, cups of coffee, and lunches. And I managed to buttonhole people with far better things to do than talk to me.

But I wouldn't have been able to pull it together without the generous support of the Dubai School of Government and its dean, Tarik Yousef, to whom I am indebted for extending blind support to my project.

Also at DSG, I'm grateful for the help of Sahar Jawad for her superb English translations of hours of Sharjah Radio broadcasts; to Huda Sajwani, Paul Dyer, and Fadi Salem for factual help; and to my best carpool buddy, Christine Assaad, who so often did the driving.

I'd also like to thank historian and archaeologist Peter Hellyer in Abu Dhabi for graciously correcting my historical inaccuracies and putting up with my diatribes defending them; and Christopher Davidson at the University of Durham, whose two excellent books paved the way for mine, and who responded with patience to my incessant e-mails. David Butter at the Economist Intelligence Unit in London patiently corrected several factual errors and offered numerous improvements.

Other expert voices who honed my portrayals include the political scientist Abdulkhaleq Abdulla—whose prescient insights I've relied on for four years—as well as scholars Anisa al-Sharif and Valerie Marcel; ambassador extraordinaire Anthony Harris; the ever-gracious Nabil al-Yousuf at The Executive Office; Chip Cummins at the *Wall Street Journal*, Simeon Kerr at the *Financial Times*, and Bill Spindle and Jim Calderwood at *The National*.

Charley Kestenbaum's patient insights into U.S. policy were particularly helpful. Liza Darnton's comments on my manuscript were a sunbeam in the dark. Aisha Ahli and Hamda bin Demaithan opened doors to some warm and fascinating people. Peyman Pejman ushered me into the wonderful Emirates collection at Zayed University's library. My old traveling pal Kamran Jebreili took some great photos for this book, while unveiling the intricate political shadings of Iranian expatriates. I'd also like to thank Ibrahim Alabed at the National Media Council; Brian Kerrigan at *The National*; and friends Mike Charlton and John Hollingsworth for supplying pictures for this book.

I also owe big thank-yous to my agent, Alice Martell, in New York and to my subagent, Sara Menguc, in London for going far beyond the call in so many ways. And to my editor, Michael Flamini, whose enthusiasm spurred me on.

Finally, I've got to give serious thanks to my mom, Noël Werle, and my wife, Chloe, for their nitpicky—er, meticulous—proofreading.

NOTES

1. The Sands of Time

1. Frauke Heard-Bey, *From Trucial States to United Arab Emirates: A Society in Transition*, 3rd ed. (Dubai: Motivate, 2005), 1, 24. Recent archaeology finds reviewed by Peter Hellyer at the National Media Council in Abu Dhabi could point to a temporary population surge in the seventeenth and eighteenth centuries.

2. Heard-Bey, *From Trucial States to United Arab Emirates*, 18.

3. Peter Hellyer notes that Dubai had a thriving settlement in the Iron Age (1300–300 BC). An archaeology site in the present-day Jumeirah neighborhood reveals a village in the early Islamic period.

4. Heard-Bey, *From Trucial States to United Arab Emirates*, 20–21.

5. An expedition in 1992 led by Dr. Juris Zarins, professor of anthropology at Southwest Missouri State University, discovered what it claimed were the remains of the ancient city of Ubar in Oman. The city, as described in the Quran and elsewhere, sank into the earth. The expedition found the city was built atop an underground limestone cavern that collapsed as wells drained the water it held, toward the end of the Roman period.

6. Bertram Thomas, *Arabia Felix* (London, 1932), 137; cited in Heard-Bey, 426.

7. Ibrahim Al-Abed and Peter Hellyer, eds., *United Arab Emirates: A New Perspective* (London: Trident, 1997), 57. Al-Dur lies in what is now the emirate of Umm Al-Quwain.

8. Peter Hellyer, Abu Dhabi–based archaelogist and historial, e-mail interview, 2008.

9. Heard-Bey, *From Trucial States to United Arab Emirates*, 128.

10. Al-Abed and Hellyer, *United Arab Emirates*, 79.

11. Ibid., 82–83.

12. Wilfred Thesiger, *Arabian Sands* (Dubai: Motivate, 2004; orig. 1959), 49.

13. Hendrik van der Meulen, "The Role of Tribal and Kinship Ties in the Politics of the United Arab Emirates" (PhD diss., Fletcher School of Law and Diplomacy, Tufts University, 1997), 164–65. The Zaab hometown, Jazeerat Al-Hamra, now lies abandoned, a ghost town.

14. Donald Hawley, *The Trucial States* (New York: Twayne, 1971), 70–71.

15. Ibid., 69–70.

16. Heard-Bey, *From Trucial States to United Arab Emirates*, 282.

17. Geoffrey King, "Delmephialmas and Sircorcor: Gasparo Balbi, Dalma, Julfar and a Problem of Transliteration," *Arabian Archaeology and Epigraphy* Vol. 17, issue 2 (pub. 2006), 249.

18. Aquil A. Kazim, "Historic Oman to the United Arab Emirates, from AD 600 to 1995: An Analysis of the Making, Remaking and Unmaking of a Socio-Discursive Formation in the Arabian Gulf" (PhD diss., American University, 1996), 405.

19. Graeme Wilson, *Rashid's Legacy* (Dubai: Media Prima, 2006), 24–25.

20. The UAE's minister of foreign trade and most prominent woman, Sheikha Lubna al-Qassimi, is a member of the Qawasim clan.

21. Van der Meulen, "The Role of Tribal and Kinship Ties," 203.

22. Charles Belgrave, *The Pirate Coast* (London: G. Bell and Sons, 1966); cited by Christopher M. Davidson, *The United Arab Emirates: A Study in Survival* (Boulder, CO: Lynne Rienner, 2005), 26.

23. Davidson, *The United Arab Emirates*, 28–29.

24. Ibid., 28.

25. Ibid., 30.

26. James Calderwood and Jim Krane, "US Wraps Up Massive Persian Gulf Exercises," *Army Times*, via the Associated Press, March 29, 2007; http://www.armytimes.com/news/2007/03/ap_gulf_manuevers_070328. The United States has close to 40,000 troops in the Gulf, including 25,000 in Kuwait, 6,500 in Qatar, 3,000 in Bahrain, 1,300 in the United Arab Emirates, and a few

hundred in Oman and Saudi Arabia, according to figures from the Dubai-based Gulf Research Center.

27. Anthony Harris, author interview, May 21, 2008. Sheikh Saqr, who took power in 1948, is the world's second longest serving ruler, after the Thai king Bhumipol. Sheikh Saqr in 2008 remained the ruler of Ras Al-Khaimah mostly in name. Day-to-day running of the emirate is handled by his son Sheikh Saud, the deputy ruler.

28. The map hangs on the wall in the map room at the Sheikh Saeed Al Maktoum House, a museum on the Dubai creek that once served as the ruler's residence. Description from author's visit, April 26, 2008.

29. The Maktoum family claims Liwa as its ancestral home, but historians, including Peter Hellyer, disagree, citing tribal surveys that show the family and its Bani Yas tribe living along the coastal plain. When the members of the tribe fled to Dubai, the Maktoums may have instead sailed there in dhows.

30. Heard-Bey, *From Trucial States to United Arab Emirates*, 13. In 1906 a diver from Liwa surfaced with a pearl so monstrous that a dispute over its ownership broke out, prompting the British to intervene. The diver tried to establish a claim on the pearl by dint of his tribal home, and he revealed to the English the hitherto unknown villages of the Liwa Oasis.

31. Robert Hughes Thomas, ed., *Arabian Gulf Intelligence* (London: Oleander, 1985).

32. The Maktoums of Dubai restrict themselves to a small pool of original men's names, recycling them over and over, especially Maktoum, Hasher, Hamdan, Rashid, Said, Mohammed, Ahmed, and a few others. It makes for frequent misidentification.

2. A Free Port Grows in the Desert

1. Wilson, *Rashid's Legacy*, 35.

2. Ibid.

3. Davidson, *The United Arab Emirates*, 13.

4. Ibid.; Wilson, *Rashid's Legacy*, 36.

5. Description from exhibit at Sheikh Saeed Al Maktoum's House, which is in Dubai's Shindaga, April 26, 2008.

6. Julia Wheeler, and Paul Thuysbaert, *Telling Tales: An Oral History of Dubai* (Dubai: Explorer, 2005), 44.

7. Dhow ports up and down the lower Gulf coast are also thought to be the chief

Iranian sources of everything from bootleg cigarettes to dual-use computer technology banned for export under the U.S. embargo.

8. Given 300,000 Iranians and fewer than 100,000 Emiratis.

9. Jim Krane, "Iranian Beachgoers Defy Conservatives on Party Island," Associated Press, October 2, 2006.

10. "UAE Open for Iran Business," *Iran Daily*, February 16, 2008, http://www.iran-daily.com/1386/3064/html/focus.htm, (accessed April 20, 2008).

11. Jean-François Seznec (Georgetown University professor), author interview, April 1, 2008, Abu Dhabi.

12. Dubai Chamber of Commerce and Industry figures cited in *Iran Daily* article show Dubai's non-oil exports to Iran totaling $9.8 billion in 2007, a 33.4 percent increase on $7.3 billion in exports in 2006.

13. Anthony Harris (former British ambassador to UAE), author interview, May 21, 2008.

14. "Persian Gulf Hydrology," Encyclopedia Britannica Online, http://www.britannica.com/eb/article-22739/Persian-Gulf (accessed April 27, 2008).

15. Fatma Umm Hussain, Emirati housewife living in Dubai, interview with author, April 30, 2008.

16. There are now eight: Iran, Iraq, Saudi Arabia, Kuwait, Qatar, Bahrain, UAE, and Oman.

17. J. G. Lorimer, *Gazetteer of the Persian Gulf*, 2252; cited by Davidson, *The United Arab Emirates*, 6.

18. Wilson, *Rashid's Legacy*, 50.

19. As quoted in Wheeler and Thuysbaert, *Telling Tales*, 52.

20. Davidson, *The United Arab Emirates*, 7.

21. Ibid., 35; and author interview with Christopher Davidson, political science professor at Durham University in England, April 1, 2008.

22. Nadia Rahman, "Memory of Place and Space in the Emirate Tales," undated paper by Zayed University professor.

23. Davidson, author interview, April 1, 2008.

24. Heard-Bey, *From Trucial States to United Arab Emirates*, 250.

25. Fatma al-Sayegh (history professor at UAE University), author interview, April 10, 2008.

26. Wilson, *Rashid's Legacy*, 43.

27. Rosemarie Said Zahlan, *The Origins of the United Arab Emirates: A Political and Social History of the Trucial States* (London: Macmillan, 1978), 151.

28. Ibid., 152–53.

29. Ibid., 156.

30. Christopher M. Davidson, *Dubai: The Vulnerability of Success* (New York: Columbia University Press, 2008), 35. Davidson cites British foreign office correspondence for the death toll.

31. Zahlan, *The Origins of the United Arab Emirates*, 160–61.

32. Anthony Harris, e-mail interview, June 18, 2008; Peter Hellyer confirmed November 5, 2009.

33. Wilson, *Rashid's Legacy*, 89.

34. Zahlan, *The Origins of the United Arab Emirates*, 161.

35. Davidson, *The United Arab Emirates*, 41.

36. Ibid., 40.

37. Ibid., 31–36.

38. Zahlan, *The Origins of the United Arab Emirates*, 165–66, with input from historian Peter Hellyer, UAE National Media Council.

39. Zahlan, *The Origins of the United Arab Emirates*, 163–66.

40. Ibid., 174.

41. Abdulkhaleq Abdulla (professor of political science, UAE University), author interview, May 11, 2008.

42. Heard-Bey, *From Trucial States to United Arab Emirates*, 298–99.

43. The buildings of Sharjah's 1932 aerodrome still stand, and have been turned into a museum that features a 1930s newsreel showing a triple-winged Imperial Airways (now British Airways) plane rumbling in from the sky as Bedouin on camelback stare in wonder.

44. Dubai International Airport Web page, DIA and History, http://www.dubaiairport .com/DIA/English/TopMenu/About+DIA/DIA+and+History/.

45. Van der Meulen, "The Role of Tribal and Kinship Ties," 63.

46. Davidson, *The United Arab Emirates*, 90–92.

47. Wilson, *Rashid's Legacy*, 66–67.

48. Heard-Bey, *From Trucial States to United Arab Emirates*, 300–1.

3. Oil, Slaves, and Rebellion

1. Iran's efforts to develop nuclear energy date to 1957, when it signed an agreement with America's Atoms for Peace program. See Greg Bruno, "Iran's Nuclear Program," Council on Foreign Relations, September 4, 2008. http://www.cfr.org/publication/16811/.

2. Edward Henderson, *Arabian Destiny* (Dubai: Motivate, 1988), 72.

3. Malcolm Jones Jr., "Air Conditioning," *Newsweek*, Winter 1997, http://www.facstaff.bucknell.edu/mvigeant/therm_1/AC_final/bg.htm (accessed May 25, 2008).

4. Easa Saleh Al-Gurg, *The Wells of Memory: An Autobiography* (London: John Murray, 1998), 18–20.

5. See "The (Secret) Life of Mohammed Ali Alabbar," The Kipp Report, May 2008, http://www.kippreport.com/secretlifeofemaarcombined.php?id=2&sec=bg.

6. Daniel Yergin, *The Prize: The Epic Quest for Oil, Money & Power* (New York: Free Press, 1993), 284.

7. Hawley, *The Trucial States*, 209.

8. Ibid., 209–15.

9. U.S. Department of Energy, Energy Intelligence Administration, "United Arab Emirates Country Brief," July 2007, http://www.eia.doe.gov/emeu/cabs/UAE/Oil.html (accessed May 25, 2008).

10. Ibid.

11. Hawley, *The Trucial States*, 220.

12. Heard-Bey, *From Trucial States to United Arab Emirates*, 307.

13. Wheeler and Thuysbaert, *Telling Tales*, 136.

14. Noor Ali Rashid (royal photographer), author interview, Sharjah, May 13, 2008.

15. Oxford Business Group, "Emerging Dubai, 2007," 129.

16. Economist Intelligence Unit, January 2009 UAE Country Report. Dubai figure is an estimate.

17. Heard-Bey, *From Trucial States to United Arab Emirates*, 152.

18. Hawley, *The Trucial States*, 136.

19. Heard-Bey, *From Trucial States to United Arab Emirates*, 231.

20. Ibid., 84.

21. Ibid., 89.

22. Ibid., 91–93.

23. Hawley, *The Trucial States*, 136.

24. Donald Hawley, *The Emirates: Witness to a Metamorphosis* (London: Michael Russell, 2007), 65.

25. Ibid., 65, 69.

26. Daniel Lerner, *The Passing of Traditional Society: Modernizing in the Middle East* (Toronto: Free Press, 1964), 399; Karl W. Deutsch, "Social Mobilization and Political Development," *American Political Science Review* 55, no. 6 (1961); and Samuel P. Huntington, *Political Order in Changing Societies* (New Haven, CT: Yale University Press, 1968), 140–91. All cited by Davidson, *The United Arab Emirates*, 66.

27. Davidson, author interview, April 1, 2008. Davidson cites official correspondence between Hawley and the Foreign Office in London.

28. Anthony Harris, author interview, May 21, 2008.

29. Al-Gurg, *The Wells of Memory* 73–75.

30. Nico Vellinga (economist, Zayed University), author interview, June 11, 2008.

31. Bahrain still receives half the revenue from an oilfield operated by Saudi Arabia.

32. CIA World Factbook, https://www.cia.gov/library/publications/the-world-factbook (accessed August 15, 2008). Per-capita income in Abu Dhabi reached $74,000 in 2006, according to government figures.

33. Wheeler and Thuysbaert, *Telling Tales*, 82.

34. Van der Meulen, "The Role of Tribal and Kinship Ties," 91.

4. It's Sheikh Rashid's World—We Just Live in It

1. Most of the funeral description comes from Hawley, *The Emirates*, 94–95.

2. Noor Ali Rashid, author interview, May 13, 2008.

3. Hawley, *The Emirates*, 75.

4. Ibid., 98.

5. Al-Gurg, *The Wells of Memory*, 143.

6. George Chapman, former director of Gray Mackenzie operations in Dubai, author interview, May 8, 2008.

7. Graeme Wilson, *Father of Dubai: Sheikh Rashid bin Saeed Al Maktoum* (Dubai: Media Prima, 1999), 133.

8. George Chapman, author interview, May 8, 2008.

9. Anthony Harris, author interview, June 3, 2008.

10. He was the world's eighty-sixth richest man in 2007, with a fortune of $8 billion, according to *Forbes*, http://www.forbes.com/lists/2007/10/07billionaires_Abdul-Aziz-Al-Ghurair-family_JDP8.html.

11. Hawley, *The Trucial States*, 245.

12. Ibid., 245.

13. George Chapman, author interview, May 8, 2008.

14. Hawley, *The Trucial States*, 244.

15. Davidson, *The United Arab Emirates*, 158.

16. As quoted in Jeffrey Sampler and Saeb Eigner, *Sand to Silcon: Achieving Rapid Growth Lessons from Dubai* (London: Profile Books, 2003), 174.

17. Al-Gurg, *The Wells of Memory*, 102–6.

18. Hawley, *The Trucial States*, 245–46.

19. Christopher Davidson, "Dubai: The Security Dimensions of the Region's Premier Free Port," *Middle East Policy* 15, no. 2 (Summer 2008): 144.

20. Wheeler and Thuysbaert, *Telling Tales*, 52–53.

21. Ibid.

22. See Robin Moore, *Dubai: A Novel of Gold, Oil, and Insurgency* (Garden City, NY: Doubleday, 1976).

23. Record of conversation between UK Minister of State John Profumo and Sheikh Rashid on June 8, 1959. Referenced in *Records of Dubai, 1761–1960*, Volume 8: 1959–1960 (London: Archive Editions, 2000), 34; hereinafter Profumo/Rashid conversation, June 8, 1959.

24. Davidson, "Dubai: The Security Dimensions," 144.

25. Profumo/Rashid conversation, June 8, 1959.

26. George Chapman, author interview, May 8, 2008.

27. "Making Dubai," *Al Manakh: The Dubai Guide* (Amsterdam, Moutamarat, 2007, published for the International Design Forum, May 27–29, Dubai), 154–55.

28. Qassim Sultan, *The Years of Construction and Transformation. Dubai: From*

Small Village to Global City (Dubai: Dubai Municipality, 2003). Population data taken from several pages. U.S. population figures come from the 2000 U.S. census.

29. Ray Vicker, "Is Dry Dock in Dubai to Be High and Dry and Pie in the Sky?" *Wall Street Journal*, May 6, 1980.

30. Qassim Sultan (former director, Dubai Municipality), author interview, May 15, 2008.

31. Vicker, "Is Dry Dock in Dubai to Be High and Dry and Pie in the Sky?"

32. At the time, there were discussions about moving Dubai International Airport to Jebel Ali to create synergies with the new port. The Dubai airport was already getting hemmed in by growth on the Dubai-Sharjah border. But the idea was shelved until a few years ago, when plans for Al Maktoum International Airport in Jebel Ali revived it.

33. Al-Maktoum, Mohammed bin Rashid, *My Vision: Challenges in the Race for Excellence* (Dubai: Motivate, 2006).

5. The Road to Dominance

1. Iran formally dropped its claim to Bahrain in 1970, but calls for reclaiming the island, which separated from Persia in the late eighteenth century, are still voiced periodically in Iran.

2. Davidson, *The United Arab Emirates,* 49.

3. Encylopedia Iranica online, "TONB (GREATER AND LESSER)," http://www.iranica .com/newsite/articles/ot_grp8/ot_tonb_20050606.html.

4. Zahlan, *The Origins of the United Arab Emirates*, 195.

5. Davidson, "Dubai: Security Dimensions," 153.

6. Abdulkhaleq Abdulla, author interview, May 11, 2008.

7. The UAE didn't have to wind up as a confederation of tribal autocrats. Interest groups pushed for distinct styles of governance. One group wanted an undivided state with a single government and a strong legislature. It argued that divisions among the sheikhdoms had been exacerbated by the British, who had given more power to tribal leaders than they might have seized on their own. This stance sounded too much like democracy and came at the expense of at least six ruling families. It got nowhere.

8. Thesiger, *Arabian Sands*, 234–35.

9. Al-Fahim, Mohammed, *From Rags to Riches: A Story of Abu Dhabi*, 2nd ed. (Dubai: Makarem, 2007), 132.

10. Peter Hellyer, author interview, July 8, 2008.

11. Peter Hellyer and Simon Aspinall, "Zayed: Caring Environmentalist," *Tribulus: Journal of the Emirates Natural History Group* 14, no.2 (Autumn/Winter 2004): 4.

12. Mohan Jashanmal, over lunch with author.

13. Al-Fahim, *From Rags to Riches*, 135.

14. Fatima al-Sayegh, author interview, June 23, 2008.

15. Al-Fahim, *From Rags to Riches*, 135–39.

16. Ibid., 140.

17. Anthony Harris, author interview, July 15, 2008. Similar numbers given by Peter Hellyer at the National Media Council in Abu Dhabi.

18. I heard this story from a number of people connected with the hospital and the renovation of the house.

19. Wayne White (U.S. State Department's lead intelligence analyst on the Iran-Iraq war), author interview, June 17, 2008.

20. Wilson, *Rashid's Legacy*, 475.

21. I could only use this story on condition of anonymity.

22. George Chapman, author interview, May 8, 2008.

23. Coverage of Satwa's demise appeared in "The End of Satwa," *Time Out Dubai*, May 2008.

24. Al-Gurg, *The Wells of Memory*, 102.

25. His five daughters, Mariam, Hessa, Maitha, Shaikha, and Fatima, probably also stayed close.

26. Material on Sheikh Rashid's illness from Wilson, *Rashid's Legacy*, 441–49.

6. Sprinting the Marathon

1. Mohammed bin Rashid al-Maktoum, *My Vision: Challenges in the Race for Excellence* (Dubai: Motivate, 2006).

2. Sheikh Ahmed is the product of Sheikh Saeed's late union with a second wife.

Ahmed was born in 1958, forty-five years after his eldest half-brother, Sheikh Rashid.

3. Flanagan wasn't at the meeting, but others present reported Sheikh Mohammed's statement to him.

4. Graeme Wilson, *Emirates: The Airline of the Future* (Dubai: Media Prima, 2005), 86.

5. Ibid., 248–49.

6. Ibid., 249.

7. Emirates Web site, http://www.emirates.com/uae/AboutEmirates/TheEmirates Story/TheEmiratesStory.asp. In March 2009, Emirates stopped flying A-380s to New York and shifted them to routes serving Toronto and Bangkok.

8. IATA figures for international traffic in 2007. Does not include domestic flights. When combined international and domestic figures are measured, American and United are numbers one and two, respectively.

9. Van der Meulen ("The Role of Tribal and Kinship Ties," 191) claims that Emirates' profits are mainly on paper. A footnote in his 1997 thesis alleges that the Maktoum family infuses the airline with millions of dollars to enable it to keep up its high standards, subsidies not reflected in balance sheets. The airline's financial statements, he contends, do not properly reflect its financial performance. He gives no source for these allegations. Van der Meulen, a former U.S. diplomat in the UAE, did not respond to interview requests.

10. Vivian Salama, "Passenger Increase Sees Dubai Lead Charge in Airport Retail Growth," *The National*, August 23, 2008.

11. Tom Wright (of W. S. Atkins), author interview, September 9, 2008.

12. The hotel sent a golf pro to tee off a few balls first, to make sure Tiger wouldn't bean anyone at the waterpark or on the beach.

13. Jaylyn Garcia (Dubai Tourism and Commerce Marketing Department), author interview, September 4, 2008.

14. *The Travel and Tourism Competitiveness Report 2007*, World Economic Forum, 24.

15. U.N. World Tourism Organization, *World Tourism Barometer*, June 2008.

16. *Dubai Strategic Plan—2015: Highlights* booklet.

17. Ibid.

18. Jim Krane, "Sept. 11 Factors That Hurt U.S. Economy Led to Economic Boom in Gulf," Associated Press, August 25, 2005.

19. UAE GDP growth in 2008 was 7.4 percent. Economists at Standard Chartered Bank in March 2009 predicted 0.5 percent GDP growth in 2009. The Economist Intelligence Units assessment was bleaker: a recession, with GDP dropping 1.4 percent.

20. Dubai's 565 square miles under development figure is from The Executive Office planner Abdulla al-Nedhar's personal assistant, Iman, telephone interview, September 8, 2008. That includes uninhabited land being cleared for development. The 2000 U.S. Census lists Houston's city limits as 580 square miles with nearly 2 million inhabitants, not including suburbs.

21. Joel Bowman, "Value of Gulf Projects Surges Past $2tn—Report," Arabian Business.com, March 31, 2008, http://www.arabianbusiness.com/515087-gulf-project-value-eclipses-2tn-mark.

22. Nasser Saidi (chief economist, Dubai International Financial Centre), author interview, September 22, 2008. Valuations have plummeted since then.

23. A Google search in 2008 on "world's fastest-growing city" found overwhelmingly in favor of Dubai, but the City Mayors Web site listed number one as Beihai, China.

24. Prices supplied by Better Homes on October 20, 2008.

25. Peter Riddoch, CEO Damac Properties, "Dubai Boom Isn't Over—or Is It?" *Homes Overseas*, September 1, 2008.

26. Afshin Molavi, "Profile—The Arab Sheik: Meet Dubai's Leader: Ultramodern, Apolitical, and Open for Business," *Newsweek*, August 6, 2007, http://www.msnbc.msn.com/id/20011278/site/newsweek/page/.

27. Gergawi's identity in this story comes from Afshin Molavi, "Talent, critical mass drive Dubai forward," from Bitterlemons-International.org, Dec. 27, 2007; http://www.bitterlemons-international.org/previous.php?opt=1&id=208.

28. A federal media law under consideration in 2009 proposed tough penalties, including huge fines, for coverage considered insulting to UAE royals. Most worryingly, journalists and their employers could be penalized for stories deemed to have damaged the economy. The law was widely panned inside the country and by international media watchdogs. It had not been ratified by the time this book went to press. The law does not affect international media firms operating in Media City and the free zones.

7. Almost Famous

1. Martin Hvidt, "Governance in Dubai: The Emergence of Political and Economic Ties between the Public and Private Sector" (working paper, Centre for Contemporary Middle East Studies, University of Southern Denmark, June 2006), 4.

2. Nabil al-Yousuf resigned from The Executive Office in March 2009. At the time, the office's role in running Dubai was on the wane.

3. "Dubai in World Competitiveness 2005," IMD, December 2005; also cited by Molavi, "Profile—The Arab Sheik: Meet Dubai's Leader."

4. "Suit Filed to Block Port Takeover by Arab Firm," Associated Press, February 18, 2006 (http://www.msnbc.msn.com/id/11435262/).

5. Marwan al-Shehhi, born in Ras Al-Khaimah, probably radicalized in Germany and Afghanistan; Fayez Banihammad, possibly born in Khor Fakkan, in Sharjah; may have worked as a UAE immigration officer and attended university in Saudi Arabia's Asir Province.

6. "Global Ports Connecting Global Markets," PowerPoint presentation downloaded from Dubai World Web site, http://www.dubaiworld.ae/en/Our%20Portfolio/Transport%20and%20Logistics/bu_DP%20World.html (accessed October 25, 2008).

7. Peter Overby, "Lobbyist's Last-Minute Bid Set Off Ports Controversy," *All Things Considered*, NPR News, March 8, 2006, http://www.npr.org/templates/story/story.php?storyId=5252263.

8. Doreen Hemlock, "Lauderdale Firm Maps U.S. Legal Challenge to Dubai Deal on Ports Company," *South Florida Sun-Sentinel*, March 7, 2006, http://www.redorbit.com/news/technology/419435/lauderdale_firm_maps_us_legal_challenge_to_dubai_deal_on/index.html.

9. Michael Kreitzer, lawyer representing Eller and Co., author interview, November 12, 2008.

10. Overby, "Lobbyist's Last-Minute Bid Set Off Ports Controversy."

11. Stephanie Kirchgaessner, "Bill Clinton Helped Dubai on Ports Deal," *Financial Times*, March 1, 2006, http://www.ft.com/cms/s/0/60414c4c-a95e-11da-a64b-0000779e2340.html.

12. Jamal Majid bin Thaniah, chief executive officer, DP World, author interview, September 29, 2008.

13. James Kuhnhenn, "Arabs Drop Ports Deal; S. Fla Firm in Running," *Miami Herald*, March 10, 2006.

14. Mohammed bin Rashid al-Maktoum, "Our Ambitions for the Middle East," *Wall Street Journal*, January 12, 2008.

15. No one I interviewed would reveal names of U.S. politicians who'd said they were sorry.

16. Al-Maktoum, *My Vision*.

8. Spreading Out and Going Up

1. Warren Pickering (concept designer, Nakheel), author interview, October 8, 2008.

2. Robert Lee (executive director of investment, Nakheel), author interview, September 21, 2008.

3. Ibid.

4. Sampler and Eigner, *Sand to Silicon*, 85.

5. "The Master Builder of the Middle East," *BusinessWeek*, July 2, 2007, http://www.businessweek.com/magazine/content/07_27/b4041056.htm.

6. Emaar's market capitalization sank to $8 billion in the turmoil of fall 2008.

7. "The (Secret) Life of Mohammed Ali Alabbar," The Kipp Report, May 2008.

8. Ibid.

9. Greg Sang (Emaar director of projects), author interview, October 13, 2008.

10. They've installed sensors to monitor the building movement. If it's swaying too much, the sensors slow the elevators.

9. Diamonds, Dubai, and Israel

1. Peter Meeus, CEO of Dubai-based International Diamond Laboratories, author interview, July 6, 2008, and Youri Steverlynck (CEO Dubai Diamond Exchange), author interview, July 9, 2008.

2. Peter Meeus, author interview, July 6, 2008.

3. Youri Steverlynck, author interview, July 9, 2008.

4. Nathaniel Popper, "As Dubai Heats Up, Is Israel Frozen Out?" *The Jewish Daily Forward*, December 5, 2007.

5. Jane Kinninmont (Middle East economist with Economist Intelligence Unit, London), author interview via e-mail, April 2, 2008.

6. Carmiel Arbit (Arabian Peninsula project manager, American Jewish Committee), author interview, November 3, 2008.

7. Chaim Even-Zohar, *From Mine to Mistress: Corporate Strategies and Government Policies in the International Diamond Industry* (London: Mining Communications Ltd., 2007), 618–20.

8. Ibid., 627.

9. Ernest Blom (president of the World Federation of Diamond Bourses), author interview, Dubai, November 9, 2008.

10. Carmiel Arbit, author interview, November 3, 2008. Many of the dentists failed to get UAE visas.

11. Abbas Lawati, "Israeli Jeweller Has No Trade Licence to Open Shop in Dubai," *Gulf News*, April 30, 2008; Lawati, "Embassy in Tel Aviv Sparks Protest," *Gulf News*, September 19, 2008.

12. Essa Kazim (CEO, Bourse Dubai), author interview, June 30, 2008.

10. Sheikh Mohammed: Born to Rule

1. Most material from this incident comes from Zayed University student newsletter, summer 2008.

2. Abdulla al-Mutairy (director, Sheikh Saeed al-Maktoum house), author interview, October 21, 2008.

3. Ibid.

4. "United Arab Emirates: Mohammed bin Rashid drives Dubai," Oxford Analytica report, July 3, 2007.

5. Davidson, *Dubai: The Vulnerability of Success*, (New York: Columbia University Press), 145.

6. Nassouh Nazzal, "Five Minutes That Changed a Citizen's Life," *Gulf News*, June 28, 2008.

7. Nada El Sawy, "Life on the Dole in the UAE," *Financial Times*, September 15, 2008, https://members.gulf2000.columbia.edu/?p=238418.

8. The Emirates Palace Hotel is reputed to be the most expensive hotel ever built.

9. Yasar Jarrar (government management adviser, former executive dean at Dubai School of Government), October 12, 2008, speech at Dubai School of Government to a delegation of African ministers from Zimbabwe, Zambia, Namibia, Seychelles, Malawi, Mozambique, Ghana, Swaziland, and other countries.

10. Sampler and Eigner, *Sand to Silicon*, 120.

11. Although it is unclear whether Sheikh Mohammed was married to all the women who have borne him children, it is legal under UAE and Islamic law to keep up to four simultaneous wives.

12. Sheikh Mohammed's surviving older brother, Hamdan bin Rashid, would have also been a strong candidate. He remains Dubai's deputy ruler, sharing the title with his nephew Maktoum bin Mohammed.

11. Labor Pains

1. Economist Intelligence Unit estimate, 2008. The Indian consulate in Dubai gave the rough estimate of 1.5 million Indians in the UAE, and the same amount in Saudi Arabia.

2. Venu Rajamony (consul general of India), author interview, October 13, 2008.

3. Graeme McCaig (Dutco Construction Co.; head of safety advocacy group Build Safe UAE), in conversation with the author, April 22, 2008.

4. "Site Worker Death Toll Exceeds 800," *Construction Week*, August 6–19, 2005.

5. The Dubai government reported thirty-four construction deaths in 2004 and thirty-nine in 2005, according to figures cited by Human Rights Watch in its 2006 report "Building Towers, Cheating Workers." The group said the government and companies involved appeared to be covering up the true death toll, but another source said companies were not obliged to report deaths.

6. Dubai police figures cited by Economist Intelligence Unit, United Arab Emirates Country Report, April 2007.

7. For instance, in July and August 2007, I regularly watched laborers working in blatant violation of the law from my office in the Emirates Office Tower. The violations would have also been visible to top Dubai officials working in the same building.

12. Sex and Slavery

1. Analize Viljoen (filmmaker), author interview, October 11, 2008; Viljoen interviewed the victim for a film funded by the U.S. State Department.

2. I changed her name and nationality to disguise her identity.

3. Sharla Musabih, former director, City of Hope women's shelter, Dubai, author interview, October 19, 2008.

4. Emiratis are given wide latitude to sponsor foreign workers as domestic servants. Their sponsorship quotas rise if they own businesses.

5. Anwar Gargash, UAE minister of state for foreign affairs and anti-trafficking czar, author interview, October 23, 2008.

6. Bassam Zaza, "Two Plead Innocent to Human Trafficking Charges," *Gulf News*, July 6, 2007, http://archive.gulfnews.com/articles/07/07/06/10137176 .html.

7. Simeon Kerr, "UAE in Rare Move Against Human Traffickers," *Financial Times*, December 5, 2008, http://www.ft.com/cms/s/0/d5143706-c26e-11dd-a350-000077b07658.html.

8. Zahlan, *The Origins of the United Arab Emirates*, 153.

13. The Air-Conditioned Nightmare

1. The 2006 Living Planet Report calculated the UAE's carbon footprint at 11.9 global hectares per person, 25 percent higher than number two America's 9.6 hectares and five times the global average of 2.2. The UAE figure dropped in 2008 because the WWF used more accurate population data.

2. Statistics supplied by the Emirates Environmental Group show the following: UAE water availability is among the lowest in the world, at −0.91 thousand cubic meters/person in 2007; UAE electricity consumption is the world's tenth highest, at 11,872 kilowatt-hours per capita; carbon emission are around 35 metric tons of carbon, per person, per year; Dubai's solid waste output in 2008 was around 31,000 tons per day, of which 8,000 tons are domestic waste. Dubaians produce some 1,676 kilograms per capita of solid waste per year.

3. Vesela Todorova, "Water Price Should Go Up, Says Scientist," *The National*, October 14, 2008. Consumption figures were given in liters per day: UAE, 550; United States, 485; Canada, 425; Jordan, 85.

4. David Aubrey (CEO, Woods Hole Group), author interview, September 17, 2008.

5. Eckart Woertz, economist, Gulf Research Center, Dubai, author interview, September 8, 2008.

6. Kevin Mitchell, "Constructing Fact, Fantasy and Fiction," *Al Manakh: Dubai Guide*, 30–33.

7. Sheikh Rashid's 1979 World Trade Centre is one of the few Dubai towers with window shading, designed for the fierce sun.

8. "Abu Dhabi Commits to 7 Percent Renewable Energy Target by 2020," UAE state News Agency WAM, January 18, 2009.

9. "Special Comment: Arabian Gulf Electricity Industry," report by Moody's Global Corporate Finance, October 2008.

10. Oliver Klaus, "Dubai May Allow Foreign Investors into Power Industry," Dow Jones Newswires, June 12, 2007, https://www.xing.com/app/forum?op=showarticles;id=4546170.

11. "Ras Al-Khaimah Seeks More Gas from Iran," Country Report: United Arab Emirates, Economist Intelligence Unit, March 2008, 16.

12. Tamsin Carlisle, "Ajman to Build Gulf's First Coal Plant," The National, July 17, 2008, http://www.thenational.ae/article/20080717/BUSINESS/293642699/0/NATIONAL.

13. Rahulan named the company Pacific Controls because of his boyhood fascination with the Pacific Ocean, growing up in Australia. He founded the company in Dubai, nowhere near the Pacific.

14. Dilip Rahulan, author interview, October 11, 2008.

15. Nigel Mackenzie (chief technical officer, Pacific Controls), author interview, October 11, 2008.

16. Loveday Morris, "Local Species Face Extinction," The National, October 8, 2008, http://www.thenational.ae/article/20081008/NATIONAL/89243272/0/FOREIGN.

17. Habiba al-Marashi was quoted in: Jim Krane, "Booming Development Driving away Persian Gulf Wildlife," Associated Press, July 6, 2006.

18. David Aubrey, author interview, September 17, 2008.

14. The Lawless Roads

1. Excerpt from the poem "The Dubai Driver," by Paddy Briggs, from Jumeirah Jane and Other Dubai Friends (Dubai: Zodiac Publishing, 2001), 24. Used with permission.

2. Ashfaq Ahmed, "RTA Plans to Clear Roads Faster after Minor Crashes," Gulf News, October 14, 2007, http://archive.gulfnews.com/articles/07/10/15/10160413.html.

3. The UAE had 1,056 traffic deaths in 2007, a rate of 2.9 per day, according to police figures cited by Alia al-Theeb, Maryam al-Serkal, and Rayeesa Absal, "UAE Road Accidents Claim 21 Lives in 72 Hours," Gulf News, April 7, 2008, http://archive.gulfnews.com/articles/08/04/07/10203720.html.

4. Abdulbari Bener and David Crundall, "Risk Taking Behavior in Road Traffic Accidents and Fatalities," University of Nottingham research paper, 2003, http://www.psychology.nottingham.ac.uk/IAAPdiv13/ICTTP2004papers2/Individual%20Differences/BenerB.pdf.

5. Jessica Hume, "Traffic-Related Deaths on the Increase," *The National,* Abu Dhabi, November 20, 2008. The article quotes Dr. Adnan Abbas, director of the fatalities section at Sheikh Khalifa Medical City in Abu Dhabi, as saying Abu Dhabi suffers 37.5 road deaths per year, per 100,000 residents. In comparison, heart disease kills 29.8 per 100,000 and cancer 21.7.

6. Economist Intelligence Unit, "Road Crash Highlights Weakness of Law Enforcement," United Arab Emirates Country Report, April 2008.

7. Hume, "Traffic-Related Deaths on the Increase."

8. Jonathan Somcio (Dubai Police EMT), author interview July 20, 2008.

9. Abdulbari Bener, A. Ghaffar, Abu Azab, M. Sankaran-Kutty, F. Toth, and G. Lovasz, "The Impact of Four-Wheel Drives on Road Traffic Disability and Deaths Compared to Passenger Cars," Journal of *College of Physicians & Surgeons Pakistan,* April 2006, Vol. 16: 257–60.

10. Jim Krane, "Reckless Drivers Blamed for 3,000 Mideast Traffic Deaths Per Month," Associated Press, December 13, 2005. Note that non-Arab countries in the Middle East also suffer from bad drivers. Israel reported 27 fatalities per 100,000 vehicles, versus 18 in the United States and 11 in Britain. Iran has one of the highest rates of road accidents in the world: 38 deaths per year per 100,000 people. One person is killed every 40 minutes in accidents in Iran, and one is injured every 7 minutes, according to the Iranian state news agency.

11. "Driving in Dubai" page on Web site Dubai FAQs, http://www.dubaifaqs.com/driving-in-dubai.php (accessed July 19, 2008).

12. Stephanie Vigier (Middle East Auto Analyst, Global Insight, Paris), author interview, June 24, 2008.

13. From Al Tayer Motors Web site, http://www.altayer-motors.com (accessed July 20, 2008).

14. Van der Meulen, "The Role of Tribal and Kinship Ties," 192.

15. Sada Hamad (General Motors spokeswoman), author interview, July 2, 2008.

16. Stefania Bianchi, "Dubai Metro Project Running over Budget to Avoid Delay," Dow Jones Newswires, October 15, 2008, http://www.zawya.com/printstory.cfm?storyid=ZW20081015000157&l=135350081015.

17. Survey conducted by executive recruiters GulfTalent, released June 2007.

18. Bianchi, "Dubai Metro Project Running over Budget to Avoid Delay."

15. Danger Ahead

1. U.S. Census Bureau news release, "Miami-Dade Leads Nation in Percentage of Foreign-Born," September 3, 2003, http://www.census.gov/Press-Release/www/releases/archives/american_community_survey_acs/001311.html (accessed July 9, 2008).

2. These figures are estimated as follows: Dubai's 1994 citizen population was reported by the government at 41,400 (cited by Van der Meulen); given a generous annual growth rate of 6.5 percent, the local population would have reached 100,000 by 2008. In late 2008, the Economist Intelligence Unit estimated Dubai's 2008 population at 1.92 million.

3. Other cities and states are dominated by foreigners, but not to the extent Dubai is. In Monaco, fewer than 16 percent of residents are citizens. In Abu Dhabi citizens make up 20 percent of that emirate's population, and in Doha the figure is roughly 25 percent.

4. Estimates from Economist Intelligence Unit; also, a study by the Federal National Council, an advisory body, reported that the number of UAE citizens had dwindled to just 15.4 percent of a population of 5.6 million by the end of 2006. That figure would put the Emirati population at more than 860,000. The 2005 Tedad census put UAE nationals at 825,000. The Dubai newspaper *Al Bayan* reported 875,617 UAE nationals on October 29, 2008, citing a "public figure" as its source. Emiratis formed 13.5 percent of the population; the largest group was Indians, with nearly 2.4 million.

5. In 2008, the government required *bidoun* to register with the intention of figuring out their citizenship.

6. The Economist Intelligence Unit estimates that there are 1.9 million Indians in the UAE, with 75,000 arriving per year, and 775,000 Pakistanis, with 57,000 arriving each year. The Sri Lankan community is the third largest, with 290,000, and Filipinos are fourth (230,000), followed by Egyptians (230,000).

7. Anthony Richardson and Rasha Abu Baker, "Brunch Patrol Looks for Drink Offences," *The National*, Abu Dhabi, July 7, 2008.

8. "Women Jailed for Indecent Acts," 7 Days, August 31, 2008, http://www.7days.ae/showstory.php?id=78224.

9. Source for this material is a government official who requested anonymity.

10. Matthew Brown, "U.A.E.'s Drive for Emirati-Run Economy Is Thwarted by Handouts," Bloomberg, October 4, 2007, http://www.bloomberg.com/apps/news?pid=20601109&sid=axmdijbZMi5k; Brown cites sources that put unemployment at 17 percent. I've also heard 18 percent, and much higher for women.

11. Ibid.

12. The council's nineteen members are all men.

16. Democracy and Terrorism

1. Jim Krane, "Voters in United Arab Emirates Set to Vote in Historic Elections Saturday," Associated Press, December 15, 2006.

2. Lawrence Wright, *The Looming Tower: Al-Qaeda and the Road to 9/11* (New York: Vintage Books, 2007), 280.

3. Mustafa Alani (security and terrorism analyst, Gulf Research Center, Dubai), author interview, July 15, 2008.

4. Davidson, *Dubai: The Vulnerability of Success* 297.

5. Commercial Airliner Bombings, Aerospaceweb.org, http://www.aerospaceweb .org/question/planes/q0283.shtml.

6. Davidson, *Dubai: The Vulnerability of Success*, 292; Davidson, *The United Arab Emirates*, 79. Davidson cites the *Economist* for the Hyatt Regency attack and an anonymous personal interview for the second. He gives few details on either incident. Emirati men in their white *kandouras* can still be seen drinking in bars. But one never sees a Muslim woman in a black *abaya* in a bar.

7. Daniel McGrory, "UAE Seizes al-Qaeda's Gulf Leader," *Times* online, December 24, 2002, http://www.timesonline.co.uk/tol/news/world/article805297.ece (accessed July 15, 2008).

8. Web site of the book *Ghost Plane*, by Stephen Grey, page titled "Timeline on the War on Terror as Traced by Alleged CIA Flights," http://ghostplane.net/ timeline.

9. Carol Cratty, "Military to Seek Death Penalty for USS *Cole* Suspect," CNN .com, June 30, 2008, http://www.cnn.com/2008/CRIME/06/30/cole.charges/ (accessed July 15, 2008).

10. Jim Krane, "Gulf Countries Beef Up Counter-Terror Defenses," Associated Press, September 12, 2006.

11. Mustafa Alani, author interview, July 15, 2008.

12. "United Arab Emirates: Whereabouts of Men Arrested in Raids on Coastal Towns Must Be Revealed," Amnesty International public statement, October 24, 2008, http://www.amnesty.org/en/library/info/MDE25/007/2008/en.

13. International Religious Freedom Report 2007—United Arab Emirates; U.S.

Department of State, http://www.state.gov/g/drl/rls/irf/2007/90223.htm (accessed July 19, 2008).

14. Anthony Harris, author interview, May 21, 2008.

15. Emirates news agency WAM reported on July 21, 2008, that Maj. Gen. Mohammed Ahmed al-Marri, director of the Dubai Naturalization and Residency Department, said those arrested through the iris scan system at Dubai International Airport reached 1,325 in 2006, then increased to 3,626 in 2007, and 4,382 in the first half of 2008.

16. Van der Meulen, "The Role of Tribal and Kinship Ties," 281.

17. Economist Intelligence Unit, "UAE to Reopen Embassy in Iraq," UAE Country Report, June 2008.

18. Wright, *The Looming Tower*, 329–30.

19. Good Harbor did not respond to e-mailed and telephoned interview requests.

20. Robert Elliott, "Dubai: Terrorist Target?" Security Management, March 2007, http://www.securitymanagement.com/article/dubai-terrorist-target (accessed July 15, 2008).

21. Krane, "Gulf Countries Beef Up Counter-Terror Defenses."

22. Peter Landesman, "Arms and the Man," *New York Times Magazine*, August 17, 2003.

23. Davidson, *Dubai: The Vulnerability of Success*, 281.

24. Douglas Farah, "Al-Qaeda Moved Gold to Sudan; Iran, U.A.E. Used as Transit Points," *Washington Post*, September 3, 2002.

25. Adrian Levy and Catherine Scott-Clark, *Deception: Pakistan, the United States and the Global Nuclear Weapons Conspiracy* (London: Atlantic Books, 2007), 8, 139, 282, 328, 367–68, 375.

26. From an undated story in the Dubai-based newspaper *7 Days*, http://www .daijiworld.com/news/news_disp.asp?n_id=32485&n_tit=UAE+%3A+Dh+20 +Million+Wafi+Mall+Heist+in+Dubai+-++the+Story.

27. The two former ministers are Mohammed Khalfan bin Kharbash, former minister of state for finance and former chairman of Dubai Islamic Bank and its real-estate affiliate Deyaar; he has denied any wrongdoing; Khalifa Bakhit al-Falasi, a minister of state, who was sentenced to jail in early 2009, saw his conviction overturned on appeal in May 2009.

28. Christopher Davidson, "Dubai: Spots on the Sun," June 24, 2008, article posted on the Web site of *Open Democracy* journal, http://www.opendemocracy.net/ article/dubai-the-dark-side.

17. Stuck Between America and Iran

1. Tarik Yousef, dean, Dubai School of Government, author interview, January 11, 2009.

2. Nasser Hashempour (deputy director, Iranian Business Council), author interview, November 23, 2008.

3. The sources for this material are former U.S. government employees in the UAE who wish to remain anonymous.

4. Schroen wrote a book about his exploits: *First In: An Insider's Account of How the CIA Spearheaded the War on Terror in Afghanistan* (New York: Presidia, 2005). Schroen was unable to be reached for comment.

5. Various news accounts claimed that none other than Osama bin Laden visited Dubai's American Hospital for treatment—as late as 2001—and that a subsequent CIA station chief in Dubai, Larry Mitchell, visited him there. The CIA vehemently denied the story as "sheer fantasy."

6. The director of the office, Ramin X. Asgard, did not agree to be interviewed.

7. Afshin Molavi (Iran analyst, New America Foundation), author interview, November 23, 2008. Iranian government firms in Dubai were also mentioned by Abbas Bolurfrushan (Iranian Business Council), author interview, November 24, 2008.

8. Most sanctions detail comes from Nasser Hashempour, author interview, November 23, 2008.

9. Jim Krane and James Calderwood, "Official Warns Against Trade with Iran," Associated Press, March 7, 2007.

10. An American U-2 spy plane pilot, Maj. Duane Dively of the 99th Expeditionary Reconnaissance Squadron, was killed on June 22, 2005, when his U-2 crashed on landing at Al-Dhafra Air Base. He was returning from a mission over Afghanistan.

11. Mahmoud Habboush, "US Official Affirms Strength of Military Ties with Emirates," *The National*, November 11, 2008.

18. The Meaning of Dubai

1. "Banks Express Concerns About Dubai's Property Market," Economist Intelligence Unit, UAE Country Report, August 2008, 14.

2. "GULF STATES: Property Boom Carries Social Risks," Oxford Analytica, May 30, 2008.

3. This analysis comes from Robert Lee (Nakheel's head of projects), author interview, September 21, 2008.

4. Nasser Saidi, chief economist, Dubai International Financial Centre, speaking at The Economist's World in 2009 conference, Mina A'Salaam Hotel, January 2009.

5. Matthew Brown, "Dubai May Need Help from Abu Dhabi to Fund Borrowing," Bloomberg, October 13, 2008, http://www.bloomberg.com/apps/news?pid=20601087&sid=av8CVL1H3T3U.

6. Sheikh Mohammed's speech of November 7, 2008; full English translation is available at http://www.weforum.org/pdf/GAC/speechen.pdf.

7. In 2005, London's financial services industry contributed roughly $200 billion to Britain's GDP, or roughly 9 percent of total GDP.

8. *Worldwide Centers of Commerce Index 2008*, MasterCard Worldwide, 15.

9. George Katodrytis, "The Dubai Experiment: Accelerated Urbanism," *Al Manakh: Dubai Guide*, 38–46.

10. Excerpts, some paraphrased, from Fatih A. Rifki and Amer A. Moustafa, "Madinat Jumeirah and the Urban Experience in the Private City," *Al Manakh: Dubai Guide*, 23–29.

11. The UAE's brand of diplomacy still means it stays nearly silent.

12. Hafed al-Ghwell (Dubai School of Government), author interview, June 4, 2008.

13. Al-Maktoum, *My Vision*.

Epilogue: Dubai, February 2009

1. Estimates from "Country Report: United Arab Emirates," Economist Intelligence Unit, December 2008, 6–8, and March 2009, 4.

2. Ibid., March 2009, 4.

3. Jefferies International, Wedge Alternatives, and Alternative Investment Strategies Management, as cited in "Jefferies Among 3 Companies Leaving Dubai's DIFC," Reuters, December 24, 2008.

4. "UAE Economy Poised for Abrupt Slowdown Amid Job Cuts," Reuters, December 14, 2008.

INDEX